European City Breaks

It's only just over 60 years since the end of the Second World War but the transformation of Europe in that time is nothing short of staggering. The continent that tore itself apart, then built a physical and ideological barrier through its heart before knocking it all down, may not yet be ready to embrace Churchill's vision of a 'United States of Europe' but 27 of its nations are now members of a single trading market and 12 have so far signed up to a single currency. Such startling political developments have, inevitably, had a major impact on European travel. Passport and customs checks are a thing of the past at most borders, there's no need to change currency every time you leave home and air fares have been dropping faster than the temperature on a winter's night in St Petersburg. It is now possible to fly from London to Naples for less than the cost of a pizza, see the best of the city and fly back in time for Sunday dinner. You can gaze in awe at Picasso's *Guernica* in Madrid one weekend and climb to the top of Norman Foster's Reichstag in Berlin the next; spend a night at the opera in Verona one week, and a night on the tiles in Tallinn the next. Rome or Riga? Valencia or Venice? Bratislava or Brussels? Each has its own appeal, whether it's museums and galleries stuffed with priceless treasures, delicious food, cheap booze or stunning architecture. There's so much choice it's hard to make one. So read on …

The guide

Footprint's *European City Breaks* is the perfect guide for those who want to get away but don't know where to let off steam, propose to their lover, hide, or simply wallow indulgently in a bit of luxury. The 40 cities listed in this book are all worth at least a weekend of anyone's time. We have taken the strain out of choosing where to sleep, where to eat and what to see by selecting the very top hotels and restaurants, divided into three price categories – expensive, mid-range and cheap – as well as the best bars and clubs and the pick of the sights. From the Acropolis in Athens to Bilbao's Guggenheim Museum, we've highlighted the best of Europe's heritage, old and new, artistic and technological. Throughout the guide you'll find handy star ratings in the introduction to each city which give an immediate idea of the city's strong and weak points (see also page 6). There's a festivals calendar on page 8, so you can decide whether to head for – or avoid – a place at a specific time of year, and some of the best festivals are described in more detail under the relevant city. Wherever you end up going, *European City Breaks* is there to point you in the right direction. Go on – give yourself a break.

Contents

Star cities

Where to go

We've given every city in the book scores out of 5 (1 = lowest, 5 = highest) in 8 categories: Arts and culture, Eating, Nightlife, Outdoors, Romance, Shopping, Sightseeing and Value for money so you can see their weak and their strong points. These scores are shown in the introduction to each city and should help you choose the right destination for your city break. The highest scoring cities in each category are listed below.

◉ Arts and culture

Cities that have an outstanding reputation for all-round cultural excellence, with vibrant art, literature, theatre and music scenes.

Berlin ➤➤p49	Madrid ➤➤p159
Budapest ➤➤p79	Paris ➤➤p182
Florence ➤➤p109	Rome ➤➤p210
London ➤➤p142	Venice ➤➤p255

◉ Eating

Cities that have a thriving culinary scene and a number of world-class restaurants.

Antwerp ➤➤p27	London ➤➤p142
Bologna ➤➤p61	Lyon ➤➤p153
Brussels ➤➤p71	Paris ➤➤p182

Rue St Jean, Lyon

🌓 Nightlife

The ultimate places to party after dark.

♥ Romance

The best places to propose or to enjoy a spontaneous romantic weekend.

◉ Sightseeing

The places to go for world famous sights: museums, monuments, castles, towers, Ferris wheels, etc

Galleria Vittorio Emanuele II

⛰ Outdoors

Cities that incorporate plenty of green space or provide easy access to nearby wilderness areas.

◎ Shopping

Cities with outstanding and varied retail therapy opportunities.

€ Value for money

The best places to go if you are on a tight budget.

Festivals

January
New Year's Day Concert *Vienna*
Paris Grand Parade *Paris, 1st*
Fête des Rois (Festival of Kings) *Paris, first Sun after Epiphany (6th)*
Burns Night *Edinburgh and Glasgow, 25th*
Celtic Connections (music) *Glasgow, last 2 weeks*

February
Carnival *widespread but especially in Venice, Verona, Bilbao, Lisbon and Seville, throughout Feb*
Chinese New Year *especially in Amsterdam and London, date varies*
Berlin International Film Festival *Berlin, date varies*

March
St Patrick's Day *Dublin, 17th*
Las Fallas Fire Festival *Valencia, 15-19th* ⇥p249
Spring Music Festival *Budapest, mid Mar-early Apr*

April
Settimana per la Cultura *Naples, Easter*
Semana Santa (Holy week) *Seville, Easter* ⇥p227
Feria de Abril (April Fair) *Seville, date varies* ⇥p227
Scoppio del Carro *Florence, Easter Sun*
London Marathon *London, late Apr*
Printemps Baroque du Sablon (chamber music) *Brussels, late Apr*

Koninginnedag (Queen's Day) *Amsterdam, 30th*

May
Maggio Musicale Fiorentino *Florence, late Apr-late Jun*
Fiestas de San Isidro *Madrid, 2nd week*
Prague Spring International Music Festival *Prague, mid May-early Jun*
Reykjavik Arts Festival *Reykjavik, mid May-early Jun*
Chelsea Flower Show *London, end May*
Whitsun Carnival *Copenhagen, end May*
Vogalonga (rowing competition) *Venice, end May*
Early Summer Festival *Bologna, May-Jun*
Wiener Festwochen *Vienna, May-Jun*
Vienna Opera Festival *Vienna, May-Jun*

June
Summer Dance Festival *Berlin, early Jun*
Stars of the White Nights Festival (music, opera and ballet) *St Petersburg, end May-mid Jul*
Karneval der Kulturen (Carnival of Cultures) *Berlin, Pentecost weekend*
Amsterdam Roots Festival (music) *Amsterdam, late Jun*
Festa del Naviglio (summer fête) *Milan, first Sun*

Great Irish Houses Music
Festival *Dublin, mid Jun*
Dublin Writers Festival
Dublin, mid Jun
Festos dos Santos Populares
Lisbon, 12th, and throughout Jun
Prague Fringe Festival *Prague,
end May-early Jun*
Riga Opera Festival *Riga, mid-Jun*
Festival of the Sea *Reykjavik,
1st Fri for 4 days*
**Bloomsday Festival (James
Joyce)** *Dublin, 16th*
Fête de la Musique *Paris, 21st*
**Sankt Hans Aften (St John's
Eve)** *Copenhagen, 23rd*
Roskilde Music Festival
Copenhagen, late Jun
**Calcio Storico (costumed
football)** *Florence, late Jun*
Christopher Street Day *Berlin,
late Jun* ⇥p49
**Traffic Torino Free Festival
(music)** *Turin, end Jun-early Jul*
**Istanbul Festival of Arts and
Culture** *Istanbul, Jun-Jul*
**International Istanbul Music
Festival** *Istanbul, Jun-Jul*
Glasgow Jazz Festival *Glasgow,
mid Jun*
Arena di Verona Opera Season
Verona, Jun-Aug
Zomer van Antwerpen (arts)
Antwerp, Jun-Aug
Fourvière Arts Nights *Lyon,
Jun-Aug*
Summer Festival (arts)
Barcelona, Jun-Aug
Estate Romana (music)
Rome, Jun-Sep
Hellenic Festival (arts)
Athens, Jun-Sep ⇥p31

July
Tour de France *ends Paris, dates
vary*
Neopolis Music Festival *Naples,
dates vary*
**Stockholm Jazz
Festival** *Stockholm, dates vary*
Beer Festival *Tallinn, early Jul*
Bastille Day *Paris, 14th*
**Copenhagen Jazz
Festival** *Copenhagen, 1st Fri*
**Festa del Redentore (Feast of
the Redeember)** *Venice, 3rd Sat*
ImPulsTanz Dance Festival
Vienna, Jul-Aug

La Regata di Venezia

**Ljubljana Summer Festival
(cultural events)** *Ljubljana, Jul-Aug*

August
Edinburgh Festivals *end
Jul-early Sep* ⇥p101
Sziget Music Festival *near
Budapest, mid-Aug*
Aste Nagusia (Basque festival)
Bilbao, late Aug
La Tomatina *Buñol, near Valencia,
last Wed*

Notting Hill Carnival *London,
last Sun*
Venice Film Festival *Venice,
Aug-Sep*

September
La Regata di Venezia *Venice,
1st Sun*
Flower Festival *Amsterdam, 4th*
**Festes de la Merce (street
party)** *Barcelona, 24th*
Oktoberfest (beer festival)
Munich, mid Sep-Oct ⇥p171
**Reykjavik Film and Jazz
festivals** *Reykjavik, Sep-Oct*
Autumn Festival *Prague,
Sep-Oct*
Dublin Fringe Festival *Dublin,
Sep-Oct*

October
**Budapest Autumn Music
Festival** *Budapest, late Oct*
Salon du Chocolat *Paris, late Oct*

November
**Festival of La Salute (All Saints
Day)** *Venice, 21st*

December
Christmas markets *especially
Vienna, Munich, Berlin,
Copenhagen, Prague, Antwerp
and Stockholm*
**Tivoli Gardens (Christmas
festival)** *Copenhagen, mid
Nov-end Dec*
New Year's Eve *Especially in
Athens, Berlin, Dublin, Edinburgh,
London, Paris, Prague, Stockhom
and Venice, 31st*

Currencies

Country	Currency	£ 1 =	€1 =
Czech Republic	Koruna (CZK)	CZK 41.22	CZK 28
Denmark	Krone (Kr)	Kr 10.97	Kr 7.45
Estonia	Kroon (EEK)	EEK 23.04	EEK 15.65
Euro Zone	Euro (€)	€1.47	
Hungary	Forint (HUF)	HUF 363.61	HUF 247.13
Iceland	Kronur (ISK)	ISK 129.93	ISK 88.26
Latvia	LAT (Ls)	Ls 1.03	Ls 0.70
Poland	Zloty (PLN)	PLN 5.6	PLN 3.8
Russia	Roubles (RUB)	RUB 51.51	RUB 35
Slovakia	Slovak Koruna (SKK)	SKK 49.35	SIT 33.52
Sweden	Krona (SEK)	SEK 13.56	SEK 9.22
Switzerland	Swiss Franc (CHF)	CHF 2.4	CHF 1.63
Turkey	Turkish Lira (TRY)	TRY 2.71	TRY 1.84
UK	Pound Sterling (£)		£0.68

ICELAND

NORWAY
FINLAND
RUSSIAN
SWEDEN
ESTONIA
FEDERATION

REPUBLIC OF
IRELAND
DENMARK
LATVIA

UNITED
KINGDOM

Atlantic
Ocean

NETHERLANDS
BELORUSSIA

BELGIUM
GERMANY
POLAND

CZECH
REPUBLIC
UKRAINE

FRANCE
SLOVAKIA

SWITZERLAND
AUSTRIA
HUNGARY

SLOVENIA

PORTUGAL
ROMANIA

SPAIN
CROATIA

ITALY
SERBIA
BULGARIA

Mediterranean
Sea

GREECE
TURKEY

N

200 km
200 miles

Euro Zone

Essentials

Airline information

Listed below are the major airlines for each country covered in this guide, with their main hubs. Useful websites for cheap flights include www.youfly4less.com, www.ebookers.com, www.cheap flights.co.uk, www.flightline.co.uk and www.lastminute.com. For up-to-date information on the everchanging routes of budget airlines, see www.whichbudget.com.

Airlines

Adria Airways, www.adria-airways.com.
Aer Lingus, www.aerlingus.com.
Aeroflot Russian International Airlines (SU), www.aeroflot.com. .
Air Baltic, www.airbaltic.com.
Air Europa, www.aireuropa.com.
Air France, www.airfrance.com.
Alitalia, www.alitalia.co.uk.
Austrian Airlines Group, www.aua.com, consisting of Austrian Airlines (OS), Lauda Air (NG) and Tyrolean Airways (VO).
BMI Baby, www.bmibaby.com..
British Airways, www.ba.com.
British Midland, www.flybmi.com.
Brussels Airlines, www.brusselsairlines.com.
Czech Airlines, www.csa.cz.
Easyjet, www.easyjet.com.
Estonian Air, www.estonian-air.ee.
German Wings, www.german wings.com.
Iberia, www.iberia.com.
Iceland Air, www.icelandair.net.
Iceland Express, www.iceland express.com.
Jet2.com, www.jet2.com.
KLM, www.klm.com.
Lufthansa, www.lufthansa.com.

Malev Hungarian Airlines, www.malev.com.
Olympic Airways, www.olympic airlines.com.
Portugalia Airlines, www.flypga.com.
Ryanair, www.ryanair.com.
SAS, www.scandinavian.net.
SN Brussels, www.flysn.com.
Swiss International Air Lines, www.swiss.com.
TAP Air Portugal, www.tap.pt.
Turkish Airlines, www.turkish airlines.com.

Rail information

For detailed information on rail travel throughout Europe and beyond, consult the excellent and thoroughly comprehensive **Man in Seat 61**, www.seat61.com. Note that European railways change their timetables in early June and early December each year. Thomas Cook publishes both the *Rail Map of Europe* (£8.99) and the monthly *European Rail Timetable* (£12.50, or £11.25 from www.thomascook timetables.com), which has timetables for trains, buses and boats in all European countries, as well as ships to North Africa, Israel and Mediterranean islands. For instant information on rail connections throughout Europe, check out http://reiseauskunft .bahn.de. Online rail maps can be viewed at www.europerail.net. Tickets for rail journeys within one country can usually be bought at the relevant operator's website (see below). Other international train journeys must be booked by telephone through an agency. (www.seat61.com recommends the best agency for each destination.) Reservations can usually be made up to 60 days in advance of travel (or up to 90 days on some services).

From the UK to Europe

The cheapest way to buy rail tickets from London to France, Italy, Spain or Switzerland is online at Eurostar, French Railways (SNCF) or Rail Europe websites (see below). Most rail journeys from the UK to continental Europe now include the Eurostar service from London Waterloo to either Paris Gare du Nord, Lille or Brussels Midi but this may not be the best option if you're starting from Scotland, the north of England or Wales.
Eurostar, T08705-186186, www.euro star.com. From London to Paris, Lille and Brussels, with onward connections to destinations all over Europe.
Dutch Flyer, www.dutchflyer.co.uk. All-inclusive rail and ferry service from London and East Anglia, via Harwich and the Hook of Holland, to any station in the Netherlands.
Venice Simplon Orient Express, www.orient-expresstrains.com. Luxury services from London to Paris, Venice and Rome.

Ticket agencies in the UK

Deutsche Bahn, T08702-435363, www.deutsche-bahn.co.uk. German railways booking office in the UK. For journeys from London to Germany, Austria (via Brussels/Germany), Scandinavia, Eastern Europe and Russia. Cross-channel ferry tickets not available.

European Rail, T020-7387 0444, www.europeanrail.com. Smaller specialist agency covering the whole of Europe; hefty booking fee.

International Rail, T08700-841411, www.international-rail.com. Tickets and passes for rail travel worldwide. Official UK agents for Trenitalia (Italian State Railways), www.italiarail.co.uk.

Rail Europe, T08705-848848, www.raileurope.co.uk. The biggest European rail agency, owned by SNCF. For journeys from London to France, Italy, Spain and Switzerland. Cross-channel ferry tickets not available.

Rail Traveller, T01902-326662, www.thetravelbureau.co.uk.

Railchoice, T08701-657300, www.railchoice.co.uk. For tickets across Europe, railpasses and flexipasses.

Spanish Rail UK, T020-7224 0345, www.spanish-rail.co.uk. Agents for Spanish Railways (RENFE), good for rail travel to and within Spain and Portugal.

TrainsEurope, T08717-007722, www.trainseurope.co.uk. European rail agency offering Eurostar, rail-and-sea tickets and railpasses.

Voyages SNCF, www.voyages-sncf.com. From London or Paris to anywhere in France and to major cities in Italy, Germany, Austria and Spain.

European country networks

The major network for each country covered in the guide is listed below.

Austria ÖBB (Österreichische

Bundesbahnen), www.oebb.at.

Belgium SNCB (Société Nationale des Chemins de Fer Belges), www.b-rail.be.

Czech Republic CD (Ceské Dráhy), www.cdrail.cz.

Denmark DSB, www.dsb.dk.

Estonia Edelarautee, www.edel.ee and www.elektriraudtee.ee. EVR Ekspress, www.evrekspress.ee. Sleeper trains from Tallinn to St Petersburg .

France SNCF (Société Nationale des Chemins de Fer), www.voyages-sncf.com.

Germany DB (Deutsche Bahn), www.bahn.de. ICE (Intercity Express) connects Berlin and Munich with Brussels and Vienna.

Greece OSE (Organismos Sidirodromon Ellados), www.ose.gr.

Hungary MAV (Magyar Allamvasutak), www.mav.hu.

Ireland IR (Iarnrod Eireann), www.irishrail.ie.

Italy Trenitalia (Ferrovie dello Stato), www.trenitalia.it. Italy. Trains to France, Austria, Germany and Spain.

Netherlands NS (Nederlandse Spoorwegen), www.ns.nl.

Poland PKP(Polskie Koleje Panstwowe), www.pkp.pl.

Portugal CP (Caminhos de Ferro Portugueses), www.cp.pt.

Russian Federation RZD (Russkiye Zheleznye Dorogi), www.rzd.ru.

Spain RENFE (Red Nacional de los Ferrocarriles Españoles), www.renfe.es. Sleeper trains from Paris to Madrid, Paris to Barcelona, Milan to Barcelona, Zurich to Barcelona and Madrid to Lisbon.

Slovak Republic ŽSR (železnice SR), www.zsr.sk.

Slovenia SZ (Slovenske Zeleznice), www.slo-zeleznice.si.

Sweden SJ, www.sj.se.

Turkey TCDD (Türkiye Cumhuryeti Devlet Demiryollan), www.tcdd.gov.tr.

UK National Rail, www.nationalrail.co.uk. Scotrail, www.firstscotrail.com.

Inter-European connections

Allegro, www.international-rail.com. Day and night services connecting Rome, Venice and Florence with Vienna and Salzburg.

Artesia, www.raileurope.com. Day and night services linking Rome, Milan, Turin, Florence and Venice with Paris and Lyon.

Cisalpino, www.cisalpino.com. Daytime services connecting Milan and Florence with Zurich, Basel and Stuttgart.

City Night Line, www.citynightline.ch. Hotel trains linking Zurich, Baden, Basel, Munich and Vienna with destinations in Germany, the Netherlands and Denmark.

Elipsos International, www.elipsos.com. Night 'Trenhotel' services from Madrid to Paris and from Barcelona to Paris, Milan or Zurich.

Nachtzugreise, www.nachtzug.de Sleeper trains from Germany to destinations in Austria, Denmark, France, Italy, the Netherlands, Switzerland and Eastern Europe.

Riviera, www.international-rail.com. Day and night services linking Naples,

Rome, Venice and Milan with Monte Carlo and Nice.

TGV Lyria, www.raileurope.com. French high-speed service linking Paris with Lausanne, Bern and Zurich.

Thalys, www.thalys.com. High-speed trains between Brussels, Paris, Amsterdam and Cologne.

Venice Simplon Orient Express, www.orient-expresstrains.com. Luxury journeys starting from London, Paris, Vienna or Istanbul.

X2000, www.sj.se. Connects Copenhagen and Stockholm.

European City Breaks Essentials

Ferry information

For full listings of routes check out the main carriers **Brittany Ferries** (www.brittany-ferries.com), **Irish Ferries** (www.irishferries.com), **Norfolk Line** (www.norfolkline-ferries.co.uk), **P&O** (www.poferries.com), **Stena Line**, (www.stenaline.co.uk), **DFDS Seaways** (www.dfds.co.uk). For fares on all routes see www.direct ferries.co.uk. For competitive fares from the UK to France and Spain, check out **Ferrysavers**, T0870-442 4223, www.ferrysavers.com.

From the UK to Antwerp and Brussels, P&O operates a service from Hull to Zeebrugge, from where it's 1¼ hours to each city.

P&O operates a year-round ferry service from Portsmouth to Bilbao, which they run more like a cruise so charge accordingly – a return with a car costs around £400-500. Cabins are mandatory. Prices vary hugely according to season and availability but booking in advance can be cheaper and there are occasional off-peak specials. The ferry port is at Santurtzi, 13 km from Bilbao city centre.

THE ROYAL YACHT
BRITANNIA
OCEAN TERMINAL, EDINBURGH

"Scotland's leading visitor-friendly attraction" BBC News

Audio tour of five decks • Visitor centre • Gift shop

Ocean Terminal, Leith, Edinburgh EH6 6JJ
Telephone: +44 (0)131 555 5566
www.royalyachtbritannia.co.uk

From the British mainland to Dublin, four main ferry companies run services. Irish Ferries and Stena Line operate between Holyhead and Dublin Port, while Stena Line also offers a high-speed crossing from Holyhead to Dun Laoghaire, 30 minutes' drive south of Dublin. P&O and Norfolk Line both run services from Liverpool to Dublin.

There are numerous ferry routes from the UK to France. The shortest routes include Dover to Dunkerque (3 hours' drive from Paris), which is 2 hours with Norfolk Line. P&O and Norfolk Line ferries from Dover to Calais (3 hours' drive from Paris) take just over 1 hour.

Longer services include LD Lines, www.ldlines.co.uk, who run services to Le Havre (2 hours' drive from Paris) from Portsmouth (5½ hours crossing time) and Newhaven (5 hours). Transmanche, www.tranmancheferries.com, operates ferries from Newhaven to Dieppe (4 hours). It takes 2¼ hours to drive from Dieppe to Paris.

Crossings with Brittany Ferries from Portsmouth to Caen take 5¾ hours. Caen is 2½ hours' drive from Paris. Dover to Boulogne, 2¾ hours' drive from Paris, takes 55 minutes with

Speedferries, www.speedferries.com.

From the UK to Northern Europe ferries can take 12 hours plus, with a price tag to match. From Newcastle try DFDS Seaways with routes to Denmark and Holland. From Harwich check out Stena Line who run services to the Hook of Holland, including a fast service that takes just over 6 hours.

P&O also offers a crossing from Harwich to Esbjerg (16 hours), from where it's a 3-hour drive to Copenhagen.

Visa and passport information

The information provided below is subject to change so always check with the embassy of the relevant country before travelling. British citizens can also contact www.fco.gov.uk. Countries featured in the guide are highlighted in bold.

Travelling to Schengen member states

There are no internal border controls between countries that are signatories of the Schengen Convention: **Austria**, **Belgium**, **Denmark**, **Finland**, **France**, **Germany**, **Greece**, **Italy**, **Luxembourg**, the **Netherlands**, **Portugal**, **Spain**, **Sweden**, plus **Iceland** and **Norway** (both non-EU members). Citizens of these countries can travel freely within the Schengen area, although it is recommended that they carry approved ID at all times. Citizens of other EU member states (including the UK and Ireland) still need a passport (valid for at least six months) or an approved and valid national ID card to visit the Schengen area for up to 90 days. Non-EU passport holders need to check if they

are among the 33 countries whose nationals do NOT need a visa to visit the EU for up to 90 days. All other visitors require a visa; contact the relevant embassy or consulate in your home country. Note that a visa for one Schengen member state is also valid for travel to other Schengen countries.

Travelling to non-Schengen EU member states

Citizens of EU member states, as well as citizens of Iceland, Liechtenstein, Norway and Switzerland, only need a passport (valid for at least six months) or an approved and valid national ID card for travel to non-Schengen countries within the EU: **Cyprus**, **Czech Republic**, **Estonia**, **Hungary**, **Ireland**, **Latvia**, **Lithuania**, **Malta**, **Poland**, **Slovakia**, **Slovenia** and the **UK**. Non-EU passport holders need to check whether they are among the 33 countries whose nationals do NOT need a visa to visit the EU for 90 days. Note that the list for the UK and Ireland differs slightly from other EU countries, so check with your local consulate. All other visitors require a visa and should contact the embassy or consulate in their home country.

Travelling to the Russian Federation

All foreign nationals are required to have entry visas for visits to the Russian Federation. A single-entry tourist visa, valid for up to 30 days, can be obtained from the Russian embassy or consulate before travel for about €50. Passports must be valid for six months beyond the intended stay and the visitor must hold tickets confirming return or onward travel. Proper authorization from the Passport and Visa Department (UVIR) of the Ministry of Internal Affairs or from a specially authorized travel agent is also required. Many agencies can help to organize this for a fee, including www.asla.co.uk/, www.myrussianvisa .com, www.visa torussia.com, www .gotorussia.co.uk, www.russiadirect.net.

Travelling to Switzerland

Nationals of EU member states require an approved and valid national ID card for stays of up to 90 days. Nationals of Australia, Canada, New Zealand, South Africa and the USA (among others) require a passport valid for 90 days after their intended period of stay but do not require a visa. Nationals of all other countries should contact the Swiss embassy or consulate.

Travelling to Turkey

Passport holders from Bulgaria, the Czech Republic, Denmark, Finland, France, Germany, Greece, Iceland, Israel, Japan, Liechtenstein, Luxembourg, New Zealand, Sweden and Switzerland (among others) do not require a visa for tourist visits to Turkey of up to 90 days. Passport holders from Australia, Austria, Belgium, Canada, Ireland, Italy, the Netherlands, Portugal, Slovenia, Spain, the UK and the USA (among others) require a visa. They can obtain a three-month multiple-entry visa at the port of entry for €15 (more for Canadians) or at their local Turkish consulate before travel. Nationals of all other countries should consult the Turkish embassy or consulate in their home country. Make visa applications in person one month before travel.

See also www.turkish embassy.org or www.e-konsolosluk .net/.+44

➔ Fact file

Country	Phone code	Time	Voltage (type of plug)
Austria	+43	GMT+1	230v/50Hz (2 flat pins)
Belgium	+32	GMT+1	230v/50Hz (2 round pins)
Croatia	+385	GMT+1	230v/50Hz (2 round pins)
Czech Rep	+420	GMT+1	230v/50Hz (2 round pins)
Denmark	+45	GMT+1	230v/50Hz (2 round pins)
Estonia	+372	GMT+2	230v/50Hz (2 flat pins)
France	+33	GMT+1	230v/50Hz (2 round pins)
Germany	+49	GMT+1	230v/50Hz (2 round pins)
Greece	+30	GMT+2	220v/50Hz (2/3 round pins)
Hungary	+36	GMT+1	230v/50Hz (2 round pins)
Iceland	+354	GMT-1	220v/50Hz (2 round pins)
Ireland	+353	GMT	230v/50Hz (3 rectangular pins)
Italy	+39	GMT+1	230v/50Hz (2 round pins)
Latvia	+371	GMT+2	220v/50Hz (2 round pins)
Netherlands	+31	GMT+1	230v/50Hz (2 round pins)
Poland	+48	GMT+1	230v/50Hz (2 round pins)
Portugal	+351	GMT	230v/50Hz (2 round pins)
Russia	+7	GMT+3	220v/50Hz (2 round pins)
Slovakia	+421	GMT+1	230v/50Hz (2 round pins)
Slovenia	+386	GMT+1	220v/50Hz (2 round pins)
Spain	+34	GMT+1	230v/50Hz (2 round pins)
Sweden	+46	GMT+1	230v/50Hz (2 round pins)
Switzerland	+41	GMT+1	230v/50Hz (3 round pins)
Turkey	+90	GMT+2	230v/50Hz (2 round pins)
UK	+44	GMT	230v/50Hz (3 rectangular pins)

Amsterdam

Amsterdam shouldn't really exist. The city was dragged out of marshy bogs, dried out and carved into the place we know today. It was an unconventional start and one which seems to have set the tone for things to come. Today, Amsterdam is Europe's most unconventional city. Here, locals shun the car and choose instead to career around on bicycles. Prostitution is both legal and very public, and this is the only city in the world where you can peruse a cannabis menu and smoke a joint in a coffeeshop. The Netherlands was also the first country to legalise marriage between gay couples.

Alongside these progressive ways are, conversely, some of Europe's greatest traditional attractions. The Rijksmuseum and Van Gogh Museum hold two of the finest art collections in the world, while smaller museums, such as the Anne Frank House or Rembrandthuis, provide a real insight into the city's past.

The city's future direction seems less certain. Its 'anything goes' attitude is under threat from the government's new hard line on soft drugs, which has seen a fall in the number of coffeeshops, while both main political parties are distancing themselves from the tradition of multiculturalism. Is Amsterdam becoming less tolerant, more like the rest of Europe? It somehow seems unlikely in this engaging liberal oddball of a city.

Arts & culture
★★★★

Eating
★★★

Nightlife
★★★★

Outdoors
★★

Romance
★★★

Shopping
★★★

Sightseeing
★★★★

Value for money
★★★

Overall score
★★★

At a glance

Amsterdam's old centre is hemmed in by the Ij River and Centraal Station to the north, and spreads south in a web of medieval streets and canals. The main arteries are Damrak and Ronkin, busy thoroughfares which split the centre into the **Nieuwe Zijde** (New Side), to the west of Dam Square, and the **Oude Zijde** (Old Side) to the east.

The **red-light district** lies on the Old Side and is a predictably seedy grid of streets, though not without its charm. Beyond here are the **Nieuwmarkt** and **Plantage** districts, home to Amsterdam's biggest flea market and Rembrandt's house. To the north are the **Eastern Islands**, extensively renovated docklands holding some impressively adventurous architecture.

West of Damrak, Nieuwe Zijde is Amsterdam's main shopping area and leads to the **Grachtengordel**, the

In Amsterdam, the water is the mistress and the land the vassal.

Felix Marti-Ibanez

four major canals that ring the old centre. South of the Grachtengordel is the **Museum Quarter**, full of grand old buildings, including – most famously – the enormous, neo-Gothic Rijksmuseum, overlooking the grassy Museumplein.

★ *Don't leave town without experiencing* **Gezelligheid** – *roughly translated as a cosy or relaxing time* – *in a brown café or* **bruine café**.

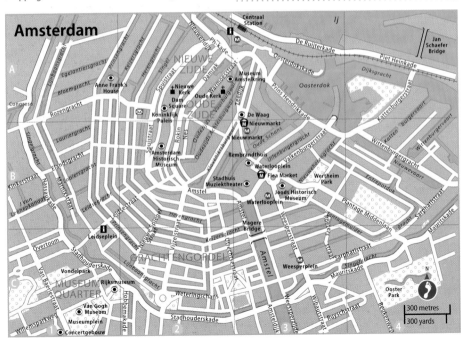

24 hours in the city

Sip a coffee at **Café Luxembourg** before heading south to the Museumsplein. Pop into the **Rijksmuseum** and ogle Rembrandt's *Nightwatch*, one of the highlights still on view while the museum undergoes renovation. A few steps along Museumplein brings you to the **Van Gogh Museum**, which warrants a good few hours. After a perk up at **Het Blauwe Theehuis**, a popular tea house near Vondelpark, wander north along the canals of the Grachtengordel to **Anne Frank's House**. Lunch at one of the pavement cafés on Nieuwmarkt and then either head south for a snoop around the **flea market** on Waterlooplein, or east to gawp at the painted ladies of the **red-light district**. (Don't miss the attic chapel in the Museum Amstelkring while you're there.) Have an early evening drink in **Café Sluyswacht**, on Jodenbreestraat, and then cross town for contemporary Dutch cuisine in the

Café de Waard, Leidseplein

history-soaked interior of **d'Vijff Vlieghen**. Finish off on the 11th floor of the former central post office, Oosterdokskade 3-5, now housing the very hip **Club 11**, and watch the city twinkling beneath you.

⊖ Travel essentials

Getting there Schiphol Airport lies 15 km southwest of the city centre. Trains run from beneath the main concourse to Centraal Station every 15 mins 0445-2400 and every hour thereafter, taking 15 mins (€3.40 single). Buses also run to the centre, including the 370 which stops in the Museum Quarter. A taxi to the centre takes around 20 mins and costs about €35. **Schiphol Travel Taxi**, T0900-8876, T038-339 4768, is a good-value shared minibus.

Centraal Station, T0900-9296, www.ns.nl, Amsterdam's main station, is right in the centre of town at the end of Damrak. There are regular international connections, including a high-speed link with Brussels Midi for connections to the Eurostar (see page 12). Another high-speed service, the Dutch Flyer, links Centraal Station with the Hook of Holland for ferries to and from Harwich (see page 13).

Getting around Most of the city's main sights are within easy walking distance of each other. The public transport system is excellent; trams are the most useful but there are also buses and a small metro (best for outlying districts). All public transport is run by the **GVB**, www.gvb.nl, which has an information and ticket office opposite Centraal Station. Its website is also a great source of travel information. Tickets can also be bought at tram stops, newsagents and on board trams and buses. Buying a strip ticket (*strippenkaart*) is much cheaper than buying individual tickets for each journey. Validate the correct number of strips when you board: 2 strips for a trip within zone 1 (Central Amsterdam); 3 strips to travel through 2 zones, and so on. A 15-part *strippenkaart* costs €6.80. Alternatively, travel passes, valid on the whole network, cost €6.50, €10.50 or €13.50 for 24, 48 and 72 hrs. Taxis have

ranks around the city but are pricey.

Tourist information The main office is opposite Centraal Station, T0900-400 4040, www.amsterdamtourist.nl, daily 0900-1700. There's another inside the station, Mon-Thu and Sat 0800-2000, Fri 0800-2100, Sun 0900-1700; and another on the corner of Leidseplein and Leidsestraat, daily 0900-1700. The **I Amsterdam Card**, www.iamsterdam card.com, offers unlimited travel on public transport, a free canal boat trip, and extensive discounts at museums. Tickets cost €33, €43 or €53 for 1, 2, or 3 days and are available from the tourist and GVB information offices.

Among the canal tours, the most useful is **Lovers Museumboat**, T020-530 1090, www.lovers.nl, a hop-on/hop-off service stopping at all major museums. Tickets cost €15 and include reduced entry to museums.

◉ Sights

Dam Square
ⓘ *Tram 4, 9, 14, 16, 24 or 25.* **🔴A2**.

Known simply as the 'Dam', this broad, tourist- and pigeon-filled square lies at the core of Amsterdam's medieval centre. It was the location of the original dam across the Amstel which gave the city its name. The **Koninklijk Paleis (Royal Palace)**, originally the town hall, was built between 1648 and 1665 in an imposing Dutch Classicist style. It became a royal residence when Louis Bonapart kicked out the mayor in 1808, during the French occupation, and it is now used for state functions. Nearby is the **Nieuwe Kerk**, dating from 1408, while, in the centre of the square, is the city's **war memorial**, a rather stark obelisk and a popular meeting place.

De Wallen red-light district
ⓘ *Tram 4, 9, 14, 16, 24 or 25.* **🔴A3**.

Amsterdam's infamous red-light district covers the area to the east of Damrak and, yes, it is just as seedy as you'd expect. Prostitutes pose in windows, groups of

Dam Square

Red-light district

beery lads barter with pimps, and touts try to entice passers-by with promises of live sex shows. But the area is also such a tourist attraction that it rarely feels threatening (at least not during the day). You'll be sharing the pavement with giggling couples and family groups wandering nonchalantly past the brothel windows. The area also has some of the city's most attractive old houses. Stroll along **Warmoesstraat** to take in the elegant façades, interspersed with sex shops and red-lit windows, and along any of the little streets branching off between **Oudezijds Voorburgwal** and **Ousezijds Achterburgwal** canals.

Two important sights in the area are, ironically, religious. Just east of Warmoesstraat is **De Oude Kerk** ⓘ *Oudekerksplein 23,* **🔴A2**, *Mon-Sat 1100-1700, Sun 1300-1700,* Amsterdam's oldest church, an attractive Gothic structure with a beautiful tower, dating from the 14th century. A few steps north is the **Museum Amstelkring** ⓘ *Oudezijds Voorburgwal 40, T020-624 6604, www.museumamstelkring.nl,* **🔴A2**, *Mon-Sat 1000-1700, Sun 1300-1700, €7,* an ordinary townhouse with an

extraordinary attic, containing the city's only surviving clandestine church. It dates from the Reformation, when public Catholic worship was outlawed.

Nieuwmarkt
ⓘ *Metro Nieuwmarkt.* **🔵B3**.

Once a major market for inhabitants from the nearby Jewish quarter – all but wiped out during the Nazi occupation – this broad square is today flanked by cafés and shops, leading to the city's Chinatown in Zeedijk, just to the north. The square is towered over by **De Waag**, a 15th-century fortress-like structure, once a city gate. During the week there's a small fruit and vegetable market and, in summer, an antique market is held every Sunday.

Waterlooplein
ⓘ *Tram 4, 9 or 14.* **🔵B3**.
Metro Waterlooplein.

Amsterdam's oldest **flea market** ⓘ *Mon-Sat 0900-1700,* is a labyrinthine sprawl of stalls, stuffed with second-hand clothes, old vinyl records and leather jackets. The square is lorded over by the 1986 Stadhuis and Muziektheater, designed by Willem

Nieuwmarkt square

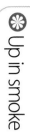

Up in smoke

Thank heavens for Bob Marley. Without Bob and the Rastafarian flag – green, gold and red stripes – tourists would have a tough time spotting a coffeeshop in Amsterdam. That's coffeeshop, not coffeehouse. The difference, of course, is that the former is permitted to sell cannabis, although it's illegal to advertise this fact. Hence all the Rasta paraphernalia, a sure-fire way to tell tourists that they've come to the right (or wrong) place, depending on their views. Amsterdam remains the only city in the world with such a liberal view on soft drugs, attracting a fare percentage of drug tourists, much to the annoyance of many locals and politicians. The law is very clear on what it will tolerate: an individual can possess 30 g and can buy up to 5 g of cannabis at a time from a licensed purveyor – any use of hard drugs (heroin, cocaine and ecstasy) is strictly illegal. Coffeeshops aren't permitted to sell alcohol and there's an age limit of 18. Recent rumblings about limiting tourists' access to coffeeshops have proved unfounded, and for now it seems this unique side of Amsterdam is here to stay.

Rembrandthuis

This graceful house was Rembrandt's home from 1639 to 1658. He lived in the elegant rooms on the ground floor and worked in the large studio upstairs during his most successful period. Today the rooms are stocked with original fittings and period furniture. Also on display is a superb collection of his etchings – over 260 pieces.

Nieuwe Zijde
ⓘ *Tram 1, 2, 13 or 17.* **A2**.

The New Side of the medieval centre was actually settled earlier than the Oude Zijde and today covers the area west of the Dam. It's a mixed area of uninspiring shopping and pretty side streets, leading to the Grachtengordel. Worth a look is the **Amsterdam Historisch Museum** ⓘ *Kalverstraat 92, T020-523 1822, www.ahm.nl,* **B2**, *Mon-Fri 1000-1700, Sat, Sun and public holidays 1100-1700, €7,* located in the old city orphanage. As well as housing some interesting paintings, the building itself, with its two courtyards and winding corridors, is fascinating.

Holzbauer and known locally as the **Stopera** (a combination of 'Stad' and 'Opera', see page 26). Although the complex was hugely controversial when it was built, the theatre now has an excellent reputation. Free concerts are held here at least once a week.

Rembrandthuis
ⓘ *Jodenbreestraat 4, T020-520 0400, www.rembrandthuis.nl,* **B3**. *Daily 1000-1700. €8. Metro to Nieuwmarkt, Hoogstraat exit. Tram 9 or 14.*

Anne Frank House
ⓘ *Prinsengracht 263, T020-556 7100, www.annefrank.org,* **A1**. *Mid-Mar to mid-Sep 0900-2100; mid-Sep to mid-Mar 0900-1900, closed Yom Kippur. €7.50. Tram 13 or 17. Bus 21, 170, 171 or 172 to Westermarkt.*

The gripping, heartbreaking story of Anne Frank is one of the most enduring accounts of life in hiding during the Second World War. The unassuming house, where the Frank family hid with friends for two years during the

Anne Frank House

Nazi occupation, provides a harrowing glimpse of the claustrophobic lives led behind blacked-out windows. The diary itself, sitting alone in a glass case, is startlingly poignant. The only survivor of the Frank family was Anne's father Otto, who returned to the house, published the diary and helped to open the museum in 1960. The entrance is now in a modern building next door.

Rijksmuseum

ⓘ *Jan Luijkenstraat 1, T020-674 7000, www.rijksmuseum.nl, ◼C1. Sat-Thu 0900-1800, Fri 0900-2200. €10. Tram 2 or 5 to Hobbemastraat, 12 to Concertgebouw, or 6, 7 or 10 to Spiegelgracht.*

Amsterdam's enormous flagship museum is undergoing extensive renovation until 2009, although parts of the museum remain open, displaying masterpieces from the collection. The building itself, designed by Pierre Cuypers, is a striking neo-Gothic riot of towers, turrets and stained glass windows and dominates the Museum Quarter. Inside, the collection is split into various sections, most famous of which is the extraordinary Dutch Golden Age collection of paintings. Other sections

Rijksmuseum

Van Gogh Museum

include sculpture, decorative arts, prints and photographs, although many of these are currently closed. The museum's prize piece, Rembrandt's *Nightwatch*, is still on show and it's worth a visit for this alone. The painting was originally called *The Militia Company of Captain Frans Banning Cocq* but became known as the *Nightwatch* as the picture darkened with grime over the years; it has since been cleaned to reveal its true daytime setting.

Van Gogh Museum

ⓘ *Paulus Potterstraat 7, T020-570 5200, www.vangoghmuseum.nl, ◼C1. Sat-Thu 1000-1800, Fri 1000- 2200. €10, €13.50 for special exhibitions. Tram 2, 3, 5 or 12 to between Paulus Potterstraat and Van Baerlestraat.*

One of Amsterdam's finest museums holds the world's largest Vincent Van Gogh collection: over 200 pieces bequeathed by his art-collector brother, Theo. The modern building is split into five periods, starting with Van Gogh's dark Dutch works and evolving, via Paris and Arles in the south of France, into the extraordinarily lively and colourful palette for which he is known. Strikingly, Van Gogh's career lasted little

longer than a decade but this marvellous collection does much to highlight how rich and productive those ten years were. Highlights include *The Potato Eaters*, *Bedroom in Arles* and *Wheatfield with Crows*. Also in the museum are the artist's sketches, as well as works by his contemporaries, including close friend Paul Gauguin; Van Gogh famously cut off his ear after an argument with his artist friend.

Joods Historisch Museum

ⓘ *Nieuwe Amstelstraat 3-5, T020-531 0310, www.jhm.nl, ◼B3. Daily 1100-1700, Thu until 2100, closed Yom Kippur. €7.50. Metro Waterlooplein. Tram 9 or 14.*

The Jewish History Museum is housed in a beautiful series of four synagogues dating from the 17th century, lined by walkways. First opened in 1930, the museum was closed and ransacked during the Second World War and it was not until the 1980s that it was restored and re-opened. It now houses a thorough collection depicting the history of Jewish life in the Netherlands, highlighting the enormous contribution Jews made to the development of Amsterdam.

Joods Historisch Museum

● Sleeping

Amsterdam's status as a hip city break destination means its vast number of beds don't often come cheap; moreover, most places get booked up, particularly in late spring (tulip season) and summer, so it's always essential to book ahead. Avoid the hotel touts, who hang around Centraal Station.

€€€ Amstel InterContinental, Professor Tulpplein 1, T020-622 6060, www.amsterdam.intercontinental.com. The city's grande dame towers on the bank of the Amstel and attracts an impressive list of rock stars and royalty. It's a classically large, elegant hotel, with posh rooms complete with Dutch wallpaper and huge beds. The Michelin-starred La Rive restaurant is highly acclaimed.

€€€ The Dylan, Keizersgracht 384, T020-530 2010, www.dylan amsterdam.com. Style guru Anouchka Hempel designed this small hotel (formerly Blakes). Rooms are individually themed, all centred on a courtyard, and there is an excellent fusion restaurant downstairs.

€€€ Hotel 717, Prinsengracht 717, T020-427 0717, www.717hotel.nl. This hotel feels like a mix between a glossy magazine shoot and the home of a rich art-collector friend. Each of the 8 rooms is impeccably designed, crammed with artwork, beautiful fabrics, pale colours and an eclectic mix of antiques. Good canalside location.

€€€-€€ Ambassade, Herengracht 341, T020-555 0222, www.ambassade -hotel.nl. Ten 17th-century canalside houses make up this hotel in a lovely spot on Herengracht. This is one for bibliophiles: regulars include John Le Carré, Umberto Eco and Salman Rushdie (check out the signed copies in the library). Rooms are traditional and plush; those in the eaves are the most appealing.

€€€-€€ Seven Bridges, Reguliersgracht 31, T020-623 1329, www.sevenbridges hotel.nl. Set in a 300-year-old house, this hotel is quiet, with rooms overlooking either the canal and the famous Seven Bridges or a small garden. Breakfast is served in your room. Book months in advance.

€€ Canal House Hotel, Keizersgracht 148, T020-622 5182, www.canalhouse.nl. Crammed with antiques, this 26-room hotel tries to maintain an early 1800s atmosphere in its lovely 17th-century shell. That means no TVs but plenty of lofty ceilings, solid furniture and homely quilts. There's an elegant breakfast room, small bar and the location on the Keizersgracht Canal is peaceful.

€ Amistad Hotel, Kerkstraat 42, T020-624 8074, www.amistad.nl. Run by husband-and-husband team, Johan and Joost, the Amistad is one of the most popular gay hotels in town. Simple, colourful rooms come with or without en suite bathrooms and have wooden floors and bright artwork. There's an internet lounge in the reception area.

€ Winston, Warmoesstraat 129, T020-623 1380, www.winston.nl. This kooky, noisy 'art hotel' has individually designed rooms. They are small (most come with bathroom) and are decorated with anything from bright primary colours to fish motifs to x-rays – check the website. Good location on the edge of the red-light district, with a bar and nightclub onsite (see page 26). Decent breakfasts are included in the price.

● Eating

Traditional Dutch fare isn't the lightest of cuisines – expect hearty meat-and-potato dishes, thick pancakes oozing all sorts of fillings, and hefty *broodjes* (sandwiches) stacked with meat, cheeses or fish. Having said that, chefs across the city are also wallowing in an orgy of fusion cuisine, which often puts French or Asian slants on Dutch dishes. Holland's colonial heritage also means lots of Indonesian flavours, and the city's multicultural population ensures plenty of Chinese, Thai, Italian and Japanese restaurants to choose from. Prices, although steeper since the introduction of the euro, remain reasonable.

Breakfast

† **De Bakkerswinkel**, Warmoesstraat 69, T020-489 8000. Breakfast and lunch only. Closed Mon. Bustling, airy deli/café serving excellent brunches, sandwiches and fat slices of quiche.

† **Winkel**, Noordermarkt 43, T020-623 0223. Breakfast and lunch only. Big breakfasts and legendary apple cake at this lively café. Be prepared to queue on Mon and Sat (market days).

Lunch

†† **Haesje Claes**, Spuistraat 273-275, T020-624 9998. Old-style Dutch comfort eating in this popular wood-panelled restaurant. *Stampot* – a filling stew of potatoes mashed with cabbage and served with sausage – is a speciality and perfect fare on a rainy afternoon. There are also good fish dishes, if you fancy something lighter.

† **Café Luxembourg**, Spui 24, T020-620 6264. Elegant café with a long marble bar and equally long menu,

inlcuding favourites like split pea soup, salmon burgers and *kroketten* (croquettes). Newspapers and a slow pace in the morning, more frenetic at lunch and dinner.

♥ Pannekoekhuis Upstairs, Grimburgwal 2, T020-626 5603. Students flock to this tiny pancake house dolling out good-value servings of filled sweet and savoury pancakes. Service can be slow.

Dinner

♥♥♥ Blauw aan de Wal, Achterburgwal 99, T020-330 2257. This is a real find, hidden away down an alley in the heart of the red-light district. Chic Mediterranean cuisine is the order of the day, with old wood floors, bare brick walls and a pretty courtyard making it all rather romantic.

♥♥♥ Christophe, Leliegracht 46, T020-625 0807, www.restaurant christophe.nl. Tue-Sat dinner. Classic restaurant in a quiet canalside location. The atmosphere is discreet and elegant (jackets are required) and the food is a sumptuous feast of French-inspired contemporary cooking. Reservations are essential.

♥♥♥ Brasserie Harkema, Nes 67, T020-428 2222, www.brasserieharkema.nl. Lunch and dinner daily. This weird fusion of traditional French-style brasserie and ultra-modern industrial styling is popular with locals, and the food is fast and good.

♥♥♥ d'Vijff Vlieghen, Spuistraat 294-302, T020-530 4060, www.thefiveflies .com. Dinner only. You won't have this place to yourself, but it's worth braving the tour groups for the food. The menu is top-notch Dutch, served in a lovely string of 17th-century houses filled with antiques and Delft tiles. Look out for the Rembrandt etchings on the walls.

♥♥♥ Kantjil en de Tijger, Spuistraat 291-293, T020-620 0994. Refreshingly free of the usual oriental decor, this large, chic space serves *rijsttafel* (rice table): an array of up to 20 Indonesian dishes. Arrive with an appetite. The spicy coconut prawns are good, too.

♥ Café Bern, Nieuwmarkt 9, T020-6220034. Dinner only. Typically laid-back brown café (see below), specializing in cheese fondues, which is an unofficial national dish hijacked from Switzerland. Punters wash this down with a shot of strong stuff.

❝❞ Don't be put off by the term *bruine cafés* (brown cafés) – these ubiquitous café-bars are the cosy mainstay of Amsterdam's nightlife.

---

❶ Nightlife

Day by Day is a useful monthly English-language listings guide produced by the tourist office, covering everything from live music and events to exhibitions and museums. Amsterdam has a huge gay and lesbian scene – many call it the gay capital of Europe – with countless gay-friendly hotels, bars and clubs. These are mostly focused on the area around Reguliersdwarsstraat.

Bars and coffeeshops

Don't be put off by the term *bruine cafés* (brown cafés) – these ubiquitous café-bars are the cosy mainstay of Amsterdam's nightlife. They're actually

called that because smoke has stained the walls with nicotine over the years. Lovely. Nevertheless, these friendly pubs, found all over the old centre and along the canals, are a great place to meet locals and try Dutch beer. Note that you are only permitted to smoke cigarettes in these and other bars. For legal cannabis, head to a coffeeshop, again found throughout the centre and identified by the leaf motif or Rasta flag in the window (see page 23). These generally have menus selling various types of cannabis. Take it easy, especially with hash cakes and cookies, which can pack a powerful punch.

For a chilled-out bar scene, often with DJs and dancing late into the night, try out some of the newer lounge bars around Nieuwezijds Voorburgwal, as well as the more traditional nightlife spots around Rembrandtplein and Leidseplein.

Clubs and live music

The club scene isn't as cutting edge as you might hope, although there are some good places in the centre. **Winston**, on Warmoesstraat, is hip at the moment (see page 25) and **Melkweg**, Lijnbaansgracht 234a, T020-531 8181, www.melkweg.nl, is a long-running favourite, functioning as a full-on arts centre, and therefore a good place to catch live music.

Classical music and theatre

The city's finest venue for opera is the **Muziektheater**, popularly known as the **Stopera**, on Waterlooplein (theatre entrance at Amstel 3), T020-551 8117, www.het-muziektheater.nl. The grand old **Concertgebouw**, T020-671 8345, www.concertgebouw.nl, is the venue for classical music and one of the world's most visited concert halls.

Antwerp

If Brussels is Belgium's biggest hitter, Antwerp is certainly a heavyweight contender. This waterfront metropolis has huge horizons: Europe's second largest port and a world centre for the diamond trade, it has reinvented itself as a modern city without forgetting its 16th- century heyday. Despite war damage, there are constant reminders of Antwerp's medieval and Renaissance past, from the impossibly delicate cathedral spire to the magnificent Rubens canvases in churches and museums. A spectacular stint as Europe's Cultural Capital in 1993 helped revive the disused quays of the Zuid – now a haven for barflies and gastronauts – and the gritty northern Eilandje. With its heritage of creative energy, Antwerp has become one of Europe's fashion hubs, and its myriad restaurants set impossibly high standards.

Arts & culture
★★★★

Eating
★★★★★

Nightlife
★★★★★

Outdoors
★★

Romance
★★★

Shopping
★★★★

Sightseeing
★★★

Value for money
★★★

Overall score
★★★★

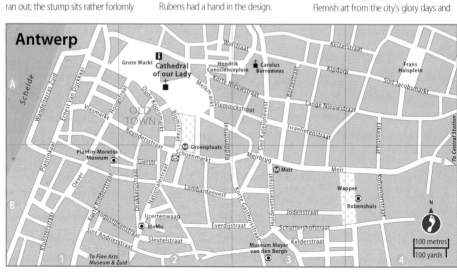

◉ Sights

Around Grote Markt ◥A2

Antwerp's grandest square is lined with guildhouses topped with scrolling gables and golden statuary. The central fountain depicts Brabo, a Roman soldier who, according to legend, chopped off the hand of a giant who imposed tolls on ships. Some say this is how the city gained its name – "hand werpen", or hand-throwing – though this is given short shrift by pedantic etymologists. Whatever the truth, it's a suitably dramatic monument, with water gushing from the tyrant's severed hand.

South of the square, the **Cathedral of Our Lady** ⓘ *Handschoenmarkt*, ◥A2, *Mon-Fri 1000-1700, Sat 1000-1500, Sun 1300-1600; carillon concerts Jun-mid Sep Mon 2100, Fri 1130, €2*, is among the most graceful pieces of medieval architecture in northern Europe. Its slender spire was supposed to have a twin, but the money ran out; the stump sits rather forlornly

Cathedral of Our Lady

next to the finished article. Inside, Rubens' cherub-rich *Descent from the Cross* is the main draw.

About 200 m east of Grote Markt, **Hendrik Conscienceplein** is the city's most charming square. Built by the Jesuits, it was dubbed Little Rome. It's dominated by the exuberantly baroque **Carolus Borromeus Church** ⓘ ◥A3 *Mon- Sat 1000-1230, 1400-1700, Sun services only*, which has an uplifting cream and gold interior. Almost inevitably, Rubens had a hand in the design.

Rubenshuis
ⓘ *Wapper 9-11, T03-201 1555, www.museum.antwerpen.be, ◥B4. Tue-Sun 1000-1700. €6.*

Although little remains as it was, this is the place to learn about Rubens and his times. When the artist-cum-diplomat built this Italianate mansion, it was the talk of the town. Roam from room to room (the audio commentary is a must) and admire the atelier before stepping into the garden, familiar from many of his paintings. It's easy to imagine the master strolling here with intellectuals and politicians, showing off a rare tulip or potato plant from the New World.

Fine Arts Museum
ⓘ *Leopold de Waelplaats, T03-238 7809, www.museum.antwerpen.be/kmska. Tue-Sat 1000-1700, Sun 1000-1800. €6.*

The city's showpiece museum is an imposing neoclassical affair in the Zuid, with a well-judged collection of (mostly) Flemish art from the city's glory days and

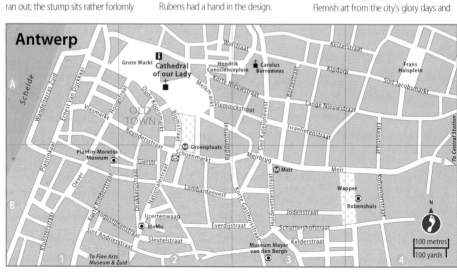

Heaven Ghent

If you're looking for Bruges without the tourists, take a 40-minute train ride to medieval Ghent. Laced with dreamy waterways, it's a university city, more youthful and alive than "Bruges-la-morte", but more reflective and less showy than Antwerp. You can easily explore the centre on foot, which is just as well, because Ghent has the highest concentration of listed monuments in the country. It has an equally impressive concentration of pubs, ranging from 'brown' taverns to sleek 1970s-style bars and cluttered bohemian hang-outs. It's suited to structureless rambling, but there are a few must-sees: **Jan Van Eyck's** *Lamb of God* ⓘ *Sint Baafsplein, T09-269 2045, Mon-Sat 0930-1630, Sun from 1300, €3*, a gloriously luminous altarpiece in St Bavo's Cathedral; the spooky **Gravensteen Castle** ⓘ *Sint-Veerleplein, T09-225 9306, Apr-Sep 0900-1800, Oct-Mar 0900-1700, €6*, built in 1180 and endlessly rebuilt; **Graslei** and **Korenlei**, rows of glittering guildhouses on either side of the Lys; and **Smak** ⓘ *Citadelpark, T09-221 1703, www.smak.be, Tue-Sun 1000-1800, €5*, Belgium's hardest-hitting contemporary art museum.

the 20th century. Upstairs are huge canvases by Rubens and his students, Van Dyck and Jordaens, as well as exquisite works by Van Eyck, Memling and Quentin Metsys. Downstairs, you can enter the disturbing world of James Ensor, whose mask-wearing grotesques and skeletons still shock, then return to normality with Rik Wouters's tender portraits of his wife.

Plantin-Moreus Museum
ⓘ *Vrijdagmarkt 22, T03-221 1450,* **⤓B1**. *Tue-Sun 1000-1700 (last entry 1600). €6.*

A sumptuous Renaissance mansion and one-time printing press, the former home of the humanist Christopher Plantin is the only museum on UNESCO's World Heritage list. Plantin's most famous work was a five-language Bible, a world first. Amid the beams, books, proofreading desks and working 16th-century presses, are the family quarters, hung with exquisite portraits by

Rubens. In summer, the inner courtyard is full of the scent of lavender and roses.

Museum Mayer van den Bergh
ⓘ *Lange Gasthuisstraat 19, T03-232 4237,* **⤓B3**. *Tue-Sun 1000-1700. €4.*

Rubenshuis

This dazzling array of paintings, statuary, tapestries and medieval missals was assembled by a 19th-century collector. Amid the many marvels are two unmissable Breughels: *Mad Meg*, a nightmarish allegory on the theme of folly, and the delightful *Twelve Proverbs*, a witty slant on popular peasant sayings.

MoMu
ⓘ *Nationalestraat 28, T03-470 2770, www.momu.be,* **⤓B2**. *Tue-Sun 1000-1800, Thu until 2100. €5.*

Home to some of the fashion world's brightest talents – Van Noten, Demeulemeester, Margiela and many more – Antwerp does expensive clothes shops well. You can find out what makes the designers tick by visiting the light-filled Modenatie building, which houses the world-famous Fashion Academy and this fascinating fashion museum with temporary exhibitions.

Travel essentials

Getting there Eurostar, www.eurostar.com, runs to Brussels Gare du Midi, from where it's a 40-min train ride to Antwerp's Central Station. Other international services currently arrive at Berchem station to the south. From Antwerp's Deurne airport, T03-285 6530, there's a shuttle bus to town (€1) or a taxi costs about €20.

Getting around The city is compact and easily walkable; there's also a good bus, tram and metro network, operated by **De Lijn**, www.delijn.be (day pass €3). You should also take full advantage of the city's cycle lanes; for rental, try **De Windroos**, Steenplein, T03-480 9388.

Tourist information The tourist office, Grote Markt, T03-232 0103, www.antwerpen.be, provides free city maps and a host of useful brochures.

Sleeping

€€€ De Witte Lelie, Keizerstraat 16-18, T03-226 1966, www.dewitte lelie.be. Antwerp's best boutique hotel: 10 ultra-stylish rooms in 3 adjacent 17th-century townhouses on a quiet street, within easy walking distance of the old centre. Parking and patio garden.

€€ Hotel t' Sandt, Zand 13-19, T03-232 9390, www.hotel-sandt.be. An elegant establishment with an alluring aura of discreet luxury. The breakfast room has the feel of a French country house, with pastel-painted antiques aplenty.

€€ Julien, Korte Nieuwstraat 24, T03-229 0600, www.hotel-julien.com. On the eastern edge of the Old Town, this designer hotel is sleek, stylized and exceedingly friendly. Pinky-green lights glow in the hallway; breakfast is served on trendy ceramics, and the rooms are calm and comfortable, with extra touches like truly thick curtains.

€ Postiljon, Blauwmoezelstraat 6, T03-231 7575. In the shadow of the cathedral, this old inn is now a cheap, cheerful, family-run affair. Some rooms have bathrooms. Great location, if you don't mind the sound of morning bells.

€ Scheldezicht, Sint-Jansvliet 10-12, T03-231 6602, www.hotelschelde zicht.be. A pretty and old-fashioned family-run hotel that doesn't stand on ceremony. The only real flourish is the extravagant spiral staircase – but it's comfortable and reasonably priced.

Eating

YYY Gin Fish, Haarstraat 9, T03-231 3207. Tue-Sat, 1800-2230. Seafood supremo Didier Garnich whips up his dishes in an open kitchen surrounded by a handful of customers on bar stools. There's no menu and everyone gets the same delicious 4-course meal, with fabulously fresh fish very much to the fore. It's almost too efficient, but it's nothing if not memorable.

YYY Kommilfoo, Vlaamse Kaai 17, T03-237 3000. Tue-Fri 1200-1400 and 1830-2200; Sat 1830-2200. This prizewinning restaurant in the Zuid has a superb 4-course Chef's Fantasy menu for €70, including wine. Expect red-onion soup with Westmalle beer, millefeuille of langoustines with parmesan or cod with cauliflower purée and fennel.

YY Le Zoute Zoen, Zirkstraat 15-17, T03-226 9220. Closed Sat lunch and Mon. A charming bistro with wax-caked candelabras, a mosaic floor and shelves cluttered with curios. The food is Belgo-French with an Italian twist and, unusually in a city that caters mainly to carnivores, it's vegetarian-friendly.

Y Bar 2, Vrijdagmarkt 19, T03-227 5436. Wed, Thu and Sat from 1000, Fri from 0800, Sun 1200-2300. A trendy, unfussy *eetcafé* that serves wok dishes, salads and excellent sandwiches, on a square that, come Fri morning, buzzes with an open-air auction.

Y Bassin, Tavernierkaai 1, T03-225 3637. Mon-Fri 1200-2300, Sat 1800-2300, Sun 1200-2200. At this cheerful riverside brasserie, north of the centre, classic Flemish cuisine is prepared "grandma's way". Try superb *stoofvlees* (beef stewed in beer), home-made prawn croquettes, cod gratinée and *stoemp* (mash) with sausages.

Y De Bloemkool, Groendalstraat 20, T03-227 3742. Mon-Tue and Sun 1130-1730, Wed 1130-1630, Fri-Sat 1130-2130. In the heart of the shopping district, this is an ideal spot for ladies and gents who lunch. There's a small terrace and a pleasant glass-roofed area at the back. The spag bol is splendid and the superior salads come with individual pots of proper dressing.

Nightlife

Finding a good bar here is like falling off a log – and after a few Belgian brews, you may well do precisely that.

The densest concentrations of drinking dens are in the Old Town and the Zuid. In town, try **De Muze**, Melkmarkt 15, for smoky jazz vibes; or **Witzli-Poetzli**, Blauwmoezelstraat 8, for scruffy boho charm. In the Zuid, **Mogador**, Graaf van Egmontstraat 57, attracts a classy pre-club crowd; **The Heming Way,** Waalse Kaai 19, serves cocktails to a cool Cuban soundtrack; and the shabby-chic **Bar Tabac**, Waalse Kaai 43, is the thinking man's choice for a late-night session.

If your last visit to Athens was before 2004, you're in for a surprise: Athens has been spruced up, refined and beautified, bringing it into the 21st century with gusto. Ancient monuments have been restored, neoclassical façades repainted, billboards and neon lighting torn down, the metro extended, tramlines added, pedestrian zones paved and trees planted. But in a city where countless layers of history sit concrete-upon-brick-upon-stone, you'll still find a curious juxtaposition of Western European, Balkan and Middle Eastern cultures, all of which are reflected in the food, the music and the architecture. This is also the city that, back in its ancient heyday, invented hedonism and you'll not be disappointed on that score now – Athens nightlife is beautiful, extravagant and inexhaustible.

Athens

Arts & culture
★★★

Eating
★★★

Nightlife
★★★★★

Outdoors
★★

Romance
★★

Shopping
★★★

Sightseeing
★★★★

Value for money
★★★

Overall score
★★

At a glance

Take the **Acropolis** as your main point of reference. If you are on a short stay, you'll probably be based in **Plaka**, Athens' oldest residential neighbourhood, skirting the Acropolis' northern and eastern slopes. The northern limit of Plaka is marked by **Ermou** (the main shopping street), which runs east–west from **Syntagma** (home to the Greek Parliament) to **Monastiraki**, best known for its Sunday morning flea market and its metro station, then proceeds to smart residential **Thissio** and **Gazi**. On the far side of Ermou lies **Psirri** and, northeast of Syntagma, the rocky mound of **Mount Lycabettus** rises above the well-to-do area of **Kolonaki**. Gazi and Psirri deserve a special mention: both former industrial zones, they have recently been transformed into night-time districts filled with happening bars, restaurants, clubs and art galleries.

Another welcome addition to Athens is the new **Archaeological Promenade**, a 4-km paved, lamp-lit walkway that now links the city's ancient sites. Starting from the new Akropolis metro station, Dionissiou Areopagitou curves around the south side of the Acropolis to join Apostolou Pavlou, which then runs alongside the Ancient Agora to bring you to Thissio. From here Adrianou runs east to Plaka, while Ermou runs west past **Kerameikos** (ancient Athens' cemetery) towards Gazi.

★ *Don't leave town without grabbing a souvlaki takeaway.*

> Athens embodies the pre-eminent quality of the antique world, Art.

Benjamin Disraeli

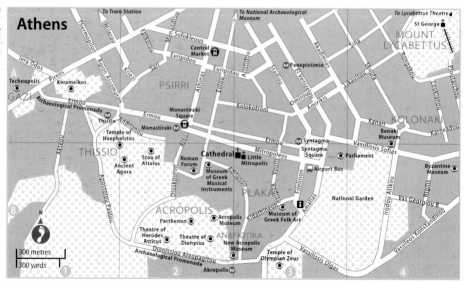

Athens

⊙ Sights

Acropolis

ⓘ *Acropolis Hill, Plaka, T210-321 0219, www.culture.gr,* **NB2**. *Summer daily 0800-1900; winter daily 0830-1700. €12 (this ticket also gives free entry to the Ancient Agora, Roman Forum, Theatre of Dionysus, Kerameikos and the Temple of Olympian Zeus and is valid for 4 days). Metro Akropolis or Monastiraki.*

Most stunning at night, when it rises above the modern city bathed in golden floodlights, the Acropolis is a rocky mound crowned by three ancient temples, symbolizing the birth of Athens and indeed of Western civilization. Today it receives some three million visitors per year and is also the biggest selling point for hotel rooms and restaurant terraces claiming to glimpse its magic.

The largest and most revered temple is the fifth-century BC **Parthenon**, built entirely from marble. Supported by 46 Doric columns, it was originally intended as a sanctuary for Athena and housed a giant gold and ivory statue of

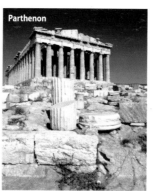
Parthenon

the goddess. The controversial Elgin Marbles (Greeks prefer to call them the Parthenon Marbles), are a series of bas-reliefs that once formed the internal frieze. In 1816 Lord Elgin, British Ambassador to Athens, which was under Ottoman occupation at the time, sold them to the British Museum in London, where they remain to this day.

Close by, you can also visit the **Acropolis Museum**, which houses many treasures, including five caryatids (columns designed to represent maidens), which once supported the **Erechtheion**, a

temple dedicated to Athena and Poseidon who are said to have fought for the patronage of Athens on this spot. Other museum offerings are stone carvings found on the site, including the Calf Bearer (a statue of a young man carrying a sacrificial calf on his shoulders), dating from 570 BC, and the Peplos Kore and Almond-Eyed Kore (statues of maidens which would have been votive offerings to Athena), dating from 550-500 BC.

Work is now underway on the **New Acropolis Museum**, opposite the Akropolis metro station in Plaka. An all-glass structure designed by Swiss architect Bernard Tschumi, it will eventually take over from the existing museum. It is scheduled to open in summer 2007.

Plaka

ⓘ *Metro Acropolis or Monastiraki.* **NB3**.

Built into the hillside below the Acropolis, Plaka is Athens' oldest residential quarter. Touristy but undeniably charming, it's made up of cobbled alleys lined with pastel-coloured neoclassical mansions dating from the late 19th century. (During this period Greece was trying to

---

⊖ Travel essentials

Getting there Athens International Airport (Eleftherios Venizelos), T210-353 0000, www.aia.gr, is 33 km northeast of the city. Express bus services to the city include the X95 to Syntagma (€3.20). Metro line 3 (blue) runs to Monastiraki (every 30 mins, €6) via Syntagma (25-30 mins). Alternatively, take the train to the main **Larissa Station** (every 15 mins 0550-2250, €6). A taxi will cost you about €25.

Getting around Most of the main attractions lie within walking distance of one another in the city centre, parts of

which are paved and pedestrian only. **Buses** are cheap and frequent but often crowded (single €0.45). There are three **metro** lines (www.ametro.gr, single €0.70), the main nodal points being Monastiraki, Syntagma and Omonia. The green line is especially useful for reaching the port at Piraeus. Two **tram lines** (single €0.60) connect Syntagma in the city centre to the coast; ideal for reaching beaches in the Glyfada area. For further information contact **OASA** (Athens Public Transport Organization), T185, www.oasa.gr. Athens' **taxis** are among

the cheapest in Europe, and Athenian taxi drivers among the most erratic. Taxis are no luxury – everyone takes them and it is quite normal to share a ride with other passengers going in a similar direction.

Tourist information Greek National Tourism Organisation (GNTO), Tsocha 2, Ambelokipi, T210-870 7000, www.gnto.gr, has a walk-in visitors' centre at Amalias 26 (close to Syntagma), T210-331 0716, Mon-Fri 0900-1900, Sat and Sun 1000-1600; also at the airport, T210-353 0448, Mon-Fri 0800-1900, Sat and Sun 1000-1600.

re-establish its cultural identity after liberation from the Ottoman Turks.) The only really old buildings remaining here are Byzantine churches. Particularly notable is the 12th-century **Little Mitropolis** ⓘ *daily 0700-1300,* ⬛B3, standing next to the far less attractive 19th-century **Cathedral** and the residential area of **Anafiotika**. Besides the countless souvenir shops and tavernas, look out for the museums of **Greek Musical Instruments** ⓘ *Diogenous 1-3,* ⬛B2, *Tue and Thu-Sun 1000-1400, Wed 1200-1800, free,* and **Greek Folk Art** ⓘ *Kidathineon 17,* ⬛B3, *Tue-Sun 1000-1400, €2,* a cluster of whitewashed Cycladic-style houses built by settlers from the island of Anafi.

Ancient Agora

ⓘ *Andrianou 24, Monastiraki, T 210-321 0185, www.culture.gr,* ⬛B2. *Summer daily 0800-1900; winter daily 0800-1700. €4. Metro Monastiraki.*

Today, Agora is a romantic wilderness of coarse grazing land and olive trees, strewn with fallen columns and crowned by an ancient temple. During the Golden Age, however, this was Athens' main

Plaka

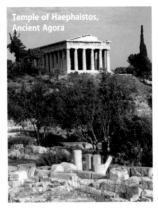

Temple of Haephaistos, Ancient Agora

marketplace, as well as the city's political, administrative and cultural heart. It was here that Socrates and St Paul made their public speeches and where democracy was born, although now you'll need some imagination to interpret it as such.

The buildings that remain recognisably intact are the remarkably well-preserved fifth-century BC **Temple of Haephaistos** and the **Stoa of Attalos**, a two-storey structure from the second century BC, which originally functioned as a trading centre but today houses the **Agora Museum**, displaying ancient finds from the site.

Central Market

ⓘ *Sofokleous and Evripidou,* ⬛A2. *Mon-Sat 0900-1500. Metro Monastiraki or Omonia.*

Modern-day Athenians shop within the halls of the vast covered market, an iron and glass structure erected in 1870. A veritable feast for the eyes, it is here that you will find stalls trading in seasonal Mediterranean fruit and vegetables, dried figs, nuts, olives and spices. In the seafood section are glittering silver-scaled fish and copious quantities of octopus and squid

displayed upon mounds of freshly ground ice, while the meat section (definitely not for the squeamish) is populated by blood-splattered butchers hacking at carcasses on tree trunks that improvise as chopping boards.

National Archaeological Museum

ⓘ *Patission 44, Omonia, T 210-821 7717, www.culture.gr. Summer daily 0800-1900; winter Mon 1300-1930, Tue-Sun 0830-1500. €7. Metro Victoria.*

Holding one of the world's finest collections of ancient Greek art, this museum is a must-see. Re-opened in 2004 after renovation, the light and airy marble-floored exhibition spaces now show off elegant classical sculpture to maximum effect. It's vast so don't try to see everything but be sure to catch the subtly coloured 16th-century BC **Thira Frescoes**, found buried below lava following a volcanic explosion on the island of Santorini, and the **Mycenaen Collection**, a hoard of gold jewellery and weaponry dating from between the 16th and 11th centuries BC.

Central Market

European City Breaks Athens

Benaki Museum

ⓘ *Vassilissis Sofias and Koumbari 1, Kolonaki, T210-367 1000, www.benaki.gr,* **ЫA4**. *Mon, Wed, Fri, Sat 0900-1700, Thu 0900- 2400, Sun 0900-1500. €6 (free Thu). Metro Syntagma.*

Born in Alexandria, Egypt, in 1873, Antonios Benakis was an avid art collector who gave this neoclassical house and his entire art collection to the Greek state before his death in 1954. A journey through the history of Greek art from 3000 BC up to the 20th century, exhibits include sculpture, ceramics, jewellery, paintings, furniture and costumes, laid out in chronological order. Top attractions include a hoard of second-century BC golden filigree jewellery inlaid with precious stones, known as the **Thessaly Treasure**, two early paintings by El Greco, and the reconstruction of two wooden-panelled living rooms from an Ottoman-inspired house in northern Greece from the 1750s.

Byzantine Museum

ⓘ *Vassilissis Sofias 22, Kolonaki, T210-723 2178, www.culture.gr,* **ЫB4**. *Tue-Sun 0830-1500. €4. Metro Evangelismos.*

National Archaeological Museum

Byzantine Museum

Hidden below the courtyard of an Italianate villa, this open-plan, split-level, underground exhibition space opened in 2004. Pieces are displayed in chronological order, following the development of the Byzantine Empire from the advent of Christianity (when many pagan symbols were absorbed by the creed) up to the fall of Constantinople in 1453. The exhibition starts with stone carvings, sculpture and mosaics taken from early basilicas. It then continues with icons depicting sultry-eyed saints against golden backgrounds, frescoes illustrating biblical events and minutely-detailed silver and gold jewellery and ecclesiastical artefacts.

Mount Lycabettus

ⓘ *Metro Evangelismos.* **ЫA4**.

Athens' highest vantage point at 295 m, Lycabettus affords panoramic views of the city, the mountains and the sea. A network of footpaths leads up through pinewoods and lush vegetation to the summit – if the hike is too steep, take a taxi or catch the **funicular** ⓘ *from Ploutarchou St in Kolonaki,* **ЫA4**, *every 30*

mins daily 0900-0300, for a two-minute whizz through a cliffside tunnel. The peak is capped by the tiny white **Church of St George** and a series of terraces hosting the **Orizontes** restaurant (page 37) and a café. Carved into the rocks on the north-facing slope, the open-air **Lycabettus Theatre** stages summer concerts. Recent performers have included Moby and Patti Smith.

Technopolis

ⓘ *Pireos 100, Gazi, T210-3460981,* **ЫA1**. *Hours vary depending on exhibitions. Free. Metro Thissio.*

Technopolis (Art City) occupies the former City Gasworks. A multi-purpose arts complex, the disused gas tanks and brick outbuildings have been converted to provide a series of spaces for exhibitions, concerts (Tindersticks and Tricky have played here) and theatre, while the towering brick chimneys are lit red at night and remain the symbol of new art in an urban environment. There's also a small **Maria Callas Museum** ⓘ *Pireos 100, Mon-Fri 0900-2100, free.*

Mount Lycabettus

European City Breaks Athens

The Hellenic Festival

Each summer, from June to the end of September, the Hellenic Festival stages open-air theatre, opera, classical music and dance at the ancient Odeon of Herodes Atticus, plus rock concerts at the hilltop Lycabettus Theatre. A stunning venue, the second-century Odeon is carved into the rocks of the southern slope of the Acropolis. The building was commissioned by the Roman consul, Herodes Atticus, in memory of his wife Regilla. The 28-m high façade serves as a backdrop to the stage, and the semicircular theatre space, with a radius of 38 m, can seat an audience of 5000. The modern festival dates back to 1955; legendary figures that have graced its stage include Maria Callas, Margot Fonteyn and Rudolph Nureyev. More recently, summer 2006 saw performances by, among others, Philip Glass, Diana Krall, Liza Minnelli and the Vienna Philharmonic Orchestra. Performances begin at 2100 (June to August) and 2030 (September). Advance booking begins three weeks prior to each performance (see www.hellenicfestival.gr for the latest programme).

Tickets are available from: **Hellenic Festival Box Office** ⓘ *39 Panepistimiou (in the arcade)*, 🚇A3, *Mon-Fri 0830-1600 and Sat 0900-1430*; **Odeon of Herodes Atticus** ⓘ *Dionysiou Areopagitou*, 🚇B2, *daily 0900-1400 and 1800-2100*; or by **telephone** ⓘ *credit card payment only, T210-928 2900, Mon-Thu 0830-2000 and Sat 0900-1430*.

● Sleeping

Syntagma is where you'll find grand expensive hotels, the Greek Parliament and lots of traffic. Kolonaki is for image-conscious shopaholics and socialites but is fun if you can take the pace. For romance, opt for Plaka. Avoid Syngrou: it's functional and impersonal and aimed primarily at business travellers.

€€€ Electra Palace, Nikodimou 18, Plaka, T210-337 0000, www.electra hotels.gr. The EP's yellow-and-white neoclassical façade, complete with wrought-iron balconies, was added during renovation for the Olympics. It's now Plaka's most stylish hotel. Some rooms have an Acropolis view. There's a spa and fitness centre, plus an outdoor infinity pool on the roof.

€€€ Fresh, Sophocleous 26 and Klisthenous, Psirri, T210-524 8511, www.freshhotel.gr. This hotel opened in 2004 and immediately featured in *Wallpaper* magazine. Close to the gritty Central Market, the look is minimalist, with fresh flowers, lounge music, and vivid orange, green and pink details adding to the fun. There's a summer rooftop bar with a pool and sundeck, and nouvelle Greek cuisine.

€€€ St George Lycabettus, Kleomenous 2, Kolonaki, T210-729 0711, www.sglycabettus.gr. On the rocky, pine-scented slopes of Mt Lycabettus, bordering chic Kolonaki, this white 1970s building offers 158 plush modern rooms, most with balconies and Acropolis views. There's a funky bar-restaurant and the top-floor Grand Balcon has stunning views. There's also a roof garden with pool.

€€ Central Hotel, Apolonos 21, Plaka, T210-323 4357, www.centralhotel.gr. On the edge of Plaka, this hotel has light and airy rooms, with minimalist Italian furniture in pale-coloured wood and puffy white duvets. There's a roof terrace with Acropolis views and a jacuzzi, plus a ground-floor restaurant.

€€ Hotel Plaka, Kapnikareas 7, Plaka, T210-322 2096, www.plakahotel.gr. Smart and discreet, this hotels lies in a side street between Monastiraki and Syntagma metro stations. The 67 rooms have pine floors, minimalist furniture and primary-coloured fabrics. There's a roof garden with a bar on summer evenings, so you can watch the sun set over the Acropolis.

€ Marble House, An Zinni 35, Koukaki, T210-922 8294/923 4058, www.marblehouse.gr. This small family-run hotel lies in a peaceful residential area, just a 10-min walk from Plaka and the Acropolis. The 16 rooms are clean and simple, with mini-bars and ceiling fans.

€ Student and Travellers' Inn, Kidathineon 16, Plaka, T210-324 4808, www.studenttravellersinn.com. Just off Plaka's prettiest square, this upscale youth hostel offers singles, doubles and quadruples, plus dorms. All the rooms are spotless and have wooden floors, a sink and mirror, and some have bathrooms. Young, friendly English-speakers run the reception. There's internet access and an internal courtyard garden with a big-screen TV.

🍴 Eating

Plaka is fine for lunch but to really tap into Athenian nightlife dine in Psirri or Gazi, where funky new eateries breathe life into standard Greek taverna fare and stay open well beyond midnight.

Breakfast

Gallery Café, Adrianou 33, Monastiraki, T210-324 9080. Overlooking the Ancient Agora, this café has a lounge atmosphere with exposed stonework, sofas and coffee tables, cool music and modern art on the walls.
Tristato, Dedalou 34 and Geronda, Plaka, T210-324 4472. In a pedestrian side street just off Platia Filomousou, this old-fashioned café is a great place for morning coffee or an afternoon pot of herbal tea.

Lunch

🍴 **O Platanos**, Diogenous 4, Plaka, T210-322 0666. One of the oldest and most hidden tavernas in Plaka, O Platanos dates back to 1932. Homely meat-and-vegetable casseroles – such as lamb with aubergine and veal with spinach – are served at tables on a bougainvillea-covered terrace, in the shade of an old plane tree, after which the restaurant is named.
🍴 **To Kouti**, Adrianou 23, Monastiraki, T210-321 3229. Playful salads, meat and seafood dishes, seasoned with spices

and aromatic herbs, are guaranteed to make your tastebuds sing. Great for dinner, or lunch after a trip to Monastiraki's Sun flea market.

Dinner

🍴🍴🍴 **Orizontes**, Mt Lycabettus, Kolonaki, T210-722 7065. The high point of Athens, 295 m above sea level, is the place to eat if you have only one night in town, plus the money to foot the bill. Perched atop Mt Lycabettus, Orizontes offers stunning views across the city and a menu of refined fusion cuisine. Reservations are recommended.
🍴🍴 **Mamacas**, Persefonis 41, Gazi, T210-346 4984. In trendy Gazi, Mamacas has a Mykonos-inspired, whitewashed-wood dining room, plus

66 99 Ask Athenians what they think their city does better than any other European capital and they will probably tell you about the nightlife.

outdoor tables backed by the silhouette of the disused gasworks. The menu features Greek taverna classics with a twist, and there's a seductive wine bar annexe.
🍴 **Zeideron**, Taki 10-12, Psirri, T210-321 5368. The perfect place to start a night out in Psirri, Zeideron serves colourful, modern taverna fare. In summer, take a table on the busy pedestrian street; in winter there's a romantic old-fashioned dining room downstairs, and a light and airy glass conservatory up top.

🌙 Nightlife

Ask Athenians what they think their city does better than any other European capital and they will probably tell you about the nightlife. All year round Psirri and Gazi are rocking. In Psirri, **Soul**, Evripidou 65, is a glamorous but fun cocktail bar in a red-walled courtyard garden with sofas and finger food, while nearby **Psirra**, Miaouli 19, pulls the grungy intellectual crowd, who drink *rakomelo* (hot raki with honey and cinnamon) at streetside tables. In upmarket Kolonaki, **Balthazar**, Tsoha 27, is a see-and-be-seen bar-restaurant in a beautifully lit walled garden, rivalled in terms of sophistication only by **Mommy**, Delphon 4, off Skoufa 62, a bar-restaurant with 1970s revival decor and a hip thirtysomething clientele. In Plaka, **Pavlos**, Platia Filomousou, is a colourful café with sofas, overlooking a leafy square; perfect for a nightcap.

The best clubs are in Gazi: **Nipiagogio**, Kleanthous 8, occupies a former kindergarten, with drinks and dancing till the last customers leave at 0600. By the sea in Voula, **Passa** is a large dance club with a restaurant and palm-lined beach, open all year.

In summer, many of the big clubs in the centre are closed as they move out to the coastal strip from Kalamaki to Varkiza. They have surprise new beach locations each year, but names to look out for include **Club 22**, **Mao** and **Envy**. Some double as swanky bathing establishments during the day, with waterside music and cocktails around sunset; the party mood sets in after midnight.

Barcelona

Barcelona dips its toes in the Mediterranean, lolls back against the Pyrenees and basks in year-round sunshine. The skyline is indelibly marked by the visionary architect Antoni Gaudí, whose delirious buildings – resembling dragons, cliffs or gingerbread houses – seem to have magically erupted across the city. And at the heart of Barcelona lie the ancient passages, gargoyles and ghostly spires of the old Gothic city, apparently untouched by modernity. Add fantastic and varied nightlife, discerning cuisine, a nose for the latest and best in fashion and design, and a population bent on having a good time and it's not surprising that, in the last decade, Barcelona has become the most visited city in Europe.

But beneath the glamorous exterior lies a city that had to work hard to get attention. Not so long ago, Gaudí's *La Pedrera* was a grime-coated bingo hall and parts of the city were too dangerous to visit. The 1992 Olympics stopped the rot and, with breathtaking energy, Barcelona reinvented itself, sloughing off the dirt and sleaze to emerge as the most seductive city on the Mediterranean. Forget flamenco, sangría and other stock Spanish clichés, Barcelona is the proud capital of the ancient kingdom of Catalunya, with a distinct language and its own customs and traditions. These are staunchly preserved and exuberantly celebrated, with fire-spitting dragons, demons and giants.

Arts & culture
★★★★

Eating
★★★★

Nightlife
★★★★★

Outdoors
★★★

Romance
★★★

Shopping
★★★★★

Sightseeing
★★★★

Value for money
★★

Overall score
★★★★★

At a glance

Finding your way around the Catalan capital isn't difficult. The Old City (Ciutat Vella) is at its heart, divided by **Les Rambles** (Las Ramblas in Castilian), the city's famous tree-lined promenade, which meanders from Plaça de Catalunya down to the port. To the east of the Ramblas is the shadowy, medieval maze of the **Barri Gòtic** – the Gothic Quarter – with the flamboyant cathedral at its centre. This has been the heart of the city since Roman times and still buzzes day and night. East of the Barri Gòtic is **El Born**, another medieval district, which has become the coolest neighbourhood in a city

Barcelona, the great enchantress.

Joan Maragall, Ode to Barcelona

famed for its addiction to fashion. Packed with uber-chic boutiques, designer stores and the trendiest restaurants, bars and clubs, it rubs shoulders with **Sant Pere**, still charmingly old-fashioned but rapidly rising in the style stakes. West of the Ramblas, **El Raval** spreads south to

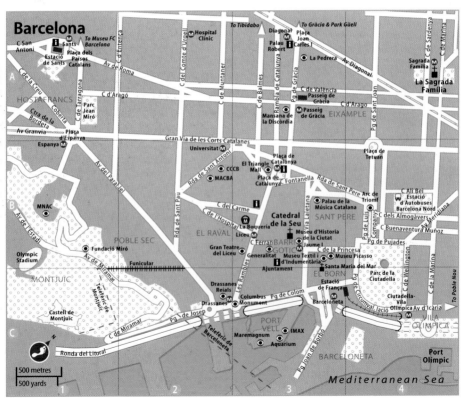

the raffish old theatre district of Paral.lel. Once a notorious red-light district, the Raval was given a massive clean-up and the glossy Museum of Contemporary Art in the 1990s and now has hip galleries, clothes stores and bohemian bars.

When the city burst out of its medieval walls in the 19th century, the rich commissioned new mansions in the airy grid of the **Eixample** (meaning extension in Catalan). Gaudí and his Modernista colleagues had a ball, leaving a spectacular legacy which now comprises one of the greatest concentrations of art nouveau architecture in the world. Beyond Eixample is **Gràcia**, once independent from the city and still with a relaxed vibe of its own. On the outskirts is **Park Güell**, Gaudí's fairytale extravaganza with magical views over the city.

To the west of the centre, overlooking the sea, is **Montjuïc Hill**, from where you can enjoy panoramic views of the city. The Olympics left their mark here with a string of excellent sporting facilities. Close by is the Fundació Miró, dedicated to the Catalan master and, at the bottom of the hill, is MNAC.

The regenerated waterfront stretches northeast from the Columbus monument at the foot of the Ramblas. **Port Vell**'s warehouses hold restaurants, museums and an entertainment complex, while the **Port Olímpic** is hugely popular, crammed with bars and seafood restaurants and flanked by sandy beaches. Beyond it lies the site of the Universal Forum of Cultures 2004, a sleek business and entertainment complex built on reclaimed land. In contrast, the traditional dock-workers' neighbourhood of **Barceloneta** is more atmospheric, with tiny tapas bars tucked away in its depths. The city's outskirts are home to parks, funfairs and museums: the best views are from **Tibidabo**, Barcelona's funfair mountain and highest peak, reached by a rickety tram and funicular.

★ *Don't leave town without having cocktails at a* xiringuito *(snack bar) on Mar Bella beach.*

El Raval

24 hours in the city

Get a feel for the city by strolling down the **Ramblas**, with a stop at **La Boquería** market on the way to take in the sights, sounds and smells. Alternatively, have a coffee at **Café de l'Òpera** and watch the world go by. Then dive into the chaotic maze of the **Barri Gòtic**, where you'll find the Gothic cathedral (take the lift to the roof for fantastic views) and plenty of great shops, bars and restaurants. If you prefer something a bit edgier, head across the Ramblas to **El Raval**, home to the excellent Museum of Contemporary Art (**MACBA**), and lots of vintage clothes stores and galleries. Have lunch on the terrace at **Plaça dels Àngels** and afterwards explore the elegant **Passeig de Gràcia**, home to the city's most emblematic Modernista buildings, including Gaudí's **Casa Batlló** and **La Pedrera**. An alternative would be to visit the extraordinary **Sagrada Família**. In the late afternoon head to the seafront for a stroll and a dip. In the evening, check out the fashionable bars and clubs of **El Born**, or take in a game at the legendary **Nou Camp** stadium – if you can get tickets.

◉ Sights

Les Rambles, llas Ramblas

ⓘ *Metro Plaça de Catalunya/Liceu,* ⬛C3.

The best introduction to Barcelona is a stroll down Les Rambles, the mile-long promenade that meanders down from Plaça de Catalunya to the port. It may look like one street but it is made up of five separate *rambles*, each with its own name and characteristics. Together they present an oddly appealing mixture of the picturesque and the tacky: street entertainers, fast-food outlets, crumbling theatres, whimsical Modernista mansions and pretty turn-of-the-century kiosks overflowing with flowers and songbirds. It's at its best early in the morning and on Sunday afternoons.

Halfway down is **La Boquería**, the city's irresistible market, with its

Mercat de la Boqueria

wrought-iron roof and Modernista sign. Inside are piles of gleaming fruit, vegetables, fish and other local specialities, plus a liberal sprinkling of tiny bars for coffee or cava. Nearer the port is the city's 19th-century opera house, the **Gran Teatre del Liceu**.

Barri Gòtic

ⓘ *Metro Liceu,* ⬛B3.

The Barri Gòtic has been the hub of the city for more than 2000 years. It's one of the best-preserved Gothic quarters in Europe, a dizzy maze of palaces, squares and churches piled on top of an original Roman settlement. The area is grubby, noisy, chaotic and packed with shops, bars and clubs. The streets are just as crowded at midnight as they are at midday.

Exploring the narrow alleyways, it's impossible to miss the **Catedral de la Seu** (Plaça Nova) with its dramatic spires and neo-Gothic façade. The cathedral dates back to the 13th century and the magnificent interior is suitably dim and hushed. A lift behind the altar swoops to the top for a bird's-eye view of huddled rooftops.

⊖ Travel essentials

Getting there Barcelona International Airport is 12 km south of the city (flights T93-298 3838, www.aena.es). International airlines use terminals A and B. The **airport train** (€2.40) runs to Estació de Sants, Passeig de Gràcia and Estació de França every 30 mins, 0600-2230. **A1 Aerobús** (€3.75) runs to Plaça de Catalunya, via Estació de Sants and Plaça d'Espanya, every 12 mins, 0600-2400. **Taxis** cost up to €25 to the centre, or more after 2200 and at weekends (supplements for luggage). **Estació de Sants** (metro Sants) is the main train station, although sleeper trains to/from Paris use **Estació de França** (metro Barceloneta). Many trains also stop at Passeig de Gràcia. For timetables and prices: T902-240202, www.renfe.es.

Getting around The Old City and Eixample, north of Plaça de Catalunya, are

easy to walk around. The Sagrada Família and Park Güell need a short bus or metro ride; Montjuïc and Tibidabo are reached by cable car or funicular.

Public transport is cheap and efficient; the main hub is Plaça de Catalunya. 6 **metro** lines run Mon-Thu 0500-2300, Fri-Sat 0500-0200, Sun 0600-2400. **Buses** run Mon-Sat 0600-2230 (less frequently Sun), and nightbuses (N) 2230-0400. Gràcia and Tibidabo are served by **FGC** train, (T93-205 1515, www.fgc.net). A single bus or metro ticket costs €1.25; a T-Dia (€5.25) allows unlimited journeys (including the airport train) for 1 day; a T-10 (€6.90) allows 10 trips and can be shared. For maps and information, visit the **TMB** office under Plaça Universitat (T93-443 0859, www.tmb.net). There's a **taxi** stand on Plaça de Catalunya, opposite the main tourist

office, or call **Barnataxi**, T93-357 7755, or **Fono-Taxi**, T93-300 1100.

Tourist information The main office is at Plaça de Catalunya, T90-630 1282, daily 0900-2100. It books hotel rooms and tours and sells discount cards and maps. It also offers themed walking tours (€8.50-10.50). There are branches at Plaça Sant Jaume, Estació de Sants and the airport. See www.barcelonaturisme.com and www.bcn.es. The **Barcelona Card** (€17 for 1 day, €30 for 5 days) gives unlimited travel by public transport plus discounts at shops, restaurants and major museums. The **Montjuïc Card** (€20) includes a day's admission to Montjuïc museums, public transport (including cable car), bike hire and other discounts. The hop-on/hop-off **Bus Turístic** (1 day €17, 2 days €21) tours the sights every 20 mins.

Close by, the imposing medieval façades of the **Generalitat** (Catalan Parliament) and the **Ajuntament** (City Council) face each other across the Plaça Sant Jaume. From here, shadowy passages, scattered with Roman ruins and ancient churches, lead to lovely squares such as Plaça Sant Just, Plaça Felip Neri and Plaça del Pi.

Museu d'Història de la Ciutat

ⓘ *Plaça del Rei s/n, T93-315 1111, www.museuhistoria.bcn.es,* **◥B3***. Oct-May Tue-Sat 1000-1400 and 1600-2000, Sun 1000-1500; Jun-Sep Tue-Sat 1000-2000, Sun 1000-1500. €4 (includes entry to Museu- Monestir de Pedralbes, Museu-Casa Verdaguer and the Interpretation Centre for the Park Güell); free 1st Sat of month. Metro Jaume I.*

This fascinating museum reveals the history of the city layer by layer. A glass lift glides down to the subterranean excavations of Roman Barcino, revealing 2000-year-old watchtowers, baths, temples, homes and businesses, discovered less than a century ago. Towards the site of the cathedral, the Roman ruins become

Barri Gòtic

MACBA

interspersed with the remnants of fifth-century Visigothic churches. Stairs lead up to the medieval Royal Palace and the Golden Age of the city's history. The echoing Saló de Tinell, built in 1359, is a masterpiece of Catalan Gothic, and the Mirador del Rei Martí watchtower offers fabulous views across the Old City.

MACBA

ⓘ *Plaça dels Àngels, El Raval, T93-412 0810, www.macba.es,* **◥B2***. 25 Sep-24 Jun Mon, Wed-Fri 1100-1930, Sat 1000-2000, Sun 1000-1500; 25 Jun-24 Sep Mon, Wed-Fri 1000-2000; Jul-Aug Thu until 2400, Sun 1000-1500. €4 for permanent collection; exhibition prices vary; Wed €3.50 for whole museum. Metro Universitat.*

Richard Meiers' huge, glassy home for MACBA was built in 1995 as a symbol of the city's urban renewal. The collection is loosely structured around three periods; the 1940s and 1950s are represented by members of the Dau al Set, a loose collection of writers and artists influenced by the Surrealists and

Joan Miró. Work from the 1960s and 1970s shows the impact of popular and consumer culture on art, while the 1980s and early 1990s are marked by a return to painting and traditional forms, plus good photographic pieces. Excellent temporary exhibitions focus on the latest digital and multimedia works. MACBA has a great bookshop and a café-bar in the spacious square that it shares with the **CCCB** (Centre of Contemporary Culture).

Passeig de Gràcia

ⓘ *Metro Passeig de Gràcia,* **◥A3**

At the heart of the Eixample is this glossy boulevard of chic boutiques, neoclassical office buildings and Modernista mansions. The most famous stretch is the **Mansana de la Discòrdia** ('block of discord') between Carrer Consell de Cent and Carrer d'Aragó, where three Modernista masterpieces nudge up against each other: **Casa Lleó i Morera**, transformed by Domènech i Montaner in 1902; **Casa Amatller**, designed by Puig i Cadafalch as a polychrome fairytale castle; and **Casa Batlló** ⓘ *T93-216 03 06,*

Casa Batlló

www.casabatllo.es, daily 0900-2000, €11, by Antoni Gaudí. Covered with shimmering *trencadis* (broken tiles) and culminating in a scaly roof, it gleams like an undersea dragon. The interior is soft and undulating, like whipped ice cream.

La Pedrera

ⓘ *C Provença 261-265, T902-400973, www.caixacatalunya.es,* ◩A3. *Daily 1000-2000, last admission 1930; guided tours daily 1100, additional tours in summer. €9, temporary exhibitions free, guided tours €3.50. Metro Diagonal.*

Casa Milà, better known as La Pedrera (the Stone Quarry), rises like a cream cliff draped with wrought-iron balconies. There's a recreation of a 1911 apartment on the first floor, with many original fittings. The attic houses **L'Espai Gaudí**, a museum of the architect's life and work in the city, but the climax of a visit is the sinuous rooftop terrace, studded with chimneys, air vents and stairwells disguised as extraordinary bulbous crosses and plump *trencadi*-covered towers. Enjoy a drink and live music on the rooftop on summer weekends.

La Pedrera rooftop

La Sagrada Família

La Sagrada Família

ⓘ *C Mallorca 401, Eixample, T93-080414, www.sagradafamilia.org,* ◩A4. *Oct-Mar daily 0900-1800; Apr-Sep daily 0900-2000. €8. Metro Sagrada Família.*

Gaudí's unfinished masterpiece, the Expiatory Temple of the Holy Family, is the most emblematic and controversial monument in Barcelona. The towers measure almost 100 m and the central spire, when finished, will soar 180 m into the sky. The temple is set for completion in 2026, the anniversary of Gaudí's death.

Gaudí designed three façades for the temple but only the Nativity façade was completed by the time of his death in 1926. The Passion façade on the other side of the church is grim and lifeless in comparison. Inside, work has begun on the construction of four huge columns to support the enormous domed roof.

There's a lift up the towers (€2); brave visitors can climb even higher, before descending via the vertiginous spiral staircase. Underneath, the crypt contains Gaudí's tomb and an interactive museum.

◉ Best of the rest

Santa María del Mar ⓘ *Pl de Santa María del Mar, El Born,* ◩C3. *Metro Jaume I.* This lovely 14th-century church is one of the purest examples of Catalan Gothic.

Museu Picasso ⓘ *C Montcada 15-23, El Born, www.museu picasso.bcn.es,* ◩B3. *Closed Sun and Mon. €6. Metro Jaume I.* Very popular collection, which is dominated by early works created in Barcelona.

Museu Tèxtil i d'Indumentària ⓘ *C Montcada 12-14, www.museu textil.bcn.es,* ◩B3. *Closed Mon. €3.50. Metro Jaume I.* Fashion exhibits from the 16th century to the present day, housed in converted Gothic palaces, with a delightful café.

CCCB ⓘ *C Montalegre 5, El Raval, www.ccb.org,* ◩B2. *Closed Mon. €4.40. Metro Universitat.* Hosts eclectic exhibitions on contemporary culture not covered by MACBA.

Drassanes Reials ⓘ *Av Drassanes s/n, www.museumaritim barcelona.com,* ◩C2. *Daily. €6. Metro Drassanes.* Vast medieval shipyards with an excellent maritime museum.

Museu FC Barcelona ⓘ *Nou Camp, www.fcbarcelona.com. €7 or €11 with tour. Metro Collblanc.* Football paraphernalia plus a guided tour of the stadium.

Tibidabo ⓘ *Mar-Sep only. FGC to Av Tibidabo, then tram Blau, then funicular.* The mountain has a great old-fashioned funfair at its summit and breathtaking views across the city.

The great rediscovery and celebration of Catalunya's cultural identity, known as the *Renaixença* (Renaissance), began in the 1850s. Architecture, literature, painting, sculpture, furniture, craft and design were galvanized by the new spirit of cultural and political optimism. This arts movement came to be known as *Modernisme* and was partly influenced by the international art nouveau and Jugenstil movements. When the medieval city walls were torn down in 1854, Ildefons Cerdà's airy grid-shaped extension (Eixample in Catalan) was constructed, giving the most influential architects of the day the chance to display their originality and virtuosity. Three names stand out: Antoni Gaudí i Cornet, Lluis Domènech i Montaner and Josep Puig i Cadafalch. You can choose your favourite in the Mansana de la Discòrdia (see page 35). The list of Modernista monuments in Barcelona is breathtakingly long; highlights include Gaudí's Casa Batlló, La Pedrera, Park Güell and the Sagrada Família; Montaner's Palau de la Música Catalana; and Puig i Cadafalch's Casa Amatller.

MNAC

ⓘ *Palau Nacional, Montjuïc , T93-622 0360, www.mnac.es,* **JB1** *. Tue-Sat 1000-1900, Sun 1000-1430. €8.50, temporary exhibitions prices vary. Metro Espanya.*

Housed in the dour Palau Nacional on Montjuïc is a magnificent collection of the best of Catalan art. The highlight is the array of spellbinding Romanesque murals gathered from Catalan churches and displayed on reconstructed church interiors. The Gothic collection reflects

MNAC

Catalunya's glory years from the 13th to the 15th centuries, with rooms devoted to the three outstanding painters of the time: Bernat Martorell, Lluís Dalmau and Jaume Huguet. Tacked on at the end is a small collection of works from the 15th to the 18th centuries, including a couple of pieces by Zurbarán, Goya and El Greco. There is also an extensive collection of 19th-century art and sculpture, including wonderful Modernista furniture and objets d'art.

Below MNAC, at the top of Avenida María Cristina, is the **Font Màgica** ⓘ *Pl de Carles Buïgas, May-Sep Thu-Sun 2000-2330, Oct and Nov Fri and Sat 1900-2100, free,* a fountain from 1929 that puts on a fabulous sound and light show; it's gloriously tacky, yet undeniably magical.

Fundació Miró

ⓘ *Parc de Montjuïc s/n, T93-443 9470, www.bcn.fjmiro.es,* **JB1** *. Oct-Jun Tue-Sat 1000-1900 (Thu until 2130), Sun 1000-1430; Jul-Aug Tue-Sat 1000-2000 (Thu until 2130). €7.50, temporary exhibitions €4. Metro Espanya or funicular from Paral.lel.*

The fabulous Fundació Miró is set in a white, light-drenched building by Josep Lluís Sert on Montjuïc. It contains the most important and comprehensive gathering of Miró's works in the world, from his early experiments with Cubism and Fauvism through to his later paintings, which are increasingly gestural and impulsive.There are spectacular sculptures from the 1960s and 1970s; some are displayed on the rooftop sculpture terrace.

Parc Güell

Park Güell

ⓘ C Olot 7, T93-130488. Nov-Feb daily 1000-1800; Mar and Oct daily 1000-1900; Apr and Sep daily 1000-2000; May-Aug daily 1000-2100. Free. Metro Lesseps, then a (signposted) 10-min walk, or bus 24.

Whimsical Park Güell is perhaps the most delightful of Gaudí's visionary creations. Two fairytale pavilions guard the entrance (one houses an exhibition, T93-285 6899, Mon-Fri 1100-1500, €2), from where stairs sweep up past the famous multi-coloured salamander, which has become one of Barcelona's best-known and best-loved symbols. The steps culminate in the **Sala Hipóstila**, also known as the Hall of a Hundred Columns because of the thick Doric columns which support its undulating roof. Gaudí's talented collaborator, the architect and mosaicist Josep Maria Jujol, was given free reign to colour the vaulted ceiling with elaborate whimsy; look carefully and you'll see the designs are made of smashed china, ceramic dolls' heads, wine glasses and old bottles. Above the hall is the main square with its snaking bench, thickly encrusted with *trencadís*, like the scales of a monstrous dragon.

Playa Barceloneta

Frank Gehry's fish

Surrounding it are porticoes and viaducts, made from unworked stone, which hug the slopes of the hillside for more than 3 km.

Just off the main esplanade is the **Casa Museu Gaudí** (T93-219 3811, €4), housed in the small Torre Rosa, Gaudí's home for the last years of his life.

Seafront

ⓘ Metro Barceloneta/Ciutadella-Vila Olímpica, **ⓒ**

Barcelona's seafront was the main focus of Olympic redevelopment in the early 1990s. A boardwalk runs from the foot of the Ramblas to the glittering **Port Vell** (Old Port) development which includes a marina, restaurants, shopping centre, IMAX and the impressive **Aquàrium** (€15). To the northeast is the old fishermen's neighbourhood of **Barceloneta**, a district of narrow streets and traditional seafood bars. From here the **Telèferic** (€9) begins its vertiginous journey over the harbour to Montjuïc. Beyond is the **Port Olímpic**, marked by Frank Gehry's shimmering copper fish.

⦿ Shop till you drop

The designer shop **Galleries Vinçon** on the Passeig de Gràcia used to have the slogan 'I shop therefore I am' emblazoned across its packaging and this seems to be the attitude of many of the city's residents, for Barcelona has more shops per capita than anywhere else in Europe. Best buys are leather, cutting-edge fashion, homewares and local wines and food. Head to **Barri Gòtic** for quirky one-off shops, **Carrer Portaferrissa** for fashion chains, **El Raval** for vintage clothes and music and **El Born** for unusual fashion and interior design shops (on and around Passeig del Born). For international fashion, designer furnishings and art galleries head to **Passeig de Gràcia** and **Diagonal**, in Eixample.

Port Olímpic

☺ Sleeping

Barcelona is one of the most popular weekend destinations in Europe and, although the number of beds has increased dramatically, you should always book as early as possible and never just turn up and hope to find somewhere to stay. Book through an agent or check out online deals at www.barcelonahotels.com and www.barcelona-on-line.com.

Most of the cheaper places are in the Old City (Barri Gòtic, El Born and El Raval); these are also the noisiest places to stay. The smartest (and quietest) places are generally concentrated in the Eixample. Hotels are ranked with one to five stars; *pensiones* have fewer facilities and are ranked with one to three stars. Note that a modest hotel may be known as a '*hostal*'; this is not the same as a 'hostel', which will have dormitory accommodation.

€€€ Arts Barcelona, C Marina 19-21, Vila Olímpica, T93-221 1000, www.hotelartsbarcelona.com. Metro Ciutadella-Vila Olímpica. One of the city's most glamorous hotels, the Arts occupies one of the enormous glassy towers at the entrance to the Port Olímpic. It was inaugurated in 1992 and offers 33 floors of unbridled luxury, including indoor and outdoor pools, a fine restaurant, a piano bar overlooking the hotel gardens and the sea, a sauna, a gym and a beauty centre.

€€€-€€ Prestige, Passeig de Gràcia 62, Eixample, T93-272 4180, www.prestigepaseodegracia.com. Metro Passeig de Gràcia. An ultra-stylish hotel in a perfect location. The building dates from the 1930s but the interior is the epitome of chic, minimalist design. High-quality fittings include Bang and Olufsen TVs and music systems, a free minibar and crisp white furnishings. Facilities include 24-hr room service, a gym and beauty centre, an oriental garden and a futuristic library full of the latest glossy coffee-table books.

€€ Actual, C Rosselló 238, Eixample, T93-552 0550, www.hotelactual.com. Metro Diagonal. On the same block as La Pedrera, Actual is decorated in the slickest minimalist style, with plenty of white marble and dark wood. The rooms are small but impeccably furnished with crisp white fabrics and ultra-modern bathrooms. It also offers triple rooms, perfect for families. There are often special offers on its website.

€€ Banys Orientals, C Argenteria 37, El Born, T93-269 8490, www.hotel banysorientals.com. Metro Jaume I. A chic boutique-style hotel close to the Museu Picasso. Rooms are a little small, but are furnished with sleek modern fabrics.

€€-€ Hostal Palacios, Rambla de Catalunya 27, Eixample, T93-301 3079, www.hostalpalacios.com. Metro Passeig de Gràcia. A lovely *hostal* with just a handful of rooms in a restored Modernista building. You'll find original floor tiles, carved wooden doors and a comfortable lounge with internet access and a piano. Bedrooms retain Modernista mouldings, while bathrooms are modern and pristine.

€ Gat Raval, C Joaquín Costa 44, El Raval, T93-481 6670, www.gat accommodation.com. Metro Universitat. A hip *hostal* painted in black, white and lime green on one of the Raval's funkiest streets. The bright, modern rooms are clean and well equipped.

€ Peninsular, C de Sant Pau 34-36, El Raval, T93-302 3138. Metro Liceu. One of the best-value options is set in an old convent. There's a charming interior patio crammed with trailing plants and Modernista detailing. The rooms are plain and basic but perfectly comfortable.

☺ Eating

Catalan dishes are simple and rely on fresh local ingredients. Meat and fish are often grilled or cooked slowly in the oven (*al forn*). There are some delicious vegetable dishes, like *escalivada*, a salad of roasted aubergine, peppers and onions. Rice dishes are also popular. Wash it all down with Catalan wine, sparkling cava or local Estrella beer.

Breakfast is usually a milky coffee (*café amb llet/café con leche*) and a pastry. Lunch is taken seriously and eaten around 1400, when many restaurants offer a fixed-price 2-course menu including a drink. Tapas are not as much of a tradition here as in other parts of Spain, but there are plenty of old-fashioned bars near the harbour that offer fresh seafood versions. Dinner is rarely eaten before 2100 and tends to be lighter than the midday meal.

Breakfast

† El Café de l'Òpera, Les Rambles 74. Metro Liceu. Opposite the Liceu Opera House, this is the perfect café for people-watching. Original Modernista fittings and an old-world ambience.

† La Pallaresa, C Petritxol 11, Barri Gòtic. Metro Liceu. This is where to get your *chocolate con churros* (thick hot chocolate with fried dough strips) in the morning – locals swear it's the best *xocolatería* in the city.

Lunch

L'Olivé, C Balmes 47, Eixample, T93-452 1990. Metro Hospital Clínic. A popular, lively restaurant serving traditional Catalan dishes, using the freshest market produce. Try *rap amb all cremat* (monkfish with roast garlic).

Sal Café, Passeig Marítim s/n, Barceloneta, T93-224 0707. With a fantastic beachside location, this trendy restaurant and bar serves contemporary Mediterranean fare. The grilled sardines are fabulous or enjoy a superb paella at lunchtime, if you book in advance.

Bar Pinotxo, Mercat de la Boquería 66-67, Les Rambles. Closed Sun. Metro Liceu. The market's best-loved counter bar, serving excellent, freshly prepared food; try the tortilla with artichokes.

Pla dels Àngels, C Ferlandina 23, El Raval, T93-329 4047. Metro Universitat. This large, popular restaurant opposite MACBA has bright, modern decor and a summer terrace. It serves extremely well-priced salads, meats and pastas, plus excellent wine.

Dinner

Beltxenea, C Mallorca 275, Eixample, T93-215 3024. Closed Sun. Metro Diagonal. A grand restaurant with a romantic terrace overlooking an immaculately manicured garden. The cuisine is as magnificent as the setting, featuring Basque classics like *merluza koskera a la vasca* (hake cheeks with clams and parsley). A real treat.

Cal Pep, Plaça Olles 8, El Born, T93-310 7961. Metro Barceloneta.

A classic: there's a smart brick-lined dining area at the back but it's more entertaining to perch at the bar, as Pepe dishes up tempting treats and holds court at the same time. Reservations essential.

Les Onze Virtuts, C/d'Ataülf 5, Barri Gòtic, T93-310 6943. Tucked away down a tiny street behind the Ayuntamiento (City Hall), this is hard to find but well worth the effort. The menu is short and simple. Try tasty salads, prawns in garlic or delicious stir-fries.

> 66 99 **El Raval has a concentration of funky bohemian clubs as well as louche bars where you can sip absinthe in timeless surroundings.**

☻ Nightlife

To find out what's on, check the listings guide *Guía del Ocio*, *B-Guided* magazine or look out for flyers. Up-to-date information is also provided at www.bcn.es.

Bars and clubs

Barcelona is a popular stop on the international DJ circuit, with cutting-edge clubs (*discotecas*) playing the very latest tunes. Some of the best clubs can be found on **Carrer Nou de Francesc** in the Barri Gòtic and along the painfully hip **Passeig del Born** in El Born. There are also several

excellent bars in the Ciutat Vella, where you can enjoy a mellow *copa* on a candlelit terrace. **El Raval** has a concentration of funky bohemian clubs as well as louche bars where you can sip absinthe in timeless surroundings. Bigger clubs, catering for the frenetic summer party crowd, can be found on **Montjuïc** and around the **Port Olímpic**, while gay clubs are clustered in the so-called **Gaixample**, east of Passeig del Gràcia.

Contemporary music

There are plenty of live music venues. Popular clubs like **Jamboree** (Plaça Reial 17, Barri Gòtic) and **Luz de Gas** (Muntaner 246, Gràcia) offer a mixed bag of musical styles. Visit **Harlem Jazz Club** (Comtessa de Sobradiel 8, Barri Gòtic) for the city's jazz scene. Latin and African music are also popular.

For lovers of electronica, the **Sónar** (www.sonar.es) summer festival of multimedia music and art is fantastic. The **BAM** festival in Sep is another great time to catch alternative sounds.

Classical music and theatre

Enjoy opera at the beautiful **Gran Teatre de Liceu** (page 42) or a rousing performance by Orfeó Català in the stunning Modernista surroundings of the **Palau de la Música** (C Sant Francesc de Paula 2, Sant Pere, T93-295 7200, www.palau musica.org). **Ciutat del Teatre** complex (Plaça Margarida Xirgu, Montjuïc) holds a dramatic arts museum and several performance spaces, including the celebrated **Teatre Lliure** (T93-228 9747, www.teatrelliure.com). In Jun and Jul, see the renowned **Festival de Barcelona Grec** (www.barcelonafestival.com).

The capital of Germany since 1999, Berlin is a city reborn – a phoenix risen from the flames of Second World War destruction and Cold War division. Arguably the hippest European capital, it attracts some of the most progressive fashionistas, artists and musicians from all over the world. The city may have needed a long period in rehab but it is now confident enough to woo British architects, Italian designers and Polish restorers to its burgeoning multinational community. These days Babylonian mosaics, French bakeries and Norman Foster creations are comfortably integrated into the buildings of Schinkel and the operas of Wagner. Anything goes in Berlin, from illegal parties held in derelict to city beaches and an open-air swimming pool on the river Spree.

Berlin

Arts & culture
★★★★

Eating
★★★★

Nightlife
★★★★★

Outdoors
★★★

Romance
★★★

Shopping
★★★

Sightseeing
★★★★

Value for money
★★★

Overall score
★★★★

At a glance

Mitte, former bohemian hub of East Berlin, is now the heart of the reunified capital and, along with its more conservative West Berlin neighbour, **Tiergarten**, is the focus of most visitors' attention. Here, the **Brandenburg Gate** and the **Reichstag** stand amid a rash of new government buildings and sprawling acres of woodland, grass and lakes, making it clear that Berlin is, once again, the capital of Germany. **Friedrichstrasse** is the main artery dividing the eastern and western halves of the city. About 15 minutes' walk east lies **Museum Island**, where you will find the city's most important museums, while **Potsdamer Platz**, south of the Brandenburg Gate, shows off Berlin's ultra-modern colours. Northeast of Mitte, **Prenzlauerberg** has become *the* hip place to live and play since the Wall came down. **Friedrichshain**, east of Mitte, is less attractive but still

> **I am so homesick for the Kurfürstendamm, for Berlin's tempo, verve and ballyhoo.**
>
> *Hildegard Knef (German singer and actress)*

on the up. **Kreuzberg**, south of Mitte, in former West Berlin, has a large Turkish population and, like its more chichi neighbour **Schöneberg**, remains a centre for the gay community. West of Tiergarten, **Charlottenburg**, once a showcase of capitalism, now competes with Mitte and Prenzlauerberg.

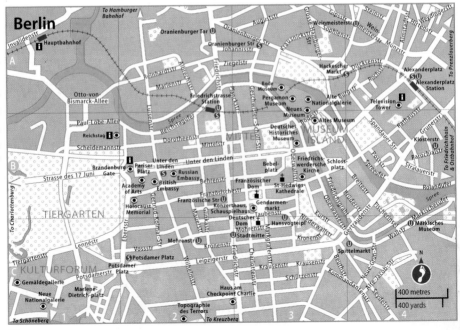

24 hours in the city

Visit the **Reichstag** first thing (open 0800-2400) and climb up to the cupola for the views. Then head to the **Adlon Hotel** for coffee, pausing to reflect at the **Brandenburg Gate**. Afterwards, head east along Unter den Linden as far as Bebelplatz (where the 1933 book burnings took place) and cross the road to spend an hour or two in the newly restored **Deutsches Historisches Museum**. Cross the river on to Museum Island and visit the outstanding **Pergamon Museum**, before having a late lunch. (Try the tasty snacks from the riverside sausage stands.) Walk through the Lustgarten, across the Schlossplatz and then cross the river again, continuing west to the **Gendarmenmarkt**, where there may be an afternoon concert in one of the cathedrals. On nearby **Friedrichstrasse**, with its stylish shops, is the museum commemorating **Checkpoint Charlie**. From here, following the fragment of the Wall west, it is

Reichstag

possible to reach the futuristic-looking **Potsdamer Platz** for a spot of dinner. Later, take a tour of the uber-chic bars and cafés around **Mitte**.

⊖ Travel essentials

Getting there Berlin has 2 main airports, www.berlin-airport.de. **Tegel (Berlin International) Airport** is 8 km northwest of the centre. Buses X9 (20 mins to Zoo) and 109 (30 mins to Zoo) run to the centre, via most of the hotels. Bus 128 is better for destinations to the north or east. The TXL express bus goes to Mitte (single €2.10). Taxis are plentiful and cost about €20 to Zoo Station or €30 to Mitte. A tip of 5-10% is normal.

Schönefeld (Berlin-Brandenburg) Airport is 20 km from the city centre. The Airport Express train runs to Berlin Hauptbahnhof every 30 mins (journey time 28 mins). Buses link the airport with southern and eastern Berlin, including No 171 to Rudow for U-Bahn line 7. There are night buses and S-Bahn services on this route. A taxi to Friedrichstrasse costs €40.

Opened in time for the 2006 World Cup, **Berlin Hauptbahnhof**, Europaplatz 1, www.hbf-berlin.de, is the state-of-the-art hub of Berlin's upgraded rail network, linking national and international services (including sleeper trains from Brussels) with the city's urban transport system. Almost all long-distance trains also stop at **Ostbahnhof**, Straße der Pariser Kommune 5 in Friedrichshain. There are 3 other long-distance stations (Gesundbrunnen, Südkreuz and Spandau), as well as regional stations. For details, see www.bahn.de.

Getting around The extensive and speedy urban rail system consists of **U-Bahn** (underground) and **S-Bahn** (overground) trains. Both operate at night. Rail services are supplemented by the 'MetroNetz' of **tram** and **bus** routes. The city is divided into 3 travel zones: A, B and C. You are only likely to visit zone C if you're going to Potsdam. A ticket for any number of journeys up to 2 hrs costs €2.10. Day passes for zones A and B cost €6.10. Tickets and passes are available at the Tegel Airport office, at the **BVG** centre at Zoo Station (T030-19449, www.bvg.de) and from machines on all platforms. The **WelcomeCard** (€16 for 48 hrs, €22 for 72 hrs), available from Berlin Infostores, offers free transport in all zones and a 25% reduction on many sights. **Taxis** are plentiful, with ranks at most U-Bahn and S-Bahn stations in the suburbs; they can be hailed in the city centre. Fares start at around €2, then cost €1 per km.

Tourist information Berlin **Infostores**, T030-250025, www.berlin-tourist-information.de, are located at the **Hauptbahnhof**, daily 0800-2200; at **Neues Kranzler Eck Passage**, Kurfürstendamm 21, Mon-Sat 1000-2000, Sun 1000-1800; at the **Brandenburg Gate**, daily 1000-1800; and in the Berlin Pavilion at the **Reichstag**, Apr-Oct daily 0830-2000, Nov-Mar daily 1000-1800. **New Berlin Tours**, www.new berlintours.com, offer excellent free tours of the city.

⊙ Sights

Brandenburg Gate
ⓘ S-Bahn Unter den Linden, ↘B2.

Built in 1791, Berlin's most famous icon has witnessed the highs and lows of German history. Left isolated by the construction of the Berlin Wall in 1961, the gate became the emblematic backdrop to that epoch-altering event on 9 November 1989 when the border was opened and young people from both sides of the city rushed forward to scale the defining symbol of the Cold War.

On the east side of the gate, **Pariser Platz** has been transformed from a concrete wilderness into an elegant diplomatic and financial centre and regained its pre-war status as one of the city's most prestigious addresses. The French embassy has been rebuilt on the north side, while opposite is the newly reopened **Academy of Arts** ⓘ Pariser Platz 4, www.adk.de. This Günther Behnisch building houses the private archives of cultural greats such as Bertolt Brecht and Günter Grass, as well as promoting German arts through

Memorial to the murdered Jews

exhibitions and performances. Next to the Academy is the unmissable **DZ bank building**, designed by Frank Gehry. Inside is an enormous sculpture whose twists and turns provide a startling contrast with the bank's façade.

South of Pariser Platz, 150 m from the Brandenburg Gate, is the **Memorial to the murdered Jews** ⓘ Wilhelmstr 22-23, information centre Tue-Sun 1000-2000 (last entrance 1915). Completed in May 2005, this 'forest of stelae', represents the gravestones of Jews murdered under the Nazi regime. It initially provoked much controversy due to its bleak design and the exclusion of graves for non-Jewish victims. However, the memorial, designed by Peter Eisenman, now elicits a positive response from most Berliners.

Reichstag
ⓘ Ebertstr, ↘B1. Daily 0800-2400 (last entry 2200). Free. S-Bahn Unter den Linden.

The imposing late-ninth-century Reichstag building has been restored to its former glory and is once again at the heart of German political life and is open to the public. The undoubted highlight is

Norman Foster's outlandish glass dome. The views from the top are not to be missed, though the long queues certainly are (get there early or visit at night to avoid them).

The Reichstag is one of many government buildings along the Spree and backs onto **Tiergarten Park**. This area has seen more redevelopment than most but, despite pressure from developers, the park's wide open spaces, lakes and woods have not been compromised.

North of Tiergarten is **Hamburger Bahnhof** ⓘ Invalidenstr 50, www.smb .spk-berlin.de, Tue-Fri 1000-1800, Sat 1100-2000, Sun 1100-1800, €8, S-Bahn Lehrter Bahnhof. Trains stopped running here in the 19th century, replaced in the late 1980s by challenging artworks, including pieces by Joseph Beuys.

Potsdamer Platz
ⓘ S-Bahn Potsdamer Platzk, ↘C2.

Once as desolate as Pariser Platz due to its proximity to the Wall, **Potsdamer Platz**, at the southeastern corner of Tiergarten park, is now almost a town in its own right; a new Manhattan of skyscrapers, cinemas, embassies and

Pariser Platz

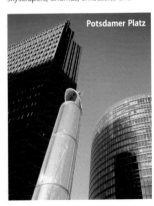
Potsdamer Platz

museums, including the **Museum für Film und Fernsehen** ① *Potsdamer Str 2, T030-300 9030, www.filmmuseumberlin.de, ⑥⑴. Tue-Sun 1000-1800, Thu 1000-2200, €6.* Just to the west lies the **Kulturforum**, which encompasses not only the **Berlin Philharmonie** but also one of the world's most prestigious art collections at the **Gemäldegallerie** ① *www.smb.spk-berlin.de, ⑥⑴, Tue, Wed, Fri-Sun 1000-1800, Thu 1000-2200 , €8,* and international and German paintings from the 20th century at the **Neue Nationalgalerie** ① *www.smb .spk-berlin.de, ⑥⑴. Tue, Wed, Fri 1000-1800, Thu 1000-2200, Sat, Sun 1100-1800, €8.*

Unter den Linden
① *S-Bahn Unter den Linden, ⑥B2.*

Unter den Linden ('Beneath the Lime Trees') runs east from the Brandenburg Gate and Pariser Platz, the trees in the centre now making a congenial pedestrian precinct between the two wide traffic lanes on either side. On the south side stands the **Russian Embassy**, an excellent example of social realism but now incongruous in a Berlin eager to forget its links with the former USSR.

Unter den Linden

Gendarmenmarkt

At the eastern end of Unter den Linden is the revamped **Deutsches Historisches Museum** ① *www.dhm.de, ⑥B3, daily 1000-1800, €2, U-Bahn Französischestr,* whose permanent exhibition covers 2000 years of German history through authentic objects and multimedia displays. Temporary exhibitions are staged in a new wing designed by I M Pei.

Gendarmenmarkt
① *U-Bahn Stadtmitte, ⑥B3.*

If there is still a tendency to judge Germany by the worst periods of its history, a stop in **Gendarmenmarkt** will show the country at its most liberal. It became the centre of a French community around 1700 when Prussia gave refuge to 6000 Huguenots. On the north side, the **Französischer Dom** (French Cathedral), now home to the **Huguenot Museum** ① *Tue-Sat 1200-1700, Sun 1100-1700, €2,* dates from this time, as does the similarly proportioned **Deutscher Dom** ① *Tue 1000-2000, Wed-Sun 1000-1800, ⑥C3,* on the south side. The **Konzerthaus**, or Schauspielhaus, in the centre of the square, was one of the earliest buildings

designed by the prolific architect, Karl Friedrich Schinkel (1781-1841).

Museum Island
① *T030-2090 5577, www.smb.museum, ⑥B3. Fri-Wed 1000-1800, Thu 1000-2200; Alte Nationalgalerie closed Mon. 1 museum €8; Museuminsel €12; free first Sun in the month. S-Bahn Hackescher Markt.*

Museum Island is an extraordinary collection of first-rate galleries in the middle of the Spree. Recognized by UNESCO as a World Cultural Heritage Site, the complex is currently undergoing a major restoration and redevelopment project that will unite all five buildings and their disparate collections by 2015.

The **Altes Museum**, Lustgarten, designed by Karl Friedrich Schinkel and considered his finest work, exhibits Greek, Roman and Etruscan antiquities plus the Ancient Egyptian collection.

The **Pergamon Museum**, Am Kupfergraben 5, houses one of the world's great archaeological collections, with entire complexes on display that are dramatically lit at night. The second-century BC Pergamon Altar and the Babylonian Street are the stars of the

Pergamon Museum

show. Some parts of the museum will close for restoration in 2008.

The **Alte Nationalgalerie**, Bodestrasse 1-3, exhibits 19th-century sculptures and paintings, while the reopened **Bode Museum**, Monbijoubrücke, houses the coin collection, sculpture collection and Byzantine art, together with Old Master paintings from the Gemäldegalerie.

The **Neues Museum** is currently closed for restoration until 2009.

Alexanderplatz
ⓘ S/U-Bahn Alexanderplatz, 🔲A4.

East of the museums, 'Alex' has, in an architectural sense, stood still for over 30 years, a time-warped legacy of old East Berlin. In the early 1970s, the best that the town could offer was here on a vast pedestrian precinct. The 365m-high **Television Tower** ⓘ www.berliner fernsehturm.de, Mar-Oct daily 0900-2400; Nov-Feb daily 1000-2400, €8, completed the image of a modern town centre. The **Weltzeituhr** (World Clock) has always been a convenient meeting point, although when it was built in 1969, it was seen by some East Berliners as a cruel reminder of all the places they could not visit.

Alexanderplatz

Olympiastadion

Charlottenberg
ⓘ S/U-Bahn Zoologischer Garten, U-Bahn Richard-Wagner or Sophie-Charlotte Platz.

Charlottenburg has lost much of its cachet since reunification but still boasts many of the institutions that made West Berlin famous. First among these is the iconic **Gedächtniskirche** (Memorial Church) ⓘ Breitscheidplatz, daily 0900-1900 for the church, Mon-Sat 1000-1600 for the exhibition, built shortly after the death of Kaiser Wilhelm in 1888 and largely destroyed by an air raid in 1943.

Lavish **Schloss Charlottenburg** (Charlottenburg Palace) ⓘ T030-320911, www.schlosscharlottenburg.de, Tue-Fri 0900-1700, Sat and Sun 1000-1700, €7, is a one-stop shop for two centuries of German architecture, from 1700 to 1900. It was built as a summer residence for Queen Charlotte (1669-1705) by her husband Friedrich I (1657-1713) and was expanded into its present baroque and rococo form in 1701 when Friedrich crowned himself King of Prussia.

A few kilometres northwest is **Olympiastadion**, which underwent a multi-million renovation for the 2006 World Cup.

◉ Best of the rest

The Story of Berlin ⓘ Kurfürsten-damm 207, www.story-of-berlin.de, daily 1000-2000, last entry 1800, €9.80, U -bahn Uhland strasse, S-bahn Savignyplatz. This brings the city's eventful past to life. Don't miss the tour of the nuclear shelter, a sealed-off underground town. **East Side Gallery** ⓘ Running along Mühlenstr to Warschauerstr, www.eastsidegallery.com. U-Bahn Warschauer Str. One of the last remaining stretches of the Wall is decorated with street art. **Sans Souci** ⓘ Tue-Sun 0900-1700, €8, S-Bahn Potsdamer Hauptbahnhof, then bus 695. Frederick the Great's summer pleasure palace.

Kreuzberg
ⓘ U-Bahn Hallesches Tor, Koch Str, Kottbusser Tor.

Once a haven of alternative living – before everyone moved to Prenzlauerberg – Kreuzberg is now home to a large Turkish community, and some of Berlin's most disturbing sights. Nazi crimes are detailed at the open-air **Topographie des Terrors** ⓘ Niederkirchnerstr, www .topographie.de, 🔲C2, daily 1000-1800, free, while the **Haus am Checkpoint Charlie** ⓘ Friedrichstr 43-45, www .mauer-museum.com, 🔲C2, daily 0900-2200, €9.50, documents East Berliners' desperate efforts to cross the border. The powerful, innovative **Jüdisches Museum** ⓘ Lindenstr 9-14, www.juedisches-museum-berlin.de, Mon 1000-2200, Tue-Sun 1000-2000, €5, shows 2000 years of German-Jewish history, with a harrowing section on the Holocaust.

Berlin's big gay pride

Berlin has welcomed the gay scene since the 'roaring twenties' when Marlene Dietrich and Christopher Isherwood lived and entertained around **Nollendorfplatz** in **Schöneberg**. Hitler's rise to power in 1933 and his deportation of gay people to the camps put a stop to this (outside Nollendorfplatz U-bahn station there is a plaque to commemorate the victims). But now, with an openly gay mayor, the city's gay and lesbian scene is more vibrant than ever. Some areas are more gay than others, but around the centre it's all quite mixed, with lots of bars and clubs catering to a gay and straight crowd. **Kreuzberg** has a very liberal feel to it, whereas Nollendorfplatz is more hardcore. **Friedrichshain** and **Prenzlauerberg** are the new kids on the block and, as a result, have quite an experimental feel to them. **Christopher Street Day**, www.csd-berlin.de, which takes place every July, is Berlin's most flamboyant festival. Loud and outrageous, this gay and lesbian parade was named after the New York Stonewall riots of 1969 and is not one for the faint-hearted.

● Sleeping

Berlin has a good selection of accommodation. Its more upmarket hotels are often large, modern affairs at the forefront of contemporary design. There are also many traditional pensions, particularly on and around the Kurfürstendamm in Tiergarten and Charlottenburg. Mitte and Prenzlauerberg have some first-rate arty and individual hotels.

€€€ Adlon, Unter den Linden 77, T030-22610, www.hotel-adlon.de. Beside the Brandenburg Gate, the Adlon is not discreet but that doesn't seem to deter a regular turnover of celebrities. They follow in hallowed footsteps: Albert Einstein, Charlie Chaplin and Theodore Roosevelt all stayed here. The current building is a replica of the original – opulent and showy but also impressively stylish.

€€€ Grand Hyatt, Marlene-Dietrich-Platz, T030-2553 1234, www.berlin.grand.hyatt.com. S/U-Bahn Potsdamer Platz, U-Bahn Mendelssohn-Bartholdy-Park. A superb combination of Oriental and Bauhaus deluxe minimalism, the angular lines of Potsdamer Platz itself are continued into the interior of this top-class hotel. More useful and personal design minutiae are everywhere and on Sun you don't have to check out until 1800.

€€ Hotel Art Nouveau, Leibnizstr 59, Charlottenburg, T030-327 7440, www.hotelartnouveau.de. U-Bahn Adenauerplatz. A friendly and helpful fourth-floor hotel in a restored art nouveau building with contemporary touches. There's a buffet breakfast and an honesty bar.

€€ Ku'Damm 101, Kurfürstendamm 101, Charlottenburg, T030-520 0550, www.kudamm101.com. U-Bahn Adenauerplatz. This bold hotel opened in 2003 and makes a good out-of-centre base. Its minimalist take on vaguely '50s and '70s themes involves curves: lots of them. Even the buffet breakfast (on the 7th floor with spectacular views) is visually striking.

€ Circus Hostels, Rosa-Luxemburg-Str 39-41 and Weinbergsweg 1a, ▶ T030-2839 1433, www.circus-berlin.de. U-Bahn Rosa-Luxemburg-Platz and Rosenthaler Platz. Very popular and for good reason. Much smarter and cleaner than most backpacker hostels and both in perfect locations.

€ mitArt Pension, Friedrichstr 127, T030-2839 0430. U-Bahn Oranienburger Tor. Still primarily a gallery, this friendly and memorably stylish hotel exhibits works of art suspended from the ceiling. Service is personal, breakfast is copious and delicious and the rooms are homely.

❼ Eating

In no other German city can you eat as well, or as internationally, as in Berlin. There are now many great restaurants and, though often pricey, they are on the whole very good value for money. As well as international cuisine, there are lots of traditional German restaurants serving generous portions of heavy but extremely tasty food.

Breakfast

🍴 **Anna Blume**, Kollwitzstr 83, corner of Sredzkistr, T030-4404 8749. Daily 1000-2400. U-Bahn Senefelderplatz. A restaurant/café/florist that smells divine. Try the 3-tier breakfast (€ 12 for 2).

Lunch

🍴🍴🍴 **Borchardt**, Französische Str 47, T030-2038 7110. Daily 1130-0100, kitchen closes at 2400. U-Bahn Französische Str. Restaurant serving international cuisine and favoured by politicians and journalists. The interior is 18th century and the mosaics and period-style floors make this Gerndarmenmarkt institution well worth a visit. The food is also first rate.

🍴🍴🍴 **Restauration 1900**, Husemannstr 1, T030-442 2494, www.restauration-1900 .de. Daily from 0930 (summer) 1100-2400 (winter). U-Bahn Eberswalder Str, Senefelder Platz. A local hang-out on Kollwitz Platz. Dishes include traditional German cuisine, such as pork knuckle and braised oxtail, but generally it has a global feel. At weekends a delicious and quite substantial brunch is served.

🍴 **Monsieur Vuong**, Alte Schönhauser Str 46, T030-872643, www.monsieur vuong.de. Mon-Sat 1200-2400, Sun 1400-0200. U-Bahn Rosa

Luxemburg Platz. Attracts prominent Berliner media types and a regular young street crowd. At €6.50 for the Indochinese menu it's no wonder why.

Dinner

🍴🍴🍴 **Schwarzenraben**, Neue Schönhauser Str 13, T030-2839 1698, www.schwarzenraben.de. S-Bahn Hackescher Markt, U-Bahn Weinmeisterstr. Daily 1000-2400. This former soup kitchen is now a fashionable bar and restaurant serving superb Italian food. There is a champagne bar downstairs where the elegant clientele while away a few self-indulgent hours.

❝❞ **The further east you go the more shabby-chic the bars tend to be; the further west the smarter and more elegant they become.**

🍴 **Yosoy**, Rosenthaler Str 37, T030-2839 1213, www.yosoy.de. S-Bahn Hackescher Markt, U-Bahn Weinmeisterstr. Daily from 1100. The feeling that you're in a North African souk is all pervasive when visiting this late-night haunt, where delicious tapas are served on tiled counters. A pleasant alternative to the super-smart Mitte bars.

🍴 **Schulter Junge**, corner Lychener Str and Danziger Str. U-Bahn Eberswalder Str. This restaurant is more like a real German *kneipe* or pub. The food is typically German, delicious and plentiful. Try *schnitzel* and *eierpfann-kuchen* (pancakes) with apple sauce.

❶ Nightlife

Berlin offers some of the best nightlife in Europe: laid-back, accessible and cutting edge at the same time. The further east you go the more shabby-chic the bars tend to be; the further west the smarter and more elegant they become. You'll never be pushed for somewhere to go. Mitte has more than its fair share of suitable watering holes, with the area around **Oranienburger Str** being particularly popular with tourists. For something a bit more authentically Berlin, **Prenzlauerberg** is the place to go. From U-Bahn Rosenthaler Platz, head up Weinbergsweg into **Kastanienallee** where you'll find many hip bars and restaurants. Bars usually open at 2200 and then close when the last guest leaves.

The club scene attracts top performers, be it LTJ Bukem at **Club Casino** or Bob Dylan at the **Columbia Halle**. Berlin also plays host to secret **Geheimtip parties**, part of the eastside nightlife. If you are lucky you might discover the location for favourites, such as the **Mittwochclub**, every Wed.

Berlin's classical music scene is world renowned. The **Berlin Philharmonic Orchestra** is based at the Berliner Philharmonie, Herbert-von-Karajan-Str 1, T030-2548 8132, www.berliner-philharmoniker.de, daily 0900-1800. Equally prestigious is the exquisitely restored **Staatsoper**, Unter den Linden 7, T030-2035 4555, www.staatsoper-berlin.org, where opera and ballet are performed. Unsold tickets are available for € 10 before a performance.

In an amazingly short time, and without losing sight of its roots, the dirty industrial city of Bilbao – a name that once conjured images of rusted pig-iron – has transformed itself with huge success into an exciting, buzzy, cultural hub. The Guggenheim Museum is the undoubted flagship of this triumphant progress. A sinuous fantasy of a building, it inspires not only because of what it is, but also because the city had the vision to put it there. While the museum has led the turnaround, much of what is enjoyable about Bilbao already existed. Bustling bar life, harmonious architecture, a superb eating culture and a sense of pride in being a working city. The exciting new developments, with constant improvement and beautification being carried out, can only add to those qualities.

Arts & culture
★★★

Eating
★★★★

Nightlife
★★★

Outdoors
★★★★

Romance
★

Shopping
★

Sightseeing
★★

Value for money
★★★

Overall score
★★★

⊙ Sights

Casco Viejo (Old Town)

ⓘ *Tram Ribera/Arriaga. Metro Casco Viejo,* 🔲A4.

Tucked into a bend in the river, Bilbao's Casco Viejo (Old Town) has something of the medina about it and evokes a cramped medieval past. Designer clothes shops occupy the ground floors where families once huddled behind the city walls, and an array of memorable bars serve up fine Spanish wine and elaborate bartop snacks, from delicious tortilla from a generations-old family recipe, to gourmet postmodern creations that wouldn't look out of place in the Guggenheim. Most Bilbaínos live and work elsewhere in the city and the true soul of the Casco emerges from early evening, when people descend on it like bees returning to the hive, strolling the

Casco Viejo

streets, listening to buskers, debating the quality of the *pintxos* (snacks) in the bars, and sipping drinks in the setting sun.

The parallel **Siete Calles** (Seven Streets) form the oldest part of town (**Somera** is particularly interesting), with the slender spire of the graceful Gothic **Catedral de Santiago** rising from the tightly packed maze. On the waterfront here is the **Mercado de la Ribera**, a lovely art deco market building with over 400 stalls of fruit, vegetables, meat and fish on three floors. **Plaza Nueva**, described by writer Miguel de Unamuno as "my cold and uniform Plaza Nueva", will appeal to lovers of symmetry. Its courtly, neoclassical arches conceal an excellent selection of restaurants and bars, serving some of the best *pintxos* in town. On Sundays there's a flea market here. On Plaza Miguel de Unamuno is **Museo Vasco** ⓘ *T944-155423,* 🔲A3, *Tue-Sat 1100-1700, Sun 1100-1400, €3 (free on Thu)*, housing an interesting, if higgledy-piggledy, series of Basque artefacts found over the centuries.

Atop a steep hill above the Casco Viejo is Bilbao's most important church, the **Basilica de Begoña** ⓘ *lift from C Esperanza (€0.25),* 🔲A4; *bear right, then turn right up C Virgen de Begoña,* home of Vizcaya's patron, the Virgin of Begoña.

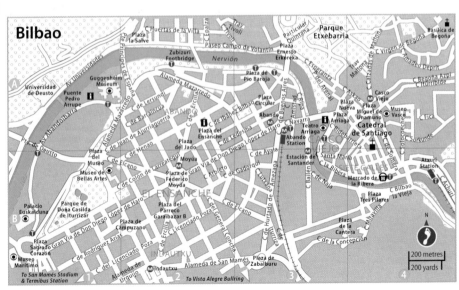

Riverbank

The riverbank is the obvious beneficiary of Bilbao's leap into the 21st century and the Nervión river has become the city's axis once more. If you only take one stroll in Bilbao, make it an evening *paseo* from the Casco Viejo west along the river to the Guggenheim Museum (see below). Highlights on the way include the fin de siècle **Teatro Arriaga** ⓘ *Tram Arriaga,* **A3**, and Calatrava's eerily skeletal **Zubizuri footbridge** ⓘ *Tram Uribitarte.*

Further downstream the bizarre **Palacio Euskalduna** opened in 1998 on the site of the last Bilbao shipyard and is now a major venue for concerts, particularly classical. Nearby is the **Museo Marítimo** ⓘ *Muelle Ramón de la Sota, T902-131000,* **B1***, Tue-Fri 1000-1400, 1600-1800, Sat and Sun 1000-1400, 1600-2000, €4, Tram Euskalduna,* a salty treat that includes a number of different boats as part of its exterior exhibition. Across the river from here is the university barrio of **Deusto**, while, just south, is **San Mamés stadium** ⓘ *C Felipe Serrate, T944-411445, Metro/tram San Mames,* home of the fervently supported Athletico Bilbao.

Basilica de Begoña

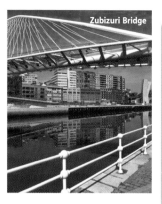
Zubizuri Bridge

Guggenheim Museum

ⓘ *Abandoibarra Etorbidea 2, T944-359000, www.guggenheim-bilbao.es,* **A1***. Tue-Sun 1000-2000, Jul-Aug also Mon. €10, combined ticket with Museo de Bellas Artes €11. Tram Guggenheim.*

More than anything else, it is this building that has thrust Bilbao firmly on to the world stage. Frank Gehry's exuberant Guggenheim brings art and architecture together. It sits among the older riverfront buildings like some unearthly vehicle that's just landed. The titanium panels are paper thin and malleable, making the whole structure shimmer like a writhing school of fish.

Outside, a pool and Fuyiko Nakaya's *FOG* sculpture interact fluidly with the river. Jeff Koons' giant floral sculpture, *Puppy*, sits eagerly greeting visitors, while, on the other side, the spider-like *Maman*, by Louise Bourgeois, guards the waterside approach. Inside are a few large-scale permanent exhibits (such as the vast, interactive *Snake*) plus touring pieces from the permanent collection of the Guggenheim Foundation and temporary exhibits.

◉ Best of the rest

At the mouth of the Nervión, 20 km from the centre, **Getxo** has a pretty old harbour and good beaches. The impressive **Puente Vizcaya**, a UNESCO World Heritage Site, zips cars and passengers across the estuary via a hanging 'gondola'. The rugged coast to the east is lined with great surf beaches and appealing fishing towns, such as **Mundaka**, a laid-back little surf village with some of Europe's best waves, and **Lekeitio**, a Basque fishing port with a picturesque harbour and good eating. Inland is the unmissable and thriving town of **Gernika**, the symbolic home of Basque nationalism. Its **Museo de la Paz** ⓘ *Pl Foru 1, T946-270213, Tue-Sat 1000-1400, 1600-1900, Sun 1000-1400, no lunchtime closing Jul-Aug, €4,* is a moving but optimistic museum detailing the brutal aerial bombardment endured by the town on 26 April 1937.

El Ensanche

Across the river from the Casco Viejo, the new town was laid out in 1876 and has an elegant European feel to it. The wealth of the city is evident here, with stately banks and classy shops lining its avenues. Here you'll find the **Museo de Bellas Artes** ⓘ *Pl del Museo 2, T944-396060,* **B1***, Tue-Sat 1000-2000, Sun 1000-1400, €4.50, Metro Moyua,* which houses modern Basque art, older pieces and temporary exhibits. On the edge of El Ensanche is the bullring and museum of **Vista Alegre** ⓘ *C Martin Agüero, T944-448698, Metro Indautxu.*

⊖ Travel essentials

Getting there Bilbao International Airport, T905-505505, designed by Santiago Calatrava, is 10 km northeast of the city. Buses run to the centre every 30 mins or so, taking 20-30 mins (€1.15). A taxi will cost about €20.

Getting around Bilbao is reasonably walkable – the Guggenheim is an easy 20-min stroll along the river from the old town – but the re-established **tram** line is a handy alternative. It runs every 10-15 mins from Atxuri station along the river, skirting the Casco Viejo and

El Ensanche, with stops at the Guggenheim and the bus station (Termibus) among other places. A single costs €1. To reach destinations further afield, including Deusto, Getxo and the beaches, use the fast, efficient **metro**. A single fare costs €1.15; a day pass is €3. **Euskotren** (T902-543210) services from Abando and Atxuri stations link Bilbao with coastal towns and Gernika. There are also buses from C Hurtado Amezaga, next to Abando station.

Tourist information Bilbao Turismo, www.bilbao.net, is at Pl Ensanche 11, T944-795760, Mon-Fri 0900-1400 and 1600-1930. There are information centres at Teatro Arriaga, on the edge of the old town, Mon-Fri 1100-1400 and 1700-1930, Sat 0930-1400 and 1700-1930, Sun 0930-1400; near the **Guggenheim** at Abandoibarra Etorbidea 2, Tue-Fri 1100-1800, Sat 1100-1900, Sun 1100-1400, and at the **airport**, T914- 710301. You can also phone for information, T944-710301, daily until 2300.

⊕ Sleeping

€€ Gran Domine, Alameda Mazarredo 61, T944-253300, www.granhotel dominebilbao.com. Tram Guggenheim. Inspiring modern hotel opposite the Guggenheim with a façade of tilted glass panels and a delightful interior.

€€ Indautxu, Pl Bombero Etxariz, El Ensanche, T944-211198, www.hoteles-silken.com. Metro Indautxu. Sister to the Gran Domine. Has bags more character than most business-level establishments.

€€ Petit Palace Arana, C Bidebarrieta 2, T944-156411, www.hthoteles.com. Metro Casco Viejo. With an unbeatable location at the mouth of the Casco Viejo warren, this beautiful building has been very sensitively converted into a smart modern hotel with great facilities.

€ Hostal Begoña, C Amistad 2, T944-230134; www.hostalbegona.com. Tram Casino. A welcoming modern hotel near Abando station, packed with flair and comfort.

€ Hotel Sirimiri, Pl de la Encarnación 3, T944-330759, www.hotelsirimiri.com. Tram Atxuri. Great hotel with a genial owner, gym, sauna and free parking.

€ Iturrienea Ostatua, C Santa María, T944-161500. Tram Arriaga. Beautiful *pensión* fitted out in stone, wood and idiosyncratic objects. Tasty breakfasts.

⊘ Eating

Casco Viejo is the best place to head for *pintxos* (bar-top snacks) and evening drinks, especially the Plaza Nueva and around the Siete Calles. In El Ensanche, there's another concentration of bars on Av Licenciado Poza, C García Rivero and C Ledesma. Restaurants are scattered throughout the Casco Viejo, Ensanche and Deusto.

₸₸₸ Guria, Gran Vía 66, El Ensanche, T944-415780. Tram Euskalduna. One of Bilbao's top restaurants; its stock-in-trade is *bacalao*. *Menús* are €41-62, otherwise it's €60 per head minimum. There's also a cheaper bistro menu and a mighty selection of brandies.

₸₸₸ Victor, Pl Nueva 2, Casco Viejo, T944-151678. Metro Casco Viejo. An elegant but relaxed place to try Bilbao's signature dish, *bacalao al pil-pil*.

₸₸ Kasko, C Santa María, Casco Viejo, T944-160311. Tram Arriaga. One of Casco Viejo's best eateries, with funky

decor inspired by the fish and high-class new Basque cuisine. Dinner is sometimes accompanied by a pianist.

₸₸ Serantes and **Serantes II**, C Licenciado Poza 16 and Alameda Urquijo 51, El Ensanche, T944-102066. Metro Moyua/Indautxu. A pair of *marisquerías* that are not as pricey as their notable reputation would suggest: very fresh fish dishes cost around the €20 mark. The daily special is usually excellent, or you could tackle some delicious *cigalas*, the 4WD of the prawn world.

₸ Café-Bar Bilbao, Pl Nueva 6, Casco Viejo, T944-151671. Metro Casco Viejo. Don't miss this sparky place with top service and a selection of some of the best *pintxos* to be had in the old town, all carefully labelled and irresistible. Try them with a *txakolí*, a slightly fizzy local wine.

₸ Saibigain, C Barrenkale Barrena 16, Casco Viejo, T944-150123. Tram Ribera. Down-to- earth, traditional Basque place with hanging hams and a good lunch for €8.50. It's worth the wait to grab a table upstairs, a less frenetic place to sit down and eat than in the bar. Closed on Sun.

With streets like embroidered cloth, threaded with the arches of continuous colonnades, the heart of Bologna is a giant cloister. Under processions of classical columns and in the shadows cast between the half-moons of its winding alleys, the city reveals her secrets to the unhurried visitor prepared to be led astray. Above and behind its chiaroscuro porticoes, Bologna is a rose-red city of bombastic churches and vainglorious palaces, a litter of monuments and masterpieces that are lasting testaments to the architectural flattery bestowed by both papal and civic forces. They both vied for control of the city, producing a legacy of political dissent which, in the 20th century, saw the city labelled red for ideological rather than aesthetic reasons.

Bologna

Arts & culture
★★★

Eating
★★★★★

Nightlife
★★★

Outdoors
★★

Romance
★★★★

Shopping
★★★

Sightseeing
★★★

Value for money
★★★

Overall score
★★★

At a glance

The heart of Bologna is its Roman core, **piazza Maggiore**, at the confluence of the city's two main roads, via Ugo Bassi and via Rizzoli. The **Centro Storico** (Old Centre) is defined by a perimeter road which follows the line of the old city walls. East of piazza Maggiore is the bustling **Quadrilatero**. To the northeast runs via Rizzoli and beyond the **due torri** (two towers) is **via Zamboni**, the heart of studentland. West along via delle Belle Arti is **La Pinacoteca**. South along the main drag, via dell'Indipendenza, is the city's **cathedral**. Southeast from piazza Maggiore is the **Santo Stefano** complex. Connected to the city by a colonnade of 666 arches,

Bologna is the Italy that works.

Charles Richards, The New Italians

the sanctuary of the **Madonna di San Luca** sits atop one of the Apennine foothills.

. . . .

★ *Don't leave town without trying some freshly made tortellini.*

. . . .

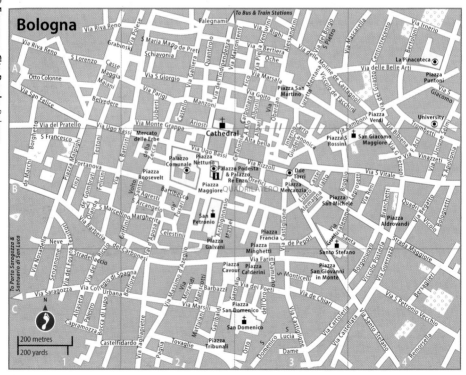

⊙ Sights

Piazza Maggiore

This grandiose square is the backdrop to a human theatre of poseurs and street artists. Standing in the middle of the entirely pedestrianized piazza you feel you could be in the central courtyard of a great castle, enclosed and protected by towers. The forbidding, late-Gothic weight of the **Basilica di San Petronio** ⓘ *T051-225442*, ▐JB2▐, *winter daily 0730-1300 and 1400-1800; summer daily 0745-1230 and 1530-1800, free*, dominates the square. As the façade and half-arches down the western exterior show, this ambitious project was never fully realised. Funded by public money, the basilica, which is a civic temple not a cathedral, was conceived as a monument of opposition to the papacy in Rome and was originally intended to be larger than St Peter's but the papacy, fearful of this ambition, diverted

Palazzo Comunale

money elsewhere. The first stone was laid in 1390 and the current state only achieved several centuries later.

On the west side, the tall, thick and crenellated mass of the **Palazzo Comunale** ⓘ *piazza Maggiore 6, T051-219 3111/Museo Morandi T051-203332,* ▐JB2▐, *Tue-Sat 0930-1830, Sun 1000-1830, entry to galleries €4, free Sat*, is the city's town hall. Built in 1287, it is more like a small city within a city and, other than its

sheer grandiosity, is most notable for its clocktower, built in 1773. Inside are some interesting rooms: especially the **Sala Farnese**, home of Bologna's public art collection, including paintings and frescoes by masters of the Bolognese school and works by Tintoretto; and the **Museo Morandi**, the largest collection of paintings by Giorgio Morandi, the city's most famous contemporary artist.

The castle-like construction in the centre of piazza Maggiore combines two buildings, **Palazzo Podesta** and **Palazzo Re Enzo**. Before becoming the governor's residence, Palazzo Podesta was designed in the early 1200s to house the city's law court. Built in 1244 as an extra wing, Palazzo Re Enzo takes its name from the man who was its prisoner for 22 years (the young king of Sardinia and illegitimate son of Frederick the Great). The building became known as Enzo's *dorata prigione* (golden prison) on account of its luxuriousness.

European City Breaks Bologna

⊖ Travel essentials

Getting there Marconi International Airport, T051-647 9615, www.bologna-airport.it, is 6 km northwest of the city centre. Taxis (€12-15) depart from a rank outside Terminal A, and a bus (€5) runs every 15 mins (0600-2340) and takes about 20 mins. **Forlì Airport**, T0543-474990, www.forliairport.com, has a direct bus service (1¼ hrs, €10) to Bologna's bus station (on piazza XX Settembre next to the train station). There are also trains from Forlì town to Bologna. For the return, direct buses from Bologna to the airport depart once a day to coincide with check-in times.

Bologna is 1½ hrs by train from Milan (www.trenitalia.com) and 3 hrs from Turin

for international rail connections. See also page 12.

Getting around Central Bologna is easily covered on foot. It takes under an hour to walk across the Centro Storico. Alternatively you could hire an old-style sit-up-and-beg bicycle. If you do want to rest your feet, the centre and suburbs are covered by an efficient network of orange buses run by the ATC, **Trasporti Pubblici Bologna**, T051-290290, www.atc.bo.it. Information on services can be found in the train and coach station in piazza XX Settembre as well as at their city office on via Marconi. Tickets costs €1 and last for an hour from the time you validate it in the machine

upon boarding. You can use it for as many journeys as you wish. The City Pass is valid for up to 7 journeys across multiple days (€8.50). Tickets can be bought at *tabacchi* (tobacconists), bars and newspaper kiosks, or on the bus in a machine (€1 coins only).

Tourist information Bologna Turismo, under Palazzo Podesta, piazza Maggiore, T051-239660, www.bolognaturismo.info. Daily 0930-1930. Provides more free maps and leaflets than you could possibly need. A **Bologna dei Musei Card** (1- or 3-day pass costing €8 or €10) allows unlimited access to Bologna's museums.

Piazza Nettuno

Alongside the Palazzo Comunale in neighbouring piazza Nettuno is Bologna's former stock exchange and only art deco building, the **Biblioteca Multimediale Sala Borsa** ⓘ *T051-219 4400*, ◥**B2**, *Mon 1200- 2130, Tue-Fri 0900-2130, Sat 0900-1900*. It's now the pride of Bologna's contemporary urban development and has a multimedia exhibition hall and library containing documentation on contemporary culture and Bologna's history. Outside on piazza Nettuno is **Fontana del Nettuno**, Bologna's bronze statue of the Roman God of the Sea, completed between 1563 and 1566, which has become a symbol of the city and a favourite backdrop for posing visitors. Also outside the Sala Borsa is a memorial to victims of the massacre by the local puppet fascist rump at the end of the Second World War.

Il Quadrilatero

The Quadrilatero is the name given to the grid of narrow streets hidden behind the east side of piazza Maggiore. These streets were home to the small businessmen of medieval Bologna and

Fontana del Nettuno

Via Ranocchi in the Quadrilatero

each street still bears the name of the powerful associations of artisans and merchants it was known for: *clavature* (locksmiths), *orefici* (jewellers), *drapperie* (textile merchants), *pescherie* (fishmongers). By day these are still among Bologna's liveliest market streets. By night they become the stage for Bologna's beautiful youth as they strut in and out of the many bars that have become some of the city's trendiest early evening nightspots.

Due Torri

ⓘ *La Torre degli Asinelli*, ◥**B3**. *Daily summer 0900-1800, winter 0900-1700. €3.*

Northeast of piazza Maggiore, down via Rizzoli are the *due torri* (two towers) that have become the city's icon. These 12th-century skyscrapers served as watchtowers to warn against an attack on the city and have wonderful views of the surrounding countryside from the top. At nearly 98 m high, **La Torre degli Asinelli** is the taller of the two. Built almost simultaneously, the leaning **Torre Garisenda** (closed to the public), was originally much higher than its current 47½ m.

Chiesa di San Giacomo Maggiore

ⓘ *piazza Rossini, T051-225970*, ◥**B4**. *Daily 0700-1200 and 1530-1830.*

Continue down via Rizzoli to reach the anarchic and bohemian atmosphere of **via Zamboni**, the heart of Bologna's student district. Along this street are the main faculty buildings and museums of Europe's oldest university, with numerous bars and cafés under its porticoes. At piazza Rossini is **Chiesa di San Giacomo Maggiore**, one of Bologna's most elegant and significant churches, with the hidden treasure in its Renaissance interior of a cycle of scenes by Lorenzo Costa, Francia and Aspertini.

La Pinacoteca Nazionale

ⓘ *via delle Belle Arti 56, T051-420 9411, www.pinacotecabologna.it*, ◥**A4**. *Tue-Sun 0900-1900. €4.*

The Pinacoteca contains the largest collection of works by artists from the 17th-century Bolognese school, including Tibaldi, Reni, the Carracci brothers, Guercino and some late Titian. The gallery was founded by Napoleon as part of his programme of cultural reform.

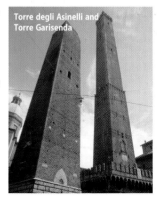
Torre degli Asinelli and Torre Garisenda

Full fat Bolognese

Bologna is to food what Milan is to fashion. The city strains with restaurants and your belt is likely to be doing the same after you have spent a few days helplessly gorging yourself on the abundant and delicious food. Italy's deeply felt regional identities are expressed through regional cuisine, and it is not unusual to hear Italians from different areas laying claim to the best food in the country; rich, substantial and varied, *la cucina bolognese* has a better claim than most. The city is the home of stuffed pastas, such as *tortellini*, *cappellacci* and *anolini*, as well as the old favourite, *lasagne*. Added to these are regional delicacies, such as *proscuitto* and *parmigiano* from Parma. Suffice it to say that food here is taken (and eaten) seriously and copiously; in a city with street names such as vicolo Baciadame (Lady-kisser Lane) and via Fregatette (Tit-rubbing Street), food is enjoyed with gastro-erotic pleasure. And as the city's nickname *la grassa* (the fat) suggests, you are likely to go home totally sated, and certainly no thinner.

Chiesa Santo Stefano

ⓘ *T051-223256, www.abbaziasanto stefano.it,* 🚌. *Daily 0930-1200, 1530-1830.*

The three arteries of via Santo Stefano, via Castiglione and Strada Maggiore, leading southeast from piazza Maggiore, are the most tranquil and picturesque part of town. You can stroll along endless arcades enjoying the shifting perspectives of palatial buildings as they are framed by each arch. The beauty of this area is nowhere more evident than in the triangular piazza Santo Stefano, site of the intricate complex of churches and maze of cloisters and chapels of the Chiesa Santo Stefano, one of the great artistic and architectural wonders of the city. Along with the Basilica di San Petronio and the Due Torri, this church is one of the must-sees of Bologna. At its peak it was a Russian doll of seven interlinked churches within churches.

Chiesa di San Domenico

ⓘ *piazza San Domenico, T051-640 0411,* 🚌. *Daily 0930-1230 and 1530-1830.*

Occupying the entire southern side of the piazza San Domenico, this church was begun in 1221 to commemorate the life of Domingo de Guzman, the founder of the Dominican Order. It

Chiesa di San Domenico

contains one of the masterpieces of Bolognese heritage: the Fabergé-esque *arca* (canopy) above Nicola Pisano's tomb of the saint in the right-hand nave. The *arca* was designed by Niccolo de Bari but completed by Michelangelo, who also sculpted the kneeling angel on the front.

Santuario di San Luca

ⓘ *T051-614 2339. Mon-Sat 0700-1230 and 1430-1900, Sun 1230-1430; closing times vary each month. Free.*

Stretching for 3.6 km and encompassing 666 arches and 15 chapels en route, the portico that leads devotees of San Luca to the Santuario (without getting sunburnt) is the longest continuous arcade in the world. It was started in 1674 and reached the summit in 1739. Follow the porticoes all the way from Porta Saragozza, in the southwest of the Centro Storico, up the colle della Guardia to San Luca for spectacular views.

Sleeping

As a conference centre Bologna has plenty of accommodation aimed at the business market and in recent years something of the hip hotel revolution has rubbed off on some of the top end addresses.

€€€ **Corona d'Oro**, via Oberdan 12, T051-745 7611, www.bolognart hotels.it. Just north of via Rizzoli, the 14th-century palazzo of the Azzoguidi family has been a hotel since the early 1800s. Recently refurbished, it retains an antique charm, thanks to its elegant Venetian-style belle époque veranda and rooms with frescoes and wood panelling. There's a breakfast room but no restaurant.

€€€ **Novecento**, piazza Galileo 4, T051-754 7311, www.bolognart hotels.it. A true boutique hotel with angular contemporary decor in Viennese secession style. A peaceful, luxurious and uniquely hip address.

€€ **Orologio**, via IV Novembre 10, T051-754 7411, www.bolognarthotels.it. On a pedestrianized street with fine views over the Palazzo Comunale, this place offers traditional, if slightly retro, luxury. The titular clock is on the façade (it doesn't strike at night).

€ **Paradise**, via Cattani 7, T051-231792, www.hotelparadisebologna.it. Off via dell' Independenza, this friendly and pretty hotel has 18 rooms; the top ones have good views and architectural character. Following a refit, all are brightly decorated. Monica and Marisa will make you feel at home.

€ **Porta San Mamolo**, vicolo del Falcone 6/8, between via Paglietta and via Miramonte Ruini, T051-583056, www.hotel- portasanmamolo.it. A small romantic hotel in a formerly seedy district of the historic centre.

Eating

♦♦♦ **Antica Osteria Romagnola**, via Rialto 13, T051-263699. Closed Mon, no lunch Tue. Comfortingly anonymous from the outside, Antonio's restaurant is rustic, welcoming and always noisy, with dark wood panels, musical instruments and mirrors on the walls. Superb local and regional cuisine is tailor-made to your taste.

♦♦♦ **Drogheria della Rosa**, via Cartoleria 10, T051-222529. Closed Sun. This cosy restaurant, run by the ebullient Emanuele Addone, used to be a food store and still has original features. Superior dishes from all over Emilia- Romagna are served in an intimate atmosphere with a superb wine list.

♦♦ **Anna Maria**, via delle Belle Arti 17, T051-266894. Closed Mon, no lunch Tue. In the lively university district, this famous and hospitable restaurant is often frequented by actors. The menu is rooted in Bolognese tradition with fresh pasta and sauces centre stage.

♦♦ **Da Fabio**, via del Cestello 2, T051-220481. Dinner only, closed Sun. Wonderful and plentiful regional dishes in this cosy, intimate and unpre-possessing little restaurant with personal service.

♦♦ **Meloncello**, via Saragozza 240, T051-614 3947. Closed Tue, no dinner Mon. It's superbly positioned in the corner of the city leading out through Porta Saragozza. Intimate and a little bit musty, it's like the extension of a family home. Essential to book ahead during the festival of San Luca in May.

♦ **Dell'Orsa**, via Mentana 1, T051-231 576. Popular student lunch hangout serving simple regional dishes until 0100. Great crostini and a range of beers.

♦ **Serghei**, via Piella 12, T051-233533. Closed Sat eve and Sun. Started as a salon for card players who wanted a snack, this small trattoria has lost nothing of its origins. It serves wholesome and abundant Bolognese dishes – perfect for famished students.

Nightlife

Bologna has had a kicking nightlife ever since the city became a university centre and the drinking traditions of Bologna's down-at-heel *osterie* go back almost 1000 years. Clubs attract international DJ names while the gay scene fuels a lot of the creativity behind Bologna's many hybrid art-dance spaces. Activity centres on 2 or 3 areas: kick off at **Rosa Rose** in the Quadrilatero, or **Café de Paris** in piazza Minghetti. Then move on to the concentration of bars in the university district, around via del Pratello, or for something smoother, to **SushiCafe** or **Farmagia** around piazza Malpighi.

Shopping

Bologna is good for everything, from books and fashion labels (Perla and Furla are local brands) to antiques and bric-a-brac, not to mention an endless supply of food and drink. For clothes, head for via M d'Azeglio, via Farini and the catwalk-like **Galleria Cavour** arcade, off Farini. Gourmets will have eyes bigger than their wallets and suitcases in the market streets of the Quadrilatero. For something more unusual and ethnic try the Momo-esque café-cum-club-cum- antiques shop, **Inde le Palais**, via Marchesana 2, home to Bologna's local commercial radio station.

Following Slovakia's 'velvet divorce' from the Czech Republic in 1993, it was tempting to see Bratislava as a poor relation to Prague in the tourism stakes. Historically, Vienna or Budapest might be more relevant comparisons – Bratislava was once an important part of the Austro-Hungarian Empire – but this is a city which deserves to be taken on its own terms. With a small but attractive old town, some fascinating galleries and museums, and rapidly developing restaurant and bar scenes, this recent addition to the EU is finally forcing tourists to sit up and take notice. There could not be a better time to discover one of Europe's newest and most easily explored capital cities.

Bratislava

Arts & culture
★★★

Eating
★★★

Nightlife
★★★

Outdoors
★★

Romance
★★★

Shopping
★★

Sightseeing
★★

Value for money
★★★★

Overall score
★★★

◉ Sights

Staré Mesto (Old Town) A3

At the pedestrianized heart of the Old Town are two interlinked squares, **Františkánska námestie** and **Hlavné námestie**, which in summer are enlivened by outdoor restaurants and cafés. Quirky statues are dotted around this area, including **Cumil**, a voyeur watching passers-by from a manhole. On one side of Hlavné namestie is the **Stará Radnica** (Old Town Hall), founded in the 15th century and gradually incorporating adjoining buildings from later periods. Look out for the cannonball fired by Napoleon's army, which is still stuck in the wall. The building houses the **Mestské múzeum** (City Museum) ⓘ *T02-5443 1473, www.muzeum.bratislava.sk,* **A3**, *Tue-Fri 1000-1700, Sat and Sun 1100-1800, 50Sk.* Although it is worth visiting to get an idea of the city's history, renovations

Cumil statue

mean that half of the rooms will be closed until at least 2008.

Nearby is the city's oldest place of worship, the **Františkánský Kostol** (Franciscan Church), its original Gothic structure largely obscured by baroque rebuilding. A little south of the main squares, **Hviezdoslavovo námestie** is lined with bars and restaurants, with the neo-Renaissance Slovak National Theatre

at one end. Further north is the only remaining city gate, **St Michael's Tower**, ⓘ *Michalská nám 24, T02-5443 3044,* **A2**, *May-Sep Tue-Fri 1000-1700 Sat and Sun 1100-1800, Oct-Apr Tue-Sun 0930-1630,* which now contains a small museum of weapons and fortifications. The main reason to visit, however, is for the wonderful view from the top.

Galéria Mesta Bratislavy
ⓘ *www.gmb.sk.*

Three of the Old Town's most impressive palaces host exhibitions for the Bratislava City Gallery. The pink **Primaciálny palác** (Primate's Palace) ⓘ *Primaciálne nám 3, T02-5935 6111,* **A3**, *Tue-Sun 1100-1700, 40Sk,* was built in the late 18th century for the city's archbishop. The ornate interior includes a mirrored room used for recitals and several 16th-century English tapestries. **Mirbachov palác** (Mirbach Palace) ⓘ *Františkánske nám 11, T02-5443 1556,* **A2**, *Tue-Sun 1100-1800, 80Sk,* houses two panelled rooms

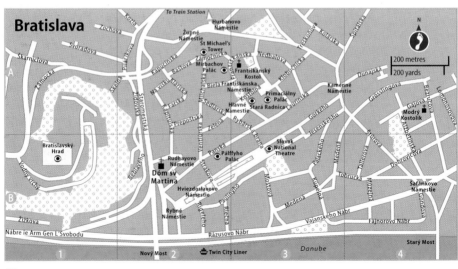

A popular day trip heads out to the 13th-century **Cervený kamen** (Red Stone Castle), T033-690 5803, www.snm.sk. Its extensive rooms are filled with period furniture, and the huge cellars, built in the 16th century to store copper but never used for that purpose, can also be visited. In summer there are falconry displays in the grounds.

The journey to the castle runs through an important part of Slovakia's wine country; it is possible to stop for a tasting and some snacks in the **Vintour cellar**, Krajinská cesta 21, Svätý Jur, T02-4497 0077, vintour@zmail.sk. It is also worth visiting the town of Pezinok to watch handmade majolica production (contact **Monika Vlašicová**, T908-308191, majolica@atlas.sk). Although it is possible to do the whole trip independently by calling ahead, it can most easily be organized through the Bratislava tourist office; see box on page 70 for contact details.

---

displaying a jumble of 18th-century prints, with several based on allegorical paintings by Rubens. The highlight of **Pálffyho palác** (Pálffy Palace) ⓘ *Panská 19, T02-5443 3627,* **B2**, which mostly holds Gothic and 19th-century painting and sculpture, is a mirrored walkway lined with books, which seems to extend forever into space.

Bratislavský Hrad

ⓘ *T02-5934 1626, www.snm-hm.sk,* **B1**. *Tue-Sun 1000-1700. 100Sk*

It's hard to miss Bratislava castle: looking a little like an upside-down table, it watches

Bratislavský Hrad

over the city from a hill close to the Danube. What is less obvious from a distance is that the building was almost entirely reconstructed in the 1950s, having been reduced to ruins by a fire in 1811. There are excellent views of the Old Town from the hill and it is possible to climb one of the towers. The castle itself displays historical exhibitions for the Slovak National Museum.

Dóm sv Martina (St Martin's Cathedral)

ⓘ *T02-5443 1359,* **B2**. *Jun-Oct Mon-Fri 0900-1145 and 1300-1645, Sat 0900-1700, Sun 1300-1645; Nov-May Mon-Fri 1000-1600, Sat 1000-1600, Sun 0800-1800.*

This small cathedral came into its own in the late 16th century, after the Turkish army took control of most of the Hungarian kingdom and Bratislava became the new capital. Hungary's kings were crowned in the cathedral until 1830. The steeple is topped with a replica of the crown of Hungary's first monarch, and golden crowns embedded in the pavement lead along the old coronation route.

Nearby is a Holocaust memorial and a black wall bearing an image of the city's

former synagogue, which fell into disuse after being desecrated by the Nazis. It was later demolished to make way for a highway.

Modrý kostolik **A4**

Well worth the short walk from the old town, the 'Blue Church' is an eye-catching art nouveau building, which was completed in 1913. Built from concrete, covered with plaster and painted in blue and white, the result is distinctively curvy. It is officially named after St Al beta (St Elizabeth), but street signs use the more descriptive nickname.

Modrý kostolik

● Sleeping

€€€ Marrol's, Tobrucká 4, T02-5778 4600, www.hotelmarrols.sk. A cosy and friendly boutique hotel decorated in elegant 1930s style, with internet-ready computers in all double rooms. The luxurious Jasmine Spa can be hired for 2 hrs for 2000Sk for up to 6 people.

€€ Art Hotel William, Laurinská 17, T02-5988 9111, www.euroagentur .com/hotels/hotel-bratislava. Opened at the end of 2006, this hotel has businesslike decor, but a very central (if slightly odd) location inside an upmarket shopping mall. Facilities are modern and impeccably clean.

€ Botel Marina, Nábre ie arm gen L'Svobodu, T02-5464 1804, www.botel marina.sk. Worth considering for novelty value alone – it's on a boat on the Danube – but also a decent hotel for the price. Rooms are on the small side, but clean and in good condition.

€ Caribic's, i kova 1/A, T02-5441 8334, www.caribics.sk. Nestled at the bottom of the castle hill, near the Danube, this comfortable and good-value pension has only six rooms and one apartment so it's best to book ahead. The restaurant serves excellent seafood.

● Eating

€€€ UFO, Nový Most, T02-6252 0300, www.u-f-o.sk. Perched on top of the new bridge, the views from the UFO are second to none. Portions are a little small and you pay a premium for the location, but the cooking is top-notch. A visit to the viewing platform costs 50Sk if you are not dining.

€€ Le Monde, Rybárska brána 8, T02-5441 5411, www.lemonde.sk. Regarded by many as the best restaurant in the city. Accomplished modern European dishes are served in tasteful surroundings, decorated with black and white photos of celebrities.

€ San Marten, T02-9113 0341, www .sanmarten.sk. An elegant but affordable Italian restaurant specializing in home-made pasta. Dining can be more or less formal, with smart white tablecloths in one room and a relaxed bar area in the other.

€ Slovenska, Hviezdoslavovo námestie 20, T02-5443 4883, www.slovrest.com. It's old fashioned, with overdone faux-rural decor, but an award-winning kitchen makes this a good place to try the national dish *bryndzové halušky* (sheep's cheese and bacon gnocchi).

● Nightlife

Bratislava is not short of places to try Slovakian beer, which is both cheap and highly drinkable. The local wine, particularly the white, is also generally pretty good. Located next door to the Academy of Arts, **Café Verne**, Hviezdoslavovo námestie 18, T02-5443 0514, has a Bohemian reputation, while **Prazdroj**, Mostová 8, T02-5441 1108, is a more down-to-earth pub. The sophisticated Cuban-themed **Malecón**, Námestie L. Štúra 4, T02-5464 0167, serves excellent cocktails and has live music every night except Sunday.

The clubbing scene is lively at the weekend, and includes oddities such as an old nuclear bunker, **Subclub**, Nábrezie arm Gen L'Svobodu 2, T02-5441 1183, www.subclub.sk.

Opera performances at the **Slovenské Národné Divadlo** (Slovak National Theatre), T02-5443 3890, www.snd.sk, are of international standard and remarkably affordable. Standby tickets are available 30 mins before the performance, typically costing around 100-300Sk.

● Travel essentials

Getting there M R Štefánik airport is 12 km northeast of the city. A taxi takes 15 mins and should cost around 400Sk; to get the best rates, book by telephone (try **Delta Taxi**, T02-16016). Alternatively take bus no 61 to the main railway station (see below) and transfer to tram No 1; this should take around 40 mins. Another option, which is sometimes cheaper, is to fly to **Schwechat** airport in Vienna then make the 50-km transfer. There are hourly trains from Vienna Südbahnhof to

Bratislava Hlavná stanica (www.slovakrail.sk), about 1 mile north of the centre. You can also combine visits to Vienna and Bratislava by catching the high-speed **Twin City Liner**, T+43 (0)1-58880, www.twincityliner.com, which cruises along the Danube Mar-Oct for € 15-27 each way (75 mins).

Getting around The Old Town is best explored on foot, while a network of buses, trolleybuses and trams serves locations further afield. Tickets are priced

according to the length of validity: 30 mins is usually enough and costs 18Sk.

Tourist information The main office of **BKIS** (Bratislava Cultural and Information Centre) is at Klobucnicka 2, T02-5441 5801, www.bkis.sk. Branches are at the airport, main railway station and passenger port. The official city website www.bratislava.sk is also useful.

Exchange rate £1=49.23Sk, € 1=33.63SK

With Brussels, it's rarely a case of love at first sight, but this is a city that soon gets under your skin. Despite its grey image, the 'capital' of Europe is not short of showpiece buildings or stunning works of art – and its shabby, slightly frayed feel could be regarded as part of its charm. The EU presence lends the city an upbeat, cosmopolitan atmosphere, while the Dutch-speaking minority adds a cultural cutting edge – and all the city's communities unite in their appreciation of the finer things in life. The cooking really is superlative, even in the humblest corner café; the beer is out of this world, and the local penchant for self-deprecating humour gives the nightlife an earthy, unpretentious vibe. Oh, and the frîtes are mighty fine, too.

Brussels

Arts & culture
★★★★

Eating
★★★★★

Nightlife
★★★

Outdoors
★

Romance
★★

Shopping
★★

Sightseeing
★★★

Value for money
★★★

Overall score
★★★★

At a glance

The core of Brussels is the plectrum-shaped **Pentagone**, home to the Upper and Lower Towns. At the Lower Town's heart is the **Grand'Place**, an awe-inspiringly opulent square graced with gilt-strewn guildhouses and a Gothic town hall. Around it bustle bars and restaurants in a warren of medieval streets known as the **Ilôt Sacré** ('Sacred Isle'). The **Upper Town**, otherwise known as the Royal Quarter, is almost oppressively monumental, its wide boulevards, mansions and palaces still lofty and inaccessible. The view back across town makes the uphill trudge worthwhile, however, and the Fine and Modern Arts Museums are essential viewing. Down rue de la Régence, under the shadow of the preposterously grandiose Palais de Justice, is the chic **Sablon** district, its main square lined with elegant houses, smart cafés and swish antiques shops. For something a little earthier, head into the **Marolles**, a traditional working-class area with a fabulous flea market. East of the Pentagone is the **European Quarter**, where quiet squares of stunning art nouveau

Let me tell you what I think: Brussels is the most, most, most city in the world.

William Cliff

architecture nestle amid the concrete colossi that house the EU institutions. To the south lie **St Gilles** and **Ixelles**, two characterful communes, laced with leafy squares, belle époque buildings, ethnic eateries and cosy cafés.

⭐ *Don't leave town without a comedy Manneken Pis corkscrew: it's the perfect souvenir for friends back home.*

⊖ Travel essentials

Getting there Brussels is well served by international trains: **Eurostar** (www.eurostar.com) runs from London to Brussels Gare du Midi (2 hr 20 mins, returns from £59), while the high-speed **Thalys** service (www.thalys.com) links the city with Paris, Amsterdam and Cologne. The city has 2 airports. **Brussels International** is served by airlines from destinations throughout Europe. From the airport, there are 4 trains an hour to the city's 3 stations; the 20-min ride costs €2.80. A taxi costs €30 each way. **Brussels South** (Charleroi) is used by some budget airlines and is a 1-hr bus ride from the capital. Alternative routes from the UK include ferry services to Zeebrugge, Ostend (both an hour's drive from

Brussels) and Calais (1½-2 hrs), or the EuroTunnel. See also pages 12 and 14.

Getting around The Pentagone is easily negotiable on foot; for journeys further afield, there's an excellent tram, bus and metro network, run by **Societé des Transports Intercommunaux Bruxellois (STIB/MIVB)**, online at www.stib.irisnet.be. A day pass for all forms of transport costs €4. You get free public transport with the **Brussels Card**, available at the Gare du Midi, the main tourist office and from hotels and museums. It offers free access to 20 museums in the city, a city map and guide and 25% discounts in shops, restaurants and bars across the city. A card costs €20 for one day, €28 for

two days or €33 for three days. Cycling in the city centre is not recommended (given the tramlines, cobbles and traffic-clogged boulevards).

Tourist information The main **Brussels International** tourist office is located in the Town Hall, on the Grand'Place, T02-513 8940, www.brussels international.be. Open Mon-Sat 0900-1800; Sun 0900-1800 in summer, 1000-1400 in winter, closed Sun Jan-Easter. It sells the Brussels Card (see above), maps and guides. There's also a room-finding service for visitors who arrive in the city without a hotel reservation.

Note that most museums are closed Mon; some are also closed at lunchtime on other days.

24 hours in the city

The die-hard Bruxellois breakfasts on beer, but a coffee on a **Grand'Place** terrace may have more appeal. Once you've drunk it all in, amble through the Ilôt Sacré, visiting the **Galeries St Hubert**, one of the world's first covered shopping arcades, and, if you can't beat the urge, paying homage to the **Manneken Pis**. Head up the Mont des Arts to the **Upper Town**, stopping at the art nouveau Old England building to visit the marvellous **Musical Instruments Museum**: the top-floor café is a good spot for lunch with a view. See the Bruegels and Magrittes at the **Fine and Modern Arts Museums**, then stroll down to the **Sablon** for a spot of window shopping; or, if you're an architecture buff, take a tram to **St Gilles** and visit the house of Victor Horta, the master architect of art nouveau. In the evening, head to the streets around tranquil **Place Ste Catherine** for fine fish and *moules-frîtes* in any of a dozen wonderful

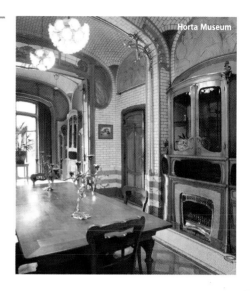
Horta Museum

places before hunkering down for some serious beer appreciation in the bountiful bars of the Old Town.

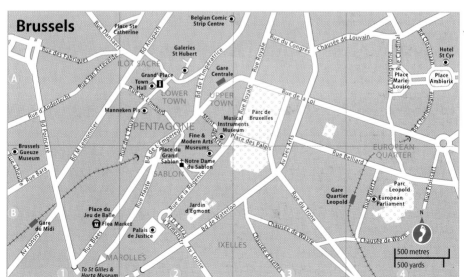

Brussels

European City Breaks Brussels

👁 Sights

Grand'Place ⬛JA2

On this jaw-droppingly gorgeous square, it's hard to know where to stare first – at the exquisite Gothic **Town Hall**, with its curlicued masonry and soaring spire, or the glorious baroque **guildhouses**, honey-coloured and dripping with gilt and leaded glass.

Jean Cocteau called the square "the greatest theatre in the world", and its story is nothing if not dramatic: Louis XIV's artillery razed the square in 1695, but the doughty burghers rebuilt it in just four years. Each house belonged to a guild, and identifying the trade from the golden statues atop each building is all part of the fun. Victor Hugo lived at **Nos 26-27** (known as '**The Pigeon**') during his exile from France; Marx brooded over the Communist Manifesto in the workers' café at **No 9**, '**The Swan**', now a swanky restaurant. The best terrace is at **Nos 1-2**, '**Le Roy d'Espagne**', formerly the bakers' guild. Drinks are not cheap, but the views are priceless.

Grand'Place

Ilôt Sacré

The jumble of medieval streets around the Grand'Place has long been anything but sacred. Their names attest to intense mercantile activity – Butchers' Street, Herring Street, Spur-Makers' Street – and they remain a blur of shops, restaurants, bars and clubs. The eateries around rue des Bouchers, with vast seafood displays outside, are expert at relieving unwary tourists of their cash and are best avoided. (If that sounds bad, night-time visitors in the 19th century were considered lucky to leave with their lives!) That said, there are other great places to eat and drink, and the atmosphere can be positively Bruegelian. The **Galeries St Hubert**, one of the world's first covered shopping arcades, is an oasis of calm amid the surrounding hubbub; a cool, airy glass structure erected in 1847, it houses a theatre, a cinema and cafés and restaurants.

Belgian Comic Strip Centre

ⓘ *Rue des Sables 20, T02-219 1980,* ⬛JA2. *Tue-Sun 1000-1800. €6.20.*

Galeries St Hubert

Tintin fans are in for a treat here; but there's more to *bande dessinée* than the intrepid boy reporter. While this marvellous museum, converted from a Horta-designed art nouveau department store, gives Hergé ample coverage, it's a great place to catch up on Belgium's other memorable comic-book creations. And, more ignominiously, the origins of the Smurfs. Parents be warned: they take the 'ninth art' seriously in Belgium, and the top-floor displays show just how grown-up the genre can be.

Manneken Pis
ⓘ *Rue de l'Etuve,* ⬛JA2

Symbol of Bruxellois irreverence, anti-war icon or shamelessly tacky photo opportunity? Here's your chance to decide, if you can force your way through the camcorder-wielding crowd that surrounds Brussels's smallest tourist attraction. Mystery surrounds his origins, but the pint-size piddler's current incarnation is a copy of a statue fashioned by Jérôme Duquesnoy in 1619 and smashed into smithereens two

Belgian Comic Strip Centre

Romantic, mysterious, lost in time: all typical epithets for Bruges, with its sleepy canals, old stone bridges, circling swans and pinkish Gothic spires. Unfortunately, "jam-packed with tourists" is another, as this dreamy medieval city, a 50-minute train ride from Brussels, pulls in the crowds in summer. Thankfully, it's at its most alluring amid a little off-season fog. Start at the city's heart, the **Markt**, to admire the soaring belfry and the elaborate 13th-century Halle (Cloth Hall), an eloquent illustration of how wealthy this Hansa city was before its river silted up in the 15th century. From here, stroll to the **Burg** for the dazzling Gothic town hall, the Romanesque Basilica of the Holy Blood and the surprisingly harmonious addition of Toyo Ito's sleek, ultra-modern pavilion, built for the city's

stint as European Capital of Culture in 2002. Don't miss the 13th-century **Church of Our Lady**, with the tallest brick spire in the world, or the **Gruuthuse**, owned by one of the 15th century's wealthiest families. The **Begijnhof**, a complex of pretty 13th-century whitewashed houses, is especially lovely when splashed with daffodils in spring; and courting couples will find it hard to resist the **Minnewater** ('Lake of Love'). Art-lovers must make time for two superb museums: the Flemish Primitives and Mannerists are the main attractions at the **Groeningemuseum** (Dijver 12) and the **Memling Museum** (Mariastraat 38).

---

centuries later. He's often decked out in costumes donated by visiting dignitaries, from the Elector of Bavaria, in 1698, to Elvis.

Manneken Pis

Fine and Modern Arts Museums

ⓘ *Place Royale 1-2, T02-508 3211, www.fine-arts-museum.be,* **ↆB2**. *Tue-Sun 1000-1700. €5*

These twin museums comprise the country's finest collection. The Fine is a conventional 19th-century gallery with a superb survey of works by the artists once grouped together as the 'Flemish Primitives': Van der Weyden, Memling, Bouts and, most important, Pieter Bruegel the Elder. It's also replete with vast Rubens canvases and superbly observed smaller works. The Modern is an unusual subterranean spiral with the world's largest collection of works by the star Surrealist René Magritte; there's also a good sample of

20th-century greats – Picasso, Matisse, Bacon, Dalí – and Belgian masters: Paul Delvaux, James Ensor, Leon Spilliaert and Constant Permeke.

Fine and Modern Arts Museums

Musical Instruments Museum

ⓘ *Rue Montagne de la Cour 2, T02-545 0130, www.mim.fgov.be,* **⑤A2**. *Tue-Fri 0930-1700, Sat-Sun 1000-1700. €5 (includes headphone hire).*

No prizes for guessing what's on show here – but the setting is a real surprise. The frills and flourishes of the ornate Old England building, a delightful art nouveau department store in glass and black iron, are an apt counterpoint to the exquisite craftsmanship of the exhibits. The painted pianos from pre-revolutionary France are a highlight, as are the weird and wonderful folk instruments. The top-floor restaurant has some of the best views in town.

Place du Grand Sablon

The Grand'Place may be the city's grandest square, but the Sablon has a little more, well, class. Although the baroque houses lack their counterparts' flamboyance, they're still drop-dead gorgeous. The antiques shops at street level are reassuringly expensive, the cafés and restaurants smart and perfect for

Musical Instruments Museum

Flea market

observing how Brussels' other half lives. There's a wonderful Gothic church, **Notre Dame du Sablon**, at the square's southeastern side.

Place du Jeu de Balle

If you find the Sablon too stuffy, head downhill to the grittier, more ramshackle Marolles, a traditionally working-class district in the shadow of the preposterously overblown Palais de Justice. It sprawls around rues Blaes and Haute (on which Bruegel lived, at No 132), but its heart is the **flea market** on place du Jeu de Balle (daily 0700-1400). Amid the mountains of tat, there are some serious bargains, especially for early birds.

Horta Museum

ⓘ *Rue Américaine 25, T02-543 0490, www.hortamuseum.be. Tue-Sun 1400-1730. €7. Tram 81 or 92.*

Victor Horta was perhaps the greatest exponent of art nouveau, and the house he built for himself in St Gilles is an eloquent reminder of his philosophy and craftsmanship. Horta believed in total

design, right down to the door knobs – he even advised clients' wives on what to wear – but he never let the style's unmistakable swirls and curls get out of control. The exterior is relatively modest but, inside, the house is a symphony of burnished wood, stained glass, delicate wrought iron and covetable antiques.

European Quarter

Home to the Commission, the Council of Europe and the European Parliament, as well as countless NGOs, lobby groups, media organizations and multinationals, this district east of the Old Town is like an entirely separate city, one where English is the lingua franca, but where you'll hear dozens of languages on every street. If possible, time your visit for a weekday; the area's deserted at weekends and the relentlessly functional post-war office blocks can deaden the soul. Amid the glass, steel and concrete boxes, however, are two lovely squares, **place Ambiorix** and **place Marie-Louise**. The Hôtel St-Cyr, at 11 place Ambiorix, is so ridiculously ornate, it's beyond parody.

European Quarter

All hail the ale

Brewing is one of Belgium's grandest traditions, and the appreciation of a really good beer, poured reverently into its special glass, is one of the high points of any visit to Brussels. Even if you don't consider yourself an ale aficionado, you'll savour a trip to the **Brussels Gueuze Museum** (i) **B1** *Cantillon brewery, rue Gheude 56, T02-521 4928, www.cantillon.be, Mon-Fri 0830-1700, Sat 1000-1700, €4*, the capital's last bastion of traditional lambic production. The basis for Belgium's fabled fruit beers, lambic is the only brew to ferment spontaneously, without yeast: the roof is left open to allow spores from the local atmosphere to infuse the liquid. Learn more on the brewery tour, marvelling at the musty ambience, the huge copper vats and the unbridled enthusiasm of the owner. Then it's tasting time: the *kriek* (cherry) and *framboise* (raspberry) beers are sharper, fruitier and more refreshing than the sweetened stuff on sale in most cafés, but the real deal is the *gueuze*, a complex blend of lambics that has a sharp, sour, almost vinegary taste. If you don't like it on the first try, you can buy 75cl bottles to enjoy at home and/or inflict on your nearest and dearest.

Sleeping

Although there are plenty of characterful establishments, the hotel trade in Brussels depends primarily on business – great news for short-breakers, as rates plummet at the weekend. Expect reductions of at least 30% and often much more. Summer prices are also extremely keen. The Old Town has a good concentration of hotels; there are also good options in the European Quarter and Ixelles. Try www.bookings.be for late deals; for B&Bs, visit www.bnb-brussels.be or www.bedandbreakfastbelgium.com.

€€€ Amigo, rue de l'Amigo 1-3, T02-547 4747, www.hotelamigo.com. Part of Rocco Forte's exclusive portfolio, this is an immensely stylish establishment near the Grand'Place. Once a prison (the poet Paul Verlaine was incarcerated here after shooting his lover, Rimbaud), it's now a liberating mix of ancient and modern, with lush tapestries and Flemish masters complemented by top-quality contemporary fabrics and fittings.

€€€ Le Dixseptième, rue de la Madeleine 25, T02-517 1717, www .ledixseptieme.be. Don't be fooled by the discreet façade – this was once the Spanish ambassador's residence. Now it's really spoiling us with a superbly restored 17th-century interior, relaxed service and 24 dreamily luxurious, classically kitted-out rooms.

€€ Saint-Michel, Grand'Place 11, T02-511 0956, www.atqp.be/hsm. The unique selling point is the address: this is the only hotel on the Grand'Place, to the left of the Town Hall. Some of the rooms have gobsmacking views. Don't bother unless you can get one, though.

€€ Welcome, rue du Peuplier 5, T02-219 9546, www.hotelwelcome.com. Amid the fish restaurants of Place Ste Catherine is this wonderful little hotel with 15 world-themed rooms. The Congo is all leopard-print fabrics; the Japan, sleek, stark and serene. It's too well done to be kitsch, and the owners have charm to spare.

€€-€ Noga, rue du Béguinage 38, T02-218 6763, www.nogahotel.com. There's a nautical theme in this quiet place on a side street near Place Ste

Catherine. The rooms are bright, boldly coloured and extremely comfortable, and the clincher is what the website calls "Noga's little extras": bike hire, a piano in the lounge, a snooker room. It's also great value.

€ Galia, place du Jeu de Balle 15-16, T02-502 4243, www.hotelgalia.com. Clean, simple rooms in a modern building at the heart of the Marolles, and handy for flea market fiends.

Eating

Even the self-deprecating Bruxellois can't help being proud of their city's culinary prowess, and with good reason: it's almost impossible to have a bad meal here, unless you're foolish enough to succumb to the wiles of the waiters on rue des Bouchers. Brasseries and cafés usually have an all-day menu, with staples such as spaghetti bolognese, omelettes and a range of croques. Portions are enormous, so go easy on the starters.

Breakfast

Het Warm Water, rue des Renards 25, T02-513 9159, www.hetwarm water.be. Sun-Tue 0800-1900, Thu-Sat 0800-2100. For brekkie, brunch and Belgian specialities, with a side order of authentic Marollien atmosphere, you can't beat this place off place du Jeu de Balle. It serves earthy, homely cuisine – Brussels soup, *pottekees*, cheese and endive omelette – as well as croissants and muesli. Brunch on Sun (1100-1500) is a riotous affair.

Lunch

Le Paon Royal, rue du Vieux Marché aux Grains 6, T02-513 0868, www.paonroyal.com. Tue-Sat 0800-2200. Lunchtime special €8.50. The Royal Peacock is the quintessence of Brussels bonhomie. Off Place Ste Catherine, it's homely with a country- pub feel, serving shrimp croquettes, veal cooked in cherry beer and eels in a pungent green sauce. Excellent beer too.

Au Bain-Marie, rue Breydel 46, T02-280 4888. Mon-Fri 1200-1500. If you really must eat healthily, you'll find it hard to better this light, airy restaurant at the heart of the European Quarter, with a meat-free mod Med menu. There's a cosmopolitan crowd from the nearby Commission building, so you can brush up on your languages while munching your bruschetta.

Dinner

La Quincaillerie, rue de Page 45, T02-533 9833, www.quincaillerie.be. Mon-Fri 1200-1430 and 1900-2400, Sat-Sun 1900-2400. An ironmonger's isn't an obvious choice for a *dîner à deux*, but this converted art nouveau hardware shop near the Horta Museum – all green wrought-iron, polished wood and gleaming copper, with a

spectacular central staircase – has romance to spare. The food's great, too, a mix of refined Franco-Belgian classics, lip-smackingly fresh fish and spectacular seafood platters. Swift but friendly service seals the deal.

Bij Den Boer, quai aux Briques 60, T02-512 6122, www.bijdenboer.com. Mon-Sat 1200-1430 and 1800-2230. There are posher and trendier places to eat fish in the Ste Catherine area but this resolutely old-fashioned restaurant has

> 66 99 **Even the self-deprecating Bruxellois can't help being proud of their city's culinary prowess, and with good reason...**

rugged charm aplenty. It's a sea of burnished wood and check tablecloths, with specials chalked up on the mirrors. House specialities include fish soup, mussels five ways, North Sea bouillabaisse and poached skate wing: it's all sea-fresh, simply prepared and sensational. The 4-course menu is great value at €25.

La Roue d'Or, rue des Chapeliers 26, T02-514 2554. Daily 1200-0000. Although its striking decor tips a (bowler) hat to Magritte and the Surrealists, the polished wood and mirrors give the game away: the Golden Wheel is basically a brasserie, and a jolly good one at that. Just off the Grand'Place, it offers a mix of French (cassoulet, andouillette AAAAA) and Belgian dishes (sausage and *stoemp*, creamy fish or chicken *waterzooi*), handling both cuisines with aplomb. The double-fried chips are to die for.

🎵 Nightlife

With so many great beers to try, it's a good job Brussels is rammed with marvellous bars. Inexplicably, the expat crowd stick to the European Quarter's Irish joints; leave them to it and focus on the Old Town. Place St Géry's terraces are a magnet for the beautiful people, but rue du Marché au Charbon has more edge, with salsa at **Cartagena** (No 70), the boho **Au Soleil** (No 86) and the LHB haven **Belgica** (No 32), among its many attractions.

The intersection of rue Dansaert and rue des Chartreux is another good crawling point: on the former, **L'Archiduc** (No 6) is a seriously cool art deco jazz bar with a liner-style interior and suitably smoky sounds; on the latter, **Le Greenwich** (No 7) is a classic old café where chess players congregate; and on nearby rue Orts, the **Beurs Café**, attached to a Flemish cultural centre, is a super-cool post-industrial space.

Beyond the Old Town, chaussée de Charleroi (tram 91 or 92) is lounge central. Try **Les Salons de l'Atalaïde** (No 89), **Le Living Room** (No 50) and **Kolya** (No 102). Off the main drag are two great conversions: **Khnopff**, rue St Bernard 1, a cooler-than-thou bar-restaurant in the titular Symbolist painter's former atelier; and the hugely romantic wine bar **Amadeus**, 13 rue Veydt, in Rodin's studio.

Finally, beer buffs should head straight for **Chez Moeder Lambic**, 68 rue de Savoie; pré-Métro Horta, a loveably scruffy St Gilles institution that stocks every Belgian brew you can think of. It's open till (at least) 0300 most nights.

Although some investment has flowed into Budapest since Hungary's EU accession in 2004, prosperity is yet to reach the doors of ordinary Hungarians. Still, the city bears the imprint of its communist years pretty lightly and shares much of the imposing grandeur of its Hapsburg neighbour, Vienna, although it is more derelict and more charming for it. The two cities Buda and Pest, joined administratively in the 19th century, are still kept apart by the grey sweep of the Danube. Above its waters lie belle époque buildings and the weathered stone of neoclassical and baroque mansions. The home of Liszt and Bartók has a rich musical heritage, as well as an underground arts and bar scene, not to mention beautiful mosaic Turkish baths where you can steam yourself back to life after a night on the town.

Budapest

Arts & culture
★★★★

Eating
★

Nightlife
★★★★

Outdoors
★★

Romance
★★★

Shopping
★

Sightseeing
★★★

Value for money
★★★★

Overall score
★★★

At a glance

Buda's Castle Hill rises just over 180 m on the west side of the Danube to offer brilliant views of both the neighbouring hilltop, **Gellért**, to the south, and the low-level sprawl of **Pest** across the river to the east. Pest incorporates two-thirds of the city and is more dynamic and grimy than its west bank rival. The Chain Bridge links Castle Hill with **Belváros** on the east bank. This is where the medieval city grew up. It is bordered by a semicircular series of roads (József Attila ut, Károly körút, Múzeum körút and Vámház körút), which together are dubbed the 'Little Boulevard'. Cutting straight through the inner city, parallel to the Danube, is the shopping street- cum-tourist zone, **Váci út**. To its northeast is **Deák Ferenc tér**, the starting point for the city's most important and grandiose thoroughfare, **Andrássy út**, which runs northeast for over 2 km to the city park, **Városliget**, and **Heroes Square** (Hösök Tere), focal point of the 1956 anti-Soviet uprising.

...beneath the noisy boom of Budapest there was that presence of a wistful and melancholy tone...

John Lukacs

The **Great Boulevard** is a broader arc that apes the semicircle of the Little Boulevard, running from Margit Hid (Margaret Bridge) at the toe-tip of Margit Island in the north, crossing Andrássy út at Oktogon, then looping back to the river at Petőfi Híd to the south of the city.

★ *Don't leave town without subjecting yourself to the elevator shaft at the House of Terror.*

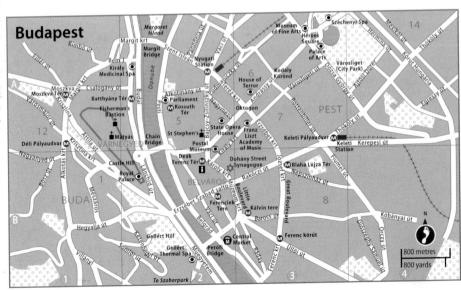

Budapest

24 hours in the city

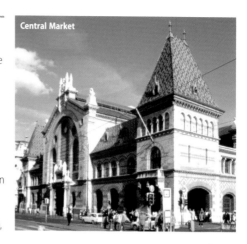
Central Market

For an early morning view of Budapest's World Heritage status head for Buda's Castle District. Enter through the northern **Vienna Gate** (Bécsi kapu tér) and stroll past the ceramic roof of the **National Archives**, before exploring the cobblestone sidestreets and ducking west for a leafy walk along the ramparts. Have a late breakfast at **Ruszwurm**, then head on towards Holy Trinity Square to see the **Mátyás Church** and the **Fishermen's Bastion**. Walk or take the funicular down the hill to the river and then take a tram south to the **Gellért** thermal spa for a swim and a pummel. After a snack lunch at the **Central Market** in Pest, head north, up Váci út, to reach **Szent István Bazilika**, and then stroll along Andrássy út to the **House of Terror**. You can recover from the horrors of the 20th century by contemplating the achievements of the Spanish masters at the **Museum of Fine Arts** on Heroes Square. Head back to the river for an early evening **cruise** before enjoying a recital at the **Opera House** or the **Liszt Academy**. Supper could be something modishly Hungarian at **Vörös és Fehér**, followed by table football and a nightcap at one of the trendy *kerts*. If that sounds too down-at-heel, try one of the bars on Liszt Ferenc Square, or the A38 boat on the river between Petőfi and Lágymányosi bridges in Buda.

⊖ Travel essentials

Getting there Ferihegy International Airport (www.bud.hu) is 16 km southeast of the city, T01-296 9696. Terminal 1 serves low-cost airlines, while Terminal 2 serves most other airlines, including Hungary's Malev. A handy **airport minibus**, T01-296 8555, runs to any address in the city 0600-2200 (HUF 2100 one way, HUF 3600 return); it's cheaper than a taxi but you must book your return journey 24 hrs in advance.

Most international express trains plus domestic trains to and from the north use **Keleti pályaudur**, VIII Kerepesi út 2-6 (M3 metro); other main stations are **Deli pályaudur**, I Krisztina körút 37 (M2 metro), and **Nyugati pályaudur**, VI Teréz körút (M3 metro). T01-461 5400, www.mav.hu, for domestic services and T01-461 5500,

www.elvira.hu, for international links, including Vienna, every 3 hrs (2½ hrs), Berlin (12 hrs) and Paris (16 hrs).

Getting around Walking around Budapest is a pleasure but the public transport network of **buses**, **trams** and **trolleybuses**, plus 3 **metro** lines, is excellent, cheap and runs 0430-2310. You can buy single journey tickets (HUF 185) or booklets at newsagents, stations and stops. A 1-day metro pass costs HUF 1150. Tickets must be validated once on board; you face a HUF 2000 on-the-spot fine if you travel without a ticket. The tourist office's **Budapest Card** gives you access to unlimited public transport in the city for 48 hrs (HUF 5200) or 72 hrs (HUF 6500), as well as discounts on sights, activities and thermal baths. **Bikes** can be

rented from many of the city's hotels and from **Velo-Touring**, T01-319 0571, www.velo-touring.hu. **Taxis** have yellow number plates and run on a meter; drivers will expect a 10% tip on top of the fare. Booking by phone is cheaper than hailing a cab on the street: try **Budataxi**, T01-233 3333; **Rádió Taxi**, T01-377 7777; **Főtaxi** T01-222 2222, or **City Taxi** T01-211 1111.

Tourist information Budapest's **Tourinform** office is at Deák tér/Sütő utca 2, T01-438 8080, www.budapest info.hu, daily 0800-2000. **Budatours**, T01-374 7070, www.budatours.hu, run a 2-hr city tour, HUF 4300, from outside Bajcsy-Zsilinskzky út metro (M1).

Exchange rate Hungarian Forint (HUF): £1 = HUF 361.65. €1 = HUF 247.87.

⊙ Sights

Várhegy and Király Palota (Castle Hill and Royal Palace)

A fortress was first built on Buda's unmistakable World Heritage hilltop following the Mongol invasion of 1241, which almost razed the settlements of low-lying Obuda and Pest. The Royal Palace occupies the southern slopes of the hill and commands regal views over the quays and boats of Pest but, although the site was successfully defended over the centuries, its buildings proved to be less resilient. The palace was destroyed first in battle with the Turks in the 17th century and, again, during the German retreat at the end of the Second World War, and each time it was rebuilt in the architectural vernacular of the day. Today, its stately neoclassical buildings and stone parapets house a rash of cultural institutes: the **Hungarian National Gallery** ⓘ *T020-439 7325, www.mng.hu,* ⬛**B2**, *Tue-Sun 1000-1800, free;* the **Budapest History Museum** ⓘ *T01-225 7809, www.btm.hu,* ⬛**A1**, *Wed-Mon 1000-1800, HUF 800;* the **National Széchényi Library** ⓘ *T01-224*

Castle Hill

Fishermen's Bastion

3700, www.oszk.hu, Tue-Fri 0900-2100, Sat 0800-2000; and the **Ludwig Museum** ⓘ *T01-555 3444, www.ludwigmuseum.hu,* ⬛**A1**, *Tue-Sun 1000-2000, HUF 1050.* Look out for the bronze sculpture of King Mátyás at the hunt, looking every inch like Errol Flynn.

Mátyás Templom, Fishermen's Bastion and Várnegyed
ⓘ *Szentháromság tér, District 1, T01-355 3657,* ⬛**A1**. *Daily 0600-2000. HUF 270-550.*

The two-thirds of Buda that wasn't taken up with palace buildings was left to the civilians. At the centre of this area is **Holy Trinity Square** (Szentháromság tér) and the lovely **Mátyás Church** ⓘ *www.matyas-templom.hu,* ⬛**A1**, *Mon-Fri 0900-1500, Sat 0900-1300, Sun 1300-1700, HUF 650.* Painted with Asian and Turkish-influenced geometric heraldic motifs, the church has had to wear a number of religious hats down the ages: it was shared between Catholics and Protestants and became a Mosque during the Turkish occupation of 1541. The Gothic body of the church was built

in the 13th century, the tower in the 15th. A facelift, timed to coincide with the 1896 millennium celebration, gave it back its eye-popping frescoes, medieval- style tiles and stained glass. The whole project was overseen by Frigyes Schulek, who also designed the neo-Romanesque trim to the church, known as the **Fishermen's Bastion**.

North of the square, in **Várnegyed**, are the squat merchants', noblemen's and courtiers' residences, painted umber, olive, yellow, ochre and cream. Heavy doors open on to courtyards, with wells and plane trees, and shallow stone reliefs decorate the façades. Parts of the area are medieval but much was rebuilt in the baroque and Louis XVI styles when the Turks left after the 1686 siege.

Orszaghaz (Parliament)
ⓘ *Kossuth Lajos tér, District 5, T01-317 9800,* ⬛**A2**. *Visits by guided tour only (tickets from the gate), daily 1000, 1200, 1400, 1800.*

The puffed-up Parliament building on the Pest embankment is a splendid piece of pomp, modelled on the Palace of Westminster, and it's as impressive inside as out: full of frescoes and sculptures,

Parliament

deep red carpets, stained-glass windows, hundred-bulb chandeliers, four-tonne monolithic granite colonnades and the crown, sceptre, orb and sword of the Hungarian coronation.

Szent István Bazilika (St Stephen's Basilica)

ⓘ *Szent István tér, District 5, T01-317 2859,* **A2**. *Summer 0900-1700; winter 1000-1600.*

Budapest's largest church, completed in 1905, is a fat neoclassical building perfumed with the myrrh of its votive candles and dominated by marble (15 different types), mosaics and paintings. If Matyas Church is Budapest's fussy Westminster Abbey, then St Stephen's is the city's St Paul's. It is named after the founder of the Hungarian state, Catholic King Szent István, whose mummified arm is kept on the left side of the chapel, and who sits carved from Italian marble on the high altar. Go up to the dome for amazing rooftop views of the **Postal Savings Bank**, designed by Ödön Lechner. What appears, at street level, to be an unremarkable white building, reveals itself from above to be a perfect aesthetic expression of the building's function: the

Postal Savings Bank

State Opera House House

bank's roof is embroidered with bees, the symbol of saving.

Magyar Állami Operaház (State Opera House)

ⓘ *Andrássy út 22, District 6, T01-332 7914, www.opera.hu,* **A2**.

Hungary punches well above its weight in terms of musical virtuosity, and the Hungarian State Opera House is an appropriate physical representation of the country's acoustic refinement. The sphinx-flanked entrance gives onto a Fabergé-egg of an interior. Built in 1884 in neo-Renaissance style to Miklós Ybl's design, the architecture is best enjoyed during a ballet or opera performance. Tickets are decidedly affordable by London standards.

Andrássy út

This UNESCO-protected boulevard runs for 2½ km, like a grandiose spoke, from inner-city Pest at Szent István's to the Hösök Tere and City Park in the northeast. It was built in the late 19th century at the time of the administrative union of Buda, Óbuda and Pest, after

the Austro-Hungarian Compromise. Its buildings are almost absurdly beautiful and can be divided loosely into three sections: closest to the Danube are four-storey residential blocks, then two-storey mansions give way to palaces and gardens the further out you get. Modelled on the Champs-Elysées and designed by Ybl, it is one of the world's finest urban landscapes. Look out particularly for the **Postal Museum** ⓘ *Andrássy út 3, T01-269 6838, www.posta muzeum.hu,* **A3**, *Tue-Sun 1000-1800, HUF 100,* which is notable for its architecture rather than its exhibits, and **Kodály Körönd**, a series of mansion blocks with amazing frescoed façades.

Terror Háza (House of Terror)

ⓘ *Andrássy út 60, District 6, T01-374 2600, www.terrorhaza.hu,* **A3**. *Tue-Fri 1000-1800, Sat-Sun 1000-1930, closed Mon. HUF 1500.*

Brace yourself: this is sightseeing as harrowing 20th-century history lesson. Number 60 Andrássy út was, from 1939 to 1944, the House of Loyalty, party HQ of the Hungarian Nazi Arrow Cross Party. Between 1945 and '56 it went on to

House of Terror

Buda bathtime

Residents on the Buda side of the city have water pressure sloshing from their taps with the force of a hardly-harnessed Niagara: Budapest lies on top of somewhere between 80 and 120 active springs and wells from which 70 million litres of water burst forth daily. The medicinal properties of the city's springs were recognized during the Turkish occupation and, by 1500, the Turks had bequeathed their Hungarian subjects some beautiful Ottoman baths, featuring high domes with shafts of light searing through the steam, and tile mosaics lining the 18°C plunge pools. Today, the baths remain a brilliant way to atone for a night on the Buda or Pest tiles, despite the off-putting appearance of most bathhouse staff. Baths tend to be single sex, although swimming pools are usually mixed. Specific treatments for rheumatism, physiotherapy and inhalation are available, but on weekends from April to September, most people head outside to lounge around and sunbathe with the papers, stirring only to complete extremely lackadaisacal laps of the swimming pool. The best baths in town are: **Gellért**, Kelenhegyi út 4-6, T01-466 6166, www.gellertbath.com, Mon-Sat 0600-1900, Sat-Sun 0600-1700, HUF 3000, which is full of art nouveau furnishings, mosaics and stained-glass windows; the neo-baroque **Széchenyi Spa**, Állatkerti út 11, District 14, T01-363 3210, May-Sep 0600-1900, Oct-Apr 0600-1700, HUF 2000-2300, which has chess boards in its pool, and the gay favourite, **Király Medicinal**, Fő utca 82-84, T01-202 3688, Mon, Wed, Fri 0700-1800 for women, Tue, Thu, Sat 0900-2000 for men, HUF 1100.

become the head of the Soviet terror organizations ÁVO and ÁVH. Both were remarkable for institutionalized brutality and the torture of subjects. The emphasis is on experience over mere exhibition. Nagging music and newsreel footage make this document of the crimes of the successive terror regimes so vivid as to turn your stomach. Documentary footage contrasts the order and iconography of the Nazi regime with the relative scrappiness of Soviet rule but the museum has also been criticized for describing the atrocities of the latter in detail, while providing only relatively cursory treatment of the Nazi genocide.

Magyar Conquest, with archangel Gabriel on top of a column and the seven tribal chieftains below. Across Heroes Square, the showcase for political gatherings and displays of Communist and Soviet might, sits the **Palace of Arts**. Behind is **City Park**, home to **Széchenyi spa** and the winter ice-skating rink.

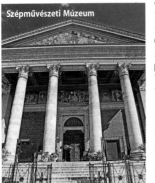
Szépművészeti Múzeum

Széchenyi spa

Szépművészeti Múzeum (Museum of Fine Arts)

ⓘ *Dózsa György út 41, Heroes Sq, District 4, T01-469 7100, www.szepmuveszeti.hu,* ⓈⒶ③. *Tue-Sun 1000-1730.*

This imitation Greek temple at the City Park end of Andrássy út houses a collection of Spanish masters including seven El Grecos and five Goyas. Its walls carry bleary oil paintings of saints, acts of martyrdom, beheadings and sermons. Outside, the **Millennium Monument** marks the 1000th anniversary of the

⊙ Sleeping

Budapest has its share of charmless Soviet-style business hotels but there are some treats too. The city also has a strong homestay tradition, as well as serviced apartments, which are available for both long-term rental and short lets.

€€€ Art'Otel, Bem Rakpart 16-19, T01-487 9487, www.artotel.de. On the Buda side of the Danube, overlooking Parliament, this hotel is spruce, slick and more minimalist than the Gresham. The 148 rooms in 4 baroque townhouses have floor-to-ceiling windows and snappy service.

€€€ Four Seasons Hotel Gresham Palace, Chain Bridge, Roosevelt tér 5-6, T01-268 6000, www.fourseasons .com/budapest. The art nouveau/ secessionist Gresham Palace was built to accommodate wealthy British aristocrats. Today, this landmark building is home to Budapest's most luxurious hotel. Rooms have huge fluffy pillows, giant bathrooms and the best views in Pest. There's also an infinity pool, gym, spa and a flawlessly polished service ethic.

€€ Danubius Hotel Gellért, Szent Gellért tér 1, T01-889 5500, www.danubiushotels.com/hu. The grand dame among Budapest's hotels. Its carpets can be dank and it reeks of the Soviet era but the views across the Liberty Bridge are splendid, and it has character in spades. Rates include admission to the excellent onsite Gellért Thermal Baths (see page 84).

€€ Hotel Pest, Paulay Ede u. 31, District 6, T01-343 1198, www.hotel pest.hu. An 18th-century apartment building just a stone's throw from the Opera House is now an elegant, 3-star hotel with 25 immaculate rooms overlooking an ivy-clad courtyard.

€€ Residence Izabella, Izabella út/ Andrássy út, T01-475 5900, www.residence-izabella.com. This residential apartment in a 19th-century building has been exactingly refurbished. Suites have 1-3 bedrooms, plus kitchen, lounge and dining room. Room service, breakfast, laundry, concierge, AV system, sauna, pool room and home theatre are all available.

€ Kalmar Bed & Breakfast, Kelenhegyi út 7-9, T01-430 0831. Something of a time warp, Kalmar is a 1900-mansion-turned-idiosyncratic pension sitting in its own garden on the southeast slope of Gellért hill, a few hundred yards back from the Danube. It's a family-run concern, with large, clean rooms. There are double rooms, suites, plus a top-floor apartment that can sleep 4; all have antique furniture, high ceilings, large windows and TVs.

❼ Eating

Hungarians know their way round a knuckle of ham, but the country that gave us goulash hasn't earned a place at the top table of global cuisine. Stout, artery-thickening dishes are the norm; most come soused in thick creamy sauces. That said, there is a lively metropolitan restaurant scene at the top end, serving fish fresh from Lake Balaton, and the countryside seems to produce so much fruit that the Hungarians have no option but to use it in spiced soups – a cool cinnamon-spiked peach broth is not uncommon in late summer. Cakes are a strong suit, as are *lángos*, a pizza-like dough that's fried, then smeared with sour cream and garlic.

⊙ Best of the rest

Gellérthegy (Gellért Hill)
ⓘ *District 6.* A symbol of Austrian supremacy, this citadel was built after the 1848 revolution.

Chain Bridge The oldest bridge to span the Danube (1849) was designed by the engineer of Hammersmith Bridge, William Tierney Clark, and built by Scotsman, Adam Clark.

Dohány Street Synagogue
ⓘ *Dohány utca 2, Mon-Thu 1000-1700 (winter 1500) Fri, Sun, 1000-1400, HUF 400-1000.* Central Europe's largest Jewish community gave rise to its largest synagogue. The Holocaust tree in the garden has metal branches and dog-collar leaves, bearing the names of Jewish lives lost.

Liszt Ferenc Zeneakadémia (Franz Liszt Academy of Music)
ⓘ *Liszt Ferenc tér 8, District 6, T01-462 4600, www.lfze.hu.* Amazing art nouveau building and one of the city's main concert halls.

Margitsziget (Margaret Island)
The lungs of the city, a favourite destination for romantics and joggers.

Szoborpark (Statue Park)
ⓘ *Balatoni út/ Szabadkai utca, District 22, T 01-424 7500, www.szoborpark.hu. 1000-sunset. HUF 600. From Ferenciek tér: No 7 or No 173 buses to Etele tér, then Volan Bus (yellow to Diosd-Erd).* 'Disneyland of Communism' displaying the vast statues that once lined the city's streets: Marx, Engels, Lenin, Hungarian labour movement heroes, plus the hammer and sickle.

♥♥♥ Vörös és Fehér, Andrássy út 41, District 6, T01-413 1545, www.voroses feher.com. Daily 1200-2400. Modish bar just opposite the Opera House that's part-owned by the Budapest Wine Society. The cellar is excellent but there's also a good Magyar/ international menu: saddles of venison, paprika catfish, filet mignon, beef consommé and goulash.

♥♥ Café Kör, Sas utca 17, Szent István Bazilika, T01-311 0053. Mon-Sat 1000-2200, closed Sun. A modest bistro on the heels of the Basilika that, in a glut of high-price showy restaurants, still attracts locals as much as passing sightseers. Flavours are Hungarian (goulash and goose liver, aubergine cream, cottage cheese dumplings with hot forest fruit sauce) with some lighter European notes. Booking is strongly recommended. Also serves breakfast.

♥♥ Gerbeaud, Vörösmarty tér 7, Deák Ferenc tér, District 5, T01-429 9000, www.gerbeaurd.hu. Daily 0900-2100. A 150-year-old institution dripping with chandeliers. The café's signature dessert is a cake with nuts, jam and apricot, covered in chocolate. Once part of the weekend ritual of the middle classes, it is now firmly etched on the tourist's itinerary.

♥ Café Gusto, Frankel Leó utca, District 2, T01-316 3970. Closed Sun. One of the tiniest cafés in Budapest has, in its relatively short lifespan (14 years), become a real local institution. Although it has only just acquired a gas cooker (so now you can get lasagne along with beef *carpaccio*), Gusto has a loyal fanbase among the city's intelligentsia. On match days, a TV is slapped on a centre table.

♥ Ruszwurm Cukrászda, Szentháromság utca 7, Várhegy, District 1, T01-375 5284, www.ruszwurm.hu.

A glory clock hangs behind the old-world cherrywood counter at this perfect Biedermeier relic. Gilt chandeliers, velvet banquettes, 19th-century ornaments and chinaware – this is the place for strudels, gingerbread and salt cakes.

Central Market Hall, Fővám Krt 1-3, District 4. Pile 'em high is the philosophy at the cheap food counters ranged around the top of the grand Market Hall built in 1890. Mounds of cabbage, stews of butter beans, stringy pickles and plenty of sordid looking sausages. Sophisticated it ain't.

66 99 Ten out of ten for hipness, though, goes to the *kerts*, Budapest-style late-night speakeasies …

😎 Nightlife

Bars and clubs

There are the chichi metropolitan sit-outs at **Liszt Ferenc Square**, or slightly seedier coffee shops along **Raday utca** and, in summer, there are chic and dressy clubs on **Margit Island**. The cool **A38** boat, moored on the Buda side between Lágymányosi and Petőfi bridges, T01-464 3940, www.a38.hu, is a Ukrainian stone carrier ship that stages cutting-edge concerts.

Ten out of ten for hipness, though, goes to the **kerts**, Budapest-style late-night speakeasies that set up in the disused courtyards of the city's derelict housing squares. Unpopular with sleep-deprived neighbours, they squat in uninhabitable dwellings until local opposition forces the fridge, chairs,

tables and, invariably, *fussball* tables, to move a few doors down to the next condemned and neglected ghost house. Understandably shy of publicity, they seldom have street signs or set addresses, so ask a local to direct you through the medieval district or look out for a doorman propped on a bar stool outside an otherwise unassuming doorway. The 2 longest-running venues are: **Szoda** in District 5; and **Szimpla** in the Jewish district, Kazinczy utca 14, T01-321 9119, www.szimpla.hu.

Tüzraktér Independent Cultural Centre, Tüzoltó u 54-56, District 9, http://tuzrakter.hu, is the place for VJ festivals, avant-garde art, jazz and performance, while **Kis West-Balkán**, Kisfaludy utca 36, District 8, T01-371 1807, www.west-balkan.com, is an open-air drink and dance hall.

Classical and opera

The city has fistfuls of concert venues, from the **National State Opera** house and the art nouveau **Liszt Ferenc Academy** to the state-of-the-art Russell Johnson-designed **National Concert Hall** at the Palace of Art, Komor Marcell u 1, T01-455 9000, www.muveszetek palota.hu, home of the National Philharmonic Orchestra. Tickets are available from T06-303 030999, www.tex.hu.

😎 Festivals

There's a quick marching parade of week-long festivals throughout the year, from the highbrow opera, ballet and folklore-themed **Budapest Spring Festival**, www.festivalcity.hu, to glass-clinking champagne and wine fests, and Central Europe's answer to Woodstock or Glastonbury: the island festival of **Sziget**, www.sziget.hu.

What can we say about Copenhagen, capital of the land that gave us Lego, Lurpak and the egg chair? To say it is 'understated chic' hardly raises the blood pressure. We know it's Scandinavian and that hints at the sensual and the liberated. An existentialist philosopher called Kierkegaard hailed from the city, and isn't there some statue of a mermaid that keeps getting decapitated? All this is true but it hardly opens a window on the city's soul. Surprise is the bonus that comes with a city that is not presented in tourist cellophane. Sightseeing here becomes a more personal odyssey, and Copenhagen's world-class museums and art galleries, the city's ever-so-literate awareness of architecture and design, and the everyday style and pace of life all become something to discovered and experienced as new.

Copenhagen

Arts & culture
★★★

Eating
★★★★

Nightlife
★★★★

Outdoors
★★★

Romance
★★★

Shopping
★★★★

Sightseeing
★★★

Value for money
★★

Overall score
★★★

At a glance

Rådhuspladsen is Copenhagen's Times Square, with the **Tivoli Gardens** and Central Station to the southwest. The capital's major shopping street, **Strøget**, runs northeast from here to Kongens Nytorv and **Nyhavn**. To the north are royal residences and grand boulevards in **Frederiksstaden** and **Rosenborg**. Southeast of Strøget is **Slotsholmen**, an oblong-shaped island enclosed by narrow canals that forms the historical heart of Copenhagen. Immediately west of Central Station, multicultural and semi-gentrified **Vesterbro** is good for accommodation. The tree-lined boulevards and elegant gardens of **Frederiksberg** are further to the west, while, to the north, a string of artificial lakes separates the city centre from gritty **Nørrebro**, where the sharp edge of contemporary Copenhagen is revealed. The 'free city'

Just living is not enough.
One must have sunshine,
freedom, and a little flower.

Hans Christian Andersen

of bohemian **Christiania** lies on the island of Christianshavn to the east of the centre.

★ *Don't leave town without watching the fireworks on Saturday evenings at Tivoli Gardens.*

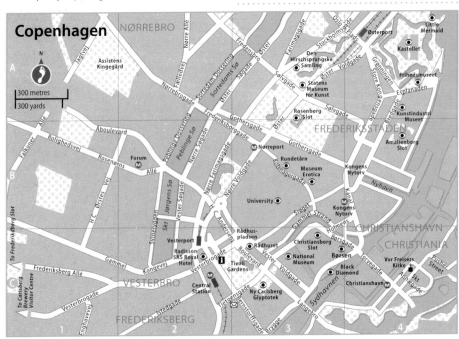

Copenhagen

◉ Sights

Tivoli Gardens

ⓘ *Vesterbrogade 3, T3315 1001, www .tivoli.dk,* **VIS**. *Mid Apr-late Sep Sun-Wed 1100-2300, Thu and Sat 1100-2400, Fri 1100- 0100; early Nov- late Dec Sun-Thu 1100-2200, Fri 1100-2300, Sat 1100-2300. Kr 75. S-tog København H.*

First opened in 1843, Tivoli pleasure gardens remain Denmark's most visited attraction and a national institution (most visitors are Danes). The tweeness has encouraged Disneyfication, but a glimmer of the original Orient-inspired magic still pervades. There is an ancient rollercoaster amongst the modern fair-ground rides, as well as fainter echoes of times past, such as the 1949 spiral lamp by Poul Henningsen near Tivoli Lake. Henningsen also designed the stunning **Glassalen**, with its hint of camp. When twilight descends, the Turkish facade of **Restaurant Nimb** is subtly illuminated, while outside is the silent fountain

Tivoli Gardens

inspired by Niels Bohr, Danish winner of the Nobel Prize for physics. The Chinese-style **Pantomime Theatre** plays host to a genuine ghost of *commedia dell'arte*.

Ny Carlsberg Glyptotek

ⓘ *Dantes Plads 7, T3341 8141, www .glyptoteket.dk,* **VIS**. *Tue-Sun 1000- 1600. Kr 50, Sun free. S-tog København H.*

This is one of Copenhagen's must-see

galleries, founded by the Carlsberg brewing magnet Carl Jacobsen at the end of the 19th century. Like other world-class museums, it contains too much to take in on a single visit, including extensive ancient Near East and Mediterranean collections. At its heart is the magnificent glass-domed Winter Garden, where Roman sarcophagi and contemporary Danish sculptures share the space with giant tropical palm trees. The 19th-century French Impressionists are housed in a purpose-built wing, added in 1996.

Nationalmuseet

ⓘ *Ny Vestergade 10, T3313 4411, www.natmus.dk,* **VIS**. *Tue-Sun 1000-1700. Free. S-tog København H.*

Denmark's National Museum showcases four floors of world cultural history and, although the emphasis is on Denmark, it also has an expansive ethnographical collection and a floor devoted to Near Eastern and Classical antiquities. Highlights include some astounding

---

◉ Travel essentials

Getting there Copenhagen International Airport, T3231 3231, flight information T3247 4747, www.cph.dk, is 9 km from the city and 12 mins from Central Station by train every 20 mins (Mon-Fri 0500-2400, Sat 0530- 2400, Sun 0630-2400, Kr27). Some stop at Nørreport, where a metro links with Kongens Nytorv for accommodation around Nyhavn. A city bus service, 250S, costs about the same as the train but takes 25 mins. Night bus N96 runs every 30 mins-1 hr to the centre (Kr 45). A taxi from outside the arrivals hall will cost about Kr180-200. International trains arrive in the heart of the city at **Central Station**, T7013 1415, www.dsb.dk; long-distance coaches also arrive here.

Getting around Public transport tickets cover buses, S-Tog trains and the metro, within designated zones. The basic ticket costs Kr18 and is valid for up to 1 hr within any 2 zones (which covers most of the sights and places of interest). Tickets and maps showing the zones are available from machines or ticket offices in train stations and from bus drivers. If you intend to do a lot of travelling about the city you can buy a *klippekort*, valid for 10 rides or a 24-hr unlimited travel card (Kr105). Another alternative is to buy a **Copenhagen Card**, which offers unlimited travel in greater Copenhagen and free admission to some museums and sights. It's valid for 24-72 hrs and costs Kr199-429. It is

also easy to get around the various sights on foot. From Central Station it takes about 30 mins to walk the length of Strøget and reach Nyhavn. From around Istedgade or Vesterbrogade it takes 20 mins to reach Slotsholmen.

Tourist information Wonderful Copenhagen tourist office, T7022 2442, www.visitcopenhagen.dk, is on the corner of Vesterbrogade and Bernstorffsgade, close to Central Station. May-Jun and Sep Mon-Sat 0900-1800; Jul-Aug Mon-Sat 0900-2000, Sun 1000-1800; Oct-Apr Mon-Sat 0900-1600, Sat 0900-1400. There is a smaller tourist office at the airport.

Exchange rate Danish Kroner (Kr). £1 = Kr10.91. €1 = Kr7.45.

3000-year-old artefacts, Viking silver ornaments, jewellery, coins and skin cloaks, an Eskimo hunter's anorak made of sealskin and a metope from the outer frieze of the Parthenon, purchased by a Danish naval officer in the 17th century.

Slotsholmen

The island of Slotsholmen is where Bishop Absalon first built a stone castle in 1167. Today it is crowded with buildings that chart the evolution of the city from the 12th century to the present. At its heart is **Christiansborg Slot** ⓘ *Christiansborg Slotsplads, T3392 6492, www.ses.dk,* 🚉, *May-Sep daily 1000-1600 (tours 1100-1500), Oct-Apr Tue-Sun 1000-1600 (tours 1200-1500), ruins Kr40, reception rooms Kr60,* the 20th- century incarnation of a palace first built by Christan VI in the 1730s. It now houses the Danish parliament, Royal Reception Rooms and an absorbing exhibition on the excavation of Absalon's original fort.

Among the many other museums and interesting buildings here, seek out the 17th-century **Børsen** (stock exchange), with its whimsical decorations;

Christiansborg Slot

Rådhuspladsen

Den Sorte Diamant (Black Diamond) ⓘ *Søren Kierkegaards Plads 1, T3347 4747,* 🚉, *daily 0800-2300,* a stunning black granite and smoked glass extension to the Royal Library, and the peaceful enclave of the **Bibliotekshaven** (Royal Library Garden).

Strøget and the Latin Quarter

The wide open space of **Rådhuspladsen** is best explored before mid morning, when there's only a gentle buzz of commuters. Dominating the late 19th- and early 20th-century square is the brown-brick **Rådhuset** (City Hall) ⓘ *T3366 2582,* 🚉, *access to tower Oct-May Mon-Sat 1200; Jun-Sep Mon-Fri 1000-1400, Sat 1200, Kr20, S-tog Vesterport.* Check out the fine views from the tower and the intricate cogs and wheels of **Jen Olsen's World Clock** near the entrance.

Copenhagen's most hyped street, pedestrianized **Strøget**, runs northeast from here. By lunchtime, its cafés, restaurants and cobbled squares heave with people and street performers. To get away from the crowds, explore

the narrow side streets where medieval Copenhagen developed. For a more tangible feel of the past, move on a few centuries and explore the **Latin Quarter** around the university with some grand 19th-century churches and a studious atmosphere. Strøget continues its long, shop-laden route along **Østergade** to Kongens Nytorv, while the small streets to the north are filled with speciality stores and restaurants. Købmagergade caters to hedonists and consumers, with more prestigious shops and the unique **Museum Erotica** ⓘ *Købmagergade 24, T3312 0311, www.museumerotica.dk,* 🚉, *May-Sep daily 1000-2300, Oct-Apr daily 1100-2000, Kr 69, Metro Kongens Nytorv.* Also here is the **Rundetårn** ⓘ *Købmagergade 52a, T3373 0373, www.rundetaarn.dk,* 🚉, *Sep-May Mon-Sat 1000-1700, Sun 1200-1700; Jun-Aug Mon-Sat 1000-2000, Sun 1200-2000, Kr25, Metro/S-tog Nørreport,* built as an observatory by Christian IV. Ascend the spiral walkway for good views of the city centre.

Frederiksstaden

A populist atmosphere characterizes the north side of the **Nyhavn** canal, where

Nyhavn

Across the water from Slotsholmen is the island of Christianshavn and the multi-faceted community of Christiania (www.christiania.org). Much more than a bohemian social experiment, Christiania is a buzzing area that mixes anarchists with hard-nosed dealers, and canny careerists with 21st-century hippies. It came into existence over 30 years ago, when hippies and activists moved into abandoned military buildings. Over the years, it has experienced numerous clashes with the authorities but now up to 1000 people work or live here tax-free, in homes most have designed and built themselves. Christiania attracts visitors intrigued by the possibility of an alternative community flourishing in the heart of a modern bourgeois state. The makeshift entrance and a few down-and-outs can be off putting but, around Pusher Street, you'll find cafés and stalls selling jewellery and T-shirts. A few years ago numerous types of cannabis were on sale here but a major clean-up campaign has stopped the open selling of drugs on the streets. While you're here, don't miss the baroque splendour of **Vor Frelsers Kirke**, with its wacky external staircase that twists around a spiral tower.

colourful Dutch-style houses and a cluster of eateries encourage visitors to sit on the quayside and soak up the sun. Around the corner, on stately **Bredgade**, the mood changes abruptly amidst the many reminders of inherited influence. **Frederiksstaden**, laid out by Frederik V in the mid-18th century, has many palaces and churches, such as the Danish royal residence at **Amalienborg Slot** and the remains of an old fortress, **Kastellet**. The most absorbing museums are **Frihedsmuseet** ⓘ *Churchillparken, T3313 7714, www.natmus.dk,* map-A4, *Oct-Apr Tue-Sun 1000-1500, May-Sep Tue-Sun 1000-1700, free, S-tog Østerport,* chronicling Danish resistance to Nazi occupation, and **Kunstindustrimuseet** ⓘ *Bredgade 68, T3318 5656, www.kunstindustri museet.dk,* map-A4, *Tue-Sun 1200-1600, Kr40,* with its exquisite collections of decorative art.

Rosenborg

West of Frederiksstaden lies the much-visited **Rosenborg Slot** ⓘ *Øster Voldgade, T3315 3286, www.rosenborg slot.dk,* map-A3, *Nov-mid Dec and Jan-Apr Tue- Sun 1100-1600, May, Sep and Oct*

Rosenborg Slot

daily 1000-1600, Jun-Aug daily 1000-1700, closed late Dec, Kr50, Metro/S-tog Nørreport, built by Christian IV in the 17th century. The castle is stuffed full of overblown furniture, tapestries and trinkets and is surrounded by the manicured greenery of the **Kongens Have** (Royal Gardens).

To the northwest are two top-notch art galleries: the esteemed **Statens Museum for Kunst** ⓘ *Sølvgade 48, T3374 8494, www.smk.dk,* map-A3, *Tue-Sun 1000-1700, Wed 1000-2000, closed public hols, free, S-tog Østerport,* which houses the national collection of major works of European art; and the lesser-known but highly rewarding **Den Hirschsprungske Samling** ⓘ *Stockholmsgade 20, T3542 0336, www.hirschsprung.dk,* map-A3, *Wed-Mon 1100-1600, Kr 50, free Wed, S-tog Østerport,* a veritable treasure trove of Danish art from the last two centuries.

Sleeping

The main hotel areas are Vesterbro and Frederiksberg, where smart and comfortable double rooms can be found for below Kr1000. Classier hotels tend to be around Nyhavn and Kongens Nytorv.

€€€ Radisson SAS Royal Hotel, Hammerichsgade 1, T3342 6000, www.radissonas.com. You wouldn't think so from the outside but the most stylish rooms in town are to be found here. Arne Jacobsen's original designs have been recently remodelled by Yasmine Mahmoudieh.

€€€-€€ 71 Nyhavn, T3343 6200, www.71nyhavnhotelcopenhagen.dk. 2 warehouses have been converted into this smart, 150-room hotel. Original beams lend a rustic touch to the luxury interior, including the bar and the above-average restaurant.

€€ DGI-byens, Tietgensgade 65, T3329 8070, www.dgi-byen.dk. A hotel that fulfils one's expectations of Scandinavian style and Danish modernism – sleek and uncluttered. Superb swimming pool and sports facilities adjoin the hotel.

€€ Hotel Bethel Sømandshjem, Nyhavn 22, T3313 0370. Characterful old seaman's hotel. Cheap rooms come without a harbour view, but for a little more you get a spacious corner room with a grand view. Showers not baths. Café and nearby Nyhavn nightlife.

€ Cab inn City, Mitchellsgade 14, T3539 8400, www.city@cabinn.dk. Pristine, budget rooms: tiny but perfectly formed with all you need contained in an amazingly small space. Very central, with a good coffee bar and 24-hr reception. Possibly the best value in town.

Eating

Gammel Strand opposite Slotsholmen has some upmarket fish restaurants and cafés. Nyhavn offers a more democratic mood for wining and dining, while in Vesterbro you'll find everything from Danish bakeries to kebab shops to specialist eateries. **Værnedamsvej, off Vesterbrogade, has several non-touristy places.**

¶¶¶ Noma, Strandgade 93, Christianshavn, T3296 3297, www.noma.dk. Mon and Sat 1800-2200, Tue-Fri 1230-1330 and 1800-2200. Set in a converted 18th-century warehouse overlooking the harbour, this ultra-minimalist room is offset by the excellent and creative modern Scandinavian cuisine.

¶¶¶ Truffle Café and Restaurant, Vestergade 29-31, T3313 1500. Mon-Sat 1130-2200, Sun 1130-1500. Superb variety of food in this slinky, smart restaurant. The set meals for 2 in the café are almost half the price of those in the restaurant. Try sushi with a Kirin in a tall glass.

¶¶ Nørrebro Bryghus, Ryesgade 3, Nørrebro, T3530 0530, www.noerrebro bryghus.dk. Mon-Wed, Sun 1100-2200, Thu-Sat 1200-0200. An old factory converted into a stylish restaurant and microbrewery with live music in the basement, superlative service in the great dining hall and sleek steel vats and pipes gurgling away beside you in the brewery itself. Inventive modern Californian-Danish food.

¶¶-¶ Nytorv Restaurant and Café, Nytorv 15, T3311 7706, www.nytorv.dk. Daily 1100-2200. One of the city's oldest restaurants, this is one of the few places left specializing in the much-heralded open sandwich. At lunch, it's full of Danes enjoying this *smørrebrød*.

¶ Rizraz, Kompagnistræde 20, T3315 0575, www.rizraz.dk. Daily 1130-2400. A vast warren of a place with a huge vegetarian all-you-can-eat Mediterranean buffet and tasty meat dishes. Possibly the best value in town.

Nightlife

Copenhagen boasts a lively, ever-changing bar and club scene, based around Vesterbro, Nørrebro, Østerbro and the centre. The great thing is that the city is small enough to allow you to sample a selection of several venues in any one night. The most popular club in town is **Vega**, Enghavevej 40, T3325 7011, www.vega.dk, in Vesterbro, which incorporates a nightclub at weekends, plus a lounge bar, concert venue and cocktail bar. In Nørrebro are 2 good places to choose from: **Rust**, Guldbergs gade 8, T3524 5200, www.rust.dk, another multi- venue place where good music takes precedence over the weekly cattle market, and **Stengade 30**, T3536 0938, www.stengade30.dk, the more underground version of the same. In the city centre, **Park Café**, Østerbrogade 79, T3542 6248, www.parkcafe.dk, has 3 dance floors and attracts an upwardly mobile crowd.

Copenhageners don't start to kick their heels until at least 2400-0100, particularly at weekends, but lounge bars (**Ideal Bar**, T3325 7011, opposite Vega in Vesterbro, and **Stereo Bar**, Linnesgade 16A, T3313 6113, in Nørrebro, are among the best) will keep you in an intimate and inviting atmosphere until then. Special one-off and try-out club and bar nights are plentiful. The weekly *Copenhagen Post*'s 'In & Out' guide contains a good day-by-day rundown in English.

From struggling provincial backwater to the city that never sleeps, Dublin has been riding one hell of a roller coaster in recent years. Ireland's capital has regained a European presence that it last experienced in the 18th century. Every day planeloads of visitors arrive in this city ready to party. While Temple Bar ladles on the blarney as thick as the head on a pint of Guinness, the statue of the 19th-century nationalist Daniel O'Connell overlooks wood-panelled Edwardian pubs, designer bars and clubs, chic shops and high-tech arts centres. Yet, amid the sophisticated gloss, the fiddly-diddly music and the political wheeler-dealing is a city whose secrets are still waiting to be explored. And through the heart of it all snakes the Liffey: dark, unfathomable and just a little bit muddier than we'd like to admit.

Dublin

Arts & culture
★★★

Eating
★★★

Nightlife
★★★★

Outdoors
★★★

Romance
★★

Shopping
★★

Sightseeing
★★★

Value for money
★★

Overall score
★★★

At a glance

Georgian **Grafton Street** runs from **Trinity College** south to **St Stephen's Green**. This area and the streets to the east are the centre of tourist Dublin, where you'll find most of the most significant sights and the city's best restaurants and hotels. **Temple Bar**, with its ancient, redeveloped streets, **Dublin Castle** and **Christchurch Cathedral** lie to the west, while to the southwest is an odd mishmash of areas, loosely defined as the **Liberties** and barely touched by the Celtic Tiger phenomenon.

North of the Liffey, **O'Connell Street**, one of the city's oldest and grandest boulevards, is now cluttered with shop signs and statuary. It's less tourist-focused than areas south of the river but has a great deal to offer thanks to its powerful historical associations and impressive literary connections. You'll also find much of the city's cheapest accommodation here. Northwest of the Liffey is a relatively unvisited area

Good puzzle would be to cross Dublin without passing a pub.

Leopold Bloom, as he wanders around Dublin in James Joyce's 'Ulysses'

with a long history, an ancient church, the city's Four Courts and **Smithfield market**. Further west still are the old **Collins Barracks**, which house a branch of the National Museum, and, beyond that again, is **Phoenix Park**, the largest enclosed public space in Europe. Victorian and Edwardian **Ballsbridge**, southeast of the centre, is the poshest part of Dublin with some good restaurants and lively bars.

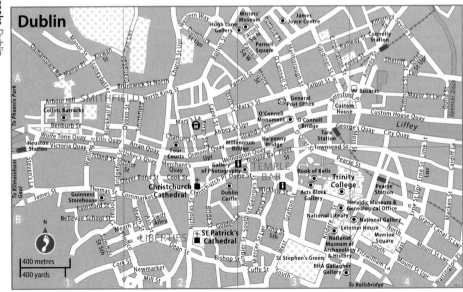

European City Breaks Dublin

24 hours in the city

Begin your day with a full Irish breakfast, guaranteed to slow you down to the Irish pace of life for a few hours at least. Spend the morning marvelling at the collection of gold in the **National Museum**, followed by a quick peek at the Picasso in the **National Gallery** and a really classy lunch at **The Commons**. In the afternoon stroll around the shops and alleys of Temple Bar before hopping on a bus to the **Guinness Storehouse** to enjoy a bird's eye view of the city – and a pint of Guinness to boot. In the evening head back to Temple Bar to sample modern Irish cuisine at **Eden**. After dinner enjoy a drink at **Oliver St John Gogarty's**, where you've a good chance of catching some traditional Irish music, or grab a cab over to the **Brazen Head**, Dublin's oldest bar. The next port of call for nightowls should be **Harcourt Street**, where the clubs get going around 2300. **POD**, **Crawdaddy** and **Tripod** are some of the hippest joints in town.

Trinity College

★ *Don't leave town without goggling at the amazing hoards of gold in the National Museum of Archaeology and History.*

European City Breaks Dublin

☉ Travel essentials

Getting there Dublin International Airport, T01-814 1111, www.dublin-airport.com, is 12 km north of the city centre. **Aircoach**, www.aircoach.ie, runs to and from city centre hotels 24 hrs daily. Tickets can be bought on board and cost €7 single or €12 return, journey time 35 mins. A taxi costs about €25. At the mouth of the Liffey, **Dublin Port** is used by ferries to and from Holyhead (Terminal 1) and Liverpool (Terminal 3); bus 53/53A runs into the centre. Other ferry services use **Dun Laoghaire** harbour, 30 mins south of the city and accessible on the DART.

Getting around The centre of Dublin is easy enough to negotiate on foot but if you get tired, local buses run by **Dublin Bus**, T01-873 4222, www.dublinbus.ie, are frequent and cheap. Bus stops are green and fares (exact change only to the driver) start at €0.95 for a short hop within the city. A 1-day pass costs €5 (3- and 5-day passes €10 and €16.50 respectively). An excellent bus map of the city is available free from Dublin Bus or the tourist office. Dublin Bus also operates the hop-on, hop-off **Dublin City Tour**, which starts on O'Connell Bridge. The complete tour takes over an hour and visits 16 sights around the city. A ticket (€14) includes discounts at each of the sights and is valid for a day. The electric tram system, the **Luas**, www.luas.ie, is designed for commuters but the red line, from Connolly Street through the shopping streets north of the river and then along the quays to Phoenix Park and Heuston station, can be useful. Tickets are available at each stop; a single ticket is valid for only 90 mins, a return for the whole day. The all-zone combi ticket for bus and Luas costs €6.20 for 1 day.

The **DART** (Dublin Area Rapid Transit), T01-703 3504, www.dart.ie, is a suburban rail service that links the coastal suburbs with the city centre. It is useful for travel between the south and north of the city and for transport to some suburban areas. There are **taxi** ranks on O'Connell Street, Dame Street and St Stephen's Green.

Tourist information Dublin Tourism Centre, St Andrew's Church, Suffolk St, www.visitdublin.com, Jun-Sep Mon-Sat 0900-2030, Sun 1100-1700; Oct-May Mon-Sat 0930-1730, offers accommodation advice and bookings, ferry and concert tickets, car hire, bureau de change, free leaflets and guidebooks for sale. There's also a **Temple Bar information centre** at 12 East Essex St, www.visit-templebar.ie.

95

◉ Sights

Trinity College

ⓘ *College Green, www.tcd.ie, [B3]. Campus tours May -Sep daily 1015-1455, 30 mins, €5 or €10 with Book of Kells.*

Trinity College is a time capsule of smooth lawns, cobblestones, statuary and formal buildings, looking more like Oxford's dreaming spires than some of the Oxford colleges themselves. It was founded in 1592 by Elizabeth I, in an attempt to prevent young Protestant intellectuals of the Pale going to Europe and discovering Catholicism. Its squares are dominated by the campanile tower, beside which is a Henry Moore statue, *Reclining Connected Form*. To the right is the finest building on the campus, the 18th-century **Old Library**, home to the **Book of Kells Exhibition** ⓘ *T01-608 2308, [B3], May-Sep Mon-Sat 0930-1700, Sun 0930-1630, Oct-Apr Mon-Sat 0930-1700, Sun 1200-1630, closed for Christmas and New Year, €8.* Two pages of the ninth-century illuminated manuscript are on show each day, accompanied

Oscar Wilde, Merrion Square

National Library

by displays explaining its religious symbolism and manufacture. Upstairs is the magnificent 65-m **Long Room**, where 200,000 of the library's oldest books are held.

Across Fellowes Square is the Arts Block, built in 1980, and showing collections of conceptual and avant-garde art in its **Douglas Hyde Gallery** ⓘ *T01-896 1116, www.douglashyde gallery.com, [B3], Mon-Fri 1100-1800, Thu 1100-1900, Sat 1100-1645, free.*

National Museum of Archaeology and History

ⓘ *Kildare St, T01-677 7444, www.museum.ie/archaeology/, [B3]. Tue-Sat 1000-1700, Sun 1400-1700. Free.*

The area south of Trinity College and east of Kildare Street is tightly packed with museums and other places to visit. At its heart is **Leinster House**, which is home to the Republic's two Houses of Parliament: the Dáil and the Seanad. The house was built around 1745 by James Fitzgerald, Earl of Kildare (later Duke of Leinster), as an escape from Parnell Square in north Dublin, which

had become a little too nouveau riche for his liking. In the 19th century, Leinster House was sold to the Royal Dublin Society, which added two new wings on either side, designed in 1884-1890 by Deane and Son, to form the **National Library** ⓘ *Kildare St, T01-603 0200, www.nli.ie, [B3], Mon-Wed 1000-2100, Thu and Fri 1000-1700, Sat 1000-1300, free,* and the National Museum of Ireland.

The museum is full of wonderful things, including a stunning hoard of Bronze Age gold, guarded by two stone *sheela-na-gigs*. Upstairs, you'll find Viking and medieval artefacts, a display of ancient Egyptian embalming techniques and 'The Road to Independence' exhibition.

National Gallery

ⓘ *Merrion Sq, T01-661 5133, www.nationalgallery.ie, [B4]. Mon-Wed, Fri and Sat 0930-1730, Thu 0930-2030, Sun 1200-1730. Free.*

Merrion Square, the Georgian heartland of Dublin, was one-time home to Daniel O'Connell at No 58, W B Yeats at 82 and Oscar Wilde at No 1. On

National Museum

its western side is the country house façade of Leinster House and the entrance to the National Gallery, where the big names of European art are well represented. There are works by Caravaggio, Degas, El Greco, Fra Angelico, Goya, Mantegna, Monet, Picasso, Rembrandt, Tintoretto, Titian, Velasquez and Vermeer for starters. Then there is also a decent display of English art and a marvellous collection by Irish artists. Although the gallery always functioned on a hand-to-mouth basis, more prosperous times saw the opening of a Millennium Wing in 2002.

St Stephen's Green

Nowadays the city's playground, and great for a picnic on a sunny day with occasional music from the bandstand, St Stephen's Green, south of Trinity College, has had many incarnations over the centuries. Until the 1660s it was an expanse of open ground where people grazed their cattle and public executions took place. As the surrounding area began to be developed the green was partly fenced in and became a park. In 1814 the public were excluded and

St Stephen's Green

National Gallery

only residents of the grand houses overlooking the park could use it. In 1877 Lord Ardilaun, one of the Guinness family, introduced a bill to Parliament making it a public park again and put up the cash to make it happen.

Dublin Castle
ⓘ Dame St, T01-677 7129, www.dublin castle.ie, **B2**. Open by guided tour only (40 mins) Mon-Fri 1000-1700; Sat, Sun and bank hols 1400-1700; last admission 1hr before closing. €4.50; free admission to Castle Yard, Chapel Royal and Dubh Linn Garden.

It is difficult to surmise from the hand-tufted carpets and 18th-century plasterwork that this was once Dublin's biggest stronghold, built in 1204 to defend the city against the native Irish. It must have looked the part, too, because, apart from a Fitzgerald attack in 1534 and an aborted attempt at seizing it in 1641, the castle has seen very little action. The most exciting thing to take place here must have been the night during the Black and Tan War, when Michael Collins infiltrated the records office. In 1922

the castle was officially handed over to him as Commander in Chief of the Irish Army. The guided tour explores the State Apartments then passes into the Upper Yard, where you can see the Statue of Justice over the gateway, unblindfolded and with her back to the city she should have been defending. Until she was mended in the 1980s, her scales of justice regularly tipped when they filled with rainwater. From here you visit the **Undercroft**, where you can see the remains of Viking fortifications, part of the old medieval city wall, the moat, postern steps for deliveries and a dribble of the River Poddle itself.

Housed in a beautifully converted clocktower within the castle walls is the stunning **Chester Beatty Library** ⓘ T01-407 0750, www.cbl.ie, **B2**, Oct-Apr Tue-Fri 1000-1700, Sat 1100-1700, Sun 1300-1700, May-Sep also Mon 1000-1700, closed public hols, free, a priceless collection of cultural and religious treasures – icons, papyrus texts, Buddhas and ancient copies of the Bible and the Koran – bequeathed to the state by the Irish-American mining magnate, Chester Beatty.

Dublin Castle

Christchurch Cathedral

ⓘ *Christchurch Pl, T01-679 8991, www.cccdub.ie, ⬛B2. Jun-Aug Mon-Fri 0900-1800, Sat 1000-1630, Sun 1245-1445; Sep-May Mon-Fri 0945-1700/1800, Sat 1000-1630, Sun 1245-1445. €5.*

This is Dublin's oldest building, pre-dating the castle by a century or so. However, the original wooden construction is long gone and, although the crypt, north wall and south transept date from the 12th century, most of what you see is 19th-century stone cladding. Inside there are lovely faux ancient floor tiles, a 16th-century replica of the tomb of Strongbow (Richard de Clare, the Norman conqueror of Ireland) and lots of stuff to admire in the 'Treasures of Christchurch' exhibition in the crypt. If you stand in the choir by the bishop's throne and look back towards the entrance, you'll notice that the north wall (to your right) is seriously out of kilter.

Temple Bar

The landmark **Ha'penny Bridge** over the River Liffey is a cast-iron footbridge built in 1816 and named after the toll

Christchurch Cathedral

Ha'penny Bridge

levied on it until 1919. On the south side of the bridge, **Merchant's Arch** leads into the hub of streets and alleys that define Temple Bar. Nowadays a vibrant tourist ghetto, this network of narrow lanes, named after its 17th-century developer, Sir William Temple, criss-crosses between the river and Dame Street and from Fishamble Street to Fleet Street. Despite all the redevelopment, a few remnants of the old city are still intact. Look out for **Sunlight Chambers**, on the corner of Parliament Street and Essex Quay, with multi-coloured terracotta reliefs displaying the benefits of soap.

The **Gallery of Photography** ⓘ *Meeting House Sq, T01-671 4654, www.irishphotography.com, ⬛B3, Tue-Sat 1000-1800, free,* is a carefully-lit, purpose-built venue with a permanent collection of 20th-century Irish photographs, plus changing monthly exhibitions by Irish and international artists. The **Irish Film Centre** on Eustace Street shows art house films in a post-modern conversion of a Quaker Meeting House.

O'Connell Street and around

Most of the hyped tourist spots are in

ⓞ Best of the rest

St Patrick's Cathedral ⓘ *Patrick's Cl, T01-453 9472, www.stpatricks cathedral.ie, ⬛B2.* Despite its ugly exterior, the national cathedral of the Church of Ireland is the more interesting of Dublin's two cathedrals.

Guinness Storehouse ⓘ *St James' Gate, T01-408 4800, www.guinness- storehouse.com, ⬛B1. Sep-Jun daily 0930-1700; Jul and Aug daily 0930-1700 and 1930-2000. €14.* A temple to the famous Irish drink and brand.

National Museum of Decorative Arts and History ⓘ *Collins Barracks, Benburb St, T01-677 7444, www.museum.ie/decorative, ⬛A1. Tue-Sat 1000-1700, Sun 1400-1700. Free.* A former military barracks houses exquisite pieces from the Museum of Ireland's decorative arts collection.

James Joyce Museum ⓘ *Sandycove, 13 km south of the centre, T01-280 9265. Mar-Oct Mon-Sat 1000-1300 and 1400-1700; Sun and public holidays 1400-1800. €6.50.* A Martello tower houses literary memorabilia associated with Joyce and *Ulysses*.

the southern half of the city but the north has lots to offer and fewer crowds; there is also a more genuine, earthy feel to it because it is less geared up to the tourist market. The area has strong historical and literary associations and boasts some of the city's earliest Georgian buildings.

The **General Post Office**, O'Connell Street's most famous building, was gutted by fire and shelling in 1916 and suffered further damage in 1922 during the Civil

Republican city

Built in 1792 and opened just in time to incarcerate any surviving rebels of the 1798 uprising, **Kilmainham Gaol** saw hundreds of men suffer and die for their belief in independence in the uprisings of 1798, 1803, 1848, 1867, 1916 and 1922. Most of the big names in Republican history spent time in here and some of them died here. The last man to walk out was Eamon de Valera at the end of the Civil War in 1923, whereupon the gaol was closed. Forty years later a group of history buffs decided to restore it and Kilmainham was opened to the public. A museum covers the early 20th-century political history of Ireland, prison memorabilia and a guided tour. It takes you around the dungeons, tiny cells, the chapel where Joseph Plunkett was married three hours before his execution and the grim yard where Connolly, Plunkett and 15 other leaders of the 1916 uprising were executed. ⓘ *Inchicore Rd, T01-453 5984, www.heritageireland.ie. Apr-Sep daily 0930-1700; Oct-Mar Mon-Sat 0930-1600, Sun 1000-1700. €5.30.*

War before being rebuilt in 1929. Inside the functioning post office is a series of paintings depicting scenes from the 1916 Easter Rising.

At the north end of O'Connell Street are the excellent **Hugh Lane Gallery** ⓘ *Charlemont House, Parnell Sq North, T01-874 1903, www.hughlane.ie,* ▣▲③, *Tue-Thu 0930-1800, Fri and Sat 0930-1700, Sun 1100-1700, free,* with its fine collection of modern art, and the attractive **Writers' Museum** ⓘ *18-19 Parnell Sq, T01-872 2077, www.writersmuseum.com,* ▣▲③, *Mon-Sat 1000-1700, Sun and public holidays 1100-1700, later opening Jun-Aug, €6.70.*

Nearby, homage can be paid to Dublin's most famous writer at the **James Joyce Centre** ⓘ *35 North Great George St, T01-878 8547, www.jamesjoyce.ie,* ▣▲③, *Tue-Sat 1000-1700, closed Christmas and New Year, €5.*

● Sleeping

Hotel rooms in Dublin don't come cheap. Grafton St and Temple Bar form Dublin's chief accommodation area and prices here are pretty high, with no B&Bs. North of the river is a concentration of more affordable guesthouses – the top end of O'Connell St, around Parnell Sq, has some interesting options – but the central location and proximity of the bus and railway station mean they tend to fill up most quickly. Ballsbridge, southeast of the city centre, has a great range of top-notch hotels, quality guest houses and a cluster of good restaurants.

€€€ **The Clarence**, 6-8 Wellington Quay, T01-407 0800, www.theclarence.ie. Owned by U2, the Clarence has preserved its original wood panelling amidst modish embellishments like leather-clad lifts, Egyptian cotton on the king-size beds, and CD players in the individually designed bedrooms. Friendly staff, a bookless lounge called the Study and original artwork contribute to the strange mix of the spartan and the sybaritic. Rates from €330.

€€€ **Morrison**, 15 Ormond Quay, T01-887 2400, www.morrisonhotel.ie. This classy building sits unobtrusively on the bank of the river and vies with the Clarence for Dublin's hippest hotel award. The decor is refreshingly un-Irish, with plenty of interesting touches waiting to be noticed, not least of which is the restaurant **Halö**. In the chic, air-conditioned bedrooms you'll find CD players, mood lighting, quality fabrics and original artwork.

€€ **Merrion Hall**, 56 Merrion Rd, T01-668 1426, www.halpinsprivate hotels.com. A quiet, welcoming place with 4-poster beds, an ample lounge area, private gardens and a library of tourist literature. Award-winning breakfasts are served in the serene, sunny breakfast room.

€€-€ Ariel House, 50-54 Lansdowne Rd, T01-668 5512, www.ariel-house .net, 3 mins on foot from Lansdowne Rd DART station. Built in the 1860s, this listed red-brick Victorian building is a classy guesthouse with a choice of no-smoking rooms, all with bath and shower; 3 have 4-poster beds. American visitors adore the decor and antiques. Car park available.

€ Bewley's Hotel, Merrion Rd, T01-668 1111, www.BewleysHotels.com. Smart, spacious and comfortable accommodation in the Ballsbridge area. The red-brick Victorian building has been converted from a convent school and the original entrance opens into a roomy public area with the O'Connell's restaurant downstairs and a café. The Aircoach stop is right outside. Rooms cost around €99 for up to 3 adults or a family of 4.

€ Castle Hotel, 2-4 Gardiner Row, T01-874 6949, www.castle-hotel.ie. A real find, this is a lovingly restored Georgian building that offers so much more, and at better value, than some of the faceless hotels in town. Elegant lounge and comfortable rooms. Michael Collins is said to have used room 201, originally No 23, when sleeping in one of his familiar safe houses during the War of Independence. Parking available.

ⓕ Eating

While many of Temple Bar's restaurants are fun, fashionable and relatively inexpensive places to enjoy a meal, the area from St Stephen's Green to Merrion Square is where the real money tends to eat. Don't even look at the menus

if you're on a tight budget but for seriously fine dining and splashing out, this is the place to eat.

♛♛♛ Browne's Brasserie, 22 St Stephen's Green, T01-638 3939, www.brownesrestaurant.com. Book well in advance at this well-established and busy restaurant. All red plush and white linen, it offers modern Irish cooking with lots of inventive sauces. A good place for brown enveloping at lunch time or a romantic dinner. Excellent value Sun lunch 1230-1430.

❝❞ Pubs, bars and clubs are what Dublin does best.

♛♛♛ Peploe's, 16 St Stephen's Green, T01-676 3144, www.peploes.com. People seem to love or hate this place. It has been listed among the world's best places to eat by prestigious journals and has a growing band of addicted visitors. You can order simple, inexpensive dishes in the wine bar or snuggle into the main restaurant for an imaginative and lovingly prepared meal. Book well in advance.

♛♛ Gallagher's Boxty House, 20-21 Temple Bar, T01-677 2762. Sells the eponymous filled potato pancakes, plus lots more Irish-sourced edibles. Vegetarians will do well here. It has an old-fashioned country-kitchen feel to it, with newspapers and books to read.

♛♛ Little Caesar, 5 Chatham House, Balfe St, T01-671 8714. This institution is 15 years old, a very long time in the life of a Dublin restaurant, and, judging by the queues, it hasn't lost its touch. It serves pizzas and pastas and some old favourites such as *bistecca alla griglia*.

♛♛ Mermaid Café, 70 Dame St, T01-670 8236. One of Dublin's better restaurants,

the Mermaid has an American-influenced changing menu, featuring mussel and smoked fish chowder and pecan pie with maple ice cream. The wine list is above average.

♛♛ Nico's, 53 Dame St, T01-677 3062. Ask anyone involved in the food business in Dublin where they like to eat and they'll mention here. Good traditional Italian food, white cloths, Chianti bottles and bustling waiters.

♛ Gruel, 68a Dame St, T01-670 7119. Very popular inexpensive restaurant that serves hearty hot meals, such as beef hotpot and pan-fried sea trout, as well as simpler filled rolls and soups. Bare boards and plain tables inside.

ⓝ Nightlife

Pubs, bars and clubs are what Dublin does best. Tourists flock to **Temple Bar** to party well into the early hours every night of the week. Elsewhere, the liveliest streets are **South Great George's** and **Camden**, which, from Thu evening, turn into a huge street party. **Harcourt St** is the centre of clubland. Most clubs serve drinks until 0200 and close around 0300. For up-to-date entertainment listings, check on noticeboards or consult the excellent *Event Guide*. Live music pours out of several pubs and bars in Dublin: try **JJ Smyth's**, 12 Aungier St; **O'Donoghue's**, 15 Merrion Row; **Whelan's**, 25 Wexford St; **Eamon Doran's**, 3A Crown Alley; or the **Cobblestone**, North King St. There are also great venues for comedy and drama, including iconic names **Abbey Theatre**, 26 Lwr Abbey St, T01-878 7222, and **Gate Theatre**, 1 Cavendish Row, T01-874 4045. See **Dublin Film Festival** (www.dublin iff.com) in spring and **Dublin Theatre Festival** (www .dublintheatrefestival .com) in autumn.

Few cities make such a strong impression as Edinburgh. Scotland's ancient capital is undeniably one of the most beautiful cities in Europe, with a grandeur to match Paris or Prague, Rome or Vienna. Fittingly, such a setting provides the stage for the Edinburgh Festival, the biggest arts event on the planet. But Edinburgh is more than just the sum of its arts. Its Hogmanay party is the largest celebration in the northern hemisphere and the arrival of the new Scottish Parliament has brought confidence and vitality to a city that was always thought of as being rather straight-laced. Edinburgh's famous pursed lip has gone, replaced by a broad smile. The city is learning how to have fun, how to be stylish and, heaven forfend, how to be just a wee bit ostentatious.

Edinburgh

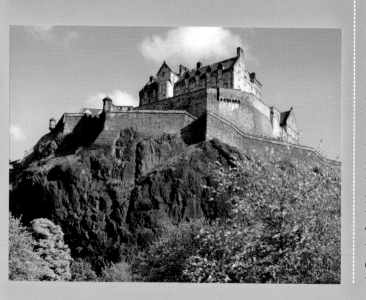

Arts & culture
★★★★

Eating
★★★★

Nightlife
★★★

Outdoors
★★★★

Romance
★★★

Shopping
★★★

Sightseeing
★★★★

Value for money
★★★

Overall score
★★★★

At a glance

South of Princes Street is the **Old Town**, a medieval Manhattan of high-rise tenements running from the castle to the Palace of Holyroodhouse. This dark and sinister rabbit warren of narrow alleys and wynds is still inhabited by the ghosts of the city's past. North of Princes Street is the elegant, neoclassical **New Town**, built in the late 18th and early 19th centuries to improve conditions in the city. The eastern New Town is bordered by **Broughton Street**, which forms one side of the so-called 'Pink Triangle', the pumping heart of the city's gay scene. Here you'll find hip bars and clubs as well as a neighbourly, laid-back atmosphere. Looming over the Pink Triangle is **Calton Hill**, whose summit and sides are studded with sublime Regency terraces and bizarre monuments. The **West End** is a seamless extension of the New Town, with perfect neoclassical symmetry and discreet old money.

It is a precipitous city but it is still, in many ways, a hidden city with its catacombs and tunnels, and citizens who don't really want to be noticed...

Ian Rankin

Northeast of the city centre is **Leith**, Scotland's major port until the shipbuilding and fishing industries decanted south. Neglected and ignored for years, Leith has undergone a dramatic transformation and now warehouse conversions, gourmet restaurants, bars and bistros jostle for position along its waterside.

★ *Don't leave town without seeing the sun rise from the top of Arthur's Seat.*

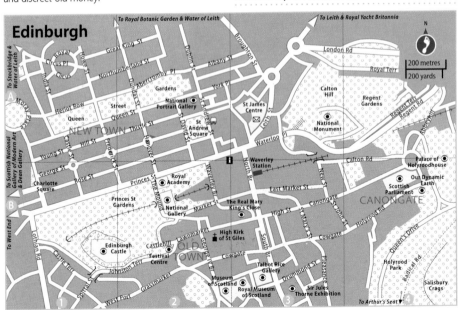

24 hours in the city

Leith quayside

Plan your day over breakfast at **Café Hub**, then take a leisurely stroll down the length of the historic **Royal Mile** before landing back in the present with a bump at the award-winning **Scottish Parliament** building. Head back up the Royal Mile for lunch at **Off The Wall**, then stretch your legs with a walk up **Calton Hill** for the stupendous views of Arthur's Seat, the Castle and across the Firth of Forth to the hills of Fife. Afterwards, indulge in some indoor aesthetic appreciation at the **National Gallery of Scotland**, then hop on a bus down to Ocean Terminal for a fascinating tour of the **Royal Yacht Britannia**. From here it's a short stroll to **Leith** for an alfresco aperitif on the quayside, followed by a superb dinner at **Martin Wishart**. Then take a cab back to the centre for a nightcap in your hotel or some late-night action in one of the many bars on or around George Street in the **New Town**.

⊖ Travel essentials

Getting there Edinburgh International Airport, T0870-040 0007, is 8 miles west of the city centre. An **Airlink** bus (www.flybybus.com) to and from Waverley Bridge leaves every 10-20 mins, takes 25 mins and costs £3 one way, £5 return. A taxi to the centre costs around £16-£17.

There are direct trains to **Edinburgh Waverley** from London King's Cross (4½ hrs), Birmingham (5 hrs) and Manchester (3½ hrs). Fares vary widely depending on the time of travel; for times, fares and bookings T08457-484950, www.thetrainline.co.uk. **Scotrail**, T0845-601 5929, www.firstscotrail.co.uk, runs the overnight Caledonian Sleeper service from London Euston (7 hrs).

Getting around Most of what you'll want to see lies within the compact city centre, which is easily explored on foot.

Public buses are generally good and efficient. Princes Street is the main transport hub and you can get a bus to any part of the city from here. An excellent way to see the sights is to take one of the guided bus tours on board an open-top double-decker bus with a multilingual guide. These depart every 10-30 mins from Waverley Bridge, the first one leaving around 0930 and the last one between 1600 and 1730, depending on the time of year. Tickets are valid for the full day and you can hop on and off any of the company's buses at any of the stops. Tickets cost £9 from **Guide Friday Tours**, T0131-556 2244, T0170-886 6000, www.guidefriday.com, or **Edinburgh Tour**, T0131-220 0770, www.edinburgh tour.com.

Taxis are not cheap, costing from around £3 for the very shortest of trips

up to around £8 from the centre to the outskirts. They also tend to be scarce at weekends so book ahead if you need one. **City Cabs** T0131-228 1211.

Tourist information Main tourist office, 3 Princes St, on top of Waverley Market, T0845-225 5121, www.edinburgh.org. Mon-Sat 0900-2000, Sun 1000-2000. It has a full range of services, including currency exchange, and will book hotel rooms, provide travel information and book tickets for various events and excursions. There's also a tourist information desk at the airport T0845-225 5121, in the international arrivals area.

For details of entertainment listings in the city, pick up a copy of *The List* from any newsagent.

⦿ Sights

Edinburgh Castle

ⓘ T0131-225 9846, www.historic-scotland
.gov.uk, **B1**. Apr-Sep daily 0930-1730;
Oct-Mar daily 0930-1630. £11.

The city skyline is dominated by
the castle, sitting atop an extinct
volcano and protected on three sides
by steep cliffs. Until the 11th century
the castle was Edinburgh, but with the
development of the royal palace from
the early 16th century, it slipped into
relative obscurity. Though mobbed for
much of the year, and expensive, the
castle is worth a visit. It encapsulates
the history of a nation, and the views
from the battlements are spectacular.
The highlight is the **Crown Room**,
where the 'Honours of Scotland' are
displayed, along with the Stone of
Destiny, the seat on which the ancient
kings of Scotland were crowned.

The Royal Mile

Running down the spine of the Old
Town, from the castle to the Palace of

Edinburgh Castle

Royal Mile

Holyroodhouse, is the Royal Mile. The
1984 regal yards comprise four separate
streets: Castlehill, Lawnmarket, the High
Street and the Canongate. Along its route
is a succession of tourist attractions –
some more worthy of the description
than others – as well as many bars,
restaurants, cafés and shops selling
everything from kilts to Havana cigars.
This is the focus of the city's tourist
activity, especially during the festival
when it becomes a mêlée of street
performers, enthralled onlookers and
alfresco diners and drinkers. One of the
main points of interest is the medieval
High Kirk of St Giles, conspicuously
placed on the High Street.

Palace of Holyroodhouse

ⓘ www.royalcollection.org.uk, **B4**.
Apr-Oct daily 0930-1800; Nov-Mar
daily 0930-1630. £8.80.

At the foot of the Royal Mile lies
Edinburgh's royal palace. The present
structure largely dates from the late
17th century when the original was
replaced by a larger building for the
Restoration of Charles II, although

the newly crowned monarch never
set foot in the place. Opposite
the Palace of Holyroodhouse
is the **Scottish parliament building**
ⓘ www.scottish.parliament.uk, which
finally opened in October 2004 after
years of delay and spiralling costs.

Holyrood Park

Edinburgh is blessed with many
magnificent open spaces but Holyrood
Park tops them all. The main feature
is the 237-m-high **Arthur's Seat**, the
igneous core of an extinct volcano. It is
a genuine bit of wilderness right in the
centre of Scotland's capital and well
worth the climb for the stupendous
views. Another dominant feature on
the skyline are the precipitous **Salisbury
Crags**, directly opposite the south gates
of Holyrood Palace.

Museum of Scotland and
Royal Museum of Scotland

ⓘ Chambers St, T0131-247 4422, www
.nms.ac.uk, **B3**. Daily 1000-1700. Free.

The Museum of Scotland is a treasure
trove of intriguing and important

Parliament building

Arthur's Seat

National Portrait Gallery

ⓘ *1 Queen St, T0131-624 6200,*
www.nationalgalleries.org, **J/A2**.
Daily 1000-1700, Thu till 1900. Free.
A free shuttle bus runs between the
National Gallery and the National
Portrait Gallery every 45 mins from
1045 to 1600.

The first of its kind in the world, this
gallery houses a collection of the great
and the good of Scottish history
in a fantastical French Gothic medieval
palace, modelled on the Doge's Palace
in Venice.

Calton Hill

Calton Hill, at the east end of Princes
Street, is another of Edinburgh's extinct
volcanoes and well worth climbing for
some of the best views in the city as
well as for the monuments at the
top. These form the four corners of
a precinct and make for a strange
collection. The most famous is the
National Monument, built to
commemorate the Scots who
died in the Napoleonic Wars.

National Portrait Gallery

artefacts, displayed chronologically
from the basement up to the sixth
floor. Though coverage is at times
patchy and incomplete, the museum
does help to take the mystery out of
Scottish history and makes for a
pleasurable few hours.

Its elderly neighbour, the Royal
Museum, holds an extensive and
eclectic range of artefacts, from Classical
Greek sculptures to stuffed elephants
and Native North American totem
poles, all housed in a wonderful
Victorian building.

National Gallery

ⓘ *The Mound, T0131-624 6200,*
www.nationalgalleries.org, **J/B2**.
Daily 1000-1700, Thu till 1900. Free.

At the junction of The Mound and
Princes Street are two of Edinburgh's
most impressive neoclassical buildings,
the National Gallery and the Royal
Academy. The former houses the
most important collection of Old Masters
in the UK outside London and boasts
many masterpieces from almost
every period in Western art.

⊛ Secret city

The spirits who haunt the
vaults and tunnels of old
Edinburgh have long drawn
tourists to the capital. Recent
research has revealed that
there may be something really
going on beneath the city's
streets. A detailed study into
paranormal activity was
carried out as part of the
**Edinburgh International
Science Festival**. Volunteers
entered the network of
ancient tunnels and reported
greatly increased paranormal
activity, such as hearing loud
breathing, seeing figures and
being touched or grabbed.
Mercat Tours (www.mercat
tours.com) runs tours of the
200-year-old haunted vaults,
Apr-Sep daily at 1200, 1400,
1500 and 1600; Oct-Mar
at 1400 and 1600. If that isn't
enough to frighten the living
daylights out of you, check
out the **City of the Dead
Haunted Graveyard Tour**
(www.blackhart.uk.com),
which involve being locked
in a haunted graveyard at
night with a bloodthirsty
poltergeist, Apr-Oct daily
at 2030, 2115 and 2200;
Nov-Mar daily at 1930 and
2030. Both tours start from
the Mercat Cross, next to St
Giles Cathedral on the High
Street, and cost £8.50.

Botanic Gardens

Scottish National Gallery of Modern Art

ⓘ *75 Belford Rd, T0131-624 6200, www.nationalgalleries.org. Daily 1000-1700. Free.*

About 20 minutes' walk from the West End is the Scottish National Gallery of Modern Art, featuring everything from the Impressionists to Hockney. It is particularly strong on Expressionism, with works by Picasso, Cézanne, Matisse, Magritte, Mondrian, Henry Moore, Kandinsky, Klee, Giacometti and Sickert all displayed, as well as the big names from Fauvism, Surrealism, Abstract Expressionism and Cubism. Alongside these are the British greats like Francis Bacon, Helen Chadwick and Damien Hirst. Opposite, the **Dean Gallery** houses one of the most complete collections of Dada and Surrealist art in Britain.

Water of Leith and the Botanic Gardens

If the weather's fair, one of the finest pleasures this city has to offer is the walk along the bucolic Water of Leith. The Water of Leith Walkway runs from the western outskirts of the city, all the way to the docks at Leith, but the most beautiful section starts from below Belford Bridge, by the Scottish National Gallery of Modern Art and Dean Gallery, and takes you to the gorgeous **Royal Botanic Gardens** ⓘ *East gate, Inverleith Row, T0131-552 7171; Mar daily 1000- 1800; Apr-Sep daily 1000-1900; Oct daily 1000-2000. Free.*

Royal Yacht Britannia

ⓘ *Ocean Terminal, Leith, T0131-555 5566, www.royalyachtbritannia.co.uk. Apr-Oct daily 0930-1630; Nov-Mar daily 1000-1530. £9.50. Britannia Tour bus from Waverley Bridge or buses 11, 22, 34, 35 and 36 from Princes St.*

The *Britannia* is a fascinating attraction and shows the Windsors in a strangely downbeat manner. The relatively steep entrance fee is well worth the outlay. The tour offers a genuine insight into the lives of Britain's best-known family and the sight of Her Majesty's bedroom, more in keeping with a Berkshire guest house than a Head of State's private quarters, comes as a real shock.

Royal Yacht Britannia

◉ Best of the rest

Our Dynamic Earth ⓘ *Holyrood Rd, www.dynamicearth.co.uk,* ▣B4. *Apr-Jun, Sep-Oct daily 1000-1700; Jul-Aug daily 1000-1800; Nov-Mar Wed-Sun 1000-1700. £8.95.* Hi-tech virtual journey through time with strong environmental message.
The Real Mary King's Close ⓘ *Warrinston's Close, High St, T0870-243 0160, www.realmary kingsclose.com,* ▣B3. *Apr-Jul, Sep and Oct daily 1000-2100; Aug daily 0900-2100; Nov-Mar Sun-Fri 1000-1600, Sat 1000-2100. £8.50.* Authentic and spooky insight into 17th-century town life.
Sir Jules Thorne Exhibition ⓘ *9 Hill Sq, T0131-527 1600, www.rcsed.ac.uk,* ▣B3. *Mon-Fri 1200-1600. £5* . Fairly grotesque but fun look through the keyhole of surgical history.
Talbot Rice Gallery ⓘ *Old College, www.trg.ed.ac.uk,* ▣B3. *Tue-Sat 1000-1700 (daily during the festival). Free.* The University's collection of Renaissance paintings, housed in a wonderful neoclassical building.
Stockbridge One of the city's most beguiling corners, with a jumble of antique shops and second-hand bookstores.
Rosslyn Chapel ⓘ *7 miles south, www.rosslyn chapel.org.uk. Mon-Fri 0930-1700, Sun 1200-1630. £7.* This 15th-century chapel is in the *Da Vinci Code* and is said to be the last resting place of the Holy Grail.
Cramond On the northwestern fringes is this 18th-century coastal village. Head along the Almond river to the Cramond Inn for some liquid refreshment.

The world's greatest arts festival

Every year Edinburgh plays host to the world's biggest arts festival, when the capital bursts into life in a riot of entertainment unmatched anywhere else. Over a million tourists descend on the city to experience a brain-sapping variety of acts performed in a frightening variety of venues. The Edinburgh Festival is actually a collection of different festivals running alongside each other, from the end of July through to the beginning of September. The **International Festival** tends to be a fairly highbrow affair and features large-scale productions of opera, ballet, classical music, dance and theatre performed in the larger venues (box office: The Hub, Castlehill, www.eif.co.uk). **The Fringe** features everything from top-class comedy to Albanian existentialist theatre performed in a lift (box office: 108 High St, www.edfringe.com). Also coming under the festival heading are the **International Jazz and Blues Festival** (www.jazzmusic.co.uk), **International Book Festival** (www.edbookfest.co.uk), **International Film Festival** (www.edfilmfest.org.uk) and **Military Tattoo** (www.edintattoo.co.uk). For details of all the events and links to other websites see www.edinburghfestivals.co.uk.

● Sleeping

Edinburgh has a huge selection of places to stay. Most of the upscale accommodation is in the New Town, West End and around Calton Hill. Many city centre hotels offer good low-season deals, especially at weekends, and also offer a standby room rate throughout the year. You'll need to book well in advance during the festival or at Hogmanay. The tourist office has a free accommodation brochure or their Central Reservations Service, T0131-473 3855, centres@eltb.org, will make a reservation for a fee of £5. Also check www.laterooms.com for last-minute deals.

€€€ **The Glasshouse**, 2 Greenside Pl, T0131-525 8200, www.theeton group.com. Luxury boutique hotel,

entered via the original façade of a Victorian church. The rooms are stylish and contemporary, in keeping with the sleek glass exterior, and most have their own balconies and great views. Guests also have the use of a 2-acre roof garden and a rooftop bar.

€€€ **Scotsman Hotel**, North Bridge, T0131-556 5565, www.thescotsman hotel.co.uk. The former offices of *The Scotsman* newspaper have been transformed into this state-of-the-art boutique hotel. Each room is distinctive and has been furnished with great attention to detail, with original art, DVD and internet. Services and facilities include valet parking, screening room, bar, brasserie and restaurant, breakfast room, private dining rooms and health club and spa.

€€€ **Tiger Lily**, 125 George St, T0131-225-5005, www.tigerlily

edinburgh.co.uk. 33 suites and rooms. Recent addition to the city's burgeoning list of boutique hotels. The Georgian exterior belies the effortlessly chic and stylish interior. There's a good restaurant and, downstairs, is the richly decadent **Lulu** bar and club with its vast cocktail menu.

€€ **Point Hotel**, 34 Bread St, T0131-221 5555, www.point-hotel.co.uk. A former Co-op department store has been stylishly refurbished to create a paradigm of chic and minimalist elegance. The suites are huge (some have jacuzzis), and rooms at the front have castle views. Handily placed for the castle and Royal Mile, its ground-floor restaurant offers high-quality bistro food. The bar and grill, **Mondobbo**, is equally stylish. Great value for this part of town.

€€ **Ricks**, 55a Frederick St, T0131-622 7801, www.ricksedinburgh.co.uk. 10 very sleek and stylish rooms are accessed via a staircase at the rear of the bar-restaurant. Decor is subtle, furnishings unfussy and in-room entertainment includes CD and DVD players and minibar.

🍴 Eating

Edinburgh has a wide range of culinary options. Most of the upmarket restaurants are in the New Town, though there are also some excellent places to be found around the Royal Mile and in Leith, which has fish restaurants and dockside bistros. During busy periods such as the festival it's best to book ahead.

Breakfast
🍴 **Café Hub**, Castlehill, T0131-473 2067. Stylish, chilled-out café with a soothing backdrop to the tasty and inventive food. There's seating outside on the terrace in summer.
🍴 **Plaisir du Chocolat**, 251-253 Canongate, T0131-556 9524. A slice of genuine Gallic gastronomic greatness and the city's finest tearoom, offering some 180 varieties of tea, hot chocolate, cakes and various French fancies. They also do a fine *petit déjeuner* and a wonderful (but not cheap at £15) weekend brunch. The *épicerie* across the road is great for tasty picnic treats.
🍴 **Valvona & Crolla**,19 Elm Row, T0131-556 6066. Great home cooking and the best cappuccino in town. The perfect place for a big Sat brunch and very popular. Authentic Italian deli.

Lunch
🍴 **The Grain Store**, 30 Victoria St,

T0131-225 7635. High-quality Scottish ingredients are served with effortless aplomb. The exuberant menu features fish, game and meat and the 2-course lunch is less than a tenner. Combined with attentive service and a relaxed ambience, this place is a real find.
🍴 **Off the Wall**, 105 High St, T0131-558 1497. Combines the finest Scottish produce with flair and imagination. Vegetarians are also well-catered for and the puddings are luscious in the extreme. Great value set lunch.

> 66 99 **Edinburgh has more pubs and bars per square mile than any other European city.**

Dinner
🍴 **Restaurant Martin Wishart**, The Shore, T0131-553 3557. Multi award-winning restaurant serving French-influenced cuisine at its very finest. A meal here is truly memorable.
🍴 **The Witchery by the Castle**, 352 Castlehill, T0131-225 5613. Dining doesn't get more atmospheric than this. The Witchery's reputation has spread far and wide, but though eating here is more of a life experience than simply a meal, style does not take precedence over content. The wine list is phenomenal, with over 900 available. Downstairs, in a converted schoolyard, is the impossibly romantic Secret Garden, which shares the same glorious Scottish menu. Lunchtime specials are good value.

🍴 **David Bann**, 5 Hunter Sq, T0131-226 1112. Daily 1100-2300. Bann's is still one the city's leading vegetarian eateries with an effortlessly cool, minimalist look and a lifestyle menu to match. They offer an imaginative and adventurous range of dishes, taking veggie food far away from the tedious, sandal-wearing days of old. Busy but laid-back and generally good value.

🎵 Nightlife

Edinburgh has more pubs and bars per square mile than any other European city. The prime drinking venue is **George St** and the streets running north and south of it. Another good destination is the area at the top of **Leith Walk** known as the 'Pink Triangle'. For more raucous boozers, head to Lothian Road and the Grassmarket. The club scene has improved dramatically and any self-respecting raver will be supplied with the latest dance floor tunes spun by some of the UK's top DJs.

For movie fans, the legendary **Filmhouse**, 88 Lothian Rd, T0131-228 2688, is the UK's most famous regional cinema and the hub of Edinburgh's International Film Festival. The café-bar is a good place to hang out. **Henry's Cellar Bar**, Morrison St, T0131-221 1228, www.henrys venue.com, is the best place to experience Edinburgh's vibrant jazz scene.

The **Traverse Theatre**, Cambridge St, T0131-228 3223, www.traverse. co.uk, is the city's most exciting theatre venue, which commissions works from contemporary playwrights from Scotland and all over the world.

For all its reputation as one of the world's most beautiful cities, Florence can seem impenetrable to the first-time visitor: a city of cramped traffic, swarms of tourists, street-hawkers and markets selling enormous quantities of belts and aprons decorated with the anatomy of Michelangelo's *David*. But it's a city that people come back to. There's good Tuscan food and wine (if you know where to look), beautiful countryside all around and a history that includes the birth of the Renaissance. But it's the art and architecture that, rightly, are most celebrated. From Michelangelo's *David* and Botticelli's *Venus* to the marginally less well known but no less impressive cloisters in Santa Croce and frescoes in Santa Maria Novella, Florence has it all. And, if you need a new belt, there are few better places.

Arts & culture
★★★★★

Eating
★★★

Nightlife
★

Outdoors
★★

Romance
★★★★

Shopping
★★★

Sightseeing
★★★★★

Value for money
★★★

Overall score
★★★

At a glance

Florence sits mostly on the northern bank of the river Arno. Many arrive in the city at **Santa Maria Novella**, the city's train station and main transport hub. The city centre spreads out southeast beyond it. To the immediate east, the area of **San Lorenzo** has streets crowded with market stalls. Just northeast of here is the **Galleria dell'Accademia**, home to many of Florence's statues. The **Duomo**, Florence's biggest landmark, lies a little further south, below which a regular grid of streets stretch towards the river and make up the heart of the antique district. At the western edge of this grid, **Palazzo Strozzi** is a hulking Renaissance building, while to the south **Piazza della Signoria** competes with the Duomo to be the city's centre point; it's surrounded by grand buildings including the **Palazzo Vecchio** and the **Uffizi**, Florence's great art gallery. Nearby, the **Ponte Vecchio**, Florence's oldest bridge, leads to the enormous Palazzo Pitti and elegant Giardino di Boboli. Also here are the churches of Santo Spirito

> This is a city of endurance,
> a city of stone.
>
> The Stones of Florence, *Mary McCarthy*

and, up a steep hill, San Miniato al Monte. Back on the northern bank of the Arno, to the east of Piazza della Signoria, is the spectacular Gothic basilica of **Santa Croce** and an area of interesting narrow streets and considerably fewer visitors.

★ *Don't leave town without climbing the steep hill to San Miniato al Monte.*

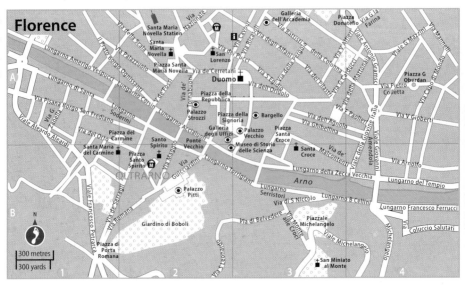

24 hours in the city

Start with a coffee and a pastry from a café (stand at the bar to drink it – many of Florence's cafés will charge you a small fortune to sit down) and allow a little time to wander across the **Ponte Vecchio** before the crowds descend. You can also stop off in **piazza della Signoria** for the obligatory photo of Michelangelo's *David*. If you plan to visit the **Uffizi**, start early to get a good place in the queue and allow the whole morning. Alternatively, the **Galleria dell'Accademia**, **Bargello** or museums and galleries of the **Pitti Palace** will give a taste of Renaissance art with less queuing time involved. Find a restaurant in the **Oltrarno**, on the other side of the river, for lunch and follow it up with a stroll in the **Giardino di Boboli**, or a climb up the hill to **San Miniato al Monte**. In the late afternoon, visit the spectacular **Duomo** and the Battistero and climb to the top of either the Campanile or the Cupola and survey the city from above, ideally with the sunshine glowing off the rooftops. Head to **Santa Croce** in the evening – if you can get there before it closes at 1730 have a look around the interior and the cloisters. Otherwise sit for a while on the steps while people gather for *aperitivi* before drinking one or

Santa Croce steps

two of your own. There are some good eating options around here, too, and you shouldn't miss an ice cream from **Vivoli**. If you want to keep going into the night, bars around Piazza Santa Croce are a good place to start, followed by a nearby club in which you can dance until dawn.

⊖ Travel essentials

Getting there Florence's **Amerigo Vespucci Airport**, T055-306 1300, www.aeroporto.firenze.it, is 4 km from the centre of Florence. A taxi to the centre will cost you about € 16; alternatively the **Vola in Bus** (every 30 mins, €4.50) connects with Santa Maria Novella railway station. Vespucci is a small airport, so flying to Pisa's **Gallileo Galilei Airport**, T050-849111, www.pisa-airport.com, or even Bologna's **Marconi Airport**, T051-647 9615, www.bologna-airport.it, may be cheaper (onward travel by train to Florence is not

difficult from either). The main station is Santa Maria Novella, Piazza Stazione, T892021, www.trenitalia.it, which also serves as the hub for the city's buses. Some international trains (including the sleeper service from Paris) use **Stazione Campo di Marte**, Via Mannelli, located northeast of the centre.

Getting around The city centre is small and doing anything other than walking has little to recommend it. Taxis can be found at ranks but they are notoriously few and far between. Buses work reasonably well but traffic

is often snarled up in jams. Cars are not allowed in some parts of the centre and trying to park is next to impossible.

Tourist information Azienda **Promozionale Turistica**, via Cavour 1, T055-290832, www.firenzeturismo.it, Mon-Sat 0815-1915, is helpful and has free maps as well as information on opening hours, prices and tours. There are also offices at **Santa Maria Novella station**, T055-212245, Mon-Sat 0830-1900, Sun and public holidays 0830-1400, and at the **airport**, T055-315874, daily 0830-2030.

● Sights

Duomo and Battistero

ⓘ *piazza del Duomo, www.opera duomo.firenze.it,* **SJA3**. *Duomo: Mon-Wed and Fri 1000-1700, Thu 1000-1530, Sat 1000-1645 (1st Sat of month 1000-1530), Sun 1330-1645; free. Campanile: daily 0830-1930; €6. Cupola: Mon-Fri 0830-1900, Sat 0830-1740; €6. Battistero: Mon-Sat 1200-1900, Sun 0830-1400; €3.*

Florence's tallest building is still its pink-and-white, marble-clad cathedral. Filippo Brunelleschi's dome was completed in 1463 and, at the time, was the biggest in the world with a span of 42 m. Brunelleschi constructed the octagonal ribbed dome without scaffolding, using bricks inside a marble skeleton. Both the cupola and the separate campanile can be climbed; there are 414 steps up the belltower and 463 steps to the top of the dome. The campanile was designed by Giotto in 1334 but not completed until after his death.

The interior of the Duomo doesn't quite match the extraordinarily beautiful exterior, although Vasari's 16th-century

Piazza della Signoria

frescoes of the Last Judgement on the inside of the dome are spectacular.

Just to the west of the Duomo, the **Battistero** (baptistry) may date from as early as the fourth century and is the city's oldest building. The interior has 13th-century mosaics and a font where Dante was baptized. The highlights, however, are the famous 14th- and 15th-century brass doors, by Pisano and Ghiberti. Those in situ are now copies; the originals are in the **Museo dell'Opera del Duomo** ⓘ *piazza del Duomo 9, T055-230 2885, Mon-Sat 0900-1930, Sun 0900-1345, €6.*

Piazza della Signoria

At the heart of the city, piazza della Signoria is a busy square which buzzes with tourists milling around the Renaissance and Roman statues and fountains. A replica of Michelangelo's *David* gets the most camera clicks but there is also the *Fontana di Nettuno* (Neptune Fountain) by Ammannati (1575) and the *Rape of the Sabine Women* by Giambologna (1583), carved, remarkably, from a single block of marble.

On the southern edge of the piazza, opposite the 14th-century, statue-filled Loggia dei Lanzi, is the **Palazzo Vecchio** ⓘ *T055-276 8224,* **SJA3**, *Fri-Wed 0900-1900, Thu 0900-1400, €6.* Originally the town hall, it also served as the residence of Duke Cosimo de Medici. Nowadays visitors can wander through some of its grand rooms.

Galleria degli Uffizi

ⓘ *piazzale degli Uffizi, T055-238 8651, www.polomuseale.firenze.it,* **SJA2**. *Tue-Sun 0815-1850. €6.50.*

Some of the longest queues in the art world are to be found outside the Uffizi gallery, so allow several hours to get in. Booking ahead is highly recommended but even this is unlikely to mean you will be able to swan straight in.

Once inside the hallowed halls of Renaissance art, highlights include: Sandro Botticelli's *Birth of Venus*, Titian's *Venus of Urbino*, Artemisia Gentileschi's *Judith Beheading Holofernes*, Michelangelo's *Holy Family*, three Caravaggios, three Leonardos and two Giottos.

The Giorgio Vasari-designed building was finished in 1581, originally intended to be offices (hence the name) of

Duomo

Galleria degli Uffizi

Excursion: Fiesole

In the hills to the northeast of Florence, Fiesole was once a more important power base than Florence itself and still likes to think of itself as a little bit superior. Certainly a little cooler, Fiesole is also more laid-back and has great views down over Florence in the valley below as well as some sights of its own. The town has a duomo which dates back to the 11th century as well as the archeological remains of a Roman theatre. The **Museo Archeologico** ⓘ *via Portigiani 1, T055-59477, summer daily 0930-1900, winter Mon and Wed-Sun 0930-1700, €6.50*), contains pieces that were uncovered at this site. The winding walk along via Vecchia Fiesolana to San Domenico is a scenic one but many choose not to move far from the central piazza Mino, which has plenty of good bars and restaurants. Bus No 7 goes between Santa Maria Novella train station in Florence and Fiesole every 15 minutes.

Florentine magistrates. It suffered significant damage as a result of a car bomb in 1993.

Ponte Vecchio

Best known for the jewellers' shops which line its sides, the Ponte Vecchio is the only Florentine bridge to have survived the Second World War. There have been shops on the bridge since it was built in 1345 – possibly originally in order to escape taxes. These days the shops are expensive tourist traps but the bridge itself remains one of the city's iconic symbols.

Palazzo Pitti and Giardino di Boboli

ⓘ *piazza Pitti, ◥B2. Tue-Sun 0815-1850 (closing time of gardens varies with dusk). Combined ticket to all museums and gardens valid for 3 days, €11.50; various other ticket combinations from €6.*

Started in 1457, the Palazzo Pitti was built by a banker, Luca Pitti as a conscious effort to outdo the Medicis, the most powerful family in Renaissance Florence. However, the enormity of the project practically bankrupted the Pitti family and the Medicis themselves moved into the palace in 1550. Already grandiose, the palace was further extended over the years, the most recent additions being the wings added in the 18th century. During Florence's brief position as capital of Italy in the 19th century, the Palazzo Pitti served as the main royal residence.

The contemporary palace houses several museums. The **Galeria Palatina** ⓘ *T055-238 8614, ◥B2*, contains many great works of Renaissance art, including

Ponte Vecchio

Palazzo Pitti Museum

paintings by Titian, Botticelli and Veronese. The **Appartamenti Monumentali** are examples of overblown opulence, and there are also museums dedicated to costume, porcelain and gold and silver.

Behind the Palazzo Pitti, **Giardino Boboli** is a large formal garden offering a peaceful, relaxed and often pleasantly cooler counterpoint to the stresses of the city centre. The gardens are the setting for musical and theatrical events in summer.

San Miniato al Monte

ⓘ *via Monte alle Croci*, 🔲**B3**. *Summer daily 0800-1930; winter daily 0800-1200 and 1500-1800. Free.*

High on a hill to the southeast of the city centre, the church of San Miniato is one of Italy's most beautiful Romanesque buildings. Construction began in 1013 and the church has changed little in the last 1000 years. The striking exterior is decorated with green and white marble. Inside the choir is raised above the crypt, creating a two-tier design, all of which is bathed in light. The nave is inlaid with mosaics and the walls have faded frescoes.

San Miniato al Monte

Santa Croce

Just down the hill, **piazzale Michelangelo**, an otherwise unremarkable car park, affords great views over the Arno and across the city. The place fills with tourists and local couples around sunset.

Santa Croce

ⓘ *piazza Santa Croce, T055-246 6105*, 🔲**B3**. *Mon-Sat 0930-1730, Sun 1300-1730. €5.*

Containing the tombs of several famous Florentines, including Michelangelo, Galileo and Machiavelli, the Gothic basilica of Santa Croce is one of Florence's most important churches.

To the right of the altar, Giotto's frescoes of the Bardi and Peruzzi chapels are the highlights of the interior. Brunelleschi's 15th-century Secondo Chiostro (second cloister) is serenely beautiful and the Capella dei Pazzi (also by Brunelleschi) is another fine example of Renaissance architecture. There is a statue of Dante outside the basilica and a funerary monument to him inside, although he was actually buried in Ravenna.

Santa Maria Novella

ⓘ *piazza Santa Maria Novella, T055-215918*, 🔲**A2**. *Mon-Thu and Sat 0900-1700. €2.70.*

Built by the Dominicans in the 13th and 14th centuries, the church of Santa Maria Novella holds a startlingly colourful fresco cycle by Ghirlandaio, illustrating the life of John the Baptist. Other highlights include Masaccio's *Trinità*, famous for its pioneering use of perspective, and the Chiostro Verde, so-called because of the green pigment used for the frescoes by the artist, Paolo Uccello. The Romanesque-Gothic façade (by Leon Battista Alberti) was added in 1470.

Galleria dell'Accademia

ⓘ *via Ricasoli 60, T055-238 8609*, 🔲**A3**. *Tue-Sun 0815-1850. €6.50.*

Famously containing Michelangelo's masterful statue of David, sculpted in 1504 (when the artist was 29 years old), the Accademia also holds unfinished Michelangelo sculptures intended for the tomb of Pope Julius II.

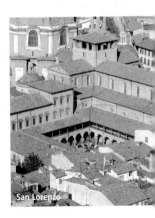
San Lorenzo

● Best of the rest

Capella Brancacci ⓘ *piazza del Carmine, T055-238 2195,* `MA1`. *Mon and Wed-Sat 1000-1700, Sun 1300-1700, reservation required. €4.* This small chapel contains some of Masaccio's 15th-century frescoes, belonging to the church of Santa Maria del Carmine.
San Lorenzo ⓘ *piazza San Lorenzo, T055-216634,* `MA2`. *Mon-Sat 1000-1700. €2.50.* In the middle of Florence's market district and so surrounded by Leonardo aprons and fake designer belts, San Lorenzo was the Medici's church in the 15th century. Brunelleschi, Donatello and Michelangelo all worked on it and it remains one of the city's most important buildings.
Oltrarno One of the most satisfying areas of the city to wander around, the south bank of the Arno has a more laid-back feel than the rest of Florence. There's a market in **Piazza Santo Spirito** on some days of the week.
Bargello ⓘ *via del Proconsolo 4, T055-238 8606,* `MA3`. *Daily 0815-1350, closed 2nd and 4th Mon in month. €4.* Built in 1255, the Bargello was later used as a prison but now holds Renaissance sculpture by Michelangelo, Donatello, Sansovino and others.
Museo di Storia della Scienza ⓘ *piazza dei Giudici 1, T055-265311, www.imss.fi.it,* `MB2`. *Jun-Sep Mon and Wed-Fri 0930-1700, Tue and Sat 0930-1300; Oct-May, Mon and Wed-Sat 0930-1700, Tue 0930-1300. €6.50.* Explores the Renaissance from a scientific viewpoint.

● Sleeping

Hotels in Florence tend to be expensive and, with notable exceptions, service can be below standard; the city's popularity means that it is a seller's market and standards tend to suffer.
€€€ Gallery Hotel Art, vicolo dell' Oro 2, T055-268557, www.lungarno hotels.com. A contemporary luxury hotel near the Ponte Vecchio, Gallery Hotel Art is a part of the Lungarno group and has a well-stocked library and a trendy bar. The place is decorated in muted tones and holds exhibitions of photography and art.
€€€ JK Place, piazza Santa Maria Novella 7, T055-264 5181, www.jkplace.com. A real fire and antique furniture meet hip design in coffee and caramel tones in this 20-room hotel on piazza Santa Maria Novella. There's an immaculate roof terrace, cakes are served in the courtyard and you'd be hard-pushed not to feel eminently fashionable, in a refined Florentine kind of way.
€€ Casa Howard Florence, via della Scala 18, T06-6992 4555, www.casa howard-florence.com. The elegant recipe of the well-known Rome hotel has been repeated in Florence – a handful of individually designed (and loosely themed) rooms, creating an intimate and homely feel. The owners have a personal and idiosyncratic style, with plenty of quality fabrics and artefacts from around the world.
€€ Torre Guelfa, borgo Santi Apostoli 8, T055-239 6338. Draped 4-poster beds, wooden floors, a roof terrace (at the top of the eponymous 13th-century tower) with views over the Florentine rooftops and large antique-filled communal areas make

Torre Guelfa good value. Its location near the Ponte Vecchio makes it an even better choice.
€ Orchidea, borgo degli Albizi 11, T055-248 0346, www.hotelorchidea florence.it. A small, friendly place with 7 rooms on one floor of a palazzo just to the east of the Duomo. Some of the large, simple rooms overlook an internal garden. It tends to fill up quickly, so book ahead.
€ Pensione Scoti, via Tornabuoni 7, T055-292128, www.hotelscoti.com. Almost opposite Palazzo Strozzi, Pensione Scoti is a smart, friendly, antique place with frescoes and large, simple, old-fashioned rooms.
€ Residenza Johanna, via Bonifacio Lupi 14, T055-481896, www.johanna.it. The cheapest of a group of 5 *residenze* in Florence (the others are Johanna II, Johlea I and II and Antica Dimora Firenze). Johanna is especially good value, with simple but classy rooms. Service is friendly, though guests are left to themselves after 1900, when staff go home.

● Eating

An abundance of good quality fresh produce lies at the heart of Tuscan cuisine and Florence's restaurants do well from it. Eating out is not especially cheap, although there are still some traditional trattorias to be found, which cater to a local market rather than the tourists.
†† **Alla Vecchia Bettola**, Vila e Ariosto 32-33, T055-224158. Closed Sun and Mon. Communal eating on benches at marble-topped tables is the style at this excellent traditional trattoria just off piazza Tasso near Santo Maria del Carmine. A daily changing menu offers top Tuscan food.

¶¶ Cibreo Trattoria, via dei Macci 122/r, T055-234 1100. Closed Sun and Mon. Also known as 'Il Cibreino', this is the little sibling of the altogether smarter **Cibreo** next door. It's cheaper and the style is more rustic, but the food is the same inventive, occasionally idiosyncratic, take on Tuscan classics.

¶¶ Fuori Porta, 10/r via del Monte alle Croci, T055-234 2483. Perfectly placed for those who plan to visit San Miniato al Monte but never make it up the hill, Fuori Porta is a wine bar that serves excellent light meals too. The outside tables are popular and, inside, you can gaze on (and of course consume) some of the enormous selection of wine on offer.

¶ Da Benvenuto, via della Mosca 16/r, T055-214833. Closed Sun. Simple but reliably good (and reliably good-value) Tuscan food in the centre of Florence.

¶ Da Nerbone, 1st floor Mercato Centrale di San Lorenzo, T055-219949. Closed Sun. Well-known for its tripe rolls (see **Tripperia da Sergio e Pierpaolo**, below), Nerbone also has excellent cheese and meat and, at lunchtime, pasta, salads, and minestrone.

¶ Il Pizzaiuolo, via dei Macci 113, T055-241171. Closed Sun. An authentic Neapolitan pizza place in Santa Croce, Il Pizzaiuolo fills up quickly in the evenings with those eager for their mouthwatering discs of tomato and mozzarella. In a city not renowned for its pizzas, this is a beacon of excellence.

¶ Osteria Santo Spirito, piazza Santo Spirito 16/r, T055-238 2383. A friendly and colourful place in the corner of the attractive piazza, which has attempted to reinvent the traditional osteria in a contemporary style. Popular with travellers.

¶ Tripperia da Sergio e Pierpaolo, via dei Macci. To the east of the city centre, some of Florence's most traditional food is served from Italy's most traditional agricultural vehicle – with no compromises to tourism or mad cow disease. From a specially adapted *ape*, usually to be found at lunchtimes outside **Cibreo Trattoria** (see above), tripe is cooked and served fresh to an increasingly young and fashionable Florentine crowd. And, to wash it down, you can help yourself to a plastic cup of wine. It's very good value and it tastes better than you might expect.

Vivoli, Via Isole delle Stinche 7, T055-292334. Closed Mon. Quite rightly one of Italy's most celebrated *gelaterias*, serving ice cream of the highest quality in generally old-fashioned flavours.

☉ Nightlife

Bars and clubs

Much of Florence's nightlife takes place around piazza Santa Croce, with other lively pockets in the Oltrarno. Clubs loosen up a little and move outside in the heat of summer but for the rest of the year, well-dressed chic predominates.

Aperitivi, usually drunk between 1900 and 2100, are often accompanied by generous buffets of complimentary snacks. Drinks are correspondingly more expensive but at places like **Negroni**, via dei Renai 17, you can just about nibble your way to an evening's sustenance.

After *aperitivi*, cocktails (or, increasingly, wine bars) take over, followed by dancing the night away at locations such as **Maramao**, via dei Macci 79/r, usually a refined rather than a raucous experience.

☉ Renaissance team

Twice Italian champions and six times cup winners, Fiorentina were, for a long time, big fish in the Italian football pond. But in 2002 they were declared bankrupt and became one of the biggest casualties of a financial crisis in Italian football. However, Fiorentina have also shown how the Italian system can be worked effectively: having been reborn as 'Florentia Viola', they made their way back up from the lower leagues and were conveniently allowed to skip one division. They bought back the rights to their old name and re-entered *Serie A* in 2004. However, their involvement in the *calciopoli* football scandal in 2006 meant they were deducted 15 points at the beginning of the 2006-7 season and only avoided relegation back to *Serie B* after an appeal. The club plays at the **Stadio Artemio Franchi** ⓘ *viale Manfredo Fanti, T055-503 0190, www.acffiorentina.it.*

Live music

The pop, rock and jazz scenes have become livelier in recent years, belying Florence's conservative reputation. Record shops are the best places to find out what's going on. Tourist offices have details of classical concerts at the **Accademia Bartolomeo Cristofori**, via di Camaldoli 7/r, T055-221646, www.accademia cristofori.it, and other venues. For opera and ballet head to the **Teatro del Maggio Musicale Fiorentino**, via Solferino 15, T055-27791, www.maggiofiorentino.com.

Glasgow is hard to define. This spontaneous free spirit has cast off its industrial past to become a modern, design-conscious city with an energy and exuberance that is simply not found anywhere else in Scotland. It is often compared to Manhattan, with its grid of streets, its tall, narrow buildings and its wisecracking citizens. It also has an air of Celtic edginess like Liverpool, a distinctive city swagger like London and a lingering sense of Victorian civic pride like Manchester. The city that reinvented itself in the 1980s is at it once again, following the discovery of St Valentine's relics in a Gorbals church: meet Glasgow, the 'City of Love', with its very own love festival on the 14th February. It gives a whole new meaning to the term 'Glasgow kiss'.

Glasgow

Arts & culture
★★★

Eating
★★★

Nightlife
★★★★

Outdoors
★★★

Romance
★★

Shopping
★★★★

Sightseeing
★★★

Value for money
★★★

Overall score
★★★

⦿ Sights

City Centre

The heart of the city is **George Square**. The tourist office and the two main train stations (Central Station and Queen Street) are all within a couple of blocks of each other. The grid of streets to the east of George Square as far as the High Street forms the **Merchant City**, the city's erstwhile trade centre, characterized by its many tobacco warehouses and elegant Palladian mansions. Money has been poured into the area's restoration and regeneration and it has now been reclaimed by the professional classes as a fashionable place to eat, drink and play.

Only a stone's throw from here is the city's **East End**, downbeat by comparison but offering a genuine slice of pure Glasgow, especially in **The Barras** ① *Sat and Sun 1000-1700,*

George Square

▶B4, a huge flea market spread out around the streets and alleys south of Gallowgate. Close by is the **People's Palace** ① *T0141-271 2962*, ▶B4, *Mon-Thu and Sat 1000-1700, Fri and Sun 1100-1700, free*, a folk museum giving a real insight into the city's social and industrial history.

At the top of the High Street is the early Gothic **Cathedral** ① *T0141-552 6891, www.historic-scotland.gov.uk,* ▶A4, *Apr-Sep Mon-Sat 0930-1730, Oct-Mar Mon-Sat 0930-1630, Sun 1300-1630, free,* the only complete medieval cathedral on the Scottish mainland.

Pedestrianized **Buchanan Street** is the city centre's main thoroughfare, running north from St Enoch Square to Sauchiehall Street. Head several blocks west along St Vincent Street to find the magnificent Roman Classical **St Vincent Street Church**, designed in 1859 by Alexander 'Greek' Thomson, one of the city's architectural geniuses. Shamefully, it's now on the World Monument Fund's list of the 100 most endangered sites.

Due north, past Blythswood Square and uphill from Sauchiehall Street, at 167 Renfrew Street, is the city's defining monument, the **Glasgow School of Art** ① *T0141- 353 4526, www.gsa.ac.uk,* ▶A3, *guided tour Apr-Sep daily 1030, 1100, 1130,*

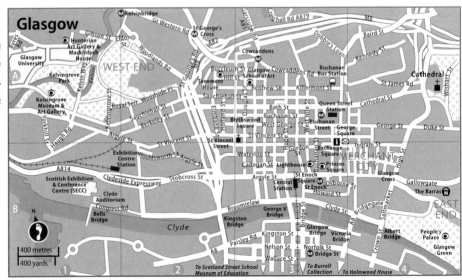

1330, 1400 and 1430, Oct-Mar Mon-Sat 1100 and 1400, £6.50. Designed by Charles Rennie Mackintosh and completed in 1907, the school is seen as his architectural masterpiece.

West End

On the other side of the M8 motorway, which cuts a swathe through the city, is the West End, an area of grand Victorian townhouses and sweeping terraces. Here, opposite Glasgow University, is the **Hunterian Art Gallery** ⓘ T0141-330 5431, **Ⓜ️A1**, Mon-Sat 0930-1700, free, which holds an important collection of European paintings as well as a huge collection of works by the American painter, James McNeill Whistler. Attached to the gallery is the **Mackintosh House**, a stunning reconstruction of the interior of the erstwhile home of chairman and his wife, Margaret MacDonald.

Glasgow's favourite art gallery, the **Kelvingrove Museum and Art Gallery** ⓘ Kelvingrove Park, T0141-276 9500, www.glasgowmuseums.com, **Ⓜ️A1**, Mon-Thu and Sat 1000-1700, Fri and Sun 1100-1700, free, reopened in July 2006

Hunterian Art Gallery

following a £28 million refurbishment. This massive red sandstone building houses one of the finest municipal collections of Scottish and European paintings in the country and should not be missed.

Burrell Collection

ⓘ Pollok Country Park, T0141-649 7151, www.glasgow.gov.uk. Daily 1000-1700. Free. The Burrell can easily be reached from the city by train or bus . Pollokshaws West train station. Bus 45, 47, 48 and 57 all stop on Pollokshaws Rd, opposite the main entrance to the park. Taxi £6-7.

Three miles southwest of the centre is Glasgow's top tourist attraction, the Burrell Collection. Among the 8500 art treasures on view are ancient Greek, Roman and Egyptian artefacts, a huge number of dazzling oriental art pieces, and numerous works of medieval and post-medieval European art. There's also an impressive array of paintings by Rembrandt, Degas, Pissaro, Bellini and Manet, amongst many others.

Buchanan Street

◉ Best of the rest

Tenement House ⓘ 145 Buccleuch St, **Ⓜ️A2**. Mar-Oct daily 1300-1700. £5. Time capsule from the first half of the 20th century.
Scotland Street School Museum of Education ⓘ Shields Rd. Apr-Sep Mon-Thu and Sat 1000-1700, Fri and Sun 1100-1700. Free. Another of Rennie Mackintosh's great works.
Holmwood House ⓘ 61-63 Netherlee Rd, Cathcart, T0141-637 2129. Apr-Oct Thu-Mon 1200-1700, phone in advance. £5. Trains to Cathcart from Central station. A bit out of the way but a work of global importance and real originality by Alexander 'Greek' Thomson.
The Lighthouse ⓘ Mitchell Lane, T0141-221 6362, **Ⓜ️B3**. Mon, Wed-Sat 1030-1700, Tue 1100-1700, Sun 1200-1700. £3. Designed by Charles Rennie Mackintosh as a newspaper office, and now housing Scotland's Centre for Architecture, Design and the City, with a Interpretation and Review Gallery and Viewing Tower.

Burrell Collection

Travel essentials

Getting there Glasgow International Airport, T0870-040 0008, www.baa.co.uk/glasgow, is 8 miles west of the city. Citylink bus No 905 goes to the centre every 10-15 mins 0600-1800 (£3.50 single, £5.30 return, taking 25-30 mins). A taxi from the airport to the city centre costs around £17. **Glasgow Prestwick**, T0871-223 0700, www.gpia.co.uk, is 30 miles southwest of the city. It is used by Ryanair for flights to/from London Stansted and numerous European destinations. Trains to and from Central Station leave every 30 mins (taking 45 mins; £3 single with Ryanair ticket, otherwise £6).

Glasgow has 2 main train stations: **Central station** is the terminus for all trains to southern Scotland, England and Wales; **Queen Street** serves the north and east of Scotland. For times, fares and bookings, contact T08457-484950, www.thetrainline.co.uk, or **Scotrail**, T0845-601 5929, www.firstscotrail.co.uk.

Getting around The best way to get around the city centre is by walking. If you want to explore the West End or South Side, you'll need to use public transport – which is generally good, efficient and reasonably priced. The city's **subway** stations are marked with a huge orange 'U' sign. There's also an extensive suburban **train** network run by Strathclyde Passenger Transport (SPT), www.spt.co.uk. **Strathclyde Travel Centre**, St Enoch Centre Sq, T0141- 332 6811, Mon-Sat 0830-1730, provides a free *Visitor's Transport Guide* with a particularly useful map of the city.

Tourist Information VisitScotland Glasgow, 11 George Sq, T0141-204 4400, www.seeglasgow.com. May daily 0900-1800; Jun and Sep daily 0900-1900; Jul-Aug daily 0900-2000; Oct-Apr Mon-Sat 0900-1800. They can help you find somewhere to stay.

Sleeping

€€€ Hotel du Vin @ One Devonshire Gardens, 1 Devonshire Gdns, T0141-339 2001, www.onedevonshiregardens.co.uk. Highly acclaimed hotel which is still the very last word in style and comfort.

€€€-€€ Abode Glasgow, 129 Bath St, T0141-221 6789, www.abodehotels.co.uk. Stylish and sleek hotel in refurbished former education authority building. Also houses the excellent **Michael Caines** restaurant. Well located and good value.

€€ Groucho Saint Judes, 190 Bath St, T0141-352 8800, www.saintjudes.com. Intimate and stylish boutique hotel with fine restaurant. Good place for a romantic break.

€€ Malmaison, 278 West George St, T0141-572 1000, www.malmaison.com. Chic, stylish urban rooms for smart 30-somethings, with a good brasserie.

€ Rab Ha's, 83 Hutcheson St, T0141-572 0400, www.rabhas.com. Best known for its food, this Merchant City institution has 4 stylish, light contemporary rooms, with crisp sheets and white bathrobes.

Eating

¶¶¶ Rogano's, 11 Exchange Pl, T0141-248 4055. Designed in the style of the Cunard liner, *Queen Mary*, this place looks like the set of a Hollywood blockbuster with prices to match, but the seafood is truly sensational.

¶¶¶-¶¶ The Ubiquitous Chip, 12 Ashton Lane, T0141-334 5007. The city's favourite restaurant. Superb Scottish cuisine, especially venison and seafood.

¶¶ Café Gandolfi, 64 Albion St, T0141-552 6813. The first of Glasgow's style bistro/brasseries and still comfortably continental, relaxed and soothing. Good place for a leisurely late breakfast.

¶¶ Fratelli Sarti, 121 Bath St, T0141-204 0440. A Glasgow institution. Good value food in authentic Italian surroundings. The pizzas are delicious.

¶¶ Mother India, 28 Westminster Terr, Sauchiehall St, T0141-221 1663. Exquisite Indian cooking at affordable prices. Friendly and informal atmosphere. Cheap set lunch.

Nightlife

Glasgow is bursting at the seams with bars and pubs to suit all tastes, from ornate Victorian watering holes to the coolest of designer bars. One of the best areas is the **West End**, with its large student population. The city centre has a great choice too, especially along **Bath St** and around the **Merchant City**. Glasgow's club scene, much of which is found in the city centre, is one of the most vibrant in the UK. Opening times are usually 2300-0300. Entry costs vary from £2-5 for smaller mainstream clubs and £5-10 for the bigger venues, up to £20 for some of the special club nights with top-class DJs. For something a little more highbrow, don't miss a night out at the **Citizens' Theatre**, 119 Gorbals St, T0141-429 0022, www.citz.co.uk, which is home to some of the UK's most exciting and innovative drama. Check out the fortnightly listings magazine, *The List* (www.thelist.co.uk), which also covers Edinburgh.

With over 25 centuries of uninterrupted history, including periods as the capital of two world empires – one Christian, the other Muslim – Istanbul is an undisputed cultural heavyweight. Castles, mosques, churches, seminaries, bazaars and palaces, plus some great museums: it has them all. Add to that a superb backdrop, cleaved by the waters of the Continent – dividing Bosphorus and the Golden Horn, with minarets and domes puncturing the skyline and the taste of salt in the air. The cosmopolitan human landscape is no less beguiling, as modernity and tradition, east and west rub shoulders and Istanbul finds its feet as a cool European city with a vibrant café culture and fancy restaurants. Be prepared – Istanbul will surprise, amaze, entertain and confound you, all in the space of an afternoon.

Istanbul

Arts & culture
★★★★

Eating
★★★

Nightlife
★★★

Outdoors
★★★

Romance
★★★★

Shopping
★★★★★

Sightseeing
★★★★★

Value for money
★★★★

Overall score
★★★★★

At a glance

Home to the Byzantine Emperors and Ottoman Sultans, **Sultanahmet** is Istanbul's historic heart. If you are only visiting for a few days, much of your time will be spent here. The area has a concentration of the city's main sights within a short stroll of its most atmospheric accommodation – think boutique Ottoman. Within walking distance are the **Grand Bazaar** and the teeming streets of **Eminönü** (where the Bosphorus ferries dock) and the **Spice Bazaar**. It's easy to spend several days exploring this part of the city, although a lot more awaits north of the Golden Horn. Across the Galata Bridge, in what was the European quarter in Ottoman times, **Galata** and **Beyoglu** have many of the city's best bars and restaurants. Formerly seedy and run-down, the narrow backstreets off pedestrianized **Istiklal Caddesi**, Istanbul's main shopping street, are dotted with atmospheric eateries, galleries and bars. At the north end of Istiklal Caddesi is **Taksim Square**, centre of the modern city but with little of interest besides its bland modern hotels. A short cab ride north is Nisantasi, an upmarket shopping district ideal for a spot of retail therapy. Down beside the Bosphorus, a string of suburbs are great to explore. The cobbled streets of **Ortaköy** lead to a waterside square overlooked by lively cafés and bars. Beyond the continent-spanning Ataturk bridge, things get progressively more exclusive, as you head towards the upmarket Bosphorus 'village' of **Bebek**, with its diminutive mosque, cafés and restaurants overlooking the expensive yachts moored offshore. Nearby is the Ottoman castle of Rumeli Hisar, built in preparation for the conquest of Constantinople, while a string of equally bucolic villages lining the Asian shore can be reached by ferry.

★ *Don't leave town without taking a boat trip on the Bosphorus.*

If one had but a single glance to give the world, one should gaze on Istanbul.

Alphonse de Lamartine,

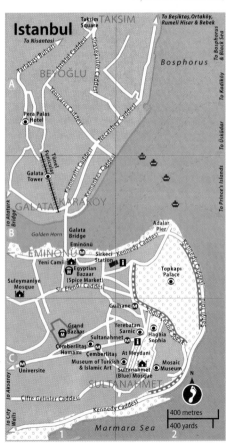

European City Breaks Istanbul

24 hours in the city

Have a lazy breakfast on your hotel roof terrace while drinking in the fantastic view. If your lodgings are one of the few in the Old City that don't have one, then try the *Hotel Uyan*. Be enthralled by the soaring symmetry of the **Sultanahmet (Blue) Mosque**, before jumping on a tram to shopaholic heaven – the **Grand Bazaar**. With lightened wallet and bag of souvenirs in hand, weave your way down through the backstreets to **Eminönü** and the **Spice Market**. Take refuge from the hustle and relax over a late lunch at the *Pandeli Restaurant*. Afterwards, wander past the fishermen on the **Galata bridge** before catching the Tünel funicular up to **Galata** and the other main shopping hub of Istanbul, **Istiklal Caddesi**. The Genoese watchtower in Galata is a great place to enjoy the sunset and a well-earned beer. After dark, jump in a taxi to **Ortaköy**, where in summer you can dine alfresco on the main square. Alternatively, the bars

and clubs of **Beyoglu** await those wanting to imbibe or boogie until the wee hours.

European City Breaks Istanbul

⊖ Travel essentials

Getting there Ataturk Airport, www.ataturkairport.com, is 25 km west of the city centre. The journey by taxi into Sultanahmet or Taksim takes 35-60 mins depending on the traffic, and costs TRY 20-30 (taxis are metered). **Havas** operates an airport bus into Taksim (every 30 mins, TRY 8.5). For Sultanahmet, get off at Aksaray and get a taxi or jump on the tram.

Getting around To get around the Old City all you need is your feet and an occasional ride on the modern **tram**, which passes Aksaray, Beyazit and the Covered Bazaar, Sultanahmet Square and Topkapı Palace (Gülhane) before terminating in Eminönü. Tokens can be bought at each station and cost TRY 1.30.

The 19th-century **funicular railway**, known as the Tünel, climbs steeply up to

Istiklal Caddesi from the north side of the Galata bridge (straight on at the end of the bridge and then bear left at the first main junction). Tokens can be bought from the ticket booths in either station, TRY 1.30. There's also a picturesque little tram that will take you the length of Istiklal Caddesi, from Tünel to Taksim Square, without stopping. For longer journeys, **taxis** are fast and cheap, but avoid road travel during rush hour.

Ferries regularly cross the Bosphorus from Eminönü and Karaköy to the suburbs of Uskudar and Kadiköy on the Asian shore. Tickets cost TRY 1.30 and the crossing takes about 15 mins. There are also 3 daily cruises up and down the Bosphorus to the Black Sea. These depart at 1030 and 1330 from Eminönü's Bogaz Hatti pier,with an extra sailing at 1200

during the summer. Tickets cost TRY 5 and the trip takes over 3 hrs, including a stop for lunch.

Tourist information The most convenient offices are in the arrivals hall at Ataturk Airport, T0212-663 0793; Sultanahmet Sq, at Divan Yolu 3, T0212-518 1802; and in Sirkeci Station, Eminönü, T0212-511 5888. They can provide maps, brochures and information on current events. For listings and city information buy a copy of *Istanbul: The Guide*.

Exchange rate Turkish New Lira (TRY). £1 = TRY 2.69. €1 = TRY 1.84.

Visas These can be bought at the airport before you go through customs. Remember to have cash ready to pay for it; euros and pounds sterling accepted. See also page 16.

⊙ Sights

Topkapı Palace

ⓘ *Topkapı Sarayi, Sultanahmet, T0212-512 0480,* **B2**. *Wed-Mon 0900-1700. TRY 17. Harem Tour TRY 15, Treasury TRY 10.*

Home of the Ottoman sultans and centre of their empire, the Topkapı Palace is one of the world's most important historical collections, as well as being one of the most popular sights in the whole country. Each year tens of thousands wander through its many halls, apartments and pavilions. Entered through the imposing **Imperial Gate** (Bab-i Humayun), the palace sprawls over a series of large courtyards, with the **Harem**, inviolate residence of the Sultans, their wives and concubines, at its core. Things can get very crowded so it is wise to visit early in the day and buy your ticket for the Harem tours, which depart every 30 minutes, as soon as you arrive. With so many other things to see, you should allow at least half a day for your wanderings. Highlights include the palace kitchens and the dazzling artefacts in the Imperial Treasury.

Topkapı Palace

Haghia Sophia

Haghia Sophia

ⓘ *Sultanahmet Meydani, T0212-522 1750,* **C2**. *Tue-Sun 0900-1700. TRY 12.*

The pinnacle of Byzantine architectural achievement was built in AD 537 at the behest of Emperor Justinian, eager to prove the pre-eminence of his 'New Rome'. Towering over the city's rooftops and topped by a whopping 30 m-wide dome, the cathedral enthralled Byzantine visitors then and continues to do so today. Despite a sacking by the Crusaders in 1204, its conversion into a mosque in 1453, then a museum in 1934, the building has a great collection of precious and ancient mosaics, some only recently rediscovered beneath Ottoman plaster. But it is the venerable atmosphere that can't help but impress.

Sultanahmet Mosque

ⓘ *Daily 0900-1900. Free.* **C2**.

Gracefully cascading domes and sharp, soaring minarets, the Sultanahmet Mosque, better known as the **Blue Mosque**, rises evocatively above the well-kept gardens of Sultanahmet Square. Built by Sultan Ahmet in 1616, it was the last of the great imperial mosques, an architectural milestone marking the beginning of the Ottoman Empire's long, inexorable decline. Controversially, the Sultan had six minarets built, instead of the usual four, an act that many saw as a mark of disrespect to the Mosques of the Prophets in Mecca, which were also graced with a half-dozen towers. As a functioning mosque you enter through a special entrance and must be dressed appropriately – shawls can be borrowed to cover exposed arms and female heads at the door. Inside, the walls are gaudily decorated with 20,000 patterned Iznik tiles, hence the building's western name.

Museum of Turkish and Islamic Art

ⓘ *At Meydani 46, Sultanahmet, T0212-518 1805,* **C2**. *Tue-Sun 0900-1700. TRY 4.*

Overlooking what was once the Byzantine Hippodrome, an arena where ceremonies, parades and races were held, and which is now known as **At Meydani**, the museum

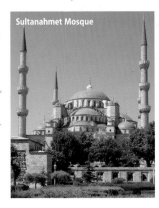

Sultanahmet Mosque

Istanbul's most famous hotel is the Pera Palas (Mesrutiyet Caddesi 98, Tepebasi, Beyoglu), built in 1892 to accommodate travellers stepping off the glittering Orient Express. The visitor's book is filled with the names of heads of state, politicians, poets, movie stars and spies: Greta Garbo, Mata Hari, Alfred Hitchcock and Jackie Onassis among them. Agatha Christie penned part of *Murder on the Orient Express* while staying, and Ataturk, the country's founder and first president, rested his head in room 101, which is kept as a mini-shrine to the great man. Small brass plaques on many of the doors identify other famous occupants. Curiosity value aside, little of the Pera Palas' original splendour survives and the high room rates are not justified by the limited facilities and rather plain rooms. It's far better to come for a look around and a drink at the hotel's long bar.

has an interesting collection covering the Middle East and Central Asia, from earliest Islamic times through to the present day. The exhibits are well labelled, organized chronologically and geographically and housed in a 16th-century palace constructed by Ibrahim Paşa, influential Grand Vizier to Suleyman the Magnificent, before he was strangled at his master's behest.

Grand Bazaar

ⓘ *www.grandbazaarturkey.com*, ◖C1.
Mon-Sat 0830-1930.

With over 5000 shops connected by a maze of covered streets and passageways, the Grand Bazaar is the largest retail area of its kind in the world. Surrender yourself to the inevitability of getting lost and just wander, browsing shops selling clothes, carpets, gold and silver, household goods and souvenirs, stopping to practice your haggling skills. Each type of shop is concentrated in a particular area, with silver and antique merchants occupying the Ic Bedestan, the historic heart of the bazaar. If you need a break there are several cafés within the bazaar.

Çemberlitaş Hamamı

ⓘ *www.cemberlitashamami.com.tr*, ◖C1.
0600-2400. TRY 12-20, plus 10% tip.

The perfect antidote to a day's sightseeing is a steam clean, followed by a massage in one of the city's many Turkish baths. Built in 1584 by master architect Mimar Sinan, and with separate sections for men and women, the Çemberlitaş Hamamı is one of the most atmospheric, as well as being close to the Grand Bazaar and Sultanahmet. Towels and cloths to wrap around you while bathing are provided, and refreshments are also available.

Egyptian Bazaar and Eminönü

ⓘ *Mon-Sat 0800-1900.* ◣B1.

Also known as the **Spice Market**, this busy arcade lined with shops selling spices, imported foods, souvenirs and herbal remedies, such as the somewhat dubious 'Turkish Viagra', gets its name from a time when it was endowed with the custom duties from Cairo. The market is part of the **Yeni Camii** (New Mosque) complex, which is surrounded by the bustling district of Eminönü. Bosphorus ferries dock

Grand Bazaar

Çemberlitaş Hamamı

at the quayside and the air is filled with the smell of juicy kebabs and the sound of itinerant traders hawking their wares from the pavements.

Istiklal Caddesi and Beyoglu

In Ottoman times Beyoglu was home to the city's Greek, Armenian and European communities, and many of their churches and consulates remain. With the departure of these communities after the establishment of the Turkish Republic, the area fell on hard times, though it has been enjoying a renaissance in recent years. Bohemian Beyoglu's narrow streets, running off the main shopping thoroughfare of Istiklal Caddesi, have lots of great restaurants, cafés and bars.

Ortaköy

Ortaköy is the first of the Bosphorus 'villages' on the European shore. Cobbled streets lined with cafés, shops and market stalls lead down to a small square overlooked by the baroque **Mecidiye mosque**, which

Istiklal Caddesi

looks like a wedding cake when lit up at night. On sunny days, the cafés are crowded, as are the bars at night. Further north, some of the city's most upmarket nightspots overlook the straits.

Rumeli Hisar and Bebek
ⓘ Tue-Sun 0900-1630. Bus 25E from Eminönü or bus 40 from Taksim.

In preparation for his attack on Constantinople in 1453, Sultan Mehmet had castles built on either side of the Bosphorus to prevent supply ships reaching the city. The larger of these was Rumeli Hisar, on the European shore north of Bebek, overlooking a bend in the Bosphorus. Today you can walk the restored 15 m-thick battlements and take imaginary pot-shots at passing ships. There are several good little cafés nearby or stroll along the coastal path to the genteel Bosphorus 'village' of Bebek, which attracts a well-heeled crowd.

Egyptian Bazaar

◉ Best of the rest

Mosaic Museum ⓘ Arasta Sokak, Sultanahmet, T0212-518 1205, ⬛C2. Tue-Sun 0900-1630. TRY 5. Byzantine mosaics displayed in situ where they were unearthed.
Yerebatan Sarnic ⓘ Yerebatan Caddesi 13, Sultanahmet, ⬛C2. Daily 0900-1800. TRY 10. Underground cistern featured in From Russian With Love.
Suleymaniye Mosque ⓘ Tiryakiler Çaşısı, Suleymaniye, T0212-522 1259, ⬛B1. Daily 0900-1900. To some, the city's finest mosque.
Galata Tower ⓘ Galata Sq, ⬛B1. Daily 0900-1900. TRY 5. A medieval Genoese watchtower with a great view.
City Walls The historic city walls have been restored and you can walk much of their 6½ km length, although it's best not to do it alone.
Dolmabahçe Palace ⓘ Dolmabahçe Caddesi, Besiktas, 0900-1600. TRY 10. Ostentatious home of the last Ottoman sultans in the twilight years of the empire.
Nisantasi An upmarket shopping and residential district north of Taksim, which has designer clothes stores and domestic chains aplenty.
Akmerkez ⓘ Nispetiye Caddesi, Etiler. Daily 1000-2200. One of the city's swankiest shopping malls.
Leanders Tower ⓘ (Also called the Maiden's Tower) Salacak Caddesi. 1200-1900. Get the ferry from Eminönü to Uskudar, from where there's a ferry to the tiny tower-topped island with a café and spectacular views.

Excursion: Prince's Islands

Off Istanbul's Asian shore are a collection of nine islands, which were a place of exile in Byzantine and Ottoman times, later becoming home to wealthy families from the city's Greek and Armenian minorities. The islands are graced with many beautiful wooden houses, churches and a Greek Orthodox monastery. They also remain blissfully car-free, with horse carts the only means of transport. The largest, **Buyukada**, is the most interesting and you can explore it by rented bicycle or hire a horse-drawn phaeton. A tour of the island takes a couple of hours on foot, taking in Leon Trotsky's home – he wrote *History of the Russian Revolution* while living here – and the hilltop St George's Monastery.

There is a beach club on the far side of the island with a small beach for cooling off. Ferries depart from Eminönü's Adalar Pier regularly for the hour-long crossing. Tickets cost TRY 4.5.

Sleeping

Istanbul has an excellent choice of accommodation from budget hotels to atmospheric Ottoman boutique places and luxury international chains. Prices are competitive in comparison with other European cities, although there are plenty of places to pamper yourself if you wish. Booking in advance is advisable at any time of year as the most popular hotels fill up quickly. Many of the city's top-notch beds are found along the Bosphorus.

€€€ **Çiragan Palace**, Çiragan Caddesi 32, Beşiktaş, T0212-326 4646, www.kempinski.com. Operated by the German Kempinski chain, this 5-star on the edge of the Bosphorus incorporates an Ottoman palace and has the city's finest swimming pool, as well as a spa and several excellent restaurants.

€€€ **Four Seasons**, Tevfikhane Sokak 1, Sultanahmet, T0212-638 8200, www.fourseasons.com. Formerly a prison, this is now one of Istanbul's most exclusive and luxurious hotels. Its 54 high-ceilinged rooms have every possible mod con and there is a great restaurant too.

€€ **Empress Zoe**, Adliye Sokak 10, Sultanahmet, T0212-518 2504, www.emzoe.com. Incorporating the ruins of 15th-century Turkish Baths, the Zoe is exquisitely decorated, with modern frescoes and wall hangings and small but comfy and well-furnished rooms. There is a scenic roof terrace bar and a lovely garden.

€€ **Sultan Ahmet Palace Hotel**, Torun 19, Sultanahmet, T0212-458 0460, www.sultanahmetpalace.com. Great location, 36 rooms, 5 with private balcony, Turkish bath in each room, minimum 2 nights, free airport transfer and also children under 6 free.

€€ **Yesil Ev**, Kabasakal Caddesi 5, Sultanahmet, T0212-517 6785. Housed in a restored Ottoman mansion on Sultanahmet Square, you can't beat the Yesil Ev (meaning Green House) for location or atmosphere. The accommodation is slightly faded and creaky, though, and don't expect a lift either. The garden café is a tranquil haven in summer.

€ **Hotel Uyan**, Utangac Sokak 25, Sultanahmet, T0212-516 4892, www.uyanhotel.com. A good choice for a budget hotel. It's set in a converted corner house with clean en suite rooms. The scenic roof terrace has stunning views.

€ **Side Hotel**, Utangac Sokak 20, Sultanahmet, T0212-517 2282, www.sidehotel.com. A well-managed place with a selection of simple pension rooms, or more expensive hotel rooms, most with their own bathrooms.

🍴 Eating

Istanbul's restaurant scene has come on leaps and bounds in recent years, with a crop of talented new Turkish chefs adding to the existing mix of traditional *meyhane* (the city's equivalent of a taverna), kebab houses and fish restaurants. Dining out is generally good value for money, though prices in some of the top-notch establishments are on a par with prices in other European cities. Alcohol is available in all but a few of the city's dining spots.

For a great evening out visit the raucous area of Kumkapi, on the coast south of Beyazit, and the Grand Bazaar, which is crowded with meze and fish restaurants, where diners are entertained by gypsy street musicians. The *meyhane* of Nevizade Sokak, reached down the Balik Pazari from Istiklal Caddesi, are very popular with local diners.

Breakfast

🍴 **Fes Café**, Halıcılar Caddesi 62, Grand Bazaar, T0212-528613. At the heart of the bazaar, this trendy café is a good spot for a cappuccino and a snack.
🍴 **Kaffehaus**, Tünel Sq 4, Beyoglu, T0212-245 4028. In a courtyard opposite the top Tünel station, this atmospheric café has tables outside and a cosy interior for the winter.

Lunch

🍴 **Haci Abdullah**, Sakizagaci Caddesi 17, T0212-293 8561, www.haciabdullah.com.tr. In a sidestreet off Istiklal Caddesi, this is a grandfather of the Istanbul restaurant scene, having served Ottoman-Turkish cuisine for over

110 years. It's also known for its pickles and preserves which are displayed in colourful jars along the walls. No alcohol served.
🍴 **Pandeli**, Misir Çarşısı (Egyptian Bazaar), Eminönü, T0212-527 3909. This atmospheric restaurant, housed in vaulted rooms above the entrance to the Spice Market, serves local Turkish dishes at lunchtime only.

❝❞ Istanbul has to be one of the great shopping cities of the world, up there, in its own way, with New York and Milan.

Dinner

🍴 **Imroz**, Nevizade Sokak 19-29, T0212-249 9073. One of the best fish and meze restaurants on a street crowded with excellent *meyhane*.
🍴 **Refik**, Sofyali Sokak 10-12, Asmalimescit, T0212-243 2834. A quintessential backstreet *meyhane* with an excellent selection of meze and meat or fish. There are tables on the street in summer.

🌙 Nightlife

You certainly won't be bored after dark in Istanbul. Beyoglu has a diverse collection of bars and clubs, catering for tastes from jazz to Turkish folk and techno. Pick up a copy of *Time Out-Istanbul* for details of the best nightspots.
Ataturk Cultural Centre, Taksim Sq, T0212-251 5600. This is the city's premier performing arts venue, hosting concerts, ballet and opera.

Babylon, Seybender Sokak 3, Asmalimescit, Beyoglu, www.babylon-ist.com. A live venue which hosts top international and Turkish acts, as well as club nights.

If you want to see where Istanbul's rich and famous strut, visit one of the super-clubs overlooking the Bosphorus in Kuruçeşme. Try **Reina**, Muallim Naci Caddesi 44, Kuruçeşme, www.reina.com.tr, but dress up and be prepared for a vertiginous bar bill.

🛍 Shopping

Istanbul has to be one of the great shopping cities of the world, up there, in its own way, with New York and Milan. The **Grand Bazaar** is of course a good place to start, but there are other areas to check out including **Arasta Bazaar**, beside Sultanahmet Mosque, for carpets, handicrafts and Iznik tiles. The **Istanbul Handicraft Centre**, on Kabasakal Caddesi 7, Sultanahmet Sq, has artisans onsite producing various traditional Ottoman crafts.

Istaklal Caddesi, the city's main drag, has a mix of department stores, clothing shops (like Mavi Jeans) and some good bookshops. For antiques, the Beyoglu district of Çukurcuma, east of Istiklal Caddesi, is dotted with little treasure troves, though remember there are restrictions on exporting real antiquities. Nişantaşi has international and home-grown fashion labels along Abdi Ipekci Caddesi and Tesvikiye Caddesi.

Across the Bosphorus in **Kadiköy**, the city's largest street market is held on Tue and Sun along Kusdili Sokak. Ask for the Salı Pazan, then follow the crowd.

Krakow

Krakow's Stare Miasto, its grand old centre, is the genteel face of Poland, a world away from the industrialized communist greyness often associated with Eastern Europe. For hundreds of years this was the Polish capital, and there's a spectacular royal castle to prove it, not to mention sumptuous churches, interesting museums and an excellent classical music scene. Krakow also has a bohemian side: it's a university city and the old Jewish quarter, Kazimierz, is packed with bars that would not look out of place in the hipper parts of London or New York. Synagogues and cemeteries, inscriptions and artefacts are all reminders of Krakow's Jewish past. Outside Krakow, Auschwitz and Birkenau death camps are chilling remnants of the Holocaust, and wandering Krakow's streets, the absence of the Jewish population is keenly felt.

Arts & culture
★★★★

Eating
★★

Nightlife
★★★

Outdoors
★

Romance
★★★★

Shopping
★★

Sightseeing
★★★

Value for money
★★★★★

Overall score
★★★

◉ Sights

Rynek Główny ⬊B1

Shaped a little like an ice-cream cone, Krakow's Stare Miasto (Old Town) centres on **Rynek Główny**, reputedly medieval Europe's biggest square. It is dominated by the **Sukiennice** (Cloth Hall), originally built in the 14th century and restructured 200 years later. These days, its market stalls sell chess sets and painted papier maché eggs. Upstairs, a gallery of Polish art is being renovated but cafés around its base remain open: Lenin was once a regular at **Noworolski**.

Rising high over the square from the northeastern corner, **Kosciól Mariacki** (St Mary's Church) ⓘ *Rynek Glówny 5, T012-422 0521, Mon-Sat 1130-1800, Sun 1400-1800, 4zl*, was built in the 14th century, replacing an earlier church destroyed by the Tartars. The taller of its two towers (81 m) was used as the city's watchtower. Every hour, a trumpeter plays from one of its topmost windows, commemorating an event in the 13th century when a watchman, trumpeting a warning of Tartar invasion, was killed mid-tune by an arrow. Inside, Veit Stoss's high altar is a late-Gothic masterpiece.

Other sights in the square include the free-standing **Wieza Ratuszowa** (Town Hall tower) ⓘ *May-Oct daily 0900-1800, 4zl*, and **Kosciól sw Wojciecha** (St Adalbert's Church), a tiny, domed structure, which is the city's oldest church, dating from the 10th century.

Around the Rynek Główny

It would be very easy to spend a couple of days exploring the atmospheric streets around the square. Heading north, **Florianska** has the big shops and is the place to buy smoked sheep's cheese from local women.

Just to the west of Florianska is the **Czartoryski Muzeum** ⓘ *ul Sw Jana 19, T012-422 5566,* ⬊A1, *May-Oct Tue and Thu 1000-1600, Wed, Fri and Sat 1000-1900, Sun 1000-1500, Nov-Apr Tue, Thu and Sun 1000-1530, Wed, Fri and Sat 1000-1800, 9zl.* Leonardo da Vinci's *Lady with an Ermine* is the clear highlight but there are also some other impressive paintings and Ancient Egyptian sarcophagi and pottery.

To the west of the square, the university district includes the 15th-century **Collegium Mauis** ⓘ *Jagiellonska 15, T012-422 0549,* ⬊B1,

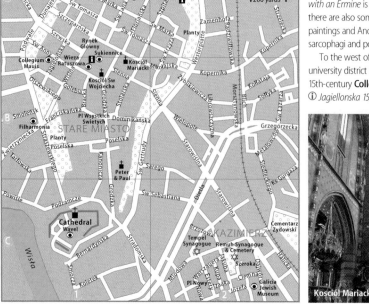

Kosciól Mariacki

The town of **Oswiecim**, 80 km west of Krakow, will forever be associated with the name the Nazis gave it after their invasion of Poland: Auschwitz. The camp and its extension ('Auschwitz II') at nearby Birkenau saw the systematic murder of around one and a half million people. **Auschwitz** itself has been turned into a museum ⓘ *www.auschwitz.org.pl, Jun-Aug daily 0800-1900, May and Sep daily 0800-1800, Apr and Oct 0800-1700, Mar and Nov 0800-1600, Dec-Feb 0800-1500, free*, with numbingly shocking displays, such as piles of shoes and watches, and cloth made from human hair. Enormous **Birkenau** is bleaker and, if anything, even more affecting. Wandering freely in and out of untouched barracks and peering through cobwebbed windows at graffitied walls and bunk beds makes the chilling reality seem starker and nearer. Day tours to Auschwitz are available from Krakow (ask at tourist information) or you could book a taxi driver for the day. Alternatively, take an hourly train to Oswiecim (about 90 minutes) and then walk or get a local bus. There's shuttle bus between Auschwitz and Birkenau.

12zl, where Copernicus once studied. It is now a museum.

Ul Grodzka runs south from the square towards the Wavel, passing the Church of Peter and Paul and the Convent of the Poor Clares en route. The Stare Miasto is ringed by a park, known as the **Planty**, which follows the route of the old walls of the city.

Wavel ⓘC1

At the southern tip of the Stare Miasto, the Wavel is the hill on which sit the royal palace and the cathedral. Home to Polish royalty for hundreds of years (most of them are still buried in sarcophagi under the cathedral), the Wavel has symbolic importance to the whole country.

The castle's grand Renaissance courtyard was built by an Italian architect, Bartolomeo Berrecci, in the 16th century. The **State Rooms** ⓘ *Tue-Sat 0930-1600, Sun 1000-1600, 15zl, free on Sun*, contain the art collection of various Polish kings, tapestries and ornately decorated rooms. The **Royal Private Apartments** ⓘ *Tue-Sat 0930-1600, 20zl*, have more art and include the king's bedchamber.

Before he became Pope John Paul II, Karol Wojtyla was archbishop at Krakow's **Cathedral** ⓘ *Mon-Sat 0900-1500, Sun 1515-1600, 10zl for the bell tower and royal tombs*. Built in 1364, the cathedral is not just a revered religious building but also a homage to the 45 Polish monarchs, all but four of whom are buried here. A climb up dark narrow stairs takes you to the 11-tonne Sigismund's bell, revealing some good views over the city.

Towards the river, a fire-breathing metal dragon is a memorial to Krak, the creature that, according to legend, once terrorized Wavel Hill.

Wavel Castle

Kazimierz ⓘC2

Further south, beyond the Wavel, is the old Jewish quarter. This is the city's most fashionable and fascinating area. Despite today's small Jewish population, it retains a definite Jewish atmosphere.

Szeroka is the area's heart, though the market square, **pl Nowy**, lined by bars, is more lively. Several synagogues can be visited, including **Remuh** ⓘ *Szeroka 40, Mon-Fri 0900-1600, 5zl*, and the rebuilt **Tempel** ⓘ *Miodowa 24, Sun-Fri 0900-1600, 5zl*. **Cmentarz Zydowski** (New Cemetery), under the railway at the eastern end of Miodowa, is a mass of moss-covered gravestones that emphasize the absence of a people.

The **Galicia Jewish Museum** ⓘ *8 Dajwór, T012-421 6842, www.galicia jewishmuseum.org, daily 0900-1800, 7zl*, is a stunning modern museum that uses contemporary photographs and accounts to look at absence, loss and memory. Photos of an old synagogue now turned into a warehouse and abandoned Jewish cemeteries with broken gravestones are especially poignant. A new exhibit looks at Poles who hid Jews from the Nazis and there is also an excellent bookshop.

⊖ Travel essentials

Getting there Krakow Balice Airport (www.lotnisko-balice.pl) is now linked to the city centre by a rickety 2-carriage train every 30 mins (20 mins; 4zl). A free bus shuttles between the arrivals hall and the train platform, but it's only a 200 m walk. A taxi to the centre is about 60zl. By rail (www.pkp.pl), the daytime intercity Wawel train and sleeper services, link Krakow with Berlin Hauptbahnhof.

Getting around Everywhere in the city centre is within reasonable walking distance and much of it is traffic-free. Should you want to try out a Polish tram or bus, tickets cost 2,50zl from news stands, or 3zl on board. Stamp your ticket when you get on.

Tourist information There is a helpful office in the Sukiennice in the main square (Rynek Glówny 1/3, T012-421 7706, www.mcit.pl, summer Mon-Fri

0900-2000, Sat 0900-1800, Sun 0900-1600, winter Mon-Fri 0900-1700, Sat 0900-1600, Sun 0900-1400; hours may vary, especially in winter), where you can also book tours. There is another information office in the Planty, near the northern end of Szpitalna (T012-432 0110). The monthly *Karnet* (4zl, available at information offices) has useful listings information.

Exchange rate £1=5.51zl, €1=3.76zl.

⊖ Sleeping

€€€ Copernicus, ul Kanonicza 16, T012-424 3400, www.hotel.com.pl /copernicus. On one of Krakow's most attractive and ancient streets, this is an elegant hotel with a brick-vaulted swimming pool in the cellar.

€€-€ Saski, ul Slawkowska 3, T012-421 4222, www.hotelsaski.com.pl. Liveried doormen and an art nouveau lift add a touch of class to this large hotel. Standard rooms are big but relatively simple; suites are far grander. Excellent breakfasts are served in the modern **Metropolitan Café**.

€ AAA Krakow Apartments, T012-6332647, www.aaakrakow.com. Good-value, modern self-catering apartments, all within a 10-minute walk of the Rynek Glówny.

€ Eden, ul Ciemna 15, T012-430 6565, www.hoteleden.pl. A friendly place near the heart of the café and bar action in Kazimierz. Rooms are bright and contemporary and the hotel has a sauna and a basement pub.

€ Klezmer Hois, ul Szeroka 6, T012-411 1245, www.klezmer.pl. A grand old Jewish hotel and restaurant on the square in Kazimierz, Klezmer Hois serves kosher wine and vodka and good food. Rooms are large, plain and comfortable.

⊖ Eating

♥♥ Wierzynek, Rynek Glówny 15, T012-424 9600, www.wierzynek .com.pl. With views over the square from the immaculate upstairs rooms, Krakow's smartest restaurant claims a lineage going back to the 14th century. The menu is posh Polish; expect tuna strudel or venison with *pierogi* and juniper berries.

♥ Balaton, ul Grodzka 37, T012-422 0469, www.balaton.krakow.pl. An old-fashioned Hungarian place just south of the square. Hearty soups arrive in flame-warmed metal bowls and generous helpings of goulash are served up on potato pancakes at long dark wood tables.

♥ Once Upon a Time in Kazimierz, Szeroka 1, T012-421 2117. Behind what could easily be mistaken for a row of old Jewish shopfronts, this candlelit, cosy place serves up simple but tasty fare such as spinach and cheese pancakes.

♥ Pod Temida, ul. Grodzka 43, T012-422 0874. An old -style milk bar or simple canteen, Pod Temida is a Polish experience with no concessions to modernity. The menu has no English so you may have to do some pointing but there's nowhere better (or cheaper) to try *pierogi*, the ubiquitous Polish ravioli-like dumplings.

⊖ Nightlife

Alchemia, ul Estery 5, T012-421 2200, www.alchemia.com.pl. Kazimierz's flagship club/bar/café hosts art and film events. There's live music downstairs (check out the flyers posted around town) and trendy Krakovians drink by candlelight upstairs.

Kawiarnia Ukrainska, ul Kanonicza 15. This central but relaxed Ukrainian café, like many places in Krakow, is sunk below street level. Warm red walls, high ceilings, mulled beer and a chilled atmosphere make it a great place to rest for an hour or two.

Moment, ul Jósefa 34, T06-6803 4000, www.momentcafe.pl. A hyper-modern cocktail bar decorated with hundreds of clocks. It also serves good food, has free Wi-Fi and will even entertain your kids for you on Fri or Sat morning (for 'the parent with a hangover').

Singer, ul Estery 22, T012-292 0622. The cosiest of all Krakow's bars and cafés has a fire in winter, dim lamps and candles, laid-back Jewish music and uses Singer sewing machines as tables.

The **Karol Szymanowski Philharmonic**, one of Poland's top orchestras, plays regularly in the grand **Filharmonia** (ul Zwieryniecka 1, T012-422 9477, www.filharmonia.krakow.pl).

European City Breaks Krakow

With its back to Europe and its soul in the 15th century, scrupulously self-effacing Lisbon has long kept a low profile while its neighbours strutted their stuff. During nearly 50 years of solitude, Salazar smothered the city in a conservative mantle but now it has emerged from its cocoon. Thanks to European funding, a stint as City of Culture in 1994 and Expo 98, which saw the arrival of the futurist Parque das Nações, Lisbon is flourishing. Appropriately, given Portugal's sea-faring, imperialist history, old and new worlds sit comfortably side by side in the capital. *Lisboetas* emerge from riverside warehouse conversions and flash fashion boutiques to board arthritic trams that still chug up ludicrous gradients, zigzagging past squat dwellings, hole-in-the-wall grocers and ancient Roman walls.

Lisbon

Arts & culture
★★★

Eating
★★★

Nightlife
★★★★

Outdoors
★★★

Romance
★★★★

Shopping
★★★

Sightseeing
★★

Value for money
★★★★

Overall score
★★★★

At a glance

Square and spare, Lisbon's downtown, **Baixa**, is the city's commercial nexus, a grid of thrusting thoroughfares built in the wake of the 1755 earthquake. Pedestrianized **Rua Augusta** is the Rambla-esque central promenade, which funnels south to handsome **Praça do Comércio**, Lisbon's Whitehall and medieval city gateway. To the north, Baixa's main square and the city's central reference point is **Rossio**. To the west, straddling one of Lisbon's seven hills, is gentrified **Chiado**. North of Rossio is the grand **Avenida da Liberdade**, which ends at **Praça Marques de Pombal**. Beyond it is Lisbon's largest park **Parque Eduardo VII** and, further north, the unassailable **Museu Calouste Gulbenkian**. West of Chiado, the **Bairro Alto** has always been Lisbon's Latin quarter, where sleek bars and fado houses line labyrinthine alleyways. Chiado's backyard to the west is the earthy neighbourhood of **São Bento**, which gives way to smarter **Estrela** and, further west still, streets climb to

Our lips meet easily across the narrow street.

Federico de Brito

haughty, diplomatic **Lapa**. East of Baixa is **Alfama**, a maze of medieval Moorish streets and where it all began. A few kilometres west of Baixa, stretching along the Tagus, **Belém** sees Portugal's imperial triumphs made stone. To the northeast, suburban sprawl gives way to sleek modernism at **Parque das Nações**, site of Expo 98.

★ *Don't leave town without visiting the Antiga Pastelaria de Belém, the cathedral to Lisbon's famed custard tart, the pastel de nata.*

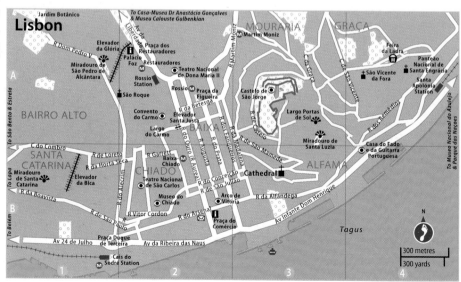

⦿ Sights

Baixa and Rossio

Surrounded by whizzing traffic, all roads seem to lead to Rossio, Baixa's central square, formally known as Praça Dom Pedro IV. The neoclassical **Teatro Nacional de Dona Maria II**, built in 1846 by Fortunato Lodi, occupies the north side of the square. During the 18th century this was the site of the Palace of the Inquisition. To the northwest stands the interlocking horseshoe arches of **Rossio station**, designed in 1887 and betraying a late 19th-century nostalgia for the period of the Discoveries. Adjacent to Rossio, **Praça da Figueira** retains more endearing old-world charm.

Southbound from Rossio, **Rua Augusta** is lined with touristy pavement cafés, international chain stores and leather emporiums. This climaxes with the overarching splendour of the **Arco de Vitória**,

Rossio Square

gateway to **Praça do Comércio** – the culmination of an enlightened despot's vision for a model city and designed to out-pomp the most regal of Europe's squares. The showpiece is a bronze equestrian statue of King Dom José I and, on the north side of the square, nestling beneath the arcaded colonnades is one of Lisbon's most famous literary landmarks, **Café Martinho do Arcado**.

On Rua Santa Justa, just south of Rossio, **Elevador de Santa Justa** ① *Daily 0900-2100*, ▉, *€1.50*, is one of Lisbon's most iconic and memorable images. Designed by an apostle of Eiffel, Raoul Mesnier du Ponsard, the 45-m vertical wrought-iron structure was built to link the Baixa with Largo do Carmo, via a 25-m walkway.

Alfama

Alfama is Lisbon's spiritual heart. It's the old Moorish quarter where ribbons of alleyways coil into blind alleys and crooked alcoves. Dominating the skyline is the iconic, if a little Disneyfied, **Castelo de São Jorge**. Ancient trams take you to **Miradouros de Santa Luzia** and **Largo Portas de Sol** from where the view of city below is breathtaking. The pristine baroque **Panteão Nacional de Santa Engrácia** and the twin bell towers of the **Igreja de São Vicente da Fora** rise amidst clusters of squat houses stacked on top of each other. Encircling the

European City Breaks Lisbon

⊖ Travel essentials

Getting there Lisbon's **Portela Airport**, T21-841 3700, www.ana-aeroportos.pt, is 6½ km from the city centre. The **AeroBus** is the cheapest and most convenient way to reach the city centre, departing every 20 mins (0745-2045) making stops en route, including Saldanha, Marquês de Pombal, Praça dos Restauradores, and arriving in Rossio in around 20-25 mins, before terminating at Cais do Sodré railway terminal. A ticket costs €3.50 and is valid on the transport network for 1 day. Buses 8, 22, 44 and 83 also operate 0600-2130 to the centre, and bus 45 runs until 0010 from outside the Cais de Sodré terminal. Bus 5 links the airport to Oriente Station. A taxi to the city centre costs €12-15 on the meter or €13 for a pre-paid taxi voucher bought in the terminal.

Getting around Most of the main sights of the Baixa, Bairro Alto, Chiado and Alfama can be reached on foot but there's also an efficient network of orange buses run by **Carris**, T21-361 3000, www.carris.pt. A *simple* (1-way) ticket bought on board costs €1.30. A ride on one of Lisbon's ancient emblematic trams is the most enjoyable way to get around. Tram 28 is an unofficial tourist tram (single €1.15; buy tickets on board). The new super tram No 15, runs from Praça da Figueira to Belém and then on to Ajuda Palace. Bright yellow Carris booths provide maps of bus and tram routes. Lisbon's metro, with 4 lines, is fast and efficient. It's best used if you are going to the north and west of the old city. A rechargeable card, '**7 Colinas**' costs an initial €0.50 and

can then be credited to cover Carris buses and trams (eg 5 day fare €3.65, 10 day fare €6.85) or the entire network including the metro (urban single €1.15; network single €1.50, 1-day network €3.35). Taxis are cheap; a trip from Rossio to the northern suburbs should be no more than €5. Fares are higher after 2200. There are ranks near Baixa-Chiado Metro station and Largo de Camões, or call **Radio Taxis**, T21-792756.

Tourist information The main office is the **Lisboa Welcome Centre**, Praça do Comércio, T21-031 2810, www.visit lisboa.com, daily 0900-2000, with other information points around the city. **Ask me Lisboa**, www.askmelisboa.com, has information on sports, the arts, palaces and museums.

church on Saturday or Tuesday is the 'thieves' **flea market**, Feira da Ladra; buy your own piece of crumbling Lisbon, a fireman's T-shirt, or a traditional basket. Surrounded by seafood restaurants, tour group-orientated fado houses and neighbourhood grocers, the **Casa do Fado e da Guitarra Portuguesa** ⓘ *Largo do Chafariz de Dentro, 1, T21-882 3470,* ▣B4*, daily 1000-1300 and 1400-1800, €2.50,* tells the history of the national song. A short bus ride away, set in the tranquil Madre de Deus Convent, the **Museu Nacional do Azulejo** ⓘ *Rua de Madre de Deus 4, T21-810 0340, www .mnazulejo-ipmuseus.pt, Tue 1400-1800, Wed-Sun 1000-1800, €3, free on Sun 1000-1400,* houses the finest collection of *azulejo* tiles in the country. For more authentic exposure to Portugal's art forms, stroll around earthy **Mouraria** to the north, the cradle of fado, or **Graça**, to the northwest, where fragments of lustrous 16th-century *azulejos* peel from façades.

Chiado

In Chiado, 19th-century old-world elegance prevails. **Rua Garrett** is studded with high fashion boutiques

Café A Brasileira

Elevador da Glória

and art nouveau jewellery stores. The literary legacy of cryptic genius Fernando Pessoa still hangs in the air, his spirit immortalized in stone at Café A Brasileira (see page 138). Devastated by fire in 1988, Chiado has been born again and now SoHo-style wrought-iron architecture is juxtaposed with the rococo elegance of the **Teatro Nacional de Sao Carlos** ⓘ *Rua Serpa Pinto, 9, T21-325 3045/6, www.saocarlos.pt,* ▣B2.

From Rua Garrett, Calçado do Sacramento leads to the peaceful **Largo do Carmo**, site of one of the most enigmatic buildings in the city, the cavernous **Convento do Carmo** ⓘ *T21-347 8629,* ▣A2*, Oct-Apr Mon-Sat 1000- 1700, May-Sep Mon-Sat 1000-1800, €3.* Heading south along Rua Serpa Pinto towards the river, the **Museu do Chiado** ⓘ *T21-343 2148, www.museodochiado -ipmuseus.pt,* ▣B2*, Tue-Sun 1000-1800, €3, free on Sun 1000-1400,* is one of the finest exhibition spaces for Portugal's 19th- and 20th-century artists.

Bairro Alto

In Lisbon's 'High Town', peeling doorways reveal sleek bars, gritty *tascas*

and fado houses. Seductive samba mingles with deep techno and black-shawled divas sing out the nation's woes. Here you'll also find baroque magnificence in the Jesuit **Igreja de São Roque** ⓘ *Largo Trindade Coelho, T21-323 5381,* ▣A1*, Tue-Sun 1000-1700, museum €1.50, free Sun,* and exotic gardens at the **Jardim Botânico** ⓘ *Rua da Escola Politécnica, www.jb.ul.pt,* ▣A1*, May-Oct 0900-2000, Nov-Apr daily 0900- 1900, €1.50.* Connecting the Baixa with Bairro Alto, the **Elevador da Glória** wheezes up to the stunning Miradouro de São Pedro de Alcântara.

On the southern edge of the Bairro Alto, Santa Catarina has some of the most endearing streets in the city. The **Miradouro de Santa Catarina** offers views across the Tagus and, from 2008, will be the new site of the acclaimed **Design and Fashion Museum (MuDe)**, which is moving from its current home in the Centro Cultural de Belém. Call T21-361 2400 for further information.

Belém

Belém, spreading west along the banks of the inky blue Tagus, is a tremendous heap of 15th- and 16th-century marvels,

Monument to the Discoveries, Belém

About 30 km from Lisbon is the UNESCO World Heritage site of Sintra. Poets have raved and pagans have revelled in its Elysian Fields, recaptured from the Moors in 1147. It's an ethereal landscape where castles rise from emerald mountain ranges. On sloping terraces, carpeted with lush pine forests, erupts a rhapsody of Bavarian kitsch in the form of the slapstick **Palácio da Pena** ⓘ *T21-910 5340, Jul-mid Sep Tue-Sun 1000- 1900; mid Sep-Jun Tue-Sun 1000-1730, last entry 30 mins before closing, €7*, the epitome of 19th-century decadence. In the valley are the cobble-stone streets and Moorish courtyards of **Sintra Vila**, the old quarter – all very chocolate box, but nonetheless alluring. The tourist magnet, however, is the sublime **Palácio Nacional** ⓘ *Largo Rainha D Amélia, T21-910 6840, Thu-Tue 1000-1730, last admission 30 mins before closing, €4*, a 14th-century royal palace steeped in Arabian myths and the imprint of cavorting kings. Trains run from Sete Rios to Sintra every 15 minutes (journey time 45 minutes; €3.60 return). The Scotturb bus No 434 runs every 20 minutes from Sintra train station through Sintra Vila to the Palácio da Pena (€4.50). A combined one-day train and bus ticket costs €12. It takes a good hour to walk up to the palace. For further information visit the tourist office at Sintra station, www.cm-sintra.pt, daily 0900-1900.

built to celebrate Vasco da Gama's discovery of the sea route to India. It is also one of the loveliest places in the city. There are breezy riverside walkways, super-sleek yachts, coloured fishing boats, and kites and frisbies flying across expansive parks. The **Mosteiro dos Jerónimos** ⓘ *Praça do Império, T21-362 0034, www.mosteiro jeronimos.pt, Oct- Apr Tue-Sun 1000-1700, May-Sep Tue-Sun 1000-1830, church free, cloisters €4.50, free Sun 1000-1400*, astounds with its sublime cloister where fantastical sea creatures and maritime emblems writhe in milky stone. By the river, the **Torre de Belém** ⓘ *Av de Brasília, T21-362 0034, Oct-Apr Tue-Sun 1000-1700, May-Sep Tue-Sun 1000-1830, €3, free Sun 1000-1400*, looks more like a chess piece washed ashore than a defensive fort.

Museu Calouste Gulbenkian

ⓘ *Av da Berna, 45a, T21-782 3461, www.gulbenkian.pt. Tue-Sun 1000-1800. €3, free Sun. Metro São Sebastião.*

Lisbon's number one attraction, as monumental in its scope as in its quality, is the Museu Calouste Gulbenkian, lying in its own serene, 17-acre garden and housing an outstanding collection of Western and Eastern art of the major periods from 2800 BC onwards.

Also north of the city centre is the decorative art museum, **Casa-Museu Dr Anastácio Gonçalves** ⓘ *Av 5 de Outubro, 6 e 8, T21-354 0823,*

Parque das Nações

www.cmag-ipmuseus.pt, Tue 1400-1800, Wed-Sun 1000-1800, €3, Metro Saldanha/Picoas. It's worth visiting for its swirling art nouveau façade alone.

Parque das Nações

This industrial wasteland has been transformed into a modernist playground, united by the theme 'The Oceans, a Heritage for the Future'. Cable cars glide up to the city's highest viewpoint, the **Torre de Vasco da Gama** ⓘ *Cais das Naus, T21-891 8000, daily 1000-2000, €2.50.*

The **Oceanarium** ⓘ *T21-891 7002, www.oceanario.pt, Mar-Oct 1000-1900, Nov-Mar 1000-1900, last entry 1 hr before closing, €10.50*, is the largest in Europe and there also the **Interactive Science museum** (Pavilhão do Conhecimento Ciência Viva) ⓘ *Alameda dos Oceanos, T21-891 7100, www.pav conhecimento.pt, Tue-Fri 1000-1800, Sat-Sun and holidays 1100-1900, €6.*

Sleeping

The most idiosyncratic places to stay are in Alfama, with its charming guest houses, arty *pensões* and a few sleeker 4-star options. Bairro Alto is in the heart of the night-time action. Many rooms overlook Rossio and Praça da Figueira, but this area is noisy. Avenida da Liberdade has most of the really swanky choices.

€€€ Le Meridien Park Atlantic, Rua Castilho, off Parque Eduardo VII 149, T21-381 8700, www.starwood hotels.com/lemeridien. Contemporary rooms and the highest standards. Sweeping views out over the Tagus.

€€ Hotel Lisboa Plaza, Travessa Salitre 7, off Av da Liberdade, T21-321 8218, www.heritage.pt. A warm hotel with an understated, luxurious atmosphere and a home-from-home feel.

€€ Hotel Metrópole, Praça do Rossio, 30, T21-321 9030, www.almeida hotels.com. Unrivalled views over Rossio, a stately 1920s classic with characterful rooms. Great value.

€ Pensão Ninho das Águias, Costa do Castelo, 74, Alfama, T21-885 4070. Just below the walls of Castelo de São Jorge is one of the best *pensãos* in the city. Comfortable rooms, some en suite. Proud owner Luís is utterly charming and devoted to the history of the place and the city in general.

€ Pensão Residencial Santa Catarina, Rua Dr Luís de Almeida e Albuquerque, 6, T21-346 6106. This temple to 1960s kitsch is just 10 mins from Bairro Alto bars and restaurants on a tranquil and picturesque street.

Eating

Chiado offers Portuguese traditional cuisine, Alfama is fado tour group territory and Bairro Alto has hip food, soul food, Portuguese staples and polycultural delicacies. Dinner is eaten late; in Bairro Alto restaurants stay open until around 0200.

††† Gambrinus, Rua Portas de Santo Antão 23e 25, Baixa, T21-342 1466. Daily 1200-0130. One of Portugal's best seafood restaurants and a local institution. Tantalizing flavours, served by knowledgeable and friendly staff.

†† Alfaia, Travessa da Queimada 22, Bairro Alto, T21-346 1232. Mon-Sat 1200-1630, 1830-0200, Sun 1830-0200. A refined Bairro Alto restaurant with international-style cuisine and superb traditional Portuguese dishes. Very popular at weekends. Booking advised.

> **❝❞ Bairro Alto is the best place to kickstart an evening. Its cobbled streets hold hundreds of bars, eateries and clubs.**

†† Bota Alta, Travessa da Queimada 35, Bairro Alto, T21-342 7959. Mon-Fri 1200-1430, 1900-2245, Sat 1900-2245. Eccentric wood-panelled tavern with a faultless repertoire of Portuguese classics. Favourites include steak in red wine and cod with port and sausages.

††† Casa do Alentejo, Rua das Porta de S Antão 58, Baixa, T21-346 9231. Daily 1200-1430, 1900-2200. Cross the Arab patio to this gem, serving delicacies from the Alentejo region.

† Antiga Pastelaria de Belém, Rua de Belém 90. Daily 0800-2300. Around 10,000 salivating locals come to worship each day at the shrine of the most famous bakery in Portugal. The best way to spend €0.75 in Lisbon.

† Café A Brasileira, Rua Garrett, Chiado, T21-8346 9541. Mon-Fri 0800-0000, Sat and Sun 0800-0200. The best place for a *bica* and *pastel de nata*. The former stomping ground of Lisbon's literati is now a popular gay meeting point.

† Café Martinho da Arcada, Praça do Comércio, 3, T21-886 6213. Mon-Sat 0800-2300. The oldest café in Lisbon, dating from 1782, is an essential stop on the trail of Fernando Pessoa. There's an expensive restaurant or you can simply order a *bica* and a *pastel de nata*.

Nightlife

Bairro Alto is the best place to kickstart an evening. Its cobbled streets hold hundreds of bars, eateries, clubs and shops. Start along the main Rua da Atalaia and explore down-to-earth *tascas*, sleek gay joints (**Frágil**, **Sétimo Céu**), jazz bars (**Catacombas**), lounge clubs (**Suave**, **Clube da Esquina**) and funky discos (**Bicaense**) that come to life after 2200. Miradouro de Santa Catarina has the best views, on the terrace or at the new **Noo Bai** rooftop bar. **B.leza** has the best African rhythms, with live music every night in Largo Conde Barão. Av 24 de Julho holds the larger, more commercial venues, like **Kremlin** or **Kapital** with pop-rock and house. East of 25th April Bridge, the Docas district of renovated warehouses on a marina has bars and clubs serving up latino sounds and tall drinks. Finally, *the* nightclub of Lisbon, **Lux**, (www.luxfragil.com), in the docks opposite Santa Apolonia train, is high-tech and spacious and offers the best in DJs, concerts, performance and video.

Finding authentic fado is tricky. Still, you can stumble across raucous amateur *fado vadio*, with no formal programme, only an orgy of emotional catharsis.

You'd be forgiven for not being entirely sure where Ljubljana is. The tiny Slovenian capital only recently caught the eye of international travellers. But like an awkward teenager who's suddenly discovered she's pretty, Ljubljana is basking in her new-found attention. The feel today is one of self-assured sophistication – the tight grid of cobbled streets and baroque townhouses is filled with trendy bars, slick museums, fashion-conscious boutiques and stylish restaurants. In summer, life spills outdoors and jazz and late-night chatter drift out over the mint-green River Ljubljanica. Some good museums and an animated cultural scene add to the air of refinement, although the delicious (and ludicrously cheap) beer is set to become a major draw. Just be sure to get there soon – before the stag parties arrive.

Ljubljana

Arts & culture
★★★

Eating
★★★

Nightlife
★★

Outdoors
★★★★

Romance
★★★★

Shopping
★★

Sightseeing
★★★

Value for money
★★★★★

Overall score
★★★

⦿ Sights

The social and historical heart of the city is **Prešernov trg**; just a few metres from the banks of River Ljubljanica, it's a lively hub where locals congregate in open-air cafés. Flanking the north of the square is the rust-red Franciscan church, with the proud statue of France Prešeren, Slovenia's greatest poet. Stroll southeast from Prešeren's feet and you'll come to Ljubljana's most photographed landmark, the **Triple Bridge**, designed by Jože Plečnik, grand architect and the city's equivalent to Barcelona's Gaudí. The three-pronged bridge crosses the narrow river to the Old Town. Turn left on the other side towards the elegant **Market Colonnade**, also designed by Plečnik, a grand curve of pale stone filled with food shops. The two squares fronting it are taken over by a bustling daily **market** and, at the far end, stands

Triple Bridge

the portly bulk of **St Nicholas's Cathedral** ⓘ *daily 0600-1200, 1500-1800,* 🚌**A3**, (look out for the rather spooky brass doors); the inside is awash with frescoes.

Dragon Bridge curves back over to the left bank, but retracing your steps brings you to **Mestni trg**, or Town Square, known for its baroque Town Hall

and the ornate **Fountain of the Three Carniolan Rivers**, created in 1751 by Francis Robba. The cobbled streets of the **Old Town** wind south from here, past Shoemaker's Bridge, site of a Sunday **flea market**, with **Ljubljana Castle** ⓘ *May-Sep daily 0900-2100, Oct-Apr 1000-1800,* 🚌**B3**, *€4.59*, towering to the east. Turn left onto Ulica Na Grad and follow the steep path to the top of **Castle Hill**; a funicular is being built, and a tourist train runs from Prešernov trg if you'd rather not walk. The castle itself is an impressive medieval hulk, with panoramic views from its tower and a 3D multimedia show of the city's history.

Back on the other side of the river, **Kongresni trg** is a leafy square flanked by the University Building and the Slovene Philharmonic, from where it's a quick stroll to the **City Museum** ⓘ *Tue-Sun 1000-1800,* 🚌**B3**, *€2.10, free with Ljubljana card.* The displays are still being developed and include the history of Ljubljana in six thematic

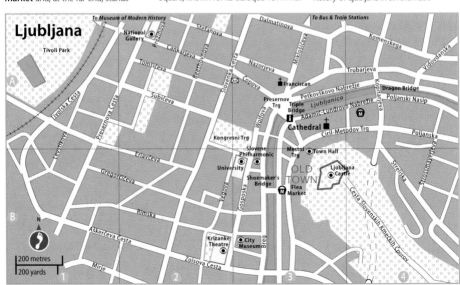

Ljubljana

sections, including its role as a centre of creativity.

Northwest of here is the **National Gallery** ① *Tue-Sun 1000-1800, www.ng-slo.si*,  *€4.20*, an ugly post-modernist lump tacked onto a Habsberg-era edifice, filled with excellent examples of Slovenian impressionists, including Ivan Grohar and Ivana Kobilca. Two blocks west is **Tivoli Park**, a lush summer playground of rolling lawns and forests, where you'll find the **Museum of Modern History** ① *Daily 1000-1800, €3.34*, housed in the bubblegum-pink Cekin Castle. It has good displays on 20th-century Slovenia.

Ljubljana Castle

⊝ Travel essentials

Getting there Brnik Aerodrome, T04-206 1000, www.lju-airport.si, is 23 km from the city centre. Buses run to the main bus terminal Mon-Fri 0520-2010, and Sat and Sun 0700-2000, taking 45 mins. A taxi costs around €25. International **rail** services link the city with Munich, Venice and Zagreb.

Getting around The best way of getting around Ljubljana is on foot; all the sights are within easy walking distance of each other. Bicycles are available for rent from Plečnikov trg, the main railway station, Tivoli railway station and Bavarski dvor square, Apr-Oct only. Buses run all over the city but the routes and schedule are confusing. The flat fare is €0.79, payable as tokens sold in newsagents' kiosks; a day ticket costs €3.75.

Tourist information The main office is Adamič Lundrovo nabrežje 2, T01-306 1215, www.ljubljana-tourism.si. Jun-Sep daily 0800-2100, Oct-May daily 0800-1900, with free maps and guides, and can book accommodation. The Ljubljana card (3 days, €12.52) offers free city bus travel and free or discounted admission to many sights.

⊜ Sleeping

€€€ Grand Hotel Union, Miklosiceva 3, T01-308 1170, www.gh-union.si. The city's grande dame and the most elegant place to stay in Ljubljana. It has a great central location and fabulous views towards the castle.
€€ City Hotel, Dalmatinova 15, T01-234 9130, www.cityhotel.si. A modern business hotel near Presernov trg, with functional rooms and a huge breakfast.
€ Celica, Metelkova 8, T01-230 9700, www.hostelcelica.com. An excellent hostel in a converted military prison, with dorms and doubles in the old cells. It's stylish and comfortable, with a great café and chill-out area downstairs.

⊘ Eating

††† **Gostlina As**, Čopova 5, T01-425 8822. A romantic fish restaurant with candlelit tables under plane trees and a cosy, vaulted interior. There's no menu; instead the waiters tell you what's on offer and recommend a wine to accompany it.
††† **Spajza**, Gornji Trg 20, T01-425 3094. Charming restaurant with a series of intimate rooms, popular with locals. Serves a good range of Mediterranean-style dishes.
†† **Gostlina Sokol**, Ciril Metodov trb 18, T01-439 6855. A labyrinthine Slovenian restaurant attracting its share of tour groups but serving authentic local food, including fresh trout from the Julian Alps, sausages and dumplings.
† **Abecedarium Café**, Ribji trg 2, T01-426 9514. Popular café in the oldest house in the city – once home to Primoz Trubar, the father of Slovenian literature. Good for late breakfasts, salads, steaks and cold cuts.
† **Zvezda Café**, Kongresni trg. A famous café serving a delectable array of cream cakes, tortes and pastries, with views over the grassy square.

⊛ Nightlife

During the summer, locals flock to the bars and cafés lining the Ljubljanica; you have to find a table wherever you can. Ljubljana's young and hip take to the city's clubs from around 2400 – the scene changes rapidly. A favourite choice with a lovely terrace is **Global**, Tomsiceva 1, T01-426 9017. The slick **Opera Bar**, Cankarjevo cesta 12, T01-421 0390, is popular with Ljubljana's smart set and stays open late. There's Australian-inspired artwork, squishy sofas and cocktails.

Chamber recitals
Between Jul and Sep the open-air Krizanke theatre hosts the **Ljubljana Summer Festival**, www.festival-lj.si, with weekend jazz performances and concerts from the Slovenian Philharmonic.

London

Somewhat to its own surprise, London is still one of the world's great cities. It's not the loveliest in the world, nor the most antique, romantic, or mysterious. Far from exotic, it's not the richest, largest, or even the most happening place on the planet either. Notwithstanding all of this, it's still impossible to resist. Civilized, improvised, sophisticated and alive, London wins all comers over in the end. A workaday, endlessly surprising mess, very much the capital of the UK, and very British, it's also a global town that has grown up thanks to other nations. Neither ancient nor modern, though erudite and grand, much of it hardly feels like a proper city at all. It's not Gotham or even Paris. The Romans, who founded Londinium in the first century AD, failed to impose any kind of order on its street plan, and no one has succeeded since. In fact London's streets, despite their enormous extent, are small, haphazard and human in scale. But they hold a world of artistic wonder within their mixed-up planning. London still does tradition, with its Tower, Buckingham Palace and Trooping the Colour, but there's a new London too: the London Eye, Tate Modern, Millennium Bridge, even the ill-fated Millennium Dome, and the new-found self-confidence afforded by the successful Olympic bid. With such magnificent trees, river views and murky weather, with its thriving culture and driven soul, like nowhere else on earth this teeming muddle works its way into your heart.

Arts & culture
★★★★★

Eating
★★★★★

Nightlife
★★★★★

Outdoors
★★★

Romance
★★★

Shopping
★★★★★

Sightseeing
★★★★★

Value for money
★★

Overall score
★★★★★

At a glance

Trafalgar Square is the centre of London. **The Strand** runs east out of the square from **Whitehall** and **Westminster**, the seat of central government, to the **City**, east of St Paul's Cathedral. Just north of the Strand is **Covent Garden** and, to the northwest of Trafalgar Square, **Leicester Square** and **Shaftesbury Avenue** are the showbiz centre of the West End with **Chinatown** next door. **Soho** is the West End's late-night party zone, with **Oxford Street** forming its northern boundary. West of Regent Street, **Mayfair** remains the swankiest end of town with the gentleman's clubland and royal stamping ground of **St James's** next door. Beyond Piccadilly Circus, **Piccadilly** heads west to Hyde Park Corner with panache. West of here, **Knightsbridge** and **South Kensington** boast luxury shopping and a trio of great museums. **Regent's Park** and **London Zoo** are northeast of Hyde Park, above **Marylebone** with its low-brow tourist attractions around **Baker**

> **New York is a great city, no question, but it will never be as pretty as London.**
>
> *Woody Allen*

Street. **Bloomsbury**, to the east, is the academic heart of London, home to the British Museum. Further east are **Holborn**, with its Law Courts, and buzzing **Clerkenwell**. South of the river, **Southwark**, **Bankside** and **Borough** are laden with attractions and reached from St Paul's across the Millennium Bridge, or along the river from the **South Bank** and the London Eye. Out in the East End, some of London's most happening nightlife is in **Shoreditch**, **Hoxton**, **Brick Lane** and **Spitalfields**, while **Greenwich**, across the river from **Docklands**, has the National Maritime Museum and Royal Observatory.

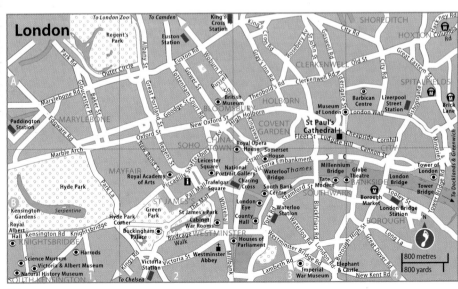

24 hours in the city

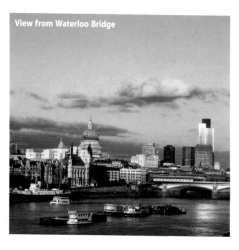

In order to see as much of London as possible in a day, it's best to avoid public transport. An easy three-mile stroll takes in several of the major sights. From **Trafalgar Square**, walk down Northumberland Avenue to the Embankment and cross over the Golden Jubilee footbridge to the **South Bank**, from where there are great views of Big Ben and Houses of Parliament. Unless you want a closer look at the attractions of **County Hall**, turn left to walk along the river, past the Royal Festival Hall and **Waterloo Bridge**, to **Tate Modern** and Shakespeare's **Globe Theatre** before heading over the Millennium Footbridge to **St Paul's Cathedral**. After a look around St Paul's, the restaurants and clubs of **Clerkenwell** and **Smithfield** or **Shoreditch** are close at hand for an evening's entertainment.

★ *Don't leave town without taking a walk over Waterloo Bridge – preferably at sunset.*

⊖ Travel essentials

Getting there London Heathrow Airport, T0870-000 0123 (Heathrow Travelcare T020-8745 7495), is 15 miles west of central London. Piccadilly Line tube trains run every 5-9 mins (roughly 0630-0100), journey time 50 mins. Heathrow Express, T0845-600 1515, www.heathrowexpress.co.uk, runs to Paddington Station, every 15 mins (0510-2340), journey time 15 mins, £14.50 single, £27 return. A black cab costs £45-50 (45 mins-1 hr). **London Gatwick Airport**, T0870-000 2468, 28 miles south of the capital. Gatwick Express, T0845- 850 1530, to and from London Victoria every 15 mins (hourly at night), £14 single, £25 return. Taxi around £70, about 1 hr. **London Luton Airport**, T01582-405100, 30 miles north of central London. Regular trains to and from London Bridge, Blackfriars, Farringdon and King's Cross stations. A taxi takes 50 mins and costs around £55. **Stansted Airport**, T0870-000 0303,

35 miles northeast. Stansted Express, T08458-500150, every 15 mins to Liverpool Street, 45 mins, £15 single, £25 open return. A taxi takes 1-1½ hrs and costs about £75.

There are 4 main train stations: King's Cross from Scotland and northeast England; Euston from the northwest; Paddington from Wales and the west; and Waterloo International for **Eurostar**, www.eurostar.com, from France and Belgium. From November 2007, Eurostar will operate from the new St Pancras International station. For train times and ticket prices call **National Rail Enquiries**, T08457-484950, or www.qjump.co.uk.

Getting around London's public transport network consists of buses and the underground (known as the Tube). It is fairly efficient, but expensive. Single Tube fares in Zone 1 (most of central London) cost £3, and single bus fares £1.50. Daily travelcards, for buses and the Tube, cost £6 (peak) and £4.70

(off-peak). Or buy an Oyster card, for the cheaper single fares on public transport. For 24-hr information on public transport and tickets call T020-7222 1234, or visit www.tfl.gov.uk. The Tube is faster, but buses are good for sightseeing as you travel around town. Car drivers must pay a congestion charge (£8) in central London Mon-Fri 0700-1830; see the website above.

Tourist information Britain and **London Visitor Centre (BLVC)**, 1 Lower Regent St, SW1 (Piccadilly Circus tube), Mon 0930-0630, Tue-Fri 0900-0630, Sat-Sun 1000-1600; Jun-Sep Sat 0900-1700, Sun 1000-1600. **London Information Centre**, in Leicester Sq, T020-7292 2333, www.london town.com, daily 0800-2300. **City Information Centre**, St Paul's Churchyard, south side of the cathedral, T020-7332 1456, Apr-Sep daily 0930-1700; Oct-Mar Mon-Fri 0930-1700, Sat 0930-1230.

◉ Sights

Trafalgar Square
ⓘ *WC2. Tube Charing Cross,*
Leicester Sq, **B2**.

Trafalgar Square is the centre of London,
avoided by Londoners whenever
possible, unless they want to make their
voices heard at demonstrations and
celebrations. Linked to Westminster and
Parliament by the breadth of Whitehall,
this is where the administrative offices
of government meet the people.
Nelson's Column, **Landseer's lions**
and the two large fountains give the
square some dignity, inspiring a sense
of occasion. The pedestrianization
of the north side of the square
has transformed access to the
National Gallery ⓘ *T020-7747 2885,*
www.nationalgallery.org.uk, **B2**,
daily 1000-1800, Wed 1000-2100, free,
guided tours from Sainsbury Wing
Level 0 daily at 1130 and 1430, also Wed
1800 and 1830, Sat 1230 and 1530, one of
the world's most comprehensive fine
art collections, with more than 2000
Western European paintings dating
from the 13th century to 1900. Behind

Trafalgar Square

Westminster Abbey

it is the **National Portrait Gallery**
ⓘ *St Martin's Pl, T020-7306 0055, ext 216,*
www.npg.org.uk, **B2**, *Mon- Wed,*
Sat-Sun 1000-1800, Thu-Fri 1000-2100,
*free.*These two treasure houses are the
best reasons for a visit to the square.

Westminster Abbey
ⓘ *SW1, information and tours T020-7654*
4834, www.westminster-abbey.org, **B2**.
Mon- Fri 0930-1645 (last admission 1545),
Sat 0930-1445 (last admission 1345).
Sun entry is for services only. £10.
Tube Westminster.

A surprisingly small church for one
of such enormous significance to
the Anglican faith and British state,
Westminster Abbey's charm lies in its age
(the oldest part is 13th century). That said,
once inside, the length and especially the
height (over 30½ m) of the nave are
awe-inspiring. Highlights include the
Coronation Chair, made to order for
Edward I and used to crown every
English monarch except three since 1308;
Henry VII's Chapel (or Lady Chapel),
dating from the early 16th century; and
Poet's Corner, with its monuments to
Shakespeare, Chaucer and other poets

and actors, as well as scientists, architects
and historians.

Buckingham Palace and St James's Park
ⓘ *T020-7766 7300, www.royal.gov.uk.*
Aug-Sep daily 0945-1800, **B2**. *£15.*
Tube Green Park, St James's Park,
Hyde Park Corner.

The Queen's official London residence
is open to the paying public for two
months of the year and, despite the
high admission prices, long queues and
disappointing tour, it attracts thousands
of people from all over the world. Next
door to the palace visitors' entrance and
open year round, the **Queen's Gallery**
ⓘ *T020-7766 7301, daily 1000-1730*
(last admission 1630), £7.50, displays
changing selections from the
Queen's collection of Old Masters
and portraiture, an extraordinary array
founded by Charles II. The **Changing
of the Guard** takes place daily on the
Palace forecourt at 1130 from 1 April
to the end of July and on alternate
days for the rest of the year.

   St James's Park, stretching out east
from the palace, is the finest and most
carefully laid out of the Royal parks

Buckingham Palace

(others include Hyde Park, Green Park, Regent's Park and Kensington Gardens). A wander around reveals surprising but carefully orchestrated vistas at every turn. Guided tours are given by its warden from April to September.

South Kensington Museums

ⓘ *SW7. Tube South Kensington,* **B1**.

Although they are located tantalisingly close together, the temptation to 'do' all three of these great museums in a day should definitely be resisted. Even two could prove too rich a treat.

The **Science Museum** ⓘ *Exhibition Rd, T0870-870 4868, www.science museum.org.uk, daily 1000-1800, free,* prides itself on being one of the most forward-thinking, interactive and accessible museums in the country. The Wellcome Wing is particularly worth visiting, with its four floors dedicated to cutting- edge science, incorporating an IMAX cinema and the first Virtual Voyage simulator in Europe.

The **Natural History Museum** ⓘ *Cromwell Rd, T020-7942 5000, www.nhm.ac.uk, daily 1000-1750, free,* housed in an extraordinary orange and blue terracotta building, is an academic

Natural History Museum

research institution that is now seriously fun packed. Divided into Life Galleries and Earth Galleries, it tells the history of our planet through a not entirely successful combination of venerable artefacts and playschool attractions. Children and adults are sure to learn something about the natural world. It never disappoints.

The **Victoria and Albert Museum** ⓘ *Cromwell Rd, T0870-906 3883, www.vam.ac.uk, Thu-Tue 1000-1745, Wed 1000-2200 (last Fri of the month 1000-2200), free,* is one of the world's greatest museums. Surprisingly, considering its grand façade, it wears that greatness lightly. It was founded in 1857 with the aim of educating the populace in the appreciation of decorative art and design by exhibiting superb examples of these. Not a narrow nationalistic enterprise, its remarkable collection was gathered, like the British Museum's, from all corners of the globe.

British Museum

ⓘ *Great Russell St, WC1, T020-7323 8000, www.thebritishmuseum.ac.uk,* **A2**. *Sat-Wed 1000-1730, Thu-Fri 1000-2030*

(late view of main floor and some upper floor galleries only); Great Court Mon-Wed 0900-2100, Thu-Sat 0900-2300, Sun 0900-1800. Free (donations appreciated), prices of temporary exhibitions vary. Tube Tottenham Court Rd.

Open to the public for free since 1753, the British Museum is one of the world's greatest cultural institutions. Norman Foster's redevelopment of the **Great Court** in 2000 turned the museum's long-hidden central quadrangle into the largest covered square in Europe. A beautiful lattice-work canopy of 3312 unique panes of glass wraps itself around the dome of the famous **Reading Room**, free-standing once again at the heart of the museum.

On entering the Great Court from the south, pick up a floorplan and get your bearings. Head to the **west wing** for Ancient Egypt, the Ancient Near East and Ancient Greece; the **east wing** for the Enlightenment and the King's Library; and the **north wing** for ethnography, Asia and the Americas. The upper floors are devoted to Ancient Rome, Europe, prehistory, Ancient Egypt, the Ancient Near East and the Japanese

Science Museum

British Museum

and Korean collections. It would be quite impossible to see everything in one day, so, apart from the guided and audio tours, it's worth joining one of the free daily 30- to 40-minute EyeOpener Gallery Talks.

St Paul's Cathedral

ⓘ T020-7236 4128, www.stpauls.co.uk, ⓈA3. Mon-Sat 0830-1600 (phone to check before visiting). £9 including cathedral crypt and galleries. Organ recitals Sun 1700, free. Tube St Paul's.

Standing proud at the top of Ludgate Hill is St Paul's Cathedral. At least the fifth church on the site, it was started in 1675 and took about 35 years to complete. Hemmed in by other buildings, Sir Christopher Wren's relatively colossal church still impresses. The redevelopment of Paternoster Square has opened up new views of St Paul's, reflecting its cleaned Portland stone in plate-glass office blocks, while the **Millennium Bridge** now provides a neat approach from Tate Modern (page 149). It's definitely worth climbing up to the **Whispering Gallery**, around the base of the inner dome, and then continuing up the dizzying cast-iron stairway to the

St Paul's Cathedral

British Airways London Eye

open-air **Golden Gallery** to soak up the tremendous wraparound views.

South Bank

ⓘ SE1. Tube Westminster, Waterloo, ⓈB3.

The **British Airways London Eye** ⓘ T0870-500 0600, www.ba-london eye.com, ⓈB3, Jun-Sep daily 1000-2100, Oct-May daily 1000-2000, £13.50, private capsule £385 (advance booking available online), is the vast spoked white observation wheel beside Westminster Bridge that dominates the London skyline. Well over 100 m in diameter, it's visible from unexpected places all around the city. There's no denying its novelty value or even, perhaps, its beauty. The half-hour 'flight' in one of its surprisingly roomy capsules, moving at 25 cm per second, provides superb 25-mile views over the city and is neither vertiginous nor at all boring.

Next door to the Eye, the magisterial **County Hall** now houses the highly acclaimed **London Aquarium** ⓘ T020-7967 8000, www.londonaquarium.co.uk, ⓈB3, daily 1000-1800 (last admission 1700), £11.75, while downstream is the **South Bank Centre**, the largest arts

◉ Best of the rest

Royal Academy of Arts ⓘ Piccadilly, T020-7300 8000, ⓈB2. Mon-Thu, Sat and Sun 1000-1800, Fri 1000-2030. Attention-grabbing exhibitions of contemporary art.
Cabinet War Rooms ⓘ King Charles St, T020-7930 6961, ⓈB2. Daily 0930-1800 (last admission 1700). £11. Nerve centre of Churchill's morale-boosting war effort.
London Zoo ⓘ Regent's Park, T020-7722 3333, www.zsl.org. Summer daily 1000-1730, winter daily 1000-1630 (last admission 1 hr before closing). £13.50.
Museum of London ⓘ 150 London Wall, T0870-444 3852, events T020-7814 5777, www.museumoflondon.org.uk, ⓈA3. Mon-Sat 1000-1750, Sun 1200-1750. Free. A refreshing visual approach to the social history of the city.
Imperial War Museum ⓘ Lambeth Rd, T020-7416 5320, www.iwm.org.uk, ⓈB3. Daily 1000-1800. Free. Dedicated to the history and consequences of all 20th-century warfare.
Somerset House ⓘ Strand, T020-7845 4600, www.somerset-house.org.uk, ⓈB3. Daily 1000-1800 (last admission 1715). 1 collection £5, any 2 collections £8, all 3 £12. An ice rink in winter and fine art and antiques all year in the Courtauld and Gilbert Collections or Hermitage Rooms.
Tate Britain ⓘ T020-7887 8888, www.tate.org.uk/britain. Daily 1000-1750, free, but special exhibitions £10. Ancient and contemporary British art.

complex of its kind in Europe. Apart from the main Royal Festival Hall (page 152), it also houses other concert venues, an exhibition space, the Poetry Library, the National Theatre (page 152), the National Film Theatre (page 151) and the cutting-edge **Hayward Gallery** ⓘ T020-7928 3144, www.hayward .org.uk, Mon, Thu, Sat and Sun 1000-1800, Tue-Wed 1000-2000, Fri 1000-2100, £5.

Tate Modern

ⓘ Bankside, SE1, ticket bookings T020-7887 8888; information T020-7887 8008, www.tate.org.uk, ◉B3 . Sun-Thu 1000-1800, Fri and Sat 1000-2200 (last admission 45 mins before closing). Free (charges for special exhibitions around £7). Tube Southwark or Blackfriars.

Tate Modern is one of the most spectacular and popular of London's attractions. The converted Bankside Power Station houses the Tate's collection of international modern art from 1900 to the present. A great solid box of brick with a single free-standing square chimney front centre, the power station was decommissioned in 1986 and left desolate until Swiss architects Herzog

Tate Modern

Tower of London

and de Meuron were appointed to adapt the building to its current role. The immense **Turbine Hall** is an astonishing space for specifically commissioned artworks on a grand scale, with the rest of the main collection permanently arranged in galleries around this central space and focusing on four themes: Still Life, Landscape, the Nude and History. Free guided tours leave from level 5 at 1100 (Nude) and 1200 (History), and from level 3 at 1400 (Still Life) and 1500 (Landscape).

Tower of London

ⓘ EC3, T0870-756 7070, www.hrp.org.uk, ◉B4 . Mar-Oct Tue-Sat 0900-1800; Mon, Sun 1000-1800; Nov-Feb Tue-Sat 0900-1700, Mon and Sun 1000-1700. Last entry 1 hr before closing. £15. Tube Tower Hill.

Londoners traditionally dislike the tower. After all, it was built 900 years ago not to protect them but to subdue them, a role it played until the mid-19th century. Nowadays, many dismiss it as a tourist trap, but it makes an enormous effort to elucidate its wealth of historical associations and bring the old buildings to life with a mix of bare Norman

stonework and 21st-century three-dimensional virtual tours. Highlights include the Norman **White Tower**, the **Royal Armouries** and the **Crown Jewels**. Nearby is the neo-Gothic extravagance of **Tower Bridge**.

Greenwich

ⓘ SE10. Cutty Sark DLR or overland train from Charing Cross or London Bridge to Greenwich train station.

With its 18th-century architecture, expansive views and royal associations, Greenwich has attracted visitors for centuries. Flanking the Renaissance Queen's House, the **National Maritime Museum** ⓘ Park Row, T020-8858 4422, www.nmm.ac.uk, daily 1000-1700, free, is dedicated to Britain's sea-faring history. Uphill from here, in Greenwich Park, is the **Royal Observatory** ⓘ T020-8858 4422, www .rog.nmm.ac.uk, daily 1000-1700, free, home of Greenwich Mean Time. Explore antique shops and market stalls in the village, and, on the waterfront, the 19th-century tea clipper **Cutty Sark** ⓘ T020-8858 3445, www.cuttysark .org.uk, closed for restoration and fire damage repair.

Royal Observatory

✳ Sex and clubs and rock'n'roll

Soho has long been associated with sex and vice. Central London's notorious one square mile district was home to some 300 prostitutes in the 1950s and, when they moved elsewhere in the 1960s, the number of strip clubs and drinking clubs increased dramatically. The most famous, Raymond Revuebar, is still doing business, though most have now closed. From the late 1960s Soho became the centre of the porn industry. While pornographic publications were whipped over from the continent in Danish Bacon lorries, the Obscene Publications Squad (OPS) was being bribed to turn a blind eye. But in 1972 a new commissioner of the Metropolitan Police was appointed to clean up Soho and the OPS was suspended. In the early 1980s new legislation requiring all sex shops to be licensed came into effect.

Soho was also one of the centres of British bohemia. Its drinking clubs are still famous: the **Colony Room**, on Dean Street, has always been a favourite haunt of hard-drinking British artists, from Francis Bacon to Damien Hirst, and the **Groucho Club**, once the epitome of Thatcherite excess, still serves the inflated egos of medialand. Soho also has mighty impressive music credentials: **Ronnie Scott's** was the first outlet in the capital for modern jazz, while the Marquee (now closed) played host to the Yardbirds and the Rolling Stones. Its dance clubs, such as **The Wag** and **Beat Route** were at the cutting edge of late 1970s and early 1980s music. Soho's most recent incarnation as the capital's big, gay heart, only confirms its status as London's Left Bank or Greenwich Village.

⬤ Sleeping

Accommodation doesn't come cheap in London – even at the budget end – but, if it's luxury, pampering and romance you're after, you'll be spoilt for choice. We've left out the really obvious big-hitters, like Claridge's, The Dorchester and The Savoy, in favour of more intimate, cosy or romantic options. All are centrally located.

€€€ **Dukes**, St James's Pl, SW1, T020-7491 4840, www.dukeshotel.com. With 89 comfortable, old-fashioned rooms and a health club, this is a very discreet luxury hotel with a cosy bar that mixes devastating Martinis.

€€€ **Hazlitt's**, 6 Frith St, W1, T020-7434 1771, www.hazlittshotel.com. Many people's London favourite with 23 individual period rooms of great character, in memory of the London essayist. No restaurant or bar but plenty nearby in the liveliest streets of Soho.

€€€ **Malmaison**, 18-21 Charterhouse Sq, EC1, T020-7012 3700, www.malmaison.com. With 97 differently shaped rooms, this hotel is comfortable, easygoing but quite flash.

€€€ **The Rookery**, Peter's Lane, Cowcross St, T020-7336 0931, www.rookeryhotel.com. A renovated old-fashioned townhouse hotel with 33 rooms in an antique building and a crow's nest of a penthouse.

€€€ **St Martin's Lane**, 45 St Martin's Lane, WC2, T020-7300 5500, www.morganshotelgroup.com. Formerly Ian Schrager's media favourite, designed by minimalist Philippe Starck. The restaurant does classic French and modern European on the side and, for drinking, there's the awesome **Light Bar** and the **Seabar**.

€€ **Aster House**, 3 Sumner Pl, SW7, T020-7581 5888, www.asterhouse.com. Sweet little guesthouse with 14 rooms, a garden and conservatory.

€€ **The Claverley**, 13-14 Beaufort Gdns, SW3, T020-7589 8541, www.claverleyhotel.co.uk. Classy and comfortable small hotel. All rooms are different, with marble bathrooms, decorated in a romantic English way. Breakfast is included.

€€ Number Sixteen, 16 Sumner Pl, SW7, T020-7589 5232, www.number sixteenhotel.co.uk. 42 rooms in 4 small townhouses. Elegant privacy and the most salubrious (and expensive) of the set in this dainty little stucco street. Part of the successful Firmdale group.

€€ Tophams Belgravia, 28 Ebury St, SW1, T020-7730 8147. A charming, small country house-style hotel, family-run with very friendly service.

🍽 Eating

London's restaurant scene continues to mature at a heady rate. The range of excellent food on offer in almost every setting and price bracket can be baffling. A good meal has become an integral part of a top night out. But the city is a notoriously pricey place in which to eat out compared to much of Europe. This is partly compensated by the sheer variety of cuisines available – from Africa to Yemen via Poland and New Zealand.

♔♔♔ Andrew Edmonds, 46 Lexington St, W1, T020-7437 5708. Excellent modern European cooking at reasonable prices is served up in a cosy, candlelit atmosphere. Booking ahead strongly recommended.

♔♔♔ Hakkasan, 8 Hanway Pl, W1, T020-7927 7000. Probably the funkiest Chinese in the capital, with its blue-lit banquettes, stylish decor and a Michelin star to boot.

♔♔♔ Moro, 34-36 Exmouth Market, EC1, T020-7833 8336. A modern Spanish restaurant that wows the area's hipsters with its artful dishes and super-fresh ingredients.

♔♔♔ Nobu, Metropolitan Hotel, 19 Old

Park Lane, W1, T020-7447 4747. Robert de Niro et al's venture at the super-fashionable Metropolitan Hotel. Sample some ultra-light Japanese- cum-South American food. Make dinner bookings up to a month ahead.

♔♔ The Eagle, 159 Farringdon Rd, T020-7837 1353. One of the first pubs to go gastro, cooking up excellent modern European food.

♔♔ Joe Allen, 13 Exeter St, WC2, T020-7836 0651. Quite hard to find but definitely worth the effort. The American menu served up in this traditional basement diner never fails to please a host of theatre-going regulars as well as tourists in the know.

♔♔ St John, 26 St John St, T020-7251 0848. Especially good offal and freshly baked bread are served up in a stark former smokery celebrating 'nose to tail' eating. **St John Bread and Wine**, 94-96 Commercial St, T020-7251 0848, is the cheaper, no-frills version.

♔ India Club, 143 Strand, WC2, T020-7836 0650. Closed Sun. Pay up to £10 for old-style curries at formica tables on linoleum floors with yellow walls. A very Indian institution, since 1950. Bring your own booze.

♔ Lahore Kebab House, 2 Umberston St, E1; T020-7488 2551. Daily till 2330. A 30-year-old family-owned informal restaurant set in the Pakistani and Bangladeshi quarters of East London. Delicious and authentic Pakistani dishes attract a multicultural crowd. Bring your own alcohol.

🎭 Nightlife

Buy *Time Out* (www.timeout.com), the weekly magazine, for the latest entertainment listings.

Bars and clubs

Some traditional pubs boast genuine Victorian interiors (**The Salisbury**, 90 St Martin's Lane, W1) while others thrive as straightforward local boozers (**Coach and Horses**, 29 Greek St, W1; **Dog and Duck**, 18 Bateman St, W1). Music bars are still jumping into the wee small hours, particularly in Shoreditch (**Big Chill Bar**, Dray Walk, off Brick Lane, E1; **Shoreditch Electricity Showrooms**, 39a Hoxton St, N1), as are the gay bars in Soho (**Freedom**, 60-66 Wardour St, W1). There are also hundreds of candlelit wine bars, swish brasseries, elegant hotel bars, sweaty dives and designer cocktail lounges. Many of the best clubs are around Old Street and Shoreditch.

Cinema

BFI London IMAX, Waterloo, SE1, T0870-787 2525, www.bfi.org.uk.
Curzon Mayfair, 38 Curzon St, W1, T0870-756 4621, www.curzon cinemas.com. Middle to highbrow mainstream movies on 1 screen.
Electric Cinema, Portobello Rd, W11, T020-7980 9696, www.electriccinema .co.uk. The epitome of cinema-going chic, and priced accordingly.
ICA Cinema, Nash House, The Mall, SW1, T020-7930 3647, www.ica.org.uk. The place for very rare or independent films, especially world cinema.
National Film Theatre (NFT), South Bank, SE1, T020-7928 3535, www.bfi.org.uk. Home to the British Film Institute.

Classical music and dance

Barbican Centre, T020-7638 8891, www.barbican.org.uk. Home of the London Symphony Orchestra.
Royal Albert Hall, Kensington Gore, T020-7589 8212. This is a grand setting

Markets

London's markets are often most evocative of the city's spirit. Here are the main ones: **Berwick Street**, W1, Mon-Sat 0900-1700), fabrics and food; **Borough**, SE1, Fri 1200-1800, Sat 0900-1600, organic food; **Brick Lane**, E1, Sun 0700-1400, just about everything; **Camden**, NW1, daily 0900-1800, furniture, gifts, clothes, accessories and general mayhem; **Columbia Road**, E1, Sun 0800-1400, flowers; **Leather Lane**, EC2, Mon-Fri 1030-1400, cheap clothes, accessories, fruit and veg; **Portobello Road**, W11, Sat 0800-1800, antiques, second-hand clothes and bric-a-brac; **Spitalfields**, E1, Mon-Fri 1000-1600, Sun 0900-1700, clothes, books, organic food, jewellery and bric-a-brac.

for a wide-ranging variety of entertainment spectacular.

Royal Opera House, Bow St, T020-7304 4000, www.royaloperahouse.org. Bastion of high culture, seats from under £20 to £115. Home to the Royal Ballet.

Sadler's Wells and **Lilian Baylis Theatre**, Rosebery Av, T020-7863 8198. Superb state-of-the-art base for dance and opera.

South Bank Centre, T0870-380 4300, www.rfh.org.uk. The **Royal Festival Hall** stages large-scale orchestral and choral concerts, while the **Queen Elizabeth Hall** and **Purcell Room** host chamber music groups.

Wigmore Hall, 36 Wigmore St, T020-7935 2141, www.wigmore-hall.org.uk. Chamber music and song.

Jazz, rock and pop

Astoria, 157 Charing Cross Rd, T020-7434 9592. Arguably London's most eminent rock and pop venue.

Brixton Academy, 211 Stockwell Rd, T020-7771 2000. Rock and pop acts.

The Jazz Café, 3 Parkway, Camden, NW1, T020-7916 6060. An eclectic mix of world, funk and folk, as well as jazz.

Ronnie Scott's, 47 Frith St, W1, T020-7439 0747. Classic jazz venue enjoying a revival after refurbishment in 2006.

Theatre

The heart of theatreland is still the **West End**, with its diet of hit musicals and populist drama. Half-price tickets are sold from a booth in Leicester Sq. **Off-West End** theatres are often a better bet for thought-provoking productions or new drama. Those with a particular good reputation include the **National Theatre**, South Bank, SE1, T020- 7452 3000, which has 3 stages for all styles and sizes of production; the **Almeida**, Almeida St, Islington, N1, T020-7359 4404, www.almeida.co.uk; the **Donmar Warehouse**, 41 Earlham St, WC2, T020-7240 4882, www.donmar warehouse.com; the **Royal Court Theatre**, Sloane Sq, SW1, T020-7565 5000, www.royalcourttheatre.com; the **Old Vic**, The Cut, SE1, T020-7928 7616, www.oldvictheatre.com; and the **Young Vic**, The Cut, SE1, T020-7928 6363, www.youngvic.org. The **Globe Theatre**, 21 New Globe Walk, SE1, T020-7902 1500, www.shakespeares-

globe.org, is also worth visiting for its authentic Elizabethan architecture and innovative open-air productions.

○ Shopping

The difficulty is knowing where to begin. **Oxford St** and **Regent St** have **Selfridges**, **Hamleys**, **Liberty** and other large department stores and big brand shops. **Tottenham Court Rd** is good for computers and electronics. Head to **Charing Cross Rd** and **Bloomsbury** for new and second-hand books and **Soho** and **Carnaby St** for urban streetwear. **Covent Garden** is good for clothes, specialist foods, toys, toiletries and gifts. Visit **Bond St** and **Mayfair** for couture fashion and expensive jewellery. For bespoke boots, suits, smoking requisites, wine and other clubby male accessories, go to St James's and **Savile Row**. For crafts and independent designers, visit **Clerkenwell**. **Knightsbridge** has high street fashion and **Harrods**. **Chelsea** and **Notting Hill** are good for one-off, independent fashion labels, second-hand clothes, music, books and gifts. See also Markets above.

In Lyon, it's all about the food. Forget sightseeing – to get a real feel for what the city's all about, step into its restaurants. Lyon has more eateries per capita than any other city in the world. Here, people swap recipes over breakfast, quarrel about chefs at lunch and debate Michelin stars over dinner. From some of the best restaurants in France to the simplest *bouchons*, you'll struggle to have a bad meal. And to walk off all that food, France's second largest city has a staggeringly beautiful Renaissance centre – so impressive that it was awarded UNESCO World Heritage Site status in 1998. Its history dates from Roman times, but its wealth came from the silk industry and Lyon still thrives today as a couture centre. Only in France could the concepts of high fashion and high calories marry so well.

Arts & culture
★★★

Eating
★★★★★

Nightlife
★★★

Outdoors
★★

Romance
★★

Shopping
★★★

Sightseeing
★★

Value for money
★★★

Overall score
★★★

At a glance

The **Presqu'île**, wedged between the Rhône and Sâone rivers, is the centre of the city, focused on smart **Bellecour** (at the centre of which is the vast place Bellecour) and **Perrache**, the area around the main train station. Just south of here is the Musée des Tissus, a highlight and an excellent introduction to the city's status as a silk capital. To the north is the Musée des Beaux-Arts and the area of **La Croix-Rousse**, once home to silk weavers and becoming a fashionable hot spot today, while to the east, on the other side of the Rhône, is the modern and commercial part of town. Sights here include the Centre d'Histoire de la Résistance et de la Déportation, L'Institut Lumière and the Musée d'Art Contemporain.

On the western banks of the Sâone is **Vieux Lyon** (Old Lyon), the Renaissance centre of the old town, the most atmospheric part of the city and the reason that Lyon is a UNESCO World Heritage Site. Here, the cobbled lanes creep up towards **Fourvière**, the hill upon which the Romans founded Lugdunum, which went on to become the most important city in Gaul. For an excellent overview of the city's layout, head to the terrace of the basilica at the top of Fourvière, which offers panoramic views over Lyon.

★ *Don't leave without rising early and seeing celebrity chefs haggling over cured ham and goldleaf-dusted chocolates at Les Halles de Lyon.*

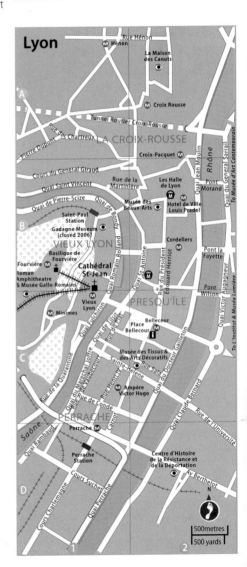

> ❝❞
>
> **Lyon is the larder of France.**
>
> *Paul Bocuse, chef*

European City Breaks Lyon

◉ Sights

Place Bellecour

This vast square – one of the largest in the country – lies at the heart of the Presqu'île, between the Rhône and Sâone rivers. In the centre is a statue of Louis XIV on horseback, dressed in Roman garb. The square is surrounded by pale gravel, grand façades and posh shops and has a tourist bureau.

Musée des Beaux-Arts

ⓘ *20 pl des Terreaux, T04-7210 1740, www.mba-lyon.fr,* **D2**. *Mon, Wed, Thu, Sat, Sun 1000-1800, Fri 1030-1830; some galleries closed at lunchtime. €6. Métro Hôtel de Ville.*

Housed in the grand Palais Saint-Pierre, this museum holds a vast collection of fine arts, second in France only to the Louvre. The collection includes pieces from ancient Greece, Rome and Egypt, continues through the Middle Ages and culminates in an excellent selection of France's finest 19th-century painters,

Place Bellecour

including Monet, Renoir and Gauguin. There's a pleasant café and the museum is all but deserted during the week.

Musée des Tissus

ⓘ *34 rue de la Charité, T04-7838 4200, www.musee-des-tissus.com,* **C2**. *Tue-Sun 1000-1730. €5. Métro Ampère Victor Hugo.*

The history of Lyon's status as a silk capital is charted in this surprisingly fascinating museum, spread across 30

rooms filled with fabrics and costumes from around the world. Included are rare Persian carpets, Coptic tapestries and silks from Italy, China and Japan, as well as some of the finest silks produced in Lyon. Next door, and included on the same ticket, is the reasonably diverting **Decorative Arts Museum** ⓘ *Tue-Sun 1000-1200 and 1400-1730*, with objets d'art and homewares from the 17th and 18th centuries.

Centre d'Histoire de la Résistance et de la Déportation

ⓘ *14 Av Berthelot, T04-7273 9906,* **D2**. *Wed-Sun 0900-1800. €4. Métro Perrache; tram T2 Centre Berthelot.*

Located in old Gestapo headquarters, this harrowing museum is a dark tour through the times of Nazi occupation, resistance and deportation during the Second World War. Lyon was a hotbed of anti-fascism, and it was in these old cells that resistance hero Jean Moulin was tortured on his arrest. Today they house displays, including the film of the trial of Klaus Barbie, head of the Gestapo.

European City Breaks Lyon

⊖ Travel essentials

Getting there Lyon-St-Exupéry Airport, T0826-800826, www.lyon .aeroport.fr, is about 25 km east of the city centre. The **Satobus**, T04-3725 3732, www.satobus.com, is a regular shuttle service from the airport to the city centre, leaving every 20 mins 0600-2340. A single ticket costs €8.60. Taxis are available from outside the terminal building; the 40-min journey should cost around €40. Both the airport and **Lyon-Part-Dieu** station are served by high-speed TGV services to and from Paris and other French and Italian cities, www.voyages-sncf.com.

Getting around The centre of town is easily explored on foot but there's also an integrated public transport system, with 4 metro lines, 2 tram lines (including the new, super-fast cross-city T3), a bus network and 2 funiculars, all run by **Transport en Commun Lyonnais (TCL)**, T0820-427000, www.tcl.fr. A single ticket, which is valid on the metro, all buses and trams, costs €1.50, and must be validated before travel (valid for 1 hr). A pack of 10 tickets costs €12.20; a 2-hr pass costs €2.10 and a day pass is €4.30. The funicular runs on separate tickets, costing €2.20 for a return.

Tourist information The **Lyon Convention and Visitors Bureau**, T04-7277 6969, www.en.lyon-france .com, is on place Bellecour. It's open Apr-Oct Mon-Sat 0900-1900, Nov-Mar Mon-Sat 1000-1730.

Lyon City Card, valid for 1, 2 or 3 days, is issued by the tourist bureau and provides free transport (including funiculars) and entry to museums, free guided tours and reductions at theatres, concerts and selected shops. One day costs €18, 2 days costs €28, and 3 days costs €38.

Vieux Lyon

ⓘ Métro Vieux Lyon, **C1**

The delightful Renaissance quarter, reached across a series of bridges, gained the city its UNESCO World Heritage Site status and is the most enjoyable area to wander around today. Vieux Lyon feels somehow more Italian than French, with cobbled lanes lined with pastel-coloured Renaissance façades, a huge number of which are given over to bustling cafés, restaurants and boutiques. Many of the roads are divided by *traboules*, tunnel- like alleys built to protect silks being carried by weavers, and used by resistance fighters during the Second World War.

Vieux Lyon

The main appeal of this area lies simply in wandering about, but there are also a handful of sights, including the **Gadagne Museum** ⓘ 1 pl du petit collège, T04-7842 0361, www.musee gadagne.com, **B1**, €3.80, incorporating the Musée Historique de Lyon and the Musée de la Marionnette, and the **Théâtre de Guignol** ⓘ 2 rue Louis Carrand, T04-7828 9257, www.guignol-lyon .com, €9, where you can see the famous local marionettes doing their thing.

The enormous **Cathédral St-Jean** is on place St-Jean, from where the

Musée des Beaux-Arts

funicular (€2.20) whisks visitors to the top of **Fourvière hill** (the gardens here are a lovely spot for a picnic) topped by the extravagant **Basilique de Fourvière**, a close imitation of Sacré Coeur in Paris. Although the interior is rather overbearing, the views over the city are tremendous. Nearby are the city's Roman remains including an impressive ruined amphitheatre, and the **Musée Gallo-Romains** ⓘ 17 rue Cléberg, T04-7453 7401, www.musees-gallo-romains.com, **C1**, Tue-Sun 1000- 1700/ 1800, €6.

La Croix-Rousse

The old silk weaver's district, on the north of Presqu'île, is rapidly undergoing a transformation. It is still to some extent a working class district but its alleys are quickly filling up with cutting-edge boutiques and restaurants. It is also riddled with *traboules* (narrow passages between houses), although many are now closed to the public for safety reasons. **La Maison des Canuts** ⓘ 10-12 rue d'Ivry, T04-7828 6204, **A2**, Tue-Sat 1000- 1830, free, is an old cooperative, where you can watch weavers at their looms and buy a variety of silk products.

L'Institut et Musée Lumière

ⓘ 25 rue du Premier Film, T04-7878 1891, www.institut-lumiere.org. Tue-Sun 1100-1830. €6.

The home of the famous Lumière brothers is located to the southeast of the centre. It charts their inspiring photographic inventions and the birth of film. The four floors of exhibits include the world's first cinematograph, which projected a film for the first time in 1895. Visitors can watch screenings, and this is also the site of a film festival.

Musée d'Art Contemporain

ⓘ Cité Internationale, 81 quai Charles de Gaulle , T04-7269 1717, www.moca -lyon.org. Wed-Sun 1200-1900. €5. Bus 4 or 47.

The contemporary arm of the Musée des Beaux-Arts lies out in the east of town in a Renzo Piano modern extension to a 1930s building. The focus here is on installation art, including sound, video and interactive pieces, with regularly changing exhibitions. The museum also hosts a biennial arts festival.

La Croix-Rousse

Lyon is the self-proclaimed – and undisputed – gastronomic capital of France, with more restaurants per head than anywhere else in the world. Its traditions are rooted in its surroundings; the region is rich in fowl, fresh fish and dairy cows, and surrounding it are the vineyards of Beaujolais (to the north) and the Côtes du Rhône (to the south). This abundant natural larder is plundered by an army of celebrated chefs, who are the hot topics of conversation and speculation amongst locals. Top of the pile is legendary **Paul Bocuse**, with no less than three Michelin stars, the inventor of nouvelle cuisine and today reigning supreme over five restaurants. Other kings of the kitchen include **Pierre Orsi** (the French swoon over his foie gras ravioli) and **Jean-Paul Lacombe**, although new chefs such as **Nicolas le Bec** are snapping at their heels. But

A bouchon

some of the finest eating experiences in Lyon can be had in its simplest establishments, known as *bouchons*. Traditionally catering for silk workers, these serve the best of Lyon's specialities, such as *quenelles*, a poached pike mousse served with béchamel sauce, and kidneys with Madeira sauce and *andouillette* (chitterling) sausage. Just don't expect to leave Lyon slimmer than when you arrived.

Sleeping

It's always a good idea to reserve your room in advance because the high number of business travellers coming to Lyon means that hotels get booked up both during the week and at weekends.

€€€ La Tour Rose, 22 rue du Boeuf, T04-7837 6910, www.slh.com. A small, opulent hotel in the Old Town, set across 3 grand 15th- and 18th-century mansions. The 12 suites all have grand furniture, exposed beams and Lyonnaise silks. The famous restaurant, headed by Philippe Chavent, is housed in a renovated chapel.

€€€ Villa Florentine, 25 Montée St-Barthelémy, T04-7256 5656, www.villaflorentine.com. This 18th-century convent has wide-reaching views over the city from its peaceful hilltop location. There's an excellent restaurant and 29 plush rooms, filled with an odd mix of antiques, chintz and modern pieces.

€€ Collège Hotel, 5 pl St-Paul, T04-7210 0505, www.college-hotel.com. Stylish hotel with quirky school theme in the centre of the Old Town. The 39 pure white minimalist rooms have flat-screen TVs. Breakfast is served at old school desks surrounded by blackboards and bookcases.

€€ Hotel Bayard, 23 pl Bellecour, T04-7837 3964, www.hotelbayard.com. A homely hotel in the centre of town, with a mix of modern and traditional rooms, some of which have original parquet floors, canopies over the beds and rickety antique furniture; rooms 2 and 4 are the most appealing.

€ Hôtel du Théâtre, 10 rue de Savoie, T04-7842 3332, www.hotel-du-theatre.fr. A friendly hotel overlooking pl des Célestins, with simple, spotless rooms, some with French windows and views of the theatre.

Eating

As you may have gathered by now, you'll eat extremely well in Lyon. Bear in mind that it's a good idea to book head at many of these restaurants, as locals like to eat out here as much as visitors.

Breakfast

Le Canut sans Cervelle, 4 bis, rue Belfort/Dumenge, T04-7830 1020. Serves a popular brunch on Sun in

its attractive Croix-Rousse location.
Le Pain Quotidien, 13-15 rue Quatre Chapeaux, T04-7838 2984. A trendy Belgian chain serving delicious breads, pastries and yoghurts, as well as their decadent trademark home-made chocolate spread.

Lunch
Brasserie Georges, 30 cours de Verdun, T04-7256 5456, www.brasserie georges.com. Cavernous art deco interior, with soaring ceilings, red banquettes and bustling waiters. Good standard fare, such as onion soup and traditional Lyonnaise sausages.
Café Chantecler, 151 blvd de la Croix Rousse, T04-7828 1369, www.cafe-chantecler.com. A good-value, old-fashioned brasserie and bar with a bohemian feel, which brews its own beers. It's an excellent choice for lunchtime specials, which are served on its outdoor terrace.

Dinner
L'Auberge du Point de Collonges, 40 quai de la Plage, Collonges-au-Mont-d'Or, T04-7242 9090, www.bocuse.fr. One of the finest restaurants in France, 4 km from Lyon. The 3 choices of menu (including the wonderfully-named Menu Bourgeois) offer superb traditional cuisine. Book several weeks in advance and be prepared to pay heftily for the privilege.
Les Terrasses, Villa Florentine, 25 Montée St-Barthélémy, T04-7256 5656. One of the best fine dining options in the city. Chef Stéphane Gaborieau is a Michelin star holder. Among the set menus are the self-explanatory scallop menu and the traditional 'Voyage Gourmand', which includes duck liver with sweetbreads, squid stewed with lobster and Dordogne veal.

Restaurant Nicolas Le Bec, 14 rue Grolée, T04-7842 1500. This Michelin-star chef is a relative newcomer to Lyon's culinary scene. Le Bec's stylish, airy restaurant feels more contemporary than many others. His menus change monthly and include a surprisingly affordable lunchtime *prix fixe* menu. For dinner, expect odd but delicious combinations, such as lobster with cocoa beans, beef braised in sea urchin stock, or hare in game sauce with hibiscus.

66 99 *A* *bouchon* is a typical Lyonnaise bistro-style restaurant serving hearty local dishes.

Happy Friends Family, 29 rue du Boeuf, T04-7240 9147. Don't be put off by the name; this fashionable place has some of the best modern food in the city. The fusion cooking mixes French, oriental and spicy north African cuisines. Book ahead.
Le Sud, 11 pl Antonin-Poncet, T04-7277 8000, www.bocuse.com. Lyon's kitchen heavyweight, Paul Bocuse, owns 4 neobrasseries: Le Nord, Le Sud, L'Est and L'Ouest. Le Sud has an appropriately Mediterranean menu.
Chabert et Fils, 11 rue des Marronniers, T04-7837 0194. A typical *bouchon* in a narrow Old Town side street. The warm, bustling atmosphere draws in the crowds with traditional dishes, such as tripe cooked with onions, or chicken livers with thyme.

Le Bouchon des Carnivores, rue des Marronniers, T04-7842 9769. Another *bouchon*, just opposite, is this meat-oriented eaterie, with a cheerful yellow interior smothered in posters and pictures of bulls. Roast beef served with morels comes recommended.

Nightlife

The streets of the Old Town get very busy in the evenings, particularly around place Bertras where there is a wide choice of bars and late-night cafés. The up-and-coming area of Croix Rousse is also increasingly popular, with trendy bars and pubs.

More sedate, but no less popular, is the excellent **Opéra National de Lyon**, T0826-305325, www.opera-lyon.com. Housed in an 18th-century building on place de la Comédie, it has a changing programme, with good-value last-minute tickets available on the actual day of performances.

Shopping

Lyon's position as a fabric and silks capital continues today; all major designers have outlets here. Clothes shops and international chains can be found along the pedestrian thoroughfare on Presqu'île, between rue Victor Hugo and rue de la République.

For fresh fruit, meat and cheese, head either to the covered market at **Les Halles de Lyon** or the open-air market, held every morning on the riverside quai St-Antoine. There is also a book market here on Sundays. Just off place Bellecour is rue Auguste Comte, lined with some excellent little antique shops.

Madrid is not a city of half-measures: Europe's highest, youngest, sunniest capital likes to boast *Desde Madrid al Cielo* ('from Madrid to Heaven'), with a matter-of-fact assumption that when you've seen Madrid, the only place left is Heaven. The city is as famous for what it lacks as for what it boasts – there's no great river, no architectural marvels, no immediate picture-postcard charm. But what it does have, it has in spades: a fabulous collection of western art held in the Prado, the Thyssen and the Reina Sofía; a crooked old centre where almost every alley is stuffed with excellent tapas bars and restaurants; a famously intense blue sky; and an even more intense nightlife that makes most other cities look positively staid.

Madrid

Arts & culture
★★★★★

Eating
★★★★

Nightlife
★★★★★

Outdoors
★★

Romance
★★★

Shopping
★★★

Sightseeing
★★★★

Value for money
★★★

Overall score
★★★★

At a glance

The leafy, elegant **Paseo del Prado** sits on the eastern side of the city, where the three big museums – the Prado, the Centro de Arte de Reina Sofía and the Thyssen-Bornemisza – are conveniently clustered. West of here is **Puerta del Sol**, Madrid's crossroads, and the cheerful, bohemian barrio of **Santa Ana**, which slopes downhill back towards the Prado. **Plaza Mayor**, west down Calle Mayor is the grand heart of old Madrid. The area around it, sprinkled with old palaces and monasteries, is known as **Hapsburg Madrid**. To the west is the enormous Bourbon **Palacio Real** and the city's beautifully restored Opera House. South of Plaza Mayor are the multicultural, edgy, traditionally working class districts of **La Latina** and **Lavapiés**, with a great flea market on Saturdays. North of the **Gran Vía**, **Chueca** and **Malasaña** are sweetly old-fashioned by

It is not the bustle of a busy people; it is the vivacity of cheerful persons, a carnival-like joy, a restless idleness, a feverish overflow of pleasure...

Edmondo de Amicis

day and unstoppably wild by night. Swanky **Salamanca**, east of here, is an elegant 19th-century grid scattered with upmarket restaurants and designer boutiques.

★ *Don't leave town without checking out the Reina Sofía's glossy new extension.*

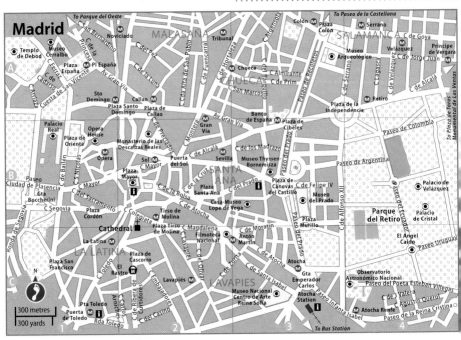

24 hours in the city

Plaza de Oriente

Have breakfast on the **Plaza de Oriente**, with views of the Palacio Real. Spend a few hours seeing the highlights at one of the big three museums – the Goyas at the **Prado**, Picasso's *Guernica* at the **Reina Sofía** or the Italian Primitives at the **Thyssen**. Trawl around the old-fashioned tapas bars in the **Plaza Santa Ana** for lunch, followed by a siesta under the trees in the **Parque del Retiro**. Take a look at some of the new galleries springing up in trendy **Chueca** or go shopping at its quirky fashion boutiques. Soak up the atmosphere at a traditional restaurant like **Casa Paco** followed by flamenco at **Casa Patas**. Alternatively, check out the Madrid club scene: celebrity spot at **Suite**, or hop onto a podium at **Coppelia**. Finish up with some traditional *churros con chocolate* at the **Chocolatería San Ginés**.

⊖ Travel essentials

Getting there Madrid's **Barajas Airport** is 15 km northeast of the city (airport information T91-305 8346). There are 2 bus lines from Terminals 1, 2 and 3 into the city centre: No 101 for Canillejas and the No 200 for Av de América. Bus No 204 also heads directly to Av de América from Terminal 4. Metro line 8 runs from Terminal 2 to the city and is being extended to Terminal 4 during 2007. Metro and bus cost the same (see below) but if you'll be using public transport during your stay it's best to get a **Metrobús ticket** (see below). Taxi ranks are outside all arrival halls. A taxi into the city costs €20-25.

Long-distance trains (including an overnight service from Paris d'Austerlitz) arrive at **Atocha station** (metro line 1), T902-240202, www.renfe.com.

Getting around Almost all Madrid's sights are clustered in the centre, an enjoyable stroll from each other. However, if you're in a hurry, the **buses** and **metro** are cheap, efficient and

user-friendly. A few places – the museums dotted around the Salamanca district and the Ventas bullring, for example – are a bit further afield but are all accessible by public transport. A single trip by bus or metro costs €1; the **Metrobús ticket** (which can be shared) costs €6.40 for 10 journeys. Tourist passes cost €3.80- €39.60 for 1-7 days' unlimited use of the bus and metro. You can buy tickets at metro stations; the Metrobús ticket is also sold at tobacconists (*estancos*). Pick up free bus and metro maps from tourist offices, metro and bus stations. Information in English is available by calling T010 or online at www.ctm- madrid.es. Good bus routes for sightseeing include: **No 2** from Plaza España, along the Gran Vía to the Retiro; **No 3** for an overview of the centre, from Puerta de Toledo to Chueco; **No 5** from Puerta del Sol up Paseo de la Castellana to Plaza de Castilla; **No 21** down Pintor Rosales in the northeast, through Chueca and to the Ventas bullring.

Tourist information The main office is in the Casa de la Panadería, Pl Mayor 27, T91-588 1636, daily 0930-2030. There are other branches at C del Duque de Medinaceli 2, T91-429 4951, Mon-Sat 0900-1900, Sun 0900-1500; Atocha train station, T91-528 4630, daily 0900-2100; Barajas Airport, Terminal 1, T91-305 8556, daily 0800-2000; Chamartín train station, Gate 16, T91-315 9976, Mon-Sat 0800-2000, Sun 0800-1400; Mercado Puerta de Toledo, Ronda de Toledo 1, T91-364 1876, Mon-Sat 0800-2000, Sun 0800-1400. Staff can provide a basic map of the city and a copy of *En Madrid What's On*, a pocket-sized magazine with helpful local information and listings. There's also a free English- language monthly newspaper *InMadrid*, with plenty of bar and club listings. The tourist information line is T902-100 007. Useful websites include: www.madrid.org, www.descubre madrid.com and www.esmadrid.com.

◉ Sights

Museo del Prado

ⓘ *Paseo del Prado, T91-330 2800, http://museoprado.mcu.es,* **B3**. *Tue-Sun 0900-2000 (last entry 1930). €6, free on Sun; Abono Paseo del Arte (for the Prado, Reina Sofía and Thyssen-Bornemisza) €14.40 . Metro Banco de España.*

The Prado houses one of the world's greatest art collections, a dazzling display of European art spanning seven centuries. When it opened in 1819, it was one of the very first public art museums, infused with the spirit of the Enlightenment and shored up by royal whim (Queen Isabel of Braganza had been impressed with the Louvre and wanted one for Spain). The collection encompasses several thousand works of art, and the sheer scale can make it a daunting prospect. Pick out some highlights or favourite painters rather than trying to see it all in one go. The museum's strength is its magnificent collection of Spanish masterpieces dating from the 12th to the 19th centuries, including works by Zurbarán, Velázquez and Goya. As part of the Prado's ongoing major renovation programme, a new

Museo Thyssen

modern wing is scheduled to open in autumn 2007.

Museo Thyssen-Bornemisza

ⓘ *Paseo del Prado 8, T91-420 3944, www.museothyssen.org,* **B3**, *Tue-Sun 1000-1900. €6, temporary exhibitions €5; Abono Paseo del Arte €14.40 . Metro Banco de España.*

Across Plaza de Cánovas del Castillo from the Prado is the **Thyssen-Bornemisza**, which perfectly complements its 'big brother'. It plugs the gaps left by the Prado, with a vast collection of western European art spanning eight centuries, as well as offering a dazzling selection of early 20th-century masters, from Braque to Kandinsky, to whet your appetite for the Reina Sofía.

Museo Nacional Centro de Arte Reina Sofía

ⓘ *C Santa Isabel 52, T91-467 5062, http://museoreinasofia.mcu.es,* **C3**. *Mon, Wed-Sat 1000-2100, Sun 1000-1430. €3.01, free Sat 1430-2100 and Sun 1000-1430; Abono Paseo del Arte €14.40. Metro Atocha.*

Housed in a former hospital close to Atocha station, Reina Sofia has been beautifully remodelled to hold the nation's collection of 20th-century art. It's a graceful, light-filled building set around a quiet, interior courtyard, with a pair of panoramic glass lifts which are almost an attraction in themselves. The second and fourth floors are devoted to the permanent exhibition and the first and third floors are used for temporary exhibitions which are usually excellent. The undoubted highlight is Picasso's celebrated *Guernica*, whose sheer scale and emotional power cannot fail to impress.

Parque del Retiro

ⓘ *Metro Banco de España/Retiro,* **B4**.

This dreamy expanse of manicured gardens, lakes, shady woods and pavilions was once the garden of the Palacio Real del Buen Retiro and is the perfect escape from the city bustle. At the centre is a vast lake (*estanque*), with a sprinkling of cafés and boats for hire. At the southern end of the park, take a peek at the bizarre *Ángel Caído* (Fallen Angel), one of only three monuments in the

Museo del Prado

Parque del Retiro

world to Satan, caught midway in his fall from Paradise. Ricardo Velázquez designed the elegant **Palacio de Velázquez** and **Palacio de Cristal** in 1882. The pavilions are now used for the Reina Sofía's temporary art exhibitions.

Plaza Santa Ana
ⓘ *Metro Antón Martín,* 🔲**B2**.

This square, flanked by restaurants, bars, theatres and hotels, has been the heart of the Barrio de los Literatos for centuries. It's been overhauled a dozen times and the latest restoration confirms Madrid's predilection for public squares.

Although not especially pretty, the square's charm lies in its vibrancy and constant animation; the pavements are lined with dozens of tapas bars complete with turn-of-the-20th-century fittings; it's one of the most popular places in Madrid for a tapas crawl (*tapeo*). On summer nights the pavements are dense with tourists, locals walking their dogs and elderly *Madrileños* sitting on benches. There are few reminders that this neighbourhood was once home

Plaza Santa Ana

Plaza Mayor

to Cervantes, Lope de Vega, Quevado and other great writers of the Golden Age, but you can visit Lope de Vega's delightful home, the **Casa-Museo Lope de Vega** ⓘ *C Cervantes 11, T91-429 9216,* 🔲**B3**, *guided tours (in Spanish) only, Tue-Fri 0930-1400, Sat 1000-1400; €2, free Sat.*

Plaza Mayor
ⓘ *Metro Sol,* 🔲**B2**.

The Plaza Mayor is vast, a huge cobbled expanse surrounded by elegant arcades and tall mansions topped with steep slate roofs. When it's bright and sunny, it's packed with terrace cafés, souvenir shops and sun-worshipping tourists; the only time you might see a *Madrileño* in the Plaza Mayor is on a Sunday morning when a stamp and coin market is held here.

Building of the square started in 1617 to designs by Felipe II's favourite architect, Juan de Herrera. This was the ceremonial centre of Madrid, a magnificent backdrop for public spectacles, coronations, executions, markets, bullfights and fiestas. (It is riddled with the subterranean torture

chambers of the Inquisition, which used the square for *autos-da-fé,* the trial of suspected heretics.) Before the square was built, a market was traditionally held in front of the **Casa de la Panadería,** the old bakery, which is now the most eye-catching building on the square. It was repainted in 1992 by Carlos Franco who covered it with a hippy-trippy fresco of floating nymphs. Arched passages lead off from here to some of 17th-century Madrid's most important thoroughfares – **Calle Toledo, Calle Mayor,** and **Calle Segovia.** Other street names still echo the trades that were once carried out here, such as **Calle Cuchilleros** (Street of the Knife Sharpeners), which incorporates part of the old city walls. This is where you'll find the traditional *mesones* (inns), which grew up to cater to merchants and travellers arriving at the city gates. **Casa Botín,** at Cuchilleros 17, opened in the 16th century and claims to be the oldest restaurant in the world.

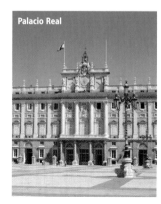

Palacio Real

Palacio Real

ⓘ *C Bailén s/n, T91-454 8803, www.patrimonionacional.es,* B1. *Oct-Mar Mon-Sat 0930-1700, Sun 0900-1400; Apr-Sep Mon-Sat 0900-1800, Sun 0900-1500. €8 (€9 with guided tour in English); free to EU citizens on Wed. Metro Opera.*

In 1734, after a fire destroyed the original Moorish alcázar, Felipe V saw a chance to build something grander and commissioned the most prestigious architects of the day to create this monumental pile. Early plans for a palace four times the size of the current one were rejected but the finished structure is still built on a staggering scale; it's no surprise that Juan Carlos I and family have chosen to live in the more modest Palacio de Zarzuela on the city's outskirts. The Royal Palace is used for official functions and can be closed at short notice; if two flags are flying, the King is at home and you won't be allowed in.

El Rastro

ⓘ *C Ribera de Curtidores. Metro Tirso de Molina or Puerta de Toledo,* C2.

South of Plaza Mayor, the districts of La Latina and Lavapiés have traditionally

El Rastro

been home to Madrid's poorest workers and immigrants. It's here that Madrid's famous flea market, **El Rastro**, takes place every Sunday morning. Stalls wind all the way up Calle Ribera de Curtidores and sell everything from tacky clothes and souvenirs to leather goods, underwear, arts and crafts and kites. The street name means Tanner's Alley and recalls the pungent trades which took place down here, out of sight (and smell) of the smart neighbourhoods at the top of the hill. Rastro itself refers to the sticky trail of blood left when the meat carcasses were hauled through the streets. The surrounding shops are mainly devoted to antiques and bric-a-brac, although you'll still find plenty of leather goods, and, although the neighbourhood is still a little shabby, it's in the process of regeneration. The atmosphere on a Sunday is wonderful; after the stallholders have packed up, everyone heads to the surrounding bars for tapas and a well-earned cold beer. Watch out for your bags, though; El Rastro is notorious for pickpockets.

Gran Vía

◉ Best of the rest

Museo Cerralbo ⓘ *C Ventura Rodríguez 17, T91-547 3646, http://museocerralbo.mcu.es,* A1. *Tue-Sat 0930-1500, Sun 1000-1500, Aug Tue-Sat 0930-1400. €2.40. Metro Ventura Rodríguez.* 19th-century palace, crammed with opulent furnishings and treasures collected by the 17th Marqués de Cerralbo.

Monasterio de las Descalzas Reales ⓘ *Pl de las Descalzas Reales 3, T91-454 8800, www.patrimonio nacional.es,* B2. *Guided tour only Tue-Thu, Sat 1030-1245, 1600-1745, Fri 1030-1245, Sun and hols 1100-1345. €5. Metro Sol.* A 16th-century convent for blue-blooded nuns, with a remarkable collection of tapestries and other artworks.

Parque del Oeste ⓘ *C Ferraz s/n, T91-366 7415,* A1. *Metro Ventura Rodríguez.* This cool, shady park spreads along the western flank of the city, north of the Plaza de España. It's most surprising sight is the Templo de Debod, a 2000-year-old gift from Egypt.

Museo Arqueológico ⓘ *C Serrano 13, Salamanca, T91-577 7912, http://man.mcu.es,* A3. *Tue-Sat 0930-2030, Sun 0930-1500. €3.01, free Sat afternoon and Sun. Metro Serrano.* Spain's most complete archaeological museum, with a collection spanning millennia.

Plaza de Toros Monumental de las Ventas ⓘ *C Alcalá 237, T91-725 1857. Museum Mar-Oct Tue-Fri 0930-1430, Sun and fight days 1000-1300; Nov-Feb Mon-Fri 0930-1430. Free. Metro Ventas.* The 1930s 'Cathedral of Bullfighting' has a 25,000-strong capacity.

Pedro Almodóvar arrived in Madrid in the late 1960s; he was just 16 but he already knew that he wanted to be a film-maker. Franco had closed Spain's only film school, so Almodóvar started making shorts on super-8. In 1978, three years after Franco's death and the year Spain signed a new democratic constitution, he made his first full-length film and began work on *Pepi, Luci, Bom*, whose subsequent success allowed Almodóvar to found his own production company. The Movida Madrileña was just getting into its stride: the city's youth, making up for decades of repression, turned music, fashion, design and art upside down, and no one knew the city's anarchic subculture better than Almodóvar. Madrid has been a recurrent feature of his work ever since, appearing in his movies as regularly as the 'las chicas de Almodóvar', the select band of actresses he favours.

In 2000, Almodóvar hit the big time, winning an Oscar for *Todo Sobre Mi Madre* (All About My Mother). The subversive director became the toast of the Hollywood establishment, cementing his success with *Hable con ella* (Talk to her) in 2002, *La Mala Educación* (Bad Education) in 2004, which was inspired by his experience of Catholic boarding school, and the award-winning *Volver* in 2006.

Sleeping

Strangely, Madrid has few hotels that are truly charming. There are a few enterprising places, with bright, modern decor and internet access, but finding accommodation here is no longer as easy as it once was; book as far in advance as possible and bring some industrial strength earplugs – Madrid is very noisy.

€€€ **Hotel Urban**, Cra de San Jerónimo 34, T91-787 7770, www.derbyhotels.com. Metro Sevilla. Currently the city's hottest hotel, in a striking glassy contemporary building, with ultra-luxurious rooms, a pool, gym, sauna and excellent restaurant.

€€€ **Orfila**, C Orfila 6, Salamanca, T91-702 7770, www.hotelorfila.com.

Metro Alonso Martínez. A luxurious 19th-century mansion offering discreet 5-star luxury. It has a beautiful, flower-scented terrace, a charming *salón de té*, and a renowned restaurant.

€€ **Galiano**, C Alcalá Galiano 6, Salamanca, T91-319 2000, www.hotel galiano.com. Metro Colón. Delightful, antique-filled hotel housed in a (much modernized) former palace, with spacious rooms and a leafy, central location.

€€ **Hotel Abalu**, C Pez 19, T91-531 4744, www.hotelabalu.com. Metro Noviciado. This is a new smart little design hotel with just 9 rooms and a suite in a great central location. The rooms are crisp and modern, with flat-screen TVs and Wi-Fi.

€€ **Hotel Mario**, C Campomanes 4, T91-548 8548, www.room-mate

hoteles.com. Metro Opera. Part of a small chain of slickly designed hotels, all offering minimalist decor, friendly service, good central locations and excellent value. Highly recommended.

€ **Hostal Cervantes**, C Cervantes 34, Santa Ana, T91-429 8365, www.hostal-cervantes.com. Metro Antón Martín. A great favourite. Friendly owners have made it feel like a home from home. There's a cosy lounge, each room has been decorated with pretty blue prints and all have en suite bathrooms.

€ **Monaco**, C Barbieri 5, T91-522 4639. Metro Chueca. This enjoyably louche former brothel is now distinctly shabby, even dilapidated, but still worth checking out. To really soak up the atmosphere, ask for room 20 or 123.

Eating

The streets around the Plaza Santa Ana – just 5 mins' walk from the Prado – are densely packed with all kinds of bars and restaurants. There are lots of traditional restaurants around the Plaza Mayor (although it's best to avoid the touristy ones on the square), as well as excellent gourmet tapas bars. Some of the cheapest and best tapas bars are in La Latina and Lavapiés.

Cafés and tapas bars

Café de los Austrias, Pl de Ramales 1, T91-559846. Daily 0900-0100, Fri and Sat 0900-0300. Metro Opera. This old-fashioned café/bar is a perfect spot to while away an afternoon.

El Jardín Secreto, C Conde Duque 2, T91-541 8023. Mon-Thu 1730-0100, Fri and Sat 1800-0230, Sun 1700-2400. Metro Plaza de España. Magical café littered with shells, candles and drapes.

Taberna de la Dolores, Pl de Jesús 4, T91-429 2243. Daily 1100-0100, Fri and Sat 1100-0200. Metro Antón Martín. Beautiful, century-old tiled tapas bar – one of the most *típico* in the city.

Restaurants

La Terraza de Casino, C Alcalá 15, T91-521 8700, www.casinodemadrid.es, Mon-Fri 1330-1530 and 2030-2300, Sat and Sun 2030-2300. Closed Aug and public hols. Metro Banco de España. This sumptuous 19th-century building has a stunning panoramic terrace and contains one of Madrid's most spectacular restaurants – part of the legendary El Bulli group. The cuisine is as exciting and creative as you would expect. Be prepared to pay around €100 per head for an unforgettable experience.

Zalacaín, C Álvarez de Baena 4, T91-561 4840. Mon-Fri 1300-1600, 2100-2400, Sat 2100-2400. Metro Gregorio Marañón. Madrid's most celebrated restaurant holds all kinds of stars and awards under the direction of chef Benjamin Urdiain. The Basque cuisine is complemented by a refined setting, perfect service and spectacular wine list.

Casa Paco, Pl Puerta Cerrada 11, T91-366 3166. Mon-Sat 1330-1600 and 2000-2400. Metro La Latina. A resolutely old-fashioned bar with a restaurant at the back. Waiters in long aprons serve sizzling grilled meats and good wines.

Palacio de Anglona, C Segovia 13, T91-366 3753. Fri and Sat until 0200. Metro La Latina. Fashionable restaurant in a 19th-century palace, with sleek, decor. Grilled meats and pasta.

Arrocería Gala, C Moratín 22, T91-429 2562. Mon-Thu 1330-1530 and 2030-0030, Fri-Sun 1330-1630 and 2030-0200. Metro Antón Martín. Valencian rice dishes, including great paella, served in a glassy patio.

La Isla del Tesoro, C Manuel Malasaña 3, T91-593 1440. Daily 1330-2330. Metro Bilbao. A wonderfully romantic spot for vegetarian food. The *menú del día* (€8.90) features the cuisine of a different country each day.

Nightlife

In Madrid it's possible to start dancing on Fri night and not stop until Mon morning. Some of the best clubs are: Low Club, Fri at **De Nombre Publico** (Pl Mostenses 11); the gay party, Ohm, Sat and Sun at **Bash** (Pl de Callao 4); and The Room, Fri at stylish **Stella** (C Arlabán 7). There's tango or salsa Mon- Fri at the **Palacio Gaviria** (C Arenal 7) and dance music or electro-pop at weekends.

Elsewhere, the **Paseo de Castellano** is famous for its summer *terrazas* where you can drink and dance outside. Madrid also has hundreds of *discobares* spread all over the city. **Santa Ana** and **Huertas** get packed, especially in summer, and though not especially fashionable barrios, you are guaranteed a good time. The streets around **Plaza de la Paja**, in the Plaza Mayor and Los Austrias area, are packed with fancy tapas joints but there's also a healthy sprinkling of down-to-earth bars. There are some very funky bars tucked away in the old working-class districts of **La Latina** and **Lavapiés**, while to the north of Gran Vía are two formerly run-down neighbourhoods that have become the focal point of the city's heady nightlife: **Chueca** is the heart of the gay district and stuffed with some ultra-stylish places – such as **Acuarela** (C Gravina 10), **El Liquid** (C Barquillo 8) and the non-gay **Star's Café** (C Marqués de Valdeiglesias 5) – while **Malasaña** is popular with students and younger people looking for a good time. For the latest news, see www.clubbingspain.com.

Shopping

As a general guide, you can find almost anything you want in the streets around **C Preciados**: department stores, chain stores and individual shops selling everything from hams to traditional Madrileño cloaks. The northwestern neighbourhoods of **Argüelles** and **Moncloa**, particularly around C Princesa, are also good for fashion chains. Smart **Salamanca** has plenty of designer boutiques and interior decoration shops, while **Chueca** is full of hip, unusual fashion and music shops.

The epitome of style and sleek design, Milan's often grey, polluted streets are an unlikely backdrop for its population of models, designers and chic businessmen. This is a functional modern Italian metropolis of football, Alfa Romeo, money and separatist politics, where industriousness is held in high esteem. Milan, however, is a city with hidden beauty. The city's courtyards, if you can get a glimpse of them, are famously attractive. The most beautiful spot in the city is on the roof of the cathedral and there is a lively Milanese cultural life, too – from the grand opera of La Scala to hip modern music venues. As a city, Milan goes against what its fashion industry might suggest: in the end, it's what's under the surface that counts.

Arts & culture
★★

Eating
★★★★

Nightlife
★★★★

Outdoors
★★

Romance
★★

Shopping
★★★★★

Sightseeing
★★

Value for money
★

Overall score
★★

👁 Sights

Duomo

The **Duomo** ⓘ *T02-8646 3456*, **◥B3**, *daily 0700-1900, free; access to roof daily 0900-1700 (until 1830 in summer), €5 lift, €3.50 steps, Metro Duomo*, is the epicentre of the city. Started in 1386, the mammoth cathedral was not completed until Napoleon ordered the addition of the façade in the 19th century. Intricately Gothic, the pale marble building has over 3000 statues, many on tall slender spires, best appreciated from the roof. Inside, a nail purportedly from Christ's cross, hangs from the ceiling.

A cathedral to the gods of shopping sits right beside the Duomo. The grand **Galleria Vittorio Emanuele II** links the northern side of the piazza del Duomo with the piazza della Scala. A vast, cross-shaped, vaulted arcade, it was opened by the eponymous first king of Italy in 1867.

It is now filled with pricey cafés and equally expensive shops. Milanesi come to strut and tourists come to marvel at the enormity of the place and, near the centre, to spin on the balls of the mosaic bull (a symbol of nearby Turin) for good luck.

Radiating out from here are several pedestrianized shopping streets, such as **corso Vittorio Emanuele II**, though the highest concentration of designer togs is to be found in the **Quadrilatero della Moda**, an area to the northeast around via Manzoni, via della Spiga, via Monte Napoleone and via Sant'Andrea. Further northest again are the Giardini Pubblici and the **Galleria d'Arte Moderna** ⓘ *Villa Reale, Via Palestro 16, T02-7600 2819*, **◥A4**, *Tue-Sun 0900-1730, free, Metro Palestro*, where works by Van Gogh, Picasso and Matisse hang in Napoleon's one-time residence. Beyond the Giardini Pubblici is the central train station.

To the northwest of the Duomo is the hulk of the **Castello Sforzesco** ⓘ *Piazza Castello 3, T02-8846 3700, www.milanocastello.it*, **◥A2**, *various museums Tue-Sun 0900-1730, €3, free Fri after 1400, Metro Cairoli, Cardorna Triennale or Lanza*, with the **Parco Sempione** beyond.

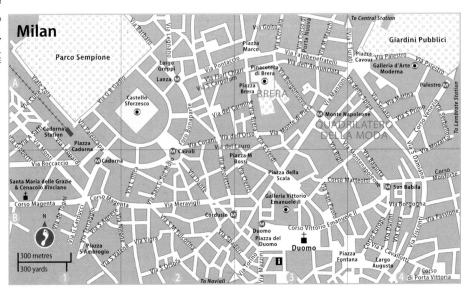

Milan

Galleria Vittorio Emanuele II

Between the castle and the Giardini Pubblici, the area of **Brera** has some of the city's oldest and most interesting streets and an excellent gallery in the **Pinacoteca di Brera** ⓘ *Via Brera 28, T02-8942 1146, www.brera.beniculturali.it,* ◖A3◗, *Tue-Sun 0830-1930, €5, Metro Lanza.* Highlights include paintings by Raphael, Caravaggio and Bellini.

Leonardo da Vinci's *Last Supper*, known as the **Il Cenacolo Vinciano** ⓘ *T02-8942 1146,* ◖B1◗, *Tue-Sun 0800-1900, €8, book by telephone at least 1 day in advance, Metro Conciliazone, Cadorna Triennale,* is located in the refectory of the Convent of Santa Maria delle Grazie, to the west of the centre. The already enormous popularity of Leonardo's innovative and dramatic masterpiece has been enhanced by the success of *The Da Vinci Code* and visitors must book ahead for their chance to see it. Most hotels in Milan will be happy to make a booking by telephone on behalf of their guests.

To the south of the centre, the **Navigli** still has remnants of Milan's old canal system and has become one of the best areas of the city for eating, drinking and shopping.

⬤ Sleeping

Many of the cheaper places to stay are in the area east of the station. Central hotels tend to be on the expensive side and often cater to a business clientele.

€€€ **Straf**, via San Raffaele 3, T02-805081, www.straf.it. A minimalist 21st-century design hotel in slate, brass and glass, a stone's throw from the Duomo.

€€ **Antica Locanda Leonardo**, corso Magenta 78, T02-4801 4197, www.anticalocandaleonardo.com. A smart and friendly place west of the centre, with wooden floors, a garden and contemporary art.

€€ **Antica Locanda Solferino**, via Castelfidardo 2, T02-657 0129, www.anticalocandasolferino.it. Stylish 19th-century bohemian hotel in the laid-back Brera area of town.

€€ **Ariston**, Largo Carrobbio 2, T02-7200 0556, www.aristonhotel.com. Bio-architecturally redesigned, the Ariston purifies the Milanese air and even the carpet glue is non-toxic. Bicycles are available for guests to use and it's only 400 m from the Duomo.

Castello Sforzesco

Quadrilatero della Moda

€€-€ **Hotel Charly**, via Settala 76, T02-204 7190, www.hotelcharly.com. Bargain elegance in 2 adjacent villas with a garden, near the station. The cheapest rooms lack en suite bathrooms.

❼ Eating

The Brera area has many of Milan's best restaurants. The Navigli, to the south, has traditional, down-to-earth places.

❚❚❚❚ **Corso Como 10**, corso Como 10, T02-653531. Closed Mon. A complex incorporating a café, photography gallery (Galleria Carla Sozzani, www.galleriacarlasozzani.org), bookshop, and fashion and perfume boutiques, Corso Como 10 really comes into its own in the evenings, when the who's who of Italian fashion troop into its courtyard restaurant to consume trendy food. It's also good for breakfast.

❚❚ **Al Pont de Ferr**, ripa di Porta Ticinese 55, T02-8940 6277. Closed Sat and Sun in winter and Sat and Sun lunch in summer. A traditional, good-value, canalside osteria lined with wine bottles. Offers country cooking and a good range of cheeses.

⊖ Travel essentials

Getting there Malpensa, T02-7485 2200, www.sea-aeroporti milano.it, Milan's main airport, is connected to the central station by bus every 20 mins (journey time around 50 mins, €5 one-way); buy tickets in arrivals or online. A taxi costs around €75, or you can travel by train every 30 mins (40 mins to Cadorna station, €11).
Linate airport, T02-7485 2200, www.sea -aeroportimilano.it, the most central, is connected to San Babila station by city bus 73 every 10 mins (about 30 mins, €1). Alternatively, **Starfly** buses run between Linate and the central station every 30 mins (€3). A taxi to the centre costs €15.

Orio al Serio, www.orio aeroporto.it, just outside Bergamo and used by **Ryanair**, has 3 bus connections to Milan central station, approximately every 30 mins, with **Autostradale** (€6.90, pay in advance at their airport office) and **Locatelli Air Pullman** (€7, pay on the bus). **Austostradale** also go, less frequently, to Lambrate station (€6.90). Or take a local bus (€1.60) into Bergamo and catch the train from there (1hr, €4.05).

International trains (including TGVs and sleeper services from Paris) arrive at **Milano Centrale**, Piazza Duca d'Aosta, www.trenitalia.com. See also page 12.

Getting around Much of the city centre's main sights are within easy walking distance of the Duomo. The **metro** is an efficient way of getting to and from the station, or down to the Navigli. There are 4 colour-coded lines, red, blue, green and yellow. Single tickets (€1) allow travel on buses and trams for 75 mins but only one metro journey. Day tickets (€4) give the freedom to use any mode of transport.

Tourist information The main tourist office, T02-7252 4301, www.milano infotourist.com, is in piazza del Duomo, on the southern side of the cathedral.

🍴 **Joia**, via P Castaldi 18, T02-2952 2124, www.joia.it. Closed Sun. A rarity in Italy: a hip, inventive vegetarian eatery, despite ludicrous names of the dishes.

🍴 **Latteria San Marco**, via San Marco 24, T02-659 7653. Closed Sun. A small traditional place in an ex-dairy in Brera serving a changing menu of Milanese food. Popular with locals and good for lunch; be prepared to wait.

🍴 **Spontini**, via Spontini 4, T02-204 7444. Closed Mon. With lots of oil and copious mozzarella, the enormously thick and tasty pizza slices in this popular and noisy place only come in 2 versions – big and bigger. There's good beer on tap and it's handy for hotels near the station.

☾ Nightlife

Bars and clubs
At *aperitivo* time, many bars compete with each other by offering ever more generous buffets of free nibbles with your drink and these can sometimes constitute a meal in themselves. Later on, Milan has a wider selection of nightclubs than most Italian cities, as well as some hip bars. Club opening hours vary with demand and the seasons but most stay open until at least 0400. Bars tend to close between midnight and 0200. The best areas for bars are **Brera** (the most unconventional), the **Navigli** (the cheapest, good on summer evenings when the area is closed to traffic) and **Corso Como** (the hippest). Notable nightspots include the immaculately smart and hip **Café Atlantique**, viale Umbria 42, www.cafe atlantique.com; and the lively, left-wing **Leoncavallo**, via Watteau 7, www.leoncavallo.org. In summer much of the nightlife decamps to **Idroscalo**, a lake near Linate airport.

Opera
La Scala, T02-7200 3744, www. teatroallascala.org. Probably the world's most famous opera house, La Scala has a Dec-Jul opera season, with classical concerts at other times. Tickets, costing €20-170, can be booked online.

The tourist office produces the bilingual monthly *Mese Milano*, with details of events and concerts.

○ Shopping

The line between Milanese street and catwalk is a fine one and it's not hard to spot the fashion set striding with hauteur around the city centre. The most famous area for Milan's designer clothing industry is the **Quadrilatero della Moda** or **Quadrilatero d'Oro** (Golden Square), an area just to the north of piazza della Scala. Quadrilatero has all the big names from Armani to Zenga and should be visited just for some window gazing even if you have no intention of making any purchases. There are, however, other parts of the city also worth visiting for the shops: the more leftfield **Navigli** is good for bargains, as is **corso Buenos Aires**, east of the station. And, if the clothes don't do it for you, on **via Durini** there are some pretty slick Italian designer kitchenware and furniture stores.

Munich knows how to have a good time. This is, after all, the beer capital of Europe. But while the merriment continues year-round in the city's bounteous beer halls, Munich manages somehow to shake off its hangover and retain a surprisingly sensible reputation for hard work and innovation. This is the home of BMW and Siemens, and is the location of some of Germany's finest museums, art galleries and theatres, lending it a rather refined and prosperous air. All this marries well with its elegant Bavarian palaces and grand churches, and its trustworthy character gave it the honour of hosting the first game of the 2006 World Cup. But look past the sharp suits and flash cars and you'll find another beer hall pounding with oompah music – an appealing reminder of Munich's mischievous side.

Arts & culture
★★★★

Eating
★★★

Nightlife
★★★

Outdoors
★★★

Romance
★★

Shopping
★★★

Sightseeing
★★★

Value for money
★★

Overall score
★★

At a glance

Munich's centre radiates out from **Marienplatz**, the Gothic heart of the **Altstadt** (Old Town). Just to the north is the **Residenz**, a former palace, surrounded by grand town houses, churches, theatres and elegant shops, while to the east is Platzl, home to the city's most famous beer hall, the Hofbräuhaus. Further east is **Museumsinsel** (Museum Island), an island on the Isar River, site of the Deutsches Museum. Back at Marienplatz, the **Viktualienmarkt**, a bustling outdoor food market, sprawls to the south of the square, while to the west is the main pedestrian shopping district, leading to **Karlsplatz** and on to the main train station. A few blocks to the north of the station is a cluster of excellent art galleries, known collectively as the **Pinakothek**, while to the south is the **Theresienwiese**, the purpose-built area that holds the huge tents of the Oktoberfest each year. Munich's best-known suburb is **Schwabing**, the lively student district, stretching to the north of the centre. The

"**O' Zapft is!**"

The mayor's declaration at the start of Oktoberfest, meaning the first beer barrel is tapped and it's time to start drinking.

tranquil, grassy **Englischer Garten** can also be found here. Further north still is **Olympiapark**, site of the 1972 Olympics, and out to the west are the sculpted grounds of **Schloss Nymphenburg**, Munich's summer palace.

★ *Don't leave town without sitting in the dappled sunshine of a beer garden tucking into a Weisswurst and frothy glass of Augustiner beer.*

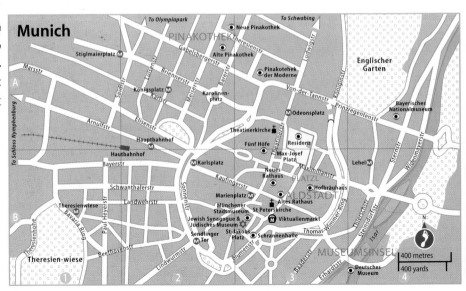

Munich

◉ Sights

Marienplatz
ⓘ *S-Bahn/U-Bahn Marienplatz, bus 52 to Marienplatz, Tram 19 to Theatinerstrasse.* ↘B3

The pulsing heart of Munich is this broad square, centred around the 17th- century **Mariensäule**, a column topped by a statue of the Virgin Mary. Flanking the north side is the gargoyled façade of the **Neues Rathaus** (New Town Hall), which holds the tourist office and has an 85-m tower offering impressive views of the city. A rather tuneless glockenspiel springs into action daily (at 1100, 1200 and 1700 in summer). Also here is the **Fischbrunnen** (Fish Fountain) and the **Altes Rathaus** (Old Town Hall), which was almost entirely destroyed during the Second World War. Today, its rebuilt bulk houses the **Spielzeugmuseum** (Toy Museum) ⓘ *daily 1000-1730, €3,* a vast collection of antique toys. In December, a traditional Christmas market takes place on the square. Overlooking Marienplatz from the west are the

Marienplatz

unmistakable domed towers of the Gothic **Frauenkirche** (Cathedral Church of Our Beloved Lady); the Alps can be seen from the top of the south tower on a clear day. South of the square is **St Peterskirche** (St Peter's Church) and **Viktualienmarkt**, a huge open-air food market. The futuristic but basic **Jewish synagogue** opened in November 2006 on nearby St-Jakobs Platz, joined by the **Jüdische Museum** (Jewish museum) in March 2007 ⓘ *T089-2339 6096,* ↘B3, *Tue-Sun 1000-1800.*

Münchener Stadtmuseum
ⓘ *Sankt-Jakobs-Platz 1, T089-2332 2370, www.stadtmuseum-online.de,* ↘B3. *Tue-Sun 1000-1800. €4. S-Bahn/U-Bahn Marienplatz.*

Near Viktualienmarkt is this excellent local history museum, which covers Munich from its official foundation in 1158 to the present, and also includes sections on fashion, musical instruments, puppets and film, with a cinema showing German and arthouse films.

Residenz and around
ⓘ *Residenzstr 1, T089-290671, www.residenz-muenchen.de,* ↘A3. *Apr-mid Oct daily 0900-1800; mid Oct-Mar daily 1000-1600. €6 (€9 with Schatzkammer) S-Bahn/U-Bahn Marienplatz, bus 52 to Odeonsplatz.*

Munich's most photographed sight is this magnificent Renaissance palace, the seat of Bavaria's rulers, the Wittelsbachs, until 1918. It is split into two sections: one open in the morning, the other in the afternoon, so you'll need a full day to take it all in. A total of 130 rooms are

---

◉ Travel essentials

Getting there Flughafen München, T089-97500, www.munich-airport.de, is 28 km northeast of the city centre. The Airport Bus runs to the centre every 20 mins and takes 45 mins. The S-Bahn (lines S1 and S8) connects the airport to the main train station and takes 45 mins.

International trains (including sleeper services from Paris) arrive at the **Hautbahnhof** central station, T+49 1805-996633, www.bahn.de.

Getting around Munich has an excellent integrated public transport system, including underground (**U-Bahn**) and overground (**S-Bahn**) trains, **trams** and buses. The Altstadt is easily explored on foot but the wider city will require you to jump on a train or tram. One ticket system covers all public transport; tickets can be bought from machines at U-Bahn/S-Bahn stations and from some bus and tram stops. A day ticket costs €4.80 for the inner city or €8.50 for up to 5 people. A 3-day ticket costs €11.80 (€20 for up to 5 people). A single trip ticket costs from €1.10, depending on the distance travelled. All tickets must be validated in the blue machines before travel. Strip tickets are useful for more than one trip; two strips need to be validated for each zone crossed.

Tourist information The main Munich Tourist Offices, T089-2339 6500, www.muenchen-tourist.de, are in the main railway station (Mon-Sat 0930-1830, Sun 1000-1800) and in the Neues Rathaus on Marienplatz (Mon-Fri 1000-2000, Sat 1000-1600).

The **CityTour Card** is a 1- or 3-day ticket for public transport in the city centre as well as discounts of up to 50% at over 30 attractions. Cards cost €9.50 (€18 for 3 days) and are available from vending machines at U- and S-Bahn stations, at some bus and tram stops, at dedicated kiosks displaying the City Tour Card sign and from many hotels.

filled with art, period furnishings and decorations, including the ancestral portrait gallery and the extravagant royal apartments. The highlight is the **Antiquarium**, a vast, arched hall resplendent with rococo swirls and murals. A separate ticket allows entry to the **Schatzkammer**, the royal treasury, crammed with jewellery and artworks from the late Greco-Roman period to the Middle Ages.

To see their modern-day counterparts, head just south to **Maximilianstrasse**, where Munich's well-heeled spend their dosh in glamorous boutiques. At the other end of Max-Joseph Platz is the baroque façade of **Theatinerkirche**, its ochre walls and green dome making a splash of colour in the pale stone surroundings.

Deutsches Museum

ⓘ *Museumsinsel 1, T089-21791, www.deutsches-museum.de,* **B4**. *Daily 0900-1700. €8.50. U-Bahn Fraunhofer-strasse, S-Bahn Isartor, tram 17 to Isartor or tram 18 to Deutsches Museum.*

Claiming to be the world's largest science and technology museum, this is certainly a gargantuan collection,

Residenz

Deutches Museum

covering everything from seafaring and space probes to the car industry and chemistry. The 55,000 sq m museum can be exhausting, but it is a sure-fire hit with children.

Pinakothek

ⓘ *Barer Str, www.pinakothek.de. U-Bahn Theresienstrasse, Odeonsplatz or Universität, tram 27 to Pinakothek, bus 154 to Schellingstrasse,* **A2**.

This series of art galleries is exceptional and regarded as one of the finest in Europe. The **Alte Pinakothek** ⓘ *No 27, T089- 2380 5216,* **A2**, *Tue 1000-2000, Wed-Sun 1000-1800, €5.50,* is a vast treasure trove of German art from the Middle Ages to the end of the rococo period. Its highlight is the exceptional collection by Dürer; look out for *The Four Apostles*, and his defining self portrait from 1500.

The **Neue Pinakothek** ⓘ *entrance on Theresienstrasse, T089-2380 5195,* **A2**, *Thu-Mon 1000-1700, Wed 1000-2000, €6,* holds a fine collection from the late 18th century to the early 20th century, including the private collection of King Ludwig I.

Open since 2002 and worth visiting for its architecture as much as its collections, is the newest addition, the **Pinakothek der Moderne** ⓘ *No 40, T089-2380 5360, www.pinakothek-der-moderne .de,* **A3**, *Tue, Wed, Sat and Sun 1000-1800, Thu and Fri 1000-2000, €9.50.* The airy concrete and glass structure has works by Dalí, Picasso and German greats such as Beckman and Polke, and architecture and design exhibits.

Englischer Garten

Wedged between the Altstadt and Schwabing is the Englischer Garten, a large city park of rolling lawns and lakes. Don't be shocked by the nude sunbathers during summer – Munich is known for its liberal views on naturism. Bare sunbathing aside, the park is a wonderful area for a stroll or picnic. The **Chinesischer Turm**, a pagoda-shaped tower, is a good landmark, set above a popular beer garden.

At the southeast corner of the Englischer Garten is the **Bayerisches Nationalmuseum** ⓘ *T089-211 2401, www.bayerisches-nationalmuseum.de,* **A4**. *Tue, Wed, Fri-Sun 1000-1700, Thu 1000-2000, €5, U-Bahn Lehel.* Although

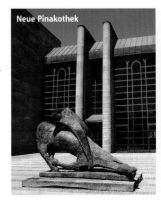
Neue Pinakothek

Oktoberfest, the world's largest beer festival, attracts a staggering – often literally – six million-plus visitors each year, who manage to knock back around six million litres of beer over two weeks. The festival actually begins in September, to much pomp from various processions and brass bands, and takes over the 'Wiesn' – the nickname for the Theresienwiese to the southwest of the city centre.

Fourteen vast tents spring up along custom-built avenues, surrounded by around 200 fairground rides and sideshows. Each tent is filled with rows of wooden tables where visitors down litre-sized Steins of beer and link arms to the pounding of oompah bands. The best time to visit is at lunch, when the tents are busy but not packed and it's possible to enjoy a big meal in relative peace (roast chicken and plates of sausages are the norm). In the evening, the pace picks up, the tents get crammed, and revellers take to dancing on the tables. Outside, the fairground rides do their best to churn the stomachs of those stumbling between tents. Although the festival attracts a fair contingent of Brits and Aussies, the majority of visitors are still Bavarian – you'll still see plenty of punters in Lederhosen and feathered caps. For more information, see **www.oktoberfest.de**.

at times rambling, it provides a worthwhile overview of the region's history. Exhibits include a fine collection of porcelain from Nymphenburg and art nouveau glassworks.

Englischer Garten

Schloss Nymphenburg

ⓘ *T089-179080, www.schloesser. bayern.de. Daily Apr-mid Oct 0900-1800, mid Oct-Mar 1000-1600. €5 museum only or €10 for museum and Marstallmuseum. Tram 17, bus 51.*

Northwest of the city centre is the summer residence of the Wittelsbachs, built in the Italian style from 1664. The main building includes the **Schönheitsgallery** (Gallery of Beauties) collected by Ludwig I, which is filled with portraits of many of the women that he considered beautiful. The **Steinerner Saal** has an elaborate frescoed ceiling and the **Marstall-museum**, housed in the court stables, includes the coronation coach of Emperor Karl VII.

Most attractive, however, are the beautiful formal gardens and pavilions surrounding the palace. Take some time to stroll around and get a feel for the place.

Schloss Nymphenburg

⊜ Sleeping

Prices for accommodation tend to be high and, be warned, they rise further during Oktoberfest, when most hotels and guesthouses get booked up months in advance.

€€€ **Bayerischer Hof**, Promenadeplatz 2-6, T089-21200, www.bayerischerhof.de. Munich's leading hotel since 1841, Bayerischer Hof has a great central location, with a grand marble lobby and huge rooms, many with 4-poster beds. There's also a roof garden with pool and spa, several bars and a nightclub.

€€ **Acanthus Hotel**, An der Hauptfeuerwache 14, T089-231880, www.acanthushotel.de. Traditional, small, family-run hotel, 10 mins' walk from the Altstadt. Rooms are floral with new bathrooms, and staff are a good source of information on the city.

€€ **Advokat**, Baaderstr 1, T089-216310, www.hotel-advokat.de. Claiming to be Munich's first boutique hotel, the Advokat is stylish and low-key, with scathingly cool staff. Excellent breakfasts served in the trendy café-bar.

€€ **Hotel Uhland**, Uhlandstr 1, T089-543350, www.hotel-uhland.de. Friendly guesthouse in a beautiful neo-Renaissance villa on a quiet street close to the Oktoberfest site. Extremely helpful staff, free bikes for rent, and cosy rooms – some with waterbeds.

€ **Euro Youth Hotel**, Senefelderstr 5, T089-5990 8811, www.euro-youth-hotel.de. Pleasant youth hostel with spotless, comfortable rooms, 50 m from the main train station. Some double rooms have private bathrooms. The Globetrotters Bar serves good breakfasts and cut-price Augustiner beer on tap.

❼ Eating

††† **Tantris**, Johann-Fichte-Str 7, T089-3619590, www.tantris.de. One of the city's finest restaurants, with a moodily-lit interior, cool retro touches and a stylish lounge bar upstairs. The menu is a mix of contemporary French and Italian, with some good value (but not cheap) lunchtime menus.

†† **Seven Fish**, Gärtnerplatz 6, T089-23000219, www.sevenfish.de. Californian-style seafood is served in this airy, bare-brick and blue-themed restaurant. Expect interesting twists, like marinated tuna with pineapple couscous or raspberry butterfish carpaccio.

† **Brotzeitstüberl**, Viktualien Markt. In the heart of the outdoor food market, this beer garden is a real social hub in summer, when locals flock here for a bout of people-watching, a cold beer and plate of the local Weisswurst and sweet mustard. Open until 2200 in summer.

† **Fraunhofer**, Fraunhoferstr 9, T089-266460. Students flock to this refreshingly tourist-free beer hall for big portions of good Bavarian food and the usual selection of beers. There's live music some nights, and a small theatre at the back.

† **Hofbräuhaus**, Platzl 9, T089-2901 3610, www.hofbraeuhaus.de. Munich's most famous beer hall has been serving for over 4 centuries, although it's suffered from its popularity and can feel very touristy. Still worth a quick visit to soak up a bit of history – and half a litre of excellent beer, of course.

† **Tresznejewski**, Theresienstr 72, T089-282349, www.tresznjewski.de. Hugely popular brasserie serving big bowls of pasta, steaks, burgers and salads. Transforms into a cocktail bar from midnight.

❶ Nightlife

Munich's nightlife has something of a split personality. On the one hand, the city is famous for its down-to-earth beer halls, where locals gather for their huge litre-glasses of beer and spill out into leafy beer gardens in summer. On the other hand, Munich has a thriving yuppie class with a correspondingly flash nightlife scene, centred on cocktail lounges and thumping clubs dotted around the centre and suburbs. The studenty area of **Schwabing** has good laid-back bars, while the gay and lesbian bar scene is based around **Gärtnerplatz**. Also worth seeing are some of the jazz and classical music venues; the city has 3 first-rate symphony orchestras, several major theatres and numerous fringe theatres. A good source of information is the monthly *Go München* magazine, www.gomuenchen.com, which also produces *München Geht Aus*, a useful guide to restaurants and bars.

❺ Shopping

The main shopping district is the pedestrian zone in the Altstadt, with streets such as **Kaufingerstrasse** between Marienplatz and Karlsplatz, lined with chain shops and department stores. The best place for food is the large open-air **Viktualienmarkt**. Also check out **Schrannenhalle**, rebuilt in 2005, with food and craft stalls and cultural events. The city's most exclusive boutiques are on **Maximilianstrasse**; nearby is trendy **Theatinerstrasse** and **Fünf Höfe**, a series of smart courtyards filled with shops. For more off-the-wall purchases, head to the second-hand shops in **Schwabing**.

Naples, wedged between the world's most famous volcano and the deep blue sea, is beautiful and ugly in equal measure. A world away from the genteel islands of Ischia and Capri that grace its bay, the city can be intimidating: anarchic and only sporadically law-abiding, the traffic is terrible and peace and quiet is hard to find. But it's an extraordinarily vivacious city, the pizzas are fantastic, music is ingrained in its culture and the treasure trove of sights hidden away in its narrow streets is overwhelming. More like Marrakech than Milan, ask an Italian from the north about Naples and they will throw up their hands in despair. But probe these gentrified folk a little more and they may tell you with something approaching admiration about the Neapolitan Renaissance, the cultural rebirth of a once-grand city.

Arts & culture
★★★★

Eating
★★★★

Nightlife
★★

Outdoors
★★★

Romance
★★★

Shopping
★★

Sightseeing
★★★★

Value for money
★★★★

Overall score
★★★

⦿ Sights

Santa Lucia

The grandest part of the city is around the giant and slightly barren **piazza del Plebiscito**. With its curved colonnade and vast, imposing space dotted with kids playing football, Vesuvius can be glimpsed between the grand 17th- and 18th-century buildings. The **Palazzo Reale** ⓘ *T848-800288,* **⬐B2**, *Thu-Tue 0900- 1900, Royal Apartments €2-4, palace courtyard and gardens free,* was built at the beginning of the 17th century for Spanish viceroys and extended by the Bourbons in the 18th century. Behind the church on the hill of **Monte di Dio**, tightly packed housing is stacked on the area where the original Parthenope was founded in around 680 BC by Greeks from nearby Cuma. **Via Chiaia**, running north of the

Piazza del Plebiscito

hill, is one of Naples' smartest shopping areas. In piazza Trento e Trieste, **Teatro di San Carlo** ⓘ *T081-797 2331, www.teatro sancarlo.it,* **⬐B2**, *daily 0900-1730, €5, tours throughout the day except during performances,* is Naples' great opera house. If you like castles, **Castel dell Ovo** ⓘ *Mon-Sat 0800-1800, Sun 0800-1400, free,* jutting out into the bay, is worth a wander round. And

Borgo Marinari, the collection of houses and (mainly) restaurants and bars surrounded by jetties beside the castle, is heaving on summer evenings.

Centro Storico

This is the true heart of Naples; its dark, narrow streets greasy, irregularly paved and overflowing with scooters, people and noise. Now a UNESCO World Heritage Site, the area still follows the ancient Greek and Roman layout of Neapolis, with three main east-west streets, or *decumani*. Long, straight **Spaccanapoli** ('Split Naples', vias Benedetto Croce, San Biagio dei Librai and Vicaria Vecchia), was once the *decumanus inferior* of the Greek city, while **via dei Tribunali** was the *decumanus major*.

The most interesting part of Spaccanapoli begins at piazza del Gesù, with late 16th-century **Gesù Nuovo**

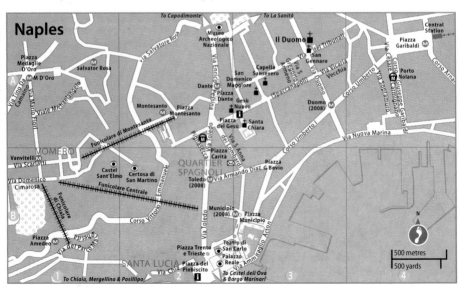

ⓘ *T081-551 8613,* ⬛JA2, *daily 0630-1300, 1600-1900.* Its brutal armoured exterior gives little hint of its spectacular interior. Next up, away from the chaotic plethora of bars, restaurants and small shops, are the city's inconceivably peaceful and colourfully tiled 14th-century cloisters of **Santa Chiara** ⓘ *via Santa Chiara 49/c, church T081-797 1235, www.santa chiara.org,* ⬛JA3, *Mon-Fri 0930-1300, 1430-1730, Sat and Sun 0930-1300; Museum/cloister T081-5521597, www.santachiara.info, Mon-Sat 0930-1830, €4.*

Other highlights of the Centro Storico include three 17th- and 18th-century spires, looking like enormously elongated wedding cakes: **Guglia dell'Immacolata**, piazza del Gesù, **Guglia di San Domenico Maggiore**, in a piazza of the same name, and **Guglia di San Gennaro**, in piazza Riario Sforza, adjacent to the Duomo. The 13th-century **Duomo** ⓘ *via del Duomo,* ⬛JA3, *Mon-Fri 0800-1230, 1630-1900, Sat 0800-1230, 1630-1930, Sun 0800-1330, 1700-1930, Scavi del Duomo €3,* is slightly less of a focus than cathedrals in other Italian cities but still an exceptionally grand building. Its chapels are especially

Santa Chiara cloisters

Via San Gregorio Armeno

interesting, one holding the famous remains of San Gennaro, the city's patron saint. Another, the fourth-century Cappella di Santa Restituta, is one of the city's oldest buildings. Under the building, in the Scavi del Duomo, some fascinating ancient remains have been unearthed.

Cappella Sansevero ⓘ *via de Sanctis 19, T081-551 8470, www.museo sansevero.it,* ⬛JA3, *Wed-Sat and Mon 1000-1740, Sun 1000-1310, €6,* originally built in 1590 but remodelled in the 18th century, is also worth a visit for some virtuoso allegorical marble sculptures, notably *Disillusion*, by Francisco Queirolo (1704-1762), and an amazingly lifelike *Veiled Christ* (1753) by Giuseppe Sanmartino.

Amongst other numerous places to wander, **via San Gregorio Armeno**, running north perpendicular to Spaccanapoli, is worth a visit. All year round shops spill their wares out onto the pavements: thousands upon thousands of figures, some smaller than others, vie for space with models of fruit baskets, mini electrically pumped water features and the occasional mechanized man-drinking-beer, or butcher- chopping-meat. Above you,

angels suspended from ceilings and doorways stare down lovingly.

Quartieri Spagnoli and Via Toledo

Via Toledo, Naples' bustling high street, runs between piazza del Plebiscito and piazza Dante. To its west, the narrow streets of the Quartieri Spagnoli are one of the city's poorest areas, and the Camorra heartland. There's a fascinating **market** every day up via Pignasecca and towards piazza Montesanto, while via Toledo heads north to the **Museo Archeologico Nazionale di Napoli** ⓘ *piazza Museo 19, T081-440 1466, www.marketplace.it/museo.nazionale,* ⬛JA2, *0900-1930, closed Tue, €6.50.* From enormous grandiose marble statues to small homely paintings, and from erotic oil lamps to a mosaic made of a million pieces, this is a staggering collection and gives an amazing idea of the look and feel of the ancient Roman world.

Mercato di Porta Nolana

Just to the west of the Circumvesuviana Terminal, this extraordinary piece of

Via Toledo

Pompeii and Herculaneum

There's a reason why **Pompeii** is the most famous of Vesuvius' victims. It may not be as well preserved as Herculaneum, but its sheer scale is staggering. Here is an entire Roman town, once home to as many as 20,000 people, ruined yes, but in many ways extraordinarily intact; a city stopped dead in its tracks in AD 79. Much of the wonder of the place is to be had simply by wandering around, looking into ordinary houses. Some of the most prosaic aspects are also the most arresting: tracks on the roads where carts have worn down the stones, shop signs advertizing their wares, mosaics warning you to 'beware of the dog'. ⓘ *T081-857 5347, www.pompeiisites.org. Apr-Oct 0830-1930, last entrance 1800, Nov-Mar 0830-1700, last entrance 1530. €11, 3-day ticket for Pompeii, Herculaneum, Oplontis and Stabia €20.*

Deep below the level of the surrounding contemporary city, **Herculaneum** (*Ercolano*) is extraordinarily unscathed; much more than Pompeii's mixture of ash and pumice, Herculaneum's mud solidified and sealed in the town below, preserving organic substance and the upper storeys of houses. ⓘ *Corso Resina 6, Ercolano, T081-739 0963. Apr-Oct 0830-0730, last entry 1800, Nov-Mar 0830-1700, last entry 1530. €11.*

Neapolitan theatre spills out every morning onto via Cesare Carmignano and via Sopramuro. It's a heady mix of fish, fruit and veg, pirated DVDs, bread, olives, contraband cigarettes, cheap beer, toy helicopters and fishing rods.

La Sanità and Capodimonte

Beyond the Museo Archeologico the road continues to the fine, green Parco di Capodimonte, where the **Reggia di Capodimonte** ⓘ *via Capodimonte, T081-749 9111, Thu-Tue 0830-1930, €7.50 (1400-1700, €6.50)*, houses the Bourbon and the Farnese art collections. On a bus there you might not even notice Dickensian La Sanità. Home to the city's ancient catacombs, it lies below and is bypassed by the bridge built by the French in 1808.

Chiaia, Mergellina and Posillipo

To the west of the centre the genteel Caracciolo seafront curves around to the yacht-filled marina of Mergellina, beyond which the exclusive residential area of Posillipo rises. Chiaia in particular is a more laid-back area of bars, cafés and restaurants and some green spaces, notably the **Villa Comunale** park.

Certosa di San Martino

ⓘ *largo San Martino 5, T081-558 5942,* **J82**. *Thu-Tue 0830-1930. €6.*

Perched high above Naples, in Vomero, with exceptional views is this 14th-century Carthusian monastery. It now contains the excellent **Museo di San Martino** and is one of Naples' most satisfying sights, containing interesting paintings, an elegant cloister, an exhibition of *presepi* (nativity scenes), one of Naples' most spectacular churches and terraced gardens. The hulking **Castel Sant'Elmo** is next door.

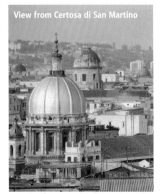
View from Certosa di San Martino

⊖ Travel essentials

Getting there Naples Airport, T081-789 6259, www.gesac.it, is 5 km from the centre. Alibus runs every 30 mins to piazza Garibaldi (central train and bus station) and piazza Municipio, by the port (€3). Taxis to Centro Storico costs around €20.

International trains, including sleeper services from Paris, arrive at **Napoli Centrale station**, piazza Garibaldi, northeast of the centre.

Getting around The city is a fairly manageable size and, despite the crazy traffic, walking is the best way to get around the Centro Storico. There are also useful **bus** routes: R2 goes from piazza Garibaldi along corso Umberto I to piazza

Trento e Trieste; R3 from piazza Carità to Mergellina past piazza Trento e Trieste and the Chiaia seafront; R4 north from the port to the Museo Archeologico. Linea 2 of the **metro** is useful for connecting piazza Garibaldi to Montesanto, Chiaia (piazza Amadeo) and Mergellina. For travel information on the city and local area, see www.unicocampania.it. Tickets, valid for 90 mins, cost €1 each but it's also possible to buy a day ticket (*Giornaliero*) for €3 (€2.50 at weekends). Four **funicular railways** go to Vomero, Centrale (via Toledo to piazza Fuga), Chiaia (via del Parco Margherita to via Cimarosa), Montesanto (piazza Montesanto to via Morghen) and Mergellina (via Mergellina to via

Manzoni). The **Circumvesuviana**, T081-772 2444, runs from Naples' piazza Garibaldi around the bay to Sorrento every 30 mins, stopping at Torre Annunziata (for Oplontis), Pompeii (Pompei Scavi) and Herculaneum (Ercolano). A daily ticket costs €6.40.

Tourist information Azienda autonoma di soggiorno, cura e turismo, piazza del Gesù, T081-552 3328. Mon-Sat 0900-2000, Sun 0900-1500. **Osservatorio Turistico-Culturale del Comune**, Portico di San Francesco di Paola, piazza Plebiscito, T081-247 1123. Mon-Fri 0900-1900, Sat 0900-1400. The useful bilingual monthly publication *Qui Napoli*, is free and full of up-to-date information.

⊜ Sleeping

€€€ Costantinopoli, via S Maria di Costantinopoli 104, T081-557 1035, www.costantinopoli104.com. Near piazza Bellini, this pristine and stylish place has a tranquil courtyard garden with a small pool. Don't miss one of its famously good breakfasts.

€€ Caravaggio, piazza Riario Sforza 157, T081-211 0066, www.caravaggio hotel.it. Modern rooms in a 17th-century building. Cosy feel and amiable staff.

€€ Soggiorno Sansevero, piazza S Domenico Maggiore 9, T081-790 1000, www.albergosansevero.it. In the heart of the Centro Storico, large rooms in a handsome old palazzo at a good price.

€ Albergo Bellini, via San Paolo 44, T081-456996. This small, exceptionally welcoming and good-value hotel has an old-fashioned feel.

€ Donnalbina7, via Donnalbina 7, T081-1956 7817, www.donnalbina7.it. Minimalistic, classy and chic but also welcoming and cosy, Donnalbina7 offers the best value in the city.

⊙ Eating

⅋⅋⅋ Pizzeria Brandi, salita Sant'Anna di Palazzo 1-2, T081-416928. Daily 1230-1500, 1930-0100. Inventors of the ubiquitous pizza Margherita. Also has a selection of traditional Neapolitan fare.

⅋ Caffè Letterario Intra Moenia, piazza Bellini 70, T081-290720. Daily 1000-0200. A literary café with a decent menu and a cultured atmosphere. Exhibitions, literary meetings, concerts and poetry evenings happen here and there's also internet access.

⅋ Da Michele, via Sersale 1, T081-553 9204. Mon-Sat 1000-2400. The purists' pizzeria supreme. There are two choices, Margherita or Marinara, and service is lightning quick.

⅋ La Cantina di Via Sapienza, via Sapienza 40/41, T081-459078. Mon-Sat 1200-1530. Great home cooking in a popular lunch-only eatery. A delicious bowl of *penne aum aum*, with tomato aubergine and mozzarella, is only €2.90.

⅋ La Vecchia Cantina, vico San Nicola alla Carità 14, T081-552 0226. Mon and

Wed-Sat 1200-1600, 1900-2200; Sun 1200-1600. Busy, traditional family place with lots of good fish dishes and exquisite *torta caprese*.

⅋ Osteria della Mattonella, via G Nicotera 13, T081-416541. Mon-Sat 1300-1500, 1930-2330. Tucked away up the hill from the piazza del Plebiscito. You may need to knock on the door and wait to be let in. Fast, friendly and informal service combined with fairly simple but delicious Neapolitan fare.

◑ Nightlife

Areas which buzz until late are: around **piazza Bellini** and via Benedetto Croce in the Centro Storico; **Borgo Marinari** (in summer), by the Castel dell'Ovo; **Chiaia**, mainly to the west of piazza dei Martiri; and **Mergellina**.

Bar Gambrinus, via Chiaia 1 (piazza Trento e Trieste), T081-417582, 0800-0130, is Naples' most refined bar and worth a visit for the luscious Liberty interior and the exceedingly good cakes.

Not a city for the faint-hearted, Paris engulfs the senses with its vibrant culture, architectural marvels, world-class galleries, stylish shopping, smoky (soon to be smoke-free) wine bars and fantastic food. With a list like this, it's hardly surprising that the city has a reputation for arrogance; something that could be called merely confidence in itself as both a historical showpiece and a fearless innovator. While it holds tight to its traditions, this modern city continues magically to evolve. Its essence is an effortless balance of old and new, of traditional elegance and creative thinking: it is Notre Dame through cherry blossom from the quai de la Tournelle and rollerblading under potted palm trees beside the Seine.

More than ever before, Paris of the 21st century is a feisty brew of peoples from around the world. Old-fashioned French flavours have not been lost, or even submerged – men in berets still play boules on the quai de la Seine and bourgeois madames still feed tasty titbits to their poodles from the restaurant table, but now there are more ingredients in the city mix, more viewpoints. (It is estimated that 20% of the two million people living in central Paris are immigrants.)

Twirling seductively to her own special tempo, with the rest of Europe gawping from the sidelines, Paris confidently expects to lead the way but is also not afraid to go against the prevailing wind.

Arts & culture
★★★★★

Eating
★★★★★

Nightlife
★★★★

Outdoors
★★

Romance
★★★★★

Shopping
★★★★★

Sightseeing
★★★★

Value for money
★★

Overall score
★★★★★

At a glance

Central Paris is divided into 20 numbered districts (*arrondissements*) and is bisected by the River Seine. At its heart are two small islands – **Île de la Cité** (home to Notre Dame Cathedral) and **Île St Louis**. This is intricate, romantic Paris. On the **Left Bank** of the Seine (*Rive Gauche*), **St Germain** still has a high concentration of publishing houses and bookshops but tourist chatter has largely replaced debates on Existentialism and Surrealism. The **Latin Quarter**, to the east, is home to the Sorbonne, while the imposing seventh *arrondissement*, to the west, has a number of key landmarks, including the **Eiffel Tower**, **Les Invalides** and the **Musée d'Orsay**. Southwest is **Montparnasse**, once a place of wild entertainment.

North of the Seine on the **Right Bank** (*Rive Droit*), the **Louvre** is a big pull for tourists who buzz around

Paris is a moveable feast.

Ernest Hemingway, 'A Moveable Feast'', 1964

the place du Carrousel snapping the glittering **Pyramide** and the **Jardin des Tuileries**. From here, the **Champs-Elysées**, long synonymous with wealth, sweeps up to the **Arc de Triomphe**. To the east of the Louvre are three adjoining *quartiers*: **Les Halles**, **Marais** and **Bastille**, while, to the north, **Montmartre** sits prettily on a hill, more like a village than anywhere else in the city and home to the fanciful **Sacré Coeur**. Thanks to some canny facelifts the working-class districts of **Belleville** and **Ménilmontant**, to the east, are now the hip places to be once the sun goes down.

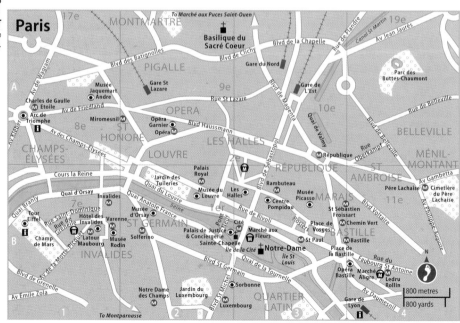

24 hours in the city

Get up early and head to the Île de la Cité for **Notre Dame** and the **Sainte-Chapelle**. Linger at the flower market, grab a delicious sorbet from the renowned **Berthillon**, then cross the Pont Neuf to the Left Bank. After a caffeine and philosophy fix in **Café de Flore**, visit the beautiful **Musée Rodin** or browse for books, antiques and fashion around **place St-Germain-des-Prés**. Treat yourself to lunch at **Ze Kitchen Gallerie** or **Les Bookinistes**, in preparation for one of the great museums: the **Louvre** or the **Musée d'Orsay**, perhaps. In the late afternoon, head for the **Marais** for window shopping or **Montmartre** for the view. After dark, **Brasserie Flo** is great for dinner, followed by jazz at **New Morning**. Alternatively, succumb to the lure of the lit-up **Eiffel Tower,** or join the beautiful people drinking the night away at the bars along **rue Oberkampf**.

Musée du Louvre

★ *Don't leave town without checking out the sculptures at the Musée Rodin.*

⊖ Travel essentials

Getting there Eurostar (www.eurostar.com) runs at least 10 trains daily from London Waterloo to **Paris Gare du Nord**. (A few services stop in Calais and Lille en route.) **Charles de Gaulle Airport**, aka Roissy, www.paris-cdg.com, is 23 km northeast of Paris. The best way into the centre is by the RER B train to Châtelet-Les-Halles (45 mins/€8.50) from Terminal 2, with a free shuttle connection from Terminal 1. There is also the **Roissybus**, T08-3668 7714 (45 mins/€8.50) to rue Scribe, near the Opéra Garnier, or regular **Air France** buses to Porte Maillot, the Arc de Triomphe, the Gare de Lyon and Gare Montparnasse. To reach the city from **Orly Airport**, 14 km south, the best bet is the **Air France** bus to Les Invalides and Montparnasse (40 mins/€7.50). Or take the free bus to RER Pont de Rungis and catch the **Orlyrail** train to the city centre (50 mins/€5.15). The RATP **Orlybus** runs to Denfert-Rochereau

(30 mins/€5.80). Ryanair flies to **Paris Beauvais Airport** to the northwest of the city, from where there's a shuttle bus to Porte Maillot (1 hr 15 mins/€13). **Paris Airports Service**, T01-5598 1080, will pick up from your hotel and charge €25 per person to the airport (half the cost of a taxi).

Getting around Note that the last two digits of a Paris postcode indicate the *arrondissement*. Central Paris is walkable but you will almost certainly need to use the **metro** system at some point. There are 16 numbered lines, plus the small cable car (*funiculaire*) up to the Sacré Coeur. Trains run daily 0530-0030. Numbered **buses** ply the streets daily 0630-2030, with a select few operating a reduced service past midnight. There are fewer buses on Sun. Timetables and routes are posted at each bus stop. Always validate your ticket in the machine at the front of the bus when you board. **Tickets** for all of central Paris

(Zones 1 and 2) are valid on buses, the metro and RER urban rail. A single costs €1.40; a carnet of 10 tickets is better value at €10.90. Tickets are sold at metro stations and some tobacconists. There are also a number of **passes** available: *Paris Visite* is valid for 1, 2, 3 or 5 days (€8.50, €13.95 €18.60 or €27.20) and can be used throughout Paris and its regions, including Disneyland Paris and Versailles. The pass comes with discount vouchers for certain sights.

Tourist information
Paris Convention and Visitors Bureau, 25 Rue des Pyramides, 75001, T08-9268 3112, www.paris-info.com, Nov-May Mon-Sat 1000-1900, Sun 1100-1900; Jun-Oct daily 0900-1900. There are other tourist offices at the Gare de Lyon (Mon-Sat 0800-1800) and the Eiffel Tower (summer daily 1100-1840). For details of city and themed tours by bike, bus, boat or on foot, consult the website,

● Sights

Île de la Cité and Notre Dame

ⓘ *6 pl du Parvis-de-Notre-Dame, 75001.
Cathedral T01-4234 5610,* ◪J83 *; Apr-Sep
daily 1000-1830; Oct-Mar daily 1000-1730;
free. Tower T01-5310 0700; daily
0930-1930; €5.70. Metro Cité.*

On an island in the Seine, France's most
famous place of worship, Notre Dame
Cathedral, was built to replace and
surpass a crumbling earlier church, on the
site where a Roman temple to Jupiter
once stood. Pope Alexander III laid the
first stone in 1163 and the cathedral took
more than 170 years to complete. The
building has a spectacular Gothic façade,
with a rose window at its western end
and magnificent flying buttresses at its
eastern end. rThe nave is at its best when
the sun shines through the stained-glass
windows, washing it with shafts of light in
reds and blues. Place du Parvis de Notre
Dame is an epicentre of tourist activity but
the gardens at the rear and to the south
are comparatively calm. Walk all the way
ound to appreciate the flying buttresses
and the cherry blossoms in spring.

Notre Dame

Les Invalides

Île de la Cité was once the seat of
royal power. Much survives from the
original medieval palace complex on the
western part of the island, namely the
Conciergerie, the Palais de Justice (still
the city's law courts) and the glittering
jewel of **Sainte-Chapelle** ⓘ *4 blvd
du Palais, 75001, T01-5373 7852,* ◪J83 *,
daily 0930-1800, €5.50*, a chapel built
by King Louis IX to house his precious
religious relics. Since the early 19th
century there has been a colourful and
sweet-smelling **Marché aux Fleurs** at
place Louis-Lépine, towards the centre
of the island (on Sundays the market
also sells caged birds and small pets).
Pont Neuf, the best-loved of all the
city's 36 bridges and the oldest
(inaugurated in 1607), straddles the
Seine at the western end of the island.

Tour Eiffel

ⓘ *Champ de Mars, 75007, T01-4411 2311,
www.tour-eiffel.fr,* ◪J81 *. 1 Jan-15 Jun
daily 0930-2345; 16 Jun-2 Sep daily
0900-0045; 3 Sep-31 Dec daily 0930-2345.
Lift to Level 1 €4.10, Level 2 €7.50, Level 3
€10.70; stairs to Levels 1-2, €3.80.
Metro Bir Hakeim.*

Gustav Eiffel won a competition to
design a 300 m tower for the Universal
Exhibition of 1889. The result was
originally reviled by Parisians and was
only meant to stand for 20 years; now
it's the city's most identifiable landmark.
The highest viewing platform is at 274 m
and, on a clear day, you can see for more
than 65 km. Take the stairs to the first
level, with a bistro, small museum and a
post office; on the second level, there are
souvenir shops and the gourmet **Jules
Verne** restaurant. To avoid long queues
(at least an hour), visit early in the
morning or late at night, when the tower
is lit up like a giant Christmas tree.

Les Invalides

Metro Invalides, Latour Maubourg

The seventh *arrondissement* breathes
extravagance from every pore. Expect
19th-century elegance and grandeur
rather than quaint backstreets and
curiosities. The avenues, mansions and
monuments proclaim their importance.
Wander rues de Grenelle, St Dominique
and Cler, east of the Champ-de-Mars, to
see where high society shops and dines.

Sitting splendidly amid the broad
avenues is **Hôtel des Invalides**

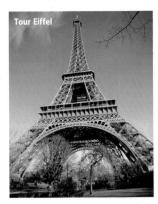

Tour Eiffel

Musée Rodin

ⓘ 129 rue de Grenelle, 75007, T01-4442 3877, www.invalides.org, ⊠B1, daily 1000-1800 (till 1700 in winter), closed first Mon of month, €7.50, Metro Latour Maubourg, Varenne, Louis XIV's hospice for war veterans. The vast Army Museum now charts French military history from prehistoric times to the present.

Around the corner, **Musée Rodin** ⓘ 77 rue de Varenne, 75007, T01-4418 6110, www.musee-rodin.fr, ⊠B1, summer Tue-Sun 0930-1745, winter Tue-Sun 0930-1645, €6, is housed in the light and airy 18th-century Hôtel Biron – the sculptor's last home. There are over 500 of Rodin's sculptures here, as well as works by Camille Claudel (his model and lover) and Rodin's own collection of paintings, including work by Van Gogh.

Musée d'Orsay

ⓘ quai Anatole France, 75007, T01-4049 4814, www.musee-orsay.fr, ⊠B2, Tue, Wed, Fri, Sun 0930-1800, Thu 0930-2145 (last entry 45 mins before closing). €7.50, Sun €5.50, extra for temporary exhibitions. Metro Solferino.

This 1900 train station-turned-art gallery is worth visiting almost as much for the building as for the great Impressionist treasures it holds. The enormous space is enhanced and illuminated by a vaulted iron-and-glass roof. There are decorative arts and Rodin sculptures on the middle level, with the most popular works, by the likes of Monet, Cézanne, Degas and Signac, on the upper level. Visit during the week to avoid the crowds.

Jardin du Luxembourg

ⓘ rue Guynemer and blvd St Michel, 75006, T01-4234 2000, ⊠B2. Summer daily 0730-1 hr before sunset; winter 0815-1 hr before sunset. Metro Notre Dame des Champs. RER Luxembourg.

The lovely Luxembourg gardens cover more than 23 ha of the Left Bank. Their centrepiece, in front of the Luxembourg Palace, is the octagonal pool, surrounded by wide paths, formal flowerbeds and terraces. On the eastern side of the garden, accessed by boulevard St Michel, is the Médicis Fountain, an open-air café and ice cream sellers. From April to August there are free daytime musical concerts at the bandstand.

In the western section, towards rue Guynemer, there is an adventure playground and a puppet theatre. Photo

Jardin du Luxembourg

◉ **Best of the rest**

Île St Louis ⓘ 75001. Metro Pont Marie, Sully Morland, ⊠B3.
This island on the Seine is like stepping into a film set for the 17th century.

Musée Picasso ⓘ Hôtel Salé, 5 rue de Thorigny, 75003, T01-4271 2521, ⊠B3. Wed-Mon 0930-1800 (until 1730 in winter). €9.50. Free 1st Sun of month. Metro Saint Paul, Chemin Vert, St Sébastien-Froissart. A chronological journey through the artist's life, including a gem from the blue period.

Canal St Martin ⓘ 75010-75019, ⊠A4. Metro République for quai de Valmy, Stalingrad for quai de la Seine. The canal was built in the 19th century as a shortcut on the Seine. Its most attractive sections have footbridges and barges.

Musée Jacquemart-André ⓘ 158 blvd Haussmann, 75008, T01-4562 1159, www.musee-jacque mart-andre.com, ⊠A1. Daily 1000-1800. €9.50. Metro Miromesnil. In 1872 the portrait artist Nélie Jacquemart painted Edouard André. Nine years later they were married and living in this magnificent mansion on boulevard Haussmann.

Cimetière du Père Lachaise ⓘ 16 rue Repos, 75020, T01-4370 7033, ⊠B4, 6 Nov-15 Mar, daily 0800-1730, 16 Mar-5 Nov, 0800-1800. Free. Metro Père Lachaise, Gambetta. The most celebrated cemetery in France and last resting place for the likes of Jim Morrison, Edith Piaf, Frédéric Chopin, Honoré de Balzac and Oscar Wilde, to name but a very few.

exhibitions are often suspended along the garden's iron railings. Bartholdi's Statue of Liberty here is a smaller model of the one given to the United States in 1885.

Musée du Louvre
ⓘ *Palais du Louvre, 75001, T 01-4020 5151, www.louvre.fr, ⓂB2, Fri-Mon 0900-1800, Wed-Thu 0900-2145. €8.50, €6 after 1800. Free 1st Sun of month. Ticket-holders can enter via Passage Richelieu. Metro Palais Royal.*

Paris's foremost art gallery is as vast as it is famous. It was constructed as a fortress in the 12th century, lived in as a palace by the late 14th century, rebuilt in the Renaissance style in the 16th century and finally converted into a museum by Napoleon. The wonderful glass pyramid entrance by I M Pei was added in 1989. Today the four floors of the three wings (Sully, Denon and Richelieu) hold some 350,000 paintings, drawings, sculptures and other items, dating from 7000 BC to the mid-19th century. Highlights include *Vénus de Milo* (2nd century BC), Rubens' *Life of Marie de Médici*, Italian sculpture in the Michelangelo Gallery and, of course, the crowd-pulling *Mona Lisa*.

Arc de Triomphe

Centre Pompidou

Champs-Elysées and Arc de Triomphe
ⓘ *pl Charles de Gaulle, 75008, T 01-5537 7377, ⓂA1. Summer daily 0930-2300; winter daily 1000-2230. €8. Free first Sun of month. Metro Charles de Gaulle-Etoile.*

The Champs-Elysées has been an international byword for glamorous living since the 19th century. The eponymous avenue is Paris's 'triumphal way', leading from the vast **place de la Concorde** to the **place Charles de Gaulle**, site of the **Arc de Triomphe**. The arch has always been the focus of parades and celebrations: Napoleon's funeral procession was held here in 1840, as were the victory celebrations of 1919 and 1944, and it's the finishing point of the Tour de France cycle race. In recent times Parisians have been snooty about the surrounding tackiness but it seems that the area's fortunes are on the up. Culturally and commercially, the area is undergoing a mini-makeover, with an influx of new restaurants, designer shops and exhibition centres.

Les Halles

With its trendy boutiques, historic squares, hip hang-outs and aristocratic-mansions-turned-museums, the Rive Droite is now fashionable and, in parts, smart. It has its low points too – the eyesore of Forum des Halles and brazenly drunken rue de Lappe in Bastille – but the good far outweighs the questionable. A highlight is the **Centre Pompidou** ⓘ *pl Beaubourg, 75004, T 01-4478 1233, www.centre pompidou.fr, ⓂB3, daily 1100-2200 (Thu till 2300), €7-9 for exhibitions, €10 internet day ticket, permanent exhibitions free on the 1st Sun of the month, Metro Rambuteau,* an architectural masterpiece of the late 1970s that still brings a buzz to the surrounding area. The multi-coloured fun carries on with the funky fountains in the neighbouring **place Igor Stravinsky**, and there are plenty of galleries to choose from along **rue Beaubourg** and **rue Quincampoix**.

Marais
Metro Chemin Vert, St Sébastien Froissart.

Sandwiched between Les Halles and Bastille is Marais, everybody's favourite place for aimless wandering, thanks to its winding medieval streets, charming tea rooms and ultra-fashionable shops. The showpiece is **Place des Vosges** ⓘ *Metro St Paul, ⓂB3,* a beautiful 17th-century square of arcaded buildings. **Rue des Rosiers**, a resolutely Jewish street, has bakeries, kosher restaurants and falafel takeaways, while the city's unabashedly gay centre is around **rue Vieille-du-Temple** and **rue des Lombards**.

Attention to retail

Shopping is an essential part of the Paris experience, even if it is only of the window variety. Inventive presentation is an art form here, especially among the city's specialist food retailers. **Place de la Madeleine** is renowned for its gourmet shops, including **Fauchon** ⓘ *Nos 28-30, T01-47 42 60 11, Mon-Sat 0900-2100,* a Parisian institution that sells cheese, wine, pastries, chocolates and more. There are also treats to be found on **Île St Louis**, such as the famous sorbets and ice cream at **Berthillon** ⓘ *31 rue St Louis-en- l'Île, Wed-Sun 1000-2000.* Don't miss the impressive architecture of the city's department stores and of **Les Galeries**, the 19th-century covered shopping arcades between boulevard Montmartre and rue St Marc. The traditional hotspots for gold-card holders are **rue du Faubourg St Honoré, rue de la paix, avenue Montaigne** and **place Vendôme**. More recently, designer names have joined the books and antiques around **place St-Germain-des-Prés**. Smaller, cheaper boutiques are to be found in the **Marais**, the **Bastille** and **Abbesses**. Streets that combine morning food markets (Tuesday-Sunday) and wonderful speciality shops include **rue Cler, rue de Buci, rue Lepic** and **rue Mouffetard**.

Fauchon

Bastille

Metro Bastille.

The winds of regeneration that the Pompidou Centre blew into Les Halles, brought the new **Opéra Bastille** to the Bastille just over a decade later. This gritty, working-class area has emerged

Basilique du...

as an after-dark hotspot and bastion of designer outlets but it still clings to its revolutionary credentials: raucous protests and demonstrations are a common sight on place de la Bastille. For a glimpse of the grittier side of life, away from trendy rue de la Roquette and rue du Faubourg St Antoine, head to the **Marché Aligre** ⓘ *place d'Aligre, 75012, ◢B4, Tue-Sat 0800-1300, 1600-1930, Sun 0800-1300, Metro Ledru Rollin,* and the surrounding streets, where old-style bars full of cigarette butts and sullen, red-faced locals are still the norm.

Basilique du Sacré Coeur

ⓘ *Parvis du Sacré Coeur, 75018, T01-5341 8900, ◢A2. Daily 0600-2230 (dome and crypt 0900-1730). Church free, dome €8. Metro Anvers, Lamarck- Caulaincourt, Abbesses plus funiculaire.*

It was the Romans who first erected a place of worship on top of this hill to the north of the city. They beheaded Denis, the first bishop of Paris, here in the third century AD. He was canonized as a result and the hill became the 'Mont des Martyrs' for early Christians. The current basilica – a glorious flurry of domes or a fanciful abomination, depending on your point of view – was designed by Paul Abadie and financed largely by national subscription. It took nearly 40 years to build, finally being consecrated in 1919, and now attracts some five million visitors each year. Inside, a golden Byzantine mosaic of Christ by Luc Olivier Merson hovers beatifically over the high altar. The spiral staircase to the dome is worth tackling, if you're partial to a long view, but you can enjoy a similar panorama from the steps of the basilica – along with the crush of tourists, hustlers and pigeons.

😊 Sleeping

Hotels near the big sights are expensive, but there are popular, mid-priced options on rue Saint-Dominique, squeezed between the Eiffel Tower and Les Invalides. The bustling streets of Marais or St Germain also have some good hotels. There are romantic corners on Île St Louis and in Montmartre, while Bastille and Oberkampf are good for night owls.

€€€ Hôtel Bourg Tibourg, 19 rue du Bourg Tibourg, 75004, T01-4278 4739, www.hotelbourgtibourg.com. Metro St Paul, Hôtel de Ville. This wonderful Marais hotel is a Costes/Jacques Garcia masterpiece. The French designer has lived in the Marais for over 20 years. The rooms are exquisitely intimate and de luxe, seamlessly combining French and Oriental influences.

€€€ Pershing Hall, 49 rue Pierre Charron, 75008, T01-5836 5800, www.pershinghall.com. Metro George V. Ultra-modern hotel designed by Andrée Putman. Minimalist in the extreme but also luxurious.

€€ Hôtel Beaumarchais, 3 rue Oberkampf, 75011, T01-5336 8686, www.hotelbeaumarchais.com. Metro Filles du Calvaire, Oberkampf. Primary colours are the defining feature of this buzzing 33-room hotel.

€€ Hôtel Danemark, 21 rue Vavin, 75006, Montparnasse, T01-4326 9378, www.hoteldanemark.com. Metro Vavin. An elegant and welcoming hotel on a lively street, lined with little cafés and shops. Rooms are cosy and at least one of the bathrooms has a jacuzzi.

€€ Hôtel des Deux-Îles, 59 rue St Louis en l'Île, 75004, T01-4326 1335, www.deuxiles-paris-hotel.com.

Metro Pont Marie. Welcoming and comfortable. Specify if you want a bath rather than a shower.

€€ Hôtel Luxembourg, 4 rue de Vaugirard 75006, T01-4325 3590, www.hotel-luxembourg.com. Metro Odéon. 33 rooms. Popular choice in Louis XIV building, with free Wi-Fi in rooms. Great location right by the eponymous gardens and the Sorbonne.

€€ Hôtel des Marronniers, 21 rue Jacob, 75006, T01-4325 3060, www.paris-hotel-marronniers.com. Metro St-Germain-des-Prés. This is in the heart of animated St Germain but is set back from the street so it's not too noisy. The rear courtyard has tables for breakfast or afternoon tea.

€€ Hôtel des Tuileries, 10 rue Saint-Hyacinthe, 75001, T01-4261 0417, www.hotel-des-tuileries.com. Metro Pyramides. An 18th-century house converted into a hotel. The 26 rooms are individual, comfortable and homely. The reception room showcases Louis XVI-style furniture.

€€ Hôtel du Vieux Marais, 8 rue du Plâtre, 75004, T01-4278 4722, www.paris-hotel-vieux-marais.com. Metro Hôtel de Ville. A family-run hotel for the past 30 years, the Vieux Marais has 30 rooms, with Poltrona Frau furniture and gleaming bathrooms.

€ Grand Hôtel Lévêque, 29 rue Cler, 75007, T01-4705 4915, www.hotel-leveque.com. Metro École Militaire, La Tour Maubourg. Located in a market street, offering clean rooms, most with en suite bathroom. Recently renovated, so reservations essential.

€ Hôtel Esmeralda, 4 rue St-Julien-le-Pauvre, 75005, T01-4354 1920. Metro St Michel. A budget option with character. Try to ignore the wonky bedside tables, the curling wallpaper and the decrepit breakfast room.

🍴 Eating

Breakfast

🍴 Le Comptoir du Commerce, 1 rue des Petits Carreaux, 75002, T01-4236 3957, www.comptoirdu commerce.com. Mon-Sat 0800-2400, Sun 1200-1900. Metro Sentier. Pine walls and shutters and cushioned seating create a country kitchen ambience. Good range of breakfasts.

🍴 Café de Flore, 172 blvd St Germain, 75006, T01-4548 5526, www.cafe-de-flore.com. Daily 0730- 0100. Metro St-Germain-des-Prés. Renowned as an unofficial philosophical forum, the Café de Flore retains its intellectual air, although today's thinkers need deeper pockets than their forebears.

Lunch

🍴 Le Dauphin, 167 rue Saint Honoré, 75001, T01-4260 4011. Winter daily 1200-1430, 1930-2230; summer daily 1200-0030. Metro Palais Royal. Hearty fare from southwest France served in an elegant setting. The house speciality is *la parillada* – meat, fish or vegetables on a hot plate.

🍴 Les Bookinistes, 53 quai des Grands Augustins, 75006, T01-4325 4594. Mon-Fri 1200-1430, 1900-2300, Sat 1900-2300. Metro St Michel. One of Guy Savoy's bistros, this place serves popular modern French cooking and overlooks Notre Dame. Healthy-sized portions of quality food, from delectable sea bass to melt-in-the-mouth scallops.

🍴 Ze Kitchen Gallerie, 4 rue des Grands Augustins, 75006, T01-4432 0032. Mon-Fri 1200-1500, 1900-2300. Metro St Michel. Inspirational and inventive, with an emphasis on the nutritious as well as the delicious. The lunchtime menu (€21-32) includes a glass of wine and coffee. Bookings essentials.

Pause Café, 41 rue de Charonne, 75011, T01-4806 8033. Mon-Sat 0800-0200, Sun 0900-2000. Metro Bastille, Ledru-Rollin. The relaxed atmosphere, large terrace and good, reasonably priced food have made this a very popular lunch spot.

Dinner

La Fermette Marbeuf, 5 rue Marbeuf, 75008, T01-5323 0800, www.fermettemarbeuf.com. Daily 1200-1500, 1900-2330. Metro Franklin D Roosevelt. An art nouveau extravaganza with ceramic panels featuring animals and flowers. When booking your table, ask to be placed in the back room, under the glass roof with its delicate stained-glass panes.

Brasserie Flo, 7 cour des Petites-Ecuries (enter 63 rue du Fg St Denis), 75010, T01-4770 1359. Daily 1200-1500, 1900-0130. Metro Château d'Eau. Excellent food in a wonderful panelled art nouveau dining room. Classic Flo dishes include oysters in a champagne sauce and steak tartare.

Le Café Noir, 65 rue Montmartre, 75002, T01-4039 0736. Daily 1200-0200. Metro Sentier. A down-to-earth corner café with large windows, red formica tables, mirrors and pictures.

⦿ Nightlife

For up-to-the-minute info on what's on check the listings magazines *Pariscope* or *L'Officiel des Spectacles*.

Bars and clubs

Paris has something to suit every taste, from authentic wine bars with red-faced old soaks propping up the zinc counter, to swish venues fit for glamorous celebrities. The **Bastille** is always a popular nightspot, although it can be overrun with tourists. **Oberkampf** is just as lively, but cheaper and more authentic. Nearby **rue St Maur** is tipped to be the new Oberkampf. A lot of clubs double as live music venues some nights of the week. Many bars also serve food, albeit a limited menu, and there are a growing number of cross-over places. **Man Ray**, 34 rue Marbeuf, 75008, www.manray.fr, Metro Franklin Roosevelt, is a classic example of a fine restaurant that is also a bar with DJs, while **Café Cheri(e)**, 44 blvd de la Villette 75019, Metro Belleville, is a trendy nightspot known locally as a great alternative to a full-blown club.

❝❞ Paris has something to suit every taste, from authentic wine bars with red-faced old soaks propping up the zinc counter, to swish venues fit for glamorous celebrities.

Dance and opera

National and international dance troupes regularly come to Paris to perform. **Opéra Garnier**, Palais Garnier, pl de l'Opéra, 75009, T08-9289 9090, www.opera-de-paris.fr, Metro Opéra, is the principal base of the Ballet de l'Opéra National de Paris, and the best place to see classical ballet and opera favourites. **Opéra Bastille**, pl de la Bastille, 75012, T08-9289 9090, www.opera-de-paris.fr, Metro Bastille, veers towards more contemporary choices, but for ground-breaking shows, with dazzling sets and musical effects, look no further than **Opéra Comique**, 5 rue Favart, 75002, T01-4244 4546, Metro Richelieu-Drouot.

Music

If you want a taste of good old-fashioned and newly fashionable *chansons*, head to **Au Lapin Agile**, 27 rue des Saules, 75018, T01-4606 8587, www.au-lapin-agile.com, Tue-Sun 2100, €24, including 1 drink, Metro Lamarck Caulaincourt. **L'Olympia**, 28 blvd des Capucines, 75009, T01-5527 1000, www.olympiahall.com, Metro Opéra, is the home of *chanson*, where Johnny Halliday and Edith Piaf once performed. It still pulls the crowds for a broad range of performers. Jazz lovers, meanwhile, will find everything they could wish for at **New Morning**, 7-9 rue des Petites-Ecuries, 75010, T01-4523 5141, www.new morning.com, Metro Château d'Eau.

L'Elysée Montmartre, 72 blvd de Rochechouart, 75018, T01-5507 0600, www.elyseemontmartre.com, Metro Anvers, features acts from all musical backgrounds. Performances start late, so be prepared to sit on the floor and drink beer beforehand.

La Maroquinerie, 23 rue Boyer, 75020, T01-4033 3505, Metro Gambetta, features world acts, from accordion players to flamenco troupes, indie bands to Middle Eastern oud ensembles.

For classical music look out for concerts in auditoriums at the **Louvre**, T01-4020 8400 (page 188) and the **Musée d'Orsay**, T01-4049 4717 (page 187), as well as the concerts, mainly chamber music, held in churches, including **Sainte-Chapelle** (page 186). For a contemporary classical sound, **Cité de la Musique**, 221 av Jean- Jaurès, 75019, T01-4484 4484, www .cite-musique.fr, Metro Porte de Pantin, has an exciting and varied programme.

Prague

Visitors get rather poetic when they first clap eyes on Prague. The 'Golden City', the 'Belle of Bohemia' and the 'City of a Thousand Spires' certainly has a lot to live up to, but the reality matches the hype. Prague remained blessedly unharmed during the two World Wars, and the Velvet Revolution of 1989 came to pass without a single shot being fired. This translates into a beautiful city with a stunning showpiece centre: winding, medieval lanes flanked by elegant Gothic, baroque and art nouveau façades. As you wander through Europe's largest castle or over famous Charles Bridge, it's hard to imagine that Prague was off limits to western visitors as little as two decades ago. But time moves quickly in this part of the world: the Czech Republic has been a member of the EU since May 2004 and a new veneer of sophistication is spreading through the capital. Locals aren't surprised; Prague was, after all, at the vanguard of European culture for much of the 19th and early 20th centuries. Vestiges of this past are the main draws today; from the cobbled streets of Staré Město and the haunting atmosphere of the Jewish cemetery to the smoky cellar bars and the graceful concert halls that launched some of Europe's greatest composers. The essence of Prague, however, is something less tangible; getting lost in the medieval Old Town on a foggy evening, or watching the sun set over terracotta roofs and soaring church spires is, quite simply, poetry.

Arts & culture
★★★★

Eating
★★★

Nightlife
★★★★

Outdoors
★★

Romance
★★★★★

Shopping
★★

Sightseeing
★★★★

Value for money
★★★

Overall score
★★★★

At a glance

The Vltava River, running from south to north through the city centre, neatly splits up the area in which visitors spend most (if not all) of their time. On the right bank is **Staré Město** (Old Town), at the heart of which is **Staroměstské náměstí** (Old Town Square), famous for its astronomical clock. North of here is the old Jewish district of **Josefov**, edged by **Parízská** boulevard. The winding, narrow streets of the Old Town fan out south of Old Town Square, opening up in the southeast at **Václavské náměstí** (Wenceslas Square), site of the 1989 Velvet Revolution. This is the main hub of **Nové Město** (New Town), Prague's business and commercial district. To the north is the busy square, **Náměstí Republiky**, while, to the south, the wide streets hold many of the biggest hotels, restaurants and department stores. Further east is the residential area of **Vinohrady**, once the royal vineyards.

On the other side of the river is **Malá Strana** (Lesser Quarter). This area of 18th-century town houses and palaces is quieter and even more atmospheric than the Old Town, its streets rolling up towards **Hradčany**, the castle district. Hradčany is completely dominated by the magnificent castle complex, with the central road of **Nerodova** (always full of tour groups trudging to the castle) running back down into **Malá Strana**. To the south is the green expanse of **Petřín**, a tranquil, leafy hill topped by a little model of the Eiffel Tower.

Prague doesn't let go.

Franz Kafka

★ *Don't leave town without sipping a cup of Prague grog – hot rum with water, lemon and sugar.*

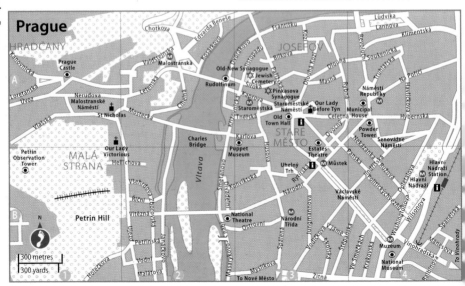

Prague

24 hours in the city

Start early with a coffee in **Old Town Square** to beat the crowds – the astronomical clock begins its daily whirrings at 0900. Look into the brooding hulk of **Our Lady Before Týn** before striking north along Parízská and into the **Josefov** district. Take a look at the **Old-New Synagogue** and the exhibitions in the **Pinkasova Synagogue** before strolling through the eerily atmospheric **Jewish Cemetery**. For a snack or early lunch, stroll back along Parízská which is lined with cafés and restaurants. Veer west and you'll hit the river and picture-postcard **Charles Bridge**, with its buskers and views of the red-roofed houses of Malá Strana creeping up towards the castle. Once across the bridge, wander along the cobbled lanes centering on **Malostranské náměstí**, the area's busiest square. Lunch at trendy *Square*, before the stiff climb up to the castle. You'll need a good few hours to stroll around the complex, after which you'll have earned a Czech beer at one of the little, smoke-filled pubs in Malá Strana.

Astronomical clock

Continue the traditional theme for dinner at *U Medvídků*, back in the Old Town, before checking out the live jazz at *AghaRTA*, Zelezna 16, or catch the Prague Symphony Orchestra at the **Municipal House**.

⊖ Travel essentials

Getting there Ruzyně Airport, www.csl.cz, is 20 km northwest of the centre. Buses run every 20 mins to the city centre, taking 20 mins. Take No 119 to Dejvicka metro station, No 100 to Zlicin metro, and No 179 to Nove Butovice metro. **CEDAZ**, T220-114296, runs a minibus shuttle to Náměstí Republiky (CZK 90 per person) every 30 mins daily 0600-2130. Private CEDAZ buses can be booked for up to 4 people and cost CZK 480. Taxis from outside the airport terminal should cost from CZK 500 to the centre.

International trains arrive at Hlavní nádraží, the city's main railway station. Call T840-112113, or see www.vlak.cz.

Getting around The Old Town is easy to walk around, as is Malá Strana, although there's a fairly steep climb to the castle. **Dopravní Podnik** (DP),

T296-191817, www.dp-praha.cz, runs Prague's limited **metro** system, extensive **tram** and **bus** network, as well as a **funicular train** to the top of Petřín hill. The metro system has 3 lines: A (green), B (yellow) and C (red), running daily 0500-2400. Trams operate daily 0430-2400; buses run at similar times. Tram Nos 51-59 and bus Nos 502-514 and 601-603 run at night. The funicular runs daily 0915-2045. Tickets need to be bought before boarding and are available from DP Information offices, some metro stations, tourist information centres and news-stands. The single ticket system is complicated, so visitors are better off buying a 1-, 3- or 7-day pass (CZK 80, CZK 220, CZK 280 respectively). Tickets must be validated in the machines at stops and in metro stations before travel.

Tourist information Prague Information Office, T12444, www.pis.cz, has several outlets. A new office has opened at Rytírská 31 (daily Apr-Oct 0900-1900, Nov-Mar 0900-1800). There is also an office in the Old Town Hall (Apr-Oct Mon-Fri 0900-1900, Sat-Sun 0900-1800; Nov-Mar Mon-Fri 0900-1800, Sat-Sun 0900-1700) and in Hlavní nádraží railway station (Apr-Oct Mon-Fri 0900-1700, Sat-Sun 0900-1600; Nov-Mar Mon-Fri 0900-1800, Sat 0900-1500). The **Prague Card** is a 4-day admission card to 40 monuments and museums, and can be purchased with or without travel on public transport; 4 days with transport costs CZK 960; 3 days without is CZK 740.

Exchange rate Czech Koruna (CZK). £1 = CZK 41.15. €1 = CZK 28.10.

👁 Sights

Pražský hrad (Prague Castle)
ⓘ *T224-373368, www.hrad.cz,* **A1**.
Castle grounds daily Apr-Oct 0500-0000;
Nov-Mar 0600-2300. Buildings daily
Apr-Oct 0900-1700; Nov-Mar 0900-1600.
Combined ticket CZK 350. Tram 12, 18,
20, 22 or 23, metro Malostranská.

Prague Castle has dominated the city's
skyline for over 1000 years. Its sprawling
complex merits at least half a day's
exploration. The first evidence of
a castle here dates back to AD 880 and,
over the following millennium, the site
became the monarchic and spiritual
powerhouse of the country. Today it
feels like a walled town and is reputedly
the world's largest castle, its courtyards
linking the palace, cathedral, several
churches, museums, galleries and a
monastery, all beautifully lit up an night.
   Your first port of call should be
St Vitus' Cathedral (Chrám sv Vita),
the seat of the Archbishop of Prague.
The interior of this magnificent Gothic
structure is delicately lit by a series of
mosaic-style stained-glass windows.

Prague Castle and
Malá Strana

St Vitus' Cathedral

Look out for **St Wenceslas's Chapel**,
resplendent with over a thousand
semi-precious stones.
   The **Old Royal Palace** (Starý
královský palác) is worth seeing for the
soaring, empty expanse of Vladislav Hall.
It once hosted coronation celebrations;
today presidents of the Republic are
sworn in here. Wander around the rest of
the palace before exiting by **St George's
Basilica** (sv Jiří), with its beautifully
preserved Romanesque interior, where
chamber music recitals are held. Next
door is the old monastery, now a gallery.
   Behind the monastery is **Golden
Lane** (Zlatá Ulička), a cobbled street,
lined with 16th-century cottages, today
filled with craft shops. (The Prague-born
writer, Franz Kafka, briefly stayed at
No 22.) At the end of the lane is the
Toy Museum (Muzeum hraček) ⓘ *daily
0930-1730, CZK 60,* filled with traditional
wooden toys and, oddly, hundreds of
Barbie dolls. Opposite is **Lobkovicz
Palace** (Lobkovický palác) ⓘ *Tue-Sun
1000-1800, CZK 40,* with its rambling
historical collection. Also worth
exploring are the castle gardens,
particularly the peaceful **Royal
Gardens**, which have beautiful views.

Malá Strana
ⓘ *Tram 12, 18, 20, 22 or 23,*
metro Malostranská, **B1**.

This wedge of land between the castle
and Vltava River, often bypassed by
visitors, is a delightful, atmospheric are
a of cobbled lanes and crumbling baroque
façades. At its heart is **Malostranské
náměstí**, a busy square fringed with
grand neoclassical houses and elegant
colonnades. In the centre is the baroque
St Nicholas church (Sv Mikuláš chrám)
ⓘ *1000-1600, CZK 50,* **A1**, built in the
early 18th century. Its prominent green
dome and tower quickly became a major
Prague landmark. The inside is quite
overwhelming, awash with hectic,
multicoloured frescoes.

Petřín
ⓘ *Tram 6, 9, 12 or 20 to Újezd,* **B1**.

A steep funicular railway, dating from the
1891 Jubilee Exhibition, climbs up green
and leafy Petřín hill. At the top of the
funicular, pause awhile to soak up the
views, then follow the path along the old
city wall, which passes a rose garden and
observatory, to the **Petřín Observation**

Petřín

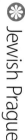

Before the Nazi occupation from 1939 to 1945, Prague's Jewish population was a thriving community, numbering some 50,000. Today, the number has dwindled to around 4,000. The focal point of the community remains the Josefov district, named after Emperor Josef II, whose 1781 reforms helped bestow civil rights to the Jewish community. The original ghetto actually dated back to the 13th century, although much of it was cleared in a huge late-19th century development project. This drove out the poorer sections of the community and transformed the winding old alleys into smart boulevards, lined with elegant mansions. With the arrival of the Nazis came forced removals, both to a new ghetto in Trezín, 60 km from the city, and, later, to concentration camps; a staggering two thirds of the population is thought to have died in camps before the end of the war. Ironically, what was left of the old ghetto was spared demolition by Nazi forces thanks to Adolph Hitler's chilling wish to preserve the area as an "exotic museum of an extinct race".

European City Breaks Prague

Tower (Petřínská rozhledna) ⓘ 🔲B1
May-Aug daily 1000-2200, Sep-Apr Mon-Fri 1000-1900, Sat-Sun 1000-1700, CZK 50. This 60-m high structure is a small-scale version of the Eiffel Tower, also dating from the Exhibition, with a viewing platform offering fabulous views over rooftops, broken by the soaring silhouettes of dozens of spires. Next door is a small neo-Gothic castle with a mirror maze (same times and prices as the tower).

Karlův most

Karlův most (Charles Bridge)

Prague's oldest bridge was founded in 1357 by Charles IV and, for many centuries, was the only link between the right and left banks. Today, it is best known for its dozens of statues, although most of these were added in the 18th century. The car-free bridge is thronged with tourists and buskers at all times of day but, at night, the bridge empties out and takes on a fairytale quality, never more so than in winter, with snowflakes drifting over the water.

Staroměstské náměstí (Old Town Square)
ⓘ *Tram 17 or 18, metro Staroměstská,* 🔲A3.

All roads in Bohemia once led to Staroměstské náměstí, still Prague's most important and jaw-dropping square, a vast cobbled expanse flanked by brightly painted baroque houses. Centrepiece is the Town Hall, home to the extraordinary **Astronomical clock** (Orloj) in a tower to the right. Crowds gather on the hour

Staroměstské náměstí

(0900-2100) to watch the figures shuffle out from little doors. They portray various saints, as well as representations of death, vanity, history and greed – the latter is a dodgy depiction of a Jew clutching money bags, albeit minus his beard, which was removed at the end of the war.

Behind the Town Hall is the looming, blackened church of **Our Lady Before Týn** (Panna Marie pred Týnem), its Gothic hulk hiding a surprisingly pretty baroque interior. In winter, a **Christmas market** selling mulled wine, souvenirs and wooden toys is held on the square.

Josefov

ⓘ *Tram 17 or 18, metro Staroměstská,* ⬛A3.

Prague's old Jewish ghetto is one of the most atmospheric quarters of the city. It's no longer the warren of old streets depicted by Kafka, but the main sights – four synagogues and the cemetery – remain. A good starting point is the **Old-New Synagogue** (Staranová synagoga) ⓘ *Cervená 2,* ⬛A3, *Sun-Thu 0930-1800, Fri 0900-1300, CZK 200,* a squat structure dating from 1275. It still functions as a synagogue, making it the

Municipal House

Old-New Synagogue

oldest still in use in Europe. The other sights in Josefov are visited as part of the **Jewish Museum** (Zidovské Muzeum) ⓘ *T221-711511, www.jewishmuseum.cz,* ⬛A3, *Sun-Fri Apr-Oct 0900-1800, Nov-Mar 0900-1630, CZK 290.* The most striking is the **Old Jewish Cemetery** (Starý zidovský hrbitov). Used from 1439 to 1787, it is the oldest and largest Jewish cemetery in Europe. It is a poignant, mysterious place, with hundreds of ancient headstones bristling from the ground at haphazard angles. The adjoining **Pinkas Synagogue** (Pinkasova sinagoga) holds a moving Holocaust memorial, with chilling pictures drawn by children from the Trezín ghetto outside Prague, most of whom were later transported to concentration camps.

Náměstí Republiky (Republic Square)

ⓘ *Tram 3, 5, 14, 24 or 26, metro Náměstí Republiky,* ⬛A4.

This busy square, in the east of Nové Město, is worth visiting for the **Municipal House** (Obecní dům) ⓘ *T222-002101, www.obecnidum.cz,* ⬛A4, the city's finest art nouveau building. An

exuberantly decorated cultural centre, it was opened in 1912 on the site of King's Court. A restaurant, opulent café and Smetana concert hall are on site. Next door is **Powder Tower** (Prasná brána) ⓘ *daily 1000-1800, CZK 50,* ⬛A4 one of a series of towers that once fortified the Old Town and were used to store gunpowder. The sharply pointed medieval tower is the starting point of the Royal Mile, along which Bohemian kings once marched towards their coronation. You can climb to the top for views over Staré Město.

Václavské náměstí (Wenceslas Square)

ⓘ *Tram 3, 9, 14 or 24, metro Muzeum or Můstek,* ⬛B4.

Site of the city's most important political protests for the last 150 years, this sloping space is more like a long, divided avenue than a square. Most famously, it was the backdrop to the Velvet Revolution of 1989, when half a million people protested against the government. At the southern end of the square is a statue of St Wenceslas, as well as the vast **National Museum** (see box opposite).

National Museum

⬤ Best of the rest

National Museum (Národní muzeum) ⓘ *T224-497111, www.nm.cz,* ⓘB4, *daily 1000-1800, closed on first Tue of every month, CZK 110.* This hulking, neo-Renaissance building houses a huge collection of almost 14 million items of natural history, art and music.

Puppet Museum (Marionette Muzeum) ⓘ *Karlova 12, T222-220913, www.puppetart.com,* ⓘA3, *daily 1200-2000.* Impressive collection of wooden puppets and a marionette theatre with regular performances (phone for times and tickets). This is also the headquarters of the international puppetry organization, UNIMA.

Church of Our Lady Victorious (Chrám Panny Marie Vítezné) ⓘ *www.pragjesu.info,* ⓘA1, *Mon-Sat 0930-1730, Sun 1300-1700.* Home of the *Infant Jesus of Prague,* a 14th-century wax statue measuring 28 cm that was presented to the Carmelites in 1628 and is revered in Catholic countries around the world. Its spangly outfits are changed regularly by the nuns.

⬤ Sleeping

Prague is crammed with characterful guesthouses and hotels; those in Staré Město tend to be more expensive, while those in Malá Strana are quieter.

€€€ **Hotel Aria**, Triziste 9, T225-334111, www.ariahotel.net. As implied by the name, this is one for music lovers. It's a baroque hotel with a contemporary interior and composer-themed rooms, a comprehensive CD library, a musical director on hand to advise on concert venues in Prague, a music salon and a rooftop café.

€€€ **Hotel Josef**, Rybná 20, Josefov, T221-700111, www.hoteljosef.com. Prague's most stylish hotel is a minimalist haven of glass, calm white lighting and the odd splash of colour. Rooms have groovy touches like DVD players and Sony Playstations. Models and rock stars make this their first port of call.

€€€ **U Pava**, U Luzického semináre 32, T257-533360, www.romantichotels.cz/upava. Characterful, historical hotel on a leafy street in Malá Strana. Rooms have heavy curtains, thick rugs on wooden floors, painted, restored ceilings and patches of over-the-top original frescoes on the walls. Views of the castle or over the old town.

€€ **Dum u Velke Boty**, Vlašská 30/333, T257-532088, www.dumuvelke boty.cz. A welcoming family-run outfit on a quiet square in Malá Strana with attractive, antique-filled rooms. There's art on the walls, simple brass beds and parquet floors. Charles Bridge is a 10-min walk away, and the owners are a great source of local information.

€€ **U Karlova Mostu**, Na Kampe 15, T257-531430, www.archibald.cz. Atmospheric, old-fashioned house just 50 m from Charles Bridge. Cosy rooms with wooden floors and stencilled walls; the room in the attic has a lovely beamed ceiling.

€€ **U Zlatého Jelena**, Celetná 11/Štuparská 6, T222-317237, www.hotel-u-zlateho-jelena.cz. Simple, airy rooms with parquet flooring, brass beds and tall windows, just a few steps from Old Town Square. Ask for a room overlooking the quiet courtyard. The staff are friendly and the breakfasts (included in the price) are substantial.

€ **Betlem Club**, Betlémskée námesti 9, T222-221 5745, www.betlemclub.cz. Good-value hotel on a quiet square, a short walk from Staroměstské náměstí. The rooms are small and comfortable, with dark wood furniture – some of it incongruously modern. Breakfast is served in a vaulted cellar.

⬤ Eating

The restaurant scene in Prague has improved immeasurably in recent years; for one thing, pork is no longer the key ingredient in all dishes. Although a traditional meal in a *pivnice* (pub) remains an essential part of a visit to Prague, there are now also a number of top-notch restaurants serving international cuisine.

Breakfast

ⓘ **Au Gourmand**, Dlouhá 10, T222-329060. Upmarket French boulangerie in the Old Town serving a delicious selection of pastries, cakes, snacks and Italian coffees in a cool, tiled interior.

ⓘ **Café Imperial**, Na Poříčí 15, T222-316012. Gorgeous high-ceilinged Hapsburg-era café, with tiled walls, rickety furniture and excellent coffee, which is served with free doughnuts in the morning. Breakfast is a big plate of eggs and sausages, and there are more substantial meals throughout the day.

Lunch

ⓘ **Nebozízek**, Petrínské sady 411, T257-315329, www.nebozizek.cz. Brilliant views from this traditional restaurant half-way up the funicular to Petřín, with a bright glass-covered terrace. Good salads and Bohemian onion soup, plus fresh fish and hearty game dishes.

Square, Malostranské náměstí 5, T296-826104, www.squarerestaurant.cz. What was once a favourite hang-out of Kafka's is today an elegant restaurant, with vaulted ceilings and a well-heeled clientele, who are lured by the Italianesque menu.

Dinner

Kampa Park, Na Kampě 8b, T296-826102, www.kampagroup.com. This is Prague's most sophisticated restaurant, with a heated terrace looking over the river. It has a contemporary menu, complemented by a 150-strong wine list. The cooking is sublime: expect dishes like langoustine ravioli and baby chicken with chanterelles and chorizo.

U Maltézských rytířů, Prokopská 10/297, T257-530075, www.umaltezsky chrytiru.cz. Snug, Gothic cellars with formal high-backed chairs and white linen tablecloths. This place feels either romantic or cold, depending on how busy it is, but the food is great – there's a melt-in-the-mouth chateaubriand and a good choice of game dishes.

U Medvídků, a Perštýň 7, T224-211916, www.umedvidku.cz. This wood-panelled and smoke-filled genuinely old-fashioned beer hall attracts a mix of local regulars and tourists. The food is traditional Czech stodge – pork, dumplings and sauerkraut – perfect for soaking up a few jars of the delicious on-tap Budvar.

☻ Nightlife

The English-language *Welcome to Prague* publication, produced by the tourist office, has basic seasonal information on up-to-date events. Tickets for the majority of venues can be bought online at www.ticket pro.cz or www.ticket portal.cz.

Bars and clubs

Traditional Prague nightlife revolves around top-notch beer and smoky pubs (*pivnice*), such as **Baráčnická rhychta** (Tržiště 23) in Malá Strana or **Kozicka** (Kozi 1) in Staré Město. The local beer is the main draw, thanks to famous names such as *Pilsner Urquell*, *Staropramen* and *Budvar*. One drawback of these good-value brews is that they attract a profusion of stag parties from the UK. Many bars and pubs now ban such groups from their premises.

Beer aside, many bars offer nightly live music; the jazz scene is thriving and it suits the vaulted, smoky cellars of the Old Town particularly well. The **Prague Jazz Festival** is held every autumn at **AghaRTA**, Zelezna 16, www.arta.cz.

> **❝❞ Music is the lifeblood of the city, and you can barely walk a step without hearing classical strains wafting out of a church, concert hall or home.**

A number of stylish cocktail bars have sprung up around the city in recent years, not to mention some dodgy Irish-themed pubs, mostly aimed at tourists. To find some of the best of the former, head to the streets around the north of Old Town Square.

Most of the city's nightclubs are yet to undergo a 21st-century style makeover but they continue to pull in the punters until the wee small hours.

Live music

The jazz scene is thriving and it suits the vaulted, smoky cellars of the Old Town particularly well.

Music lovers flock to Prague every May for **Prague Spring**, T257-312547, www.festival.cz, one of the world's leading classical music festivals. It has been running since 1946 and attracts scores of symphony, philharmonic and chamber orchestras. It begins every year on 12th May with a performance of Smetana's *Má vlast* (*My Country*) and closes three weeks later with Beethoven's 9th Symphony.

High-quality concerts can be enjoyed at other times of year, too. Prague's classical music venues are among the most beautiful buildings in the city. The Prague Symphony Orchestra plays at the **Municipal House**, on Námestí Republiky (see page 198), while the illustrious Czech Philharmonic performs at the splendid **Rudolfinum**, Alsovo nabr 12, T227-059352, www.rudolfinum.cz.

Performances of opera and ballet are held amid the neo-Renaissance magnificence of the **National Theatre** (Národní divadlo), Národní trída, T224-901448, www.narodni-divadlo.cz; at the opulent **State Opera** (Státní opera), Legerova 75, T296-117111, www.opera.cz, and at the **Estates Theater** (Stavovské divadlo), Ovocný trh, T224-215001, www.stavovskedivadlo.cz. The latter, a beautiful cream and pistachio building, is Prague's oldest theatre and hosted the premieres of Mozart's *Don Giovanni* and *La Clemenza de Tito* in the 18th century. *Don Giovanni* remains one of the most popular operas performed here to this day.

Reykjavik is the coolest of cities. And that's not just because it's the most northerly capital in the world. Set in an expanse of lava fields, close to both the largest desert and biggest glacier in Europe, this remote outpost is so far off the European map it has virtually been granted a licence to be quirky, unconventional and ground-breaking in its music, architecture, sculpture and even lifestyle. With a population of only around 113,000, it is hardly a teeming metropolis but, what it lacks in size, Reykjavik more than makes up for in the brio and creativity of its youthful population. This restless energy is reflected in powerful, subterranean forces of nature which, with typical ingenuity, have been harnessed to make life more bearable in this harsh, unforgiving environment.

Reykjavik

Arts & culture
★★★

Eating
★★

Nightlife
★★★★

Outdoors
★★★★★

Romance
★

Shopping
★

Sightseeing
★★

Value for money
★

Overall score
★★

At a glance

The bohemian old town of Reykjavik, known as **101**, is situated between two water features: the harbour and the pond. In between you'll find the heart of the city, **Austurvöllur Square**, with the historic Alþing parliament building and cathedral. Follow the main street, **Austurstraeti**, and you reach Lækjatorg Square, from where the buses leave and the roads radiate. Across the road and up the hill is **Laugavegur**, Reykjavik's busiest street, buzzing with shops, bars and cafés. Down by the harbour, you'll find the flea market at weekends, where you can try specialities such as dried cod or putrefied shark meat (only for those with strong stomachs). Towering above the city is the soaring steeple of **Hallgrímskirkja**, always useful for getting your bearings. The other dominant feature on Reykjavik's skyline is **Perlan** (the Pearl), which sits above the city's hot water tanks. To the east of 101 is **Laugardalur Valley**, where you'll find the city's largest thermal swimming pool, the botanical gardens, zoo and one of the best sculpture museums.

What angered the gods, when the lava flowed, on which we are standing now?

Kristni saga, Snorri goði

Just beyond Reykjavik itself is the vast emptiness of Iceland's weird and wonderful volcanic countryside. Even if you only have a few days, it's worth making the effort to get out of the city.

★ *Don't leave town without taking a walk along the harbour to see the viking boat sculpture, Sólfar, meaning 'Sun Voyager'.*

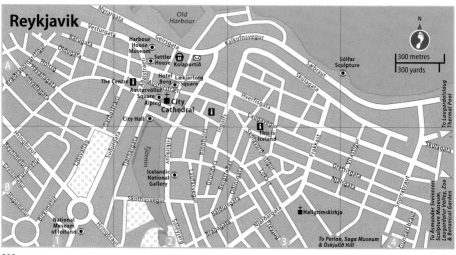

👁 Sights

Austurvöllur Square

Although Lækjatorg Square is the actual centre, Austurvöllur is the real heart of the city. The grassy space was originally six times bigger than it is today and thought to be the site of Ingólfur Arnarson's farm – Reykjavik's first settler. Today it's a popular meeting place, surrounded by cafés and bars. The small church (1787) is actually the modest city **cathedral**; next to it is the **Alþing** (Parliament House), overlooked by a stern-looking statue of **Jón Sigurdsson**, who led Iceland to independence from Denmark in 1944. In the corner of the square is **Hotel Borg**, a graceful art deco hotel, frequented by the rich and famous. Surprisingly, the Icelandic rock revolution of the 1980s began here and the hotel became a mecca for the city's young punks.

Austurvöllur Square

Aðalstræti

This is the oldest street in Reykjavik. Archaeological excavations under the Hotel Centrum have revealed the remains of what is thought to be one of the very first settler houses, dating from AD 874 to AD 930. The city's oldest surviving house, dating from 1752, is also on Aðalstræti at No 10; it's now a bar-bistro called Viðalín.

Tjörnin and around

The town pond, Tjörnin, is popular with people out for a stroll or to feed the ducks and greylag geese. It was created at the end of the last Ice Age as a sand and gravel bar, built up by the pounding waves of Faxaflói Bay. The futuristic building that seems to rise right out of the pond is the **City Hall** ① **NA2** *Mon-Fri 0820-1830, Sat and Sun 1200-1600, free.* Inside is a large relief map of Iceland, a café and a small information desk. On the east side of the pond is the **Icelandic National Gallery** ① *Fríkirkjuvegur 7, T515 9600, www.listasafn.is,* **NB2**, *Tue-Sun 1100-1700, ISK 500, free on Wed,* which has exhibitions from around the world and a small sculpture garden. On the opposite side is **Tjarnargata** street with its colourful early 20th-century timber houses.

⊖ Travel essentials

Getting there Keflavík International **Airport**, T425 0600, www.airport.is, is 48 km from Reykjavik. The reliable **Flybus** meets all incoming flights and drops you at your hotel or guesthouse, ISK 1100, 45 mins. If you're determined not to fly, it is also possible to get to Iceland by boat with **Smyril Line**, T+298-345900, www.smyril-line.com, from Denmark and Norway via the Shetland and Faroe Islands. (**NorthLink Ferries**, T+44 (0)845-600 0449, www.northlinkferries.co.uk, link Lerwick in Shetland with Aberdeen.) The ferry lands at Seyðisfjörður on the east coast, 682 km from Reykjavik.

Getting around 101 Reykjavik is small enough to walk around on foot. A stroll around town takes 20 mins; to walk to Laugavegur Valley or Öskjuhlíð

Hill takes 30 mins. The yellow **Straeto** city buses operate Mon-Fri 0700-2400, Sat and Sun 1000-2400. They are reliable and efficient, running every 20 mins, less frequently at weekends. A single fare is ISK 250. Lækjatorg Sq is the main bus terminal for local travel, where you can pick up route maps and timetables. Reykjavik is well suited to cycling as it is mainly flat. Bike rental is available from guesthouses and other places for around ISK 1700 a day. To get out of the city, it's best to hire a car (**ALP Car Rental**, T562-6060, www.alp.is) or take a tour. Otherwise, buses run from the **BSÍ** terminal, Vatnsmyrarvegur, T552 2300.

Tourist information The main tourist office is **The Centre**, Aðalstræti 2, T590 1500, www.visitreykjavik.is, Jun- Aug daily 0830-1900, Sep-May Mon-Fri 0900-1800, Sat and Sun 0900-1400. It provides all the information you could possibly need and can arrange tours, car hire and concert tickets. There's a bureau de change, internet access and tax refund centre here. Also useful is **This is Iceland**, Laugavegur 20, T561 6010, www.icetourist.is, which offers free internet and a tour booking service. A **Reykjavik Card** (ISK 1200 for 24 hrs, ISK 1700 for 48 hrs and ISK 2200 for 72 hrs) is available from the tourist office and offers free entry to the major museums and swimming pools as well as being a free bus pass.

Exchange rate Icelandic Kronur (ISK). £1 = ISK 124. €1 = ISK 85.

National Museum of Iceland

ⓘ *Suðurgata 41, T530 2200, www.natmus.is,* ◥B1. *1 May-15 Sep daily 1000-1700; 16 Sep-30 Apr Tue-Sun 1100-1700; guided tours daily 1100. ISK 600; Wed free.*

South of the pond, the National Museum is the best place to get a sense of 1200 years of Icelandic history. Tangible exhibitions and multimedia displays provide a fascinating insight into the Icelandic culture and how the nation has developed from the times of the earliest settlers to the present. The museum covers diverse aspects of the country's history, including mythology, the construction of early Viking buildings, the adoption of Christianity, the Reformation and the Census of 1703. It is well worth a visit.

Old Harbour

Although commercial fishing is now focused around Sundahöfn to the east, the old harbour area to the north of Austurvöllur Square has a certain charm (if you don't mind the lingering smell of fish) and remains busy with an influx of small fishing boats every now and then.

Sólfar (Sun Voyager)

Hallgrímskirkja

The **Kolaportið flea market** ⓘ *Geirsgata, T562 5030,* ◥B2, *Sat and Sun 1100-1700,* is held in the old customs building by the quay. Locals flock to browse through piles of bric-a-brac and second-hand clothes, and it's a good place to taste some Icelandic delicacies, such as dried cod.

Just behind the customs building, the **Harbour House Museum** ⓘ *Tryggvagata 17, T511 5155, www.listasafnreykjavikur.is,* ◥B2, *daily 1000-1700, ISK 500, free on Thu,* houses diverse exhibitions by Icelandic and foreign artists. The focus is modern and experimental, with a permanent exhibition by contemporary Icelandic artist, Erró.

Hallgrímskirkja

ⓘ *Skólavörðustígur, T510 1000, www.hallgrimskirkja.is,* ◥B3. *Daily 0900-1700. Suggested donation ISK 50, tower view ISK 350 adults.*

Dominating Reykjavik's skyline is this controversial 74 m-high church, reminiscent of a volcanic eruption. It was designed as part of a competition

and took 49 years to build. (It was completed in 1986.) While the interior is quite bare, the views from the top out over the city are wonderful. In front of the church is a statue of **Leifur Eríksson**, the Viking who is believed to have discovered America around AD1000.

Perlan and the Saga Museum

ⓘ *Öskjuhlíð Hill, T562 0200, www.perlan.is. Observatory daily 1000-2330. Free. Bus 13 from Lækjatorg Sq.*

Sitting on top of Öskjuhlíð Hill, the Pearl is the nearest thing the city has to the Eiffel Tower, with viewpoints out over the city, a café and revolving gourmet restaurant inside. The iconic circular glass building sits atop the city's hot-water storage tanks and holds regular art exhibitions, expos and concerts. It also houses one of the city's best museums, the **Saga Museum** ⓘ *T511 1517, www.saga museum.is, daily 1000-1800, winter 1200-1700, ISK 900,* which charts the early history of the country through the medieval stories of the sagas.

Down at the foot of the hill you'll find **Nauthólsvík Beach**, a quirky man-made

Perlan

Being so close to nature is a major appeal when visiting Reykjavik and it's easy to get out of the city for a half or full day. One of the most popular day trips is the Golden Circle, which takes in three of Iceland's finest natural and historic features within a day's journey of Reykjavik. It is a good way to get a taste of the country's bizarre scenery. **Þingvellir National Park**, 49 km northwest of the city, www.thingvellir.is, was the site of the ancient Viking parliament. In the centre of the park you can see a dramatic rift in the earth where the Eurasian and American continental plates are pulling part by 2 cm a year. To the northeast, **Geysir**, www.geysircenter.is, is the site of the original spouting hot spring that gave its name to all such natural features. Although it's no longer very active, another hot spring, **Strokkur**, spurts up to around 30 m, every four minutes. Ten kilometres further on, **Gulfoss** is a huge two-step waterfall that partially freezes in winter. It's best to hire a car to reach these sights, but there are plenty of tours available. **Iceland Excursions**, www.icelandexcursions.is, and the **Activity Group**, www.activity.is, offer tours and a variety of activities, including dog sledding, horse riding across lava fields, white-water rafting and snowmobiling – an exhilarating way to see the ice fields and glaciers. Whale-watching trips provide the chance to see minke, humpback and orca whales, as well as dolphins and seals.

Ásmunder Sveinsson Sculpture Museum

beach with imported yellow sand and geothermal pools. A dip here is a must, come rain or shine.

Laugardalur Valley
ⓘ *Bus 14 from Lækjatorg Sq.*

The name Reykjavik literally translates as 'smoky bay', the first settlers having mistaken the steam from the hot springs in the Laugardalur Valley for smoke. The springs are now used to feed

Laugardalslaug Thermal Pool
ⓘ *Sundlaugavegur 30a, T553 4039, Mon-Fri 0650-2130, Sat and Sun 0800-1900, ISK 300*, the city's biggest swimming pool.

Across from the Laugardalslaug pool complex is the white-domed **Ásmunder Sveinsson Sculpture Museum** ⓘ *Sigtún, T553 2155, www.listasafn reykjavikur.is, May-Sep daily 1000-1600, Oct-Apr 1300-1600, ISK 500.* Ásmunder Sveinsson was one of the pioneers of Icelandic sculpture and many of his abstract pieces draw on Icelandic literature, fairytales and nature.

Blue Lagoon
ⓘ *240 Grindavík, Reykjanes Peninsula, T420 8800, www.bluelagoon.is. 15 May-31 Aug daily 0900-2100; 1 Sep-14 May daily 1000-1900. ISK 1400. Buses Jun-Sep from BSÍ terminal and Keflavík airport.*

One of Iceland's most popular tourist attractions, the Blue Lagoon is best visited en route to the airport and is the perfect way to relax at the end of your trip. The lagoon is a steaming pool of milky turquoise water that leaches minerals from the lava bed, filling it with healing properties. Lie back, put on a mud pack and try not to let that whiff of sulphur put you off.

Blue Lagoon

⬤ Sleeping

Reykjavik has a great range of accommodation from extravagant hotels to quality guesthouses. Many hotels shut down Oct-May.

€€€ Hotel 101, Hverfisgata 10, T580 0101, www.101hotel.is. An ultra-fashionable boutique outfit with sculptures, murals, Icelandic art and an airy bar and restaurant. It's all very minimalist chic and the spa and gym downstairs will help you keep as glam as the surroundings. A futuristic, luxury experience in the heart of the city.

€€€ Hotel Borg, Pósthússtræti 11, T551 1440, www.hotelborg.is. Reykjavik's finest, an art deco hotel in Austurvöllur Sq with lovingly preserved rooms and modern art. It's a movie-star haunt: Catherine Deneuve shacked up here when she came to visit Björk and Marlene Dietrich stayed in 1944.

€€ Hotel Klöpp, Klapparstígur 26, T595 8520, www.centerhotels.is. Fashionable central 3-star hotel. Sleek modern design, neutral and beige colours and wooden floors. Klöpp means 'stone' or 'rock' and it has great views across the bay to Mt Esja.

€€ Guesthouse 101, Laugavegur 101, T562 6101, www.iceland101.com. Modern and spacious guesthouse in a large concrete building just off the main street. Moderate-sized rooms. Ideal location in the centre of the city for shopping, drinking and dining .

€ Salvation Army Guesthouse, Kirkjustræti 2, T561 3203, www.guesthouse.is. The cheapest and best-value place to stay in 101, with sleeping-bag accommodation, small shared rooms and a kitchen. Bathrooms are shared and it's a bit of a squeeze but it's in a great location.

⬤ Eating

There is plenty of Icelandic and international cuisine. Standards are high – and so are the prices.

Prir Frakkar, Baldursgata 14, T552 3939, www.3frakkar.com. Mon-Fri 1130-1430 and 1800-2200, Sat and Sun 1800-2300. Meaning the '3 Frenchmen', this seafood restaurant specializes in Icelandic classics such as puffin and whale meat. Small and traditional. Free wine if you have to wait for a table.

Siggi Hall, Thórsgata 1, T511 6677, www.siggihall.com. Tue-Thu and Sun 1800-2300, Fri and Sat 1800-0230. Reykjavik's finest restaurant. Siggi Hall is known to Icelanders for his regular weekly TV show and, now that he's opened up a city centre restaurant, for his shellfish soufflé and *bacalao* (salt cod). It's a stylish and relaxed place to dine, particularly good for its Icelandic fish, game and lamb.

Tveir Fiskar, Geirsgata 9, T511 3473, www.restaurant.is. Daily 1700- late. Refined Icelandic fish restaurant overlooking the harbour. Specialities include oyster soup, smoked puffin with pear marmalade and caviar. A high-quality gourmet affair with a feng-shui inspired interior.

Sægreifinn, Verbúð 8, T553 1500, www.saegreifinn.is. Daily 0800-1800. Run by 3 local fishermen including the 'sea baron' himself, this is actually a fish shop with a couple of wooden benches outside. The charming harbour setting and truly rustic feel make it a good, cheap spot for lunch. Try the delicious lobster soup or a barbecued fish kebab.

Baejarins Beztu, corner of Tryggvagata and Pósthússtræti. Reykjavik's original hot dog kiosk has become something of an institution. The hot dogs (*pylsur*) come with mustard, ketchup and raw or fried onions and are very tasty.

⬤ Nightlife

Check the 'what's on' section of www.icelandreview.com for details of current entertainment listings.

Bars and clubs

For many people, Reykjavik's nightlife is the main reason for coming to this cold and windswept spot. It's different to clubbing in other European destination, partly due to the size of the city, but just as the country is geologically young and dynamic, so is its nightlife. The long summer days and yawning winter nights give a whole new twist to the concept of partying till dawn. Fri and Sat are the wildest nights, with clubbing till 0800. Bars and clubs don't really fill up until 2400 as the high alcohol prices – ISK 600 for a pint of beer – force many locals to drink at home before heading into town. There are plenty of bars around Laugavegur such as bohemian **Kaffee Barinn**, Bergstadastræti 1, funky **Sirkus**, Klapparstígur 30, trendy **Oliver**, Laugavegur 20a, and lively **Vegamót**, Vegamótastígur 4. Later on, **Pravda**, Austurstræti 22, one of the larger clubs, and **Sólon**, Bankastræti 7a, are popular spots to dance. To round it all off, head for Austurvöllur Sq when the bars and clubs have closed; people tend to hang around here before going home.

Live music

It's possible to find live music being performed on every night of the week. Try **Gaukur á Stong**, Tryggvagata 22, and **Nelly's Café**, Þinghóltstræti 2, for anything from jazz to rock.

Riga

Riga has long been the largest and most cosmopolitan city in the Baltic region, a trading port on the River Daugava which was once a member of the powerful Hanseatic League. Despite having spent almost all of its 800-year history under foreign rule – most recently by Nazi Germany and the Soviet Union – Riga has retained a strong sense of its own Latvian identity. Yet for all the historical riches of this UNESCO World Heritage Site, evident in buildings ranging from Gothic to art nouveau, this is a city looking to the future. While it may not yet have regained its 1930s reputation as the 'Paris of the north', tourists are rapidly warming to Riga's attractive blend of bohemian charm and vibrant nightlife.

Arts & culture
★★★

Eating
★★

Nightlife
★★★

Outdoors
★★

Romance
★★★

Shopping
★★

Sightseeing
★★★

Value for money
★★★

Overall score
★★★

⊙ Sights

Just outside the old town, the 350-m **Freedom Monument** (Brīvības piemineklis or 'Milda'), built during the brief period of independence between the World Wars, is a good place to start. Head across the canal past the **Laima clock** (Laimas pulkstenis), a popular meeting place, and linger in bustling **Livs' Square** (Livu laukums) before climbing the steeple of **St Peter's Church** (Pētera baznīca) ⓘ *Tue-Sun 1000-1800, Ls 2,* ◥B2, to get your bearings. From here it's a short distance to **Town Hall Square** and the recently rebuilt **House of the Blackheads** (Melngalvju nams) ⓘ *Tue-Sun 1000-1700, Ls 1.50,* ◥B2. Named after an organization of unmarried merchants, the Dutch Renaissance façade makes this one of Riga's most attractive buildings; it's worth visiting the museum to check out the interior. An

Town Hall Square

ugly Soviet edifice nearby houses the sobering **Museum of the Occupation of Latvia** (Latvijas okupācijas muzejs) ⓘ *www.occupationmuseum.lv,* ◥B2, *Oct-Apr Tue-Sun 1100-1700; May-Sep daily 1100-1800, free,* detailing the horrors of the 20th century including a reconstruction of a gulag barracks. Head up Jauniela past **A&E** (No 17), the most

upmarket of Riga's many amber shops, to visit the imposing mishmash of architectural styles that is the **Dome Cathedral** (Doma baznīca) ⓘ *Sat-Tue and Thu 0900-1800, Wed and Fri 0900-1700, Ls 1.50,* ◥B2. Don't miss the cathedral's impressive cross-vaulted gallery or the nearby **Three Brothers** (Trīs brāļi), medieval buildings showcasing the styles of three different centuries. East of here, close to the canal, is the cylindrical **Powder Tower** (Pulvertornis) ⓘ *Oct-Apr Wed-Sun 1000-1700; May-Sep Wed-Sun 1000-1800, free,* ◥A2 once used to store gunpowder and now containing a war museum which is strong on 20th-century conflict. Head up Torna past the **Swedish Gate** (Zviedru vārti), built in 1698 to mark the Scandinavian occupation of Riga. It is all that remains of the old entrances to the city. **Riga Castle** (Rīgas pils) was built by crusaders and destroyed several times by the townspeople, it now houses the Latvian president as well as two museums. One

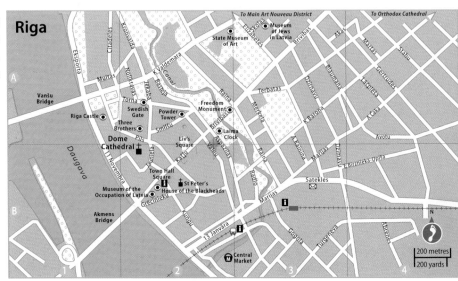

Riga

of these, the **History Museum of Latvia** (Latvijas vēstures muzejs) ⓘ *Wed-Sun 1100-1700, Ls 0.70*, provides a good introduction to the country. Crossing the canal on K Valdemara, wander down Alberta and Elizabetas to see some of Europe's best art nouveau architecture, especially at Elizabetes 10b. Return to the Freedom Monument via the small **Museum of Jews in Latvia** (Ebreji Latvijā) ⓘ *Sun-Thu 1200-1700,* **▣A3**, or the rather grander **State Museum of Art** (Valsts mākslas muzejs) ⓘ *Wed-Mon 1100-1700, Ls 1, tour Ls 5,* **▣A2**, with its collection of Latvian art. The **Orthodox Cathedral** (Pareiztičīgo katedrāle) is also worth visiting and was recently restored after being used as a planetarium in the Soviet period. Further south is the lively **Central Market** (Centrāltirgus) ⓘ *Tue-Sat 0700-1800, Sun and Mon 0700-1700,* **▣B2**, housed in five huge Zeppelin hangars. Unless time is very short, visit the **Open Air Ethnographic Museum** (Etnogrāfiskais brīvdabas muzejs) ⓘ *www.virmus.lv, daily 1000-1700; bus No 1 from corner of Merķeļa and Tērbatas to Brīvdabas, 30 mins*, which brings together rural buildings from all over Latvia. People make crafts onsite, and traditional fare is available.

Dome Cathedral

⊖ Sleeping

€€€ Hotel Bergs, Elizabetes iela 83/85, T777-0900, www.hotelbergs.lv. Formed from a pair of 19th-century buildings connected by a glass atrium, this boutique hotel in a fashionable district has been praised by *Condé Nast Traveller* and *Tatler*.

€€ Konventa Sēta, Kalēju 9/11, T708-7501, www.konventa.lv. A comfortable and central option housed in a 13th-century convent, with some rooms retaining oak beams alongside modern furnishings.

€ Viktorija, Čaka 55, T701-4111, www.hotel-viktorija.lv. This restored art nouveau building is worth the short walk from the old town. Stay in the renovated wing unless you're on a very tight budget.

⊘ Eating

⫟ Rozengrāls, Rozena 1, T722-4748, www.rozengrals.lv. Medieval dishes are served in an atmospheric cellar that dates back to the 13th century. The food is good, if a little expensive, including oddities such as baked pork tongue with cowberry sauce.

⫟ Vincents, Elizabetes 19, T733-2634. Closed Sun. Celebrity chef Martinš Ritinš prepares innovative global cuisine, attracting stars and dignitaries to one of the Baltics' best restaurants.

⫟ Lido Atpūtas Centrs, Krasta 76, T750-4420. Tram 7 or 9 from the centre. A hugely popular buffet housed in a giant log cabin, serving hearty Latvian standards – expect plenty of pork, potatoes, cabbage and bread – alongside many other dishes. There's also a restaurant and microbrewery here, and an amusement park outside.

⊖ Travel essentials

Getting there Riga International Airport is 8 km southwest of the city. There are regular buses to the centre, and taxis cost around Ls 7.

Getting around The best way to see the city centre is on foot, although there is an extensive network of buses, trolleybuses and trams with a flat fare of Ls 0.20 per journey. Minibuses ply fixed routes without a timetable and cost only a little more. Registered taxi cabs have yellow number plates.

Tourist information The main tourist office is at, Rātslaukuma 6, T703-7900, www.rigatourism.com, daily 1000-1900. There are also tourist offices in the central train station and international bus station. The inexpensive publication *Riga In Your Pocket* is highly recommended. It lists upcoming events and includes a map showing public transport routes.

Exchange rate Latvian Lats (Ls). £1 = Ls 1.03. €1 = Ls 0.70.

⫟ Sievasmātes Piradzini, Kaļķu 10. A great spot for a cheap meal of *piragi*: tasty Latvian pastries with a variety of fillings.

⊘ Nightlife

In addition to world-class events at the **National Opera**, Aspazijas bulvaris 3, T707-3777, look out for organ recitals at the **Dome Cathedral**.

Try **Depo**, Vaļņu 32, T722-0114, for live Latvian music, or enjoy a cocktail and the view from the 26th floor **Skyline** bar at the Reval Hotel Latvija, Elizabetes 55, T777-2222. Clubbing options include the trendy **Spalvas Pa Gaisu**, Grēcinieku 8, T722-0393. Note that smoking is banned in restaurants and bars, except in designated areas.

Rome

All roads lead here, it wasn't built in a day and while in the city you should do as the locals do, which might at first glance appear to be a lot of suicidal driving, sitting in piazzas drinking *aperitivi* and shopping in expensive boutiques. The Eternal City is so layered with history, sights and legend that it's unwise to aim to do much more than scratch the surface. Much of Italy's best ancient Roman remains and Renaissance art and architecture is here, sometimes alongside (or even underneath) fascist-era monstrosities. The city's baroque fountains, despite being continually draped in camera-toting tourists, are spectacularly grand. And you should leave time for markets and museums, designer shops and *pizzerie* serving the thinnest, crispest pizzas. The Vatican – the world's smallest sovereign state, beloved of quizmasters everywhere – has more of interest than many large countries, from the gasp-inducing Sistine Chapel and Raphael masterpieces to St Peter's. Massively cleaned up and restored for the millennium, Rome is beginning to regain some of its patina but still has more monuments and churches open than was the case a decade ago. Its economy is bigger than New Zealand's and as the capital of a major European country and the centre of a world religion, it has a sense of being an intensely relevant, living city – a quality sometimes lacking in other Italian cities. Surrounded by over 2000 years of history, contemporary Rome continues to blithely go about its business.

Arts & culture
★★★★★

Eating
★★★★

Nightlife
★★★★

Outdoors
★

Romance
★★★★

Shopping
★★★★

Sightseeing
★★★★★

Value for money
★★★

Overall score
★★★★

At a glance

Trains, and most of Rome's many visitors, arrive at **Termini** station, to the east of the city centre. Beyond the chaos in front of the station, via Nazionale heads from **piazza della Repubblica** southwest towards **piazza Venezia** and the main area of sights. The grandiose ugliness of the white marble **il Vittoriano** (Victor Emmanuel II monument), sits to the south of piazza Venezia, with the hill of the **Campidoglio** (one of Rome's famous seven hills, complete with great museums and a beautiful piazza) behind it. The biggest area of ancient ruins stretches east and south from the Campidoglio: the vast **Colosseo** (Colosseum) is beyond the **Foro Romano** (Forum) and the hill of the **Palatino**, effectively a single archaeological zone of temples, arches, political and civic remains. The **River Tevere** (Tiber) winds through the city, with the central areas of Pantheon, Navona and campo de' Fiori enclosed in the eastern side of a large bend. **Piazza Navona**, with grand fountains and buildings, is usually considered to be the central point of the city though the more earthy market piazza of **campo de' Fiori** just to the south has more reason to be thought of as Rome's heart. Also here are many of Rome's main sights – the **Pantheon** is the city's most complete Roman building and there are also many interesting churches and palazzi to visit. On the northeastern edge of this central area, **via del Corso** is a long straight road lined with many of the city's smartest shops, leading north to **piazza del Popolo** and the green hill of **Pincio**. On the eastern side of via

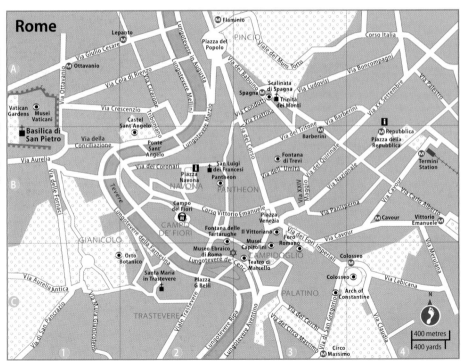

del Corso are two of the prime stopping points on tour guides' itineraries: the **Fontana di Trevi** (Trevi Fountain) and the **Scalinata Trinità dei Monti** (Spanish Steps). On the other side of the river, **Trastevere** is boho and arty and has laid-back streets filled with bars and restaurants, though there's less in the way of conventional sights. To the north, also on the western side of the river, the **Castel Sant' Angelo** stands guard over a statue-lined bridge. From here, Mussolini's grand via della Conciliazione is the best approach to San Pietro (St Peter's) and the **Vatican**.

Piazza del Popolo

All things atrocious and shameless flock from all parts to Rome.

Tacitus

View from St Peter's dome

24 hours in the city

Get up early to wander around **piazza Navona** and the fruit and vegetable market in **campo de' Fiori**. Dedicate the rest of the morning to the **Forum** and the **Palatine**, ending up in the **Colosseum**. Then head northwest through the atmospheric streets near the river for lunch. In the afternoon hit **St Peter's**, leaving enough time to queue to get in and to climb up into the dome and onto the roof for spectacular views. (Even longer queues and visitor-unfriendly opening hours mean that trying to see the Sistine Chapel and the rest of the Vatican in one day is an inefficient use of your time. If you must see them, get here as early as possible and be prepared to wait.) In the evening return to the campo de' Fiori, by this time transformed into a chic *aperitivi* spot. After a prosecco here, head across the river for food in **Trastevere**, and, if you want to party, head further south to the increasingly fashionable area of **Testaccio**.

★ *Don't leave town without wandering through the bubbling streets of Trastevere late at night.*

◉ Sights

Musei Capitolini

ⓘ *piazza del Campidoglio, T06-6710 2475, www.museicapitolini.org,* **C3**. *Tue-Sun 0900-2000.* €8.

Designed in the 16th century by Michelangelo, the handsome piazza del Campidoglio and museums on the Capitoline hill are a brilliantly conceived ensemble.

Michelangelo's regal Cordonata staircase leads up to the piazza from the via del Teatro di Marcello, just south of piazza Venezia. In placing the stairs on the western side of the piazza, Michelangelo changed its orientation: instead of facing the Forum it faces contemporary Rome.

The museums themselves are in the **Palazzo dei Conservatori** and **Palazzo Nuovo**: two buildings facing the piazza and connected by the **Galleria Congiunzione**, an underground passage opened as a part of the Millennium

Piazza del Campidoglio

celebrations and also allowing access to the Roman **Tabularium**, the archive of ancient Rome. There are good views from here over the Roman Forum.

The **Capitoline Museum** in the Palazzo dei Conservatori contains statues, bronzes and other artefacts. In its courtyard are the remnants of the enormous statue of Constantine that once stood in the Forum, including his gigantic foot. The rest of the statue was

made of wood and has not survived. The second floor has works of art including a Caravaggio and a Titian.

The **Palazzo Nuovo** contains an impressive collection of ancient marble statuary.

Foro Romano and Palatine

ⓘ *via de Fori Imperiali, T06-3996 7700,* **C3**. *Daily 0900-1 hr before sunset. Forum free, Palatine €9, combined with the Colosseum.*

Rome was almost certainly first settled on the Palatine hill, overlooking a crossing of the river Tiber. According to legend, it was here that Romulus and Remus, the founders of the city, were brought up by a she-wolf. Roman emperors built their palaces on the hill, at the bottom of which – in the Forum – commerce, worship and justice took place.

Visitors are largely free to wander among the broken columns and it's not hard to imagine the centre of the Roman Empire as it would have been 2000 years ago. There's little or no

---

⊖ Travel essentials

Getting there **Fiumicino Airport**, T06-6595 3640, www.adr.it, 25 km southwest of the city centre, is the city's main airport. The **Leonardo Express** rail service connects the airport to Rome's main train station every half an hour from around 0630-2330. It's a 35-min journey and costs €9.50. A taxi to or from the centre of the city costs €40. **Ciampino Airport**, T06-794941, www.adr.it, 15 km southeast of the centre, is the smaller airport and serves budget airlines. There are various ways of getting to Ciampino, some of which are not quite as simple or cheap as they should be. A Terravision bus service runs to coincide with Ryanair and EasyJet

flights, €7 one-way, €11.50 return. A taxi costs €30. Alternatively you can catch a bus (every 20 mins) to make the short hop to Ciampino station from where trains connect to Roma Termini every 10 mins.

International trains, including the Palatino sleeper service from Paris, arrive at the Termini station, www.trenitalia.com. See also page 12.

Getting around The same ticket system covers bus, metro and tram systems. Standard tickets cost €1 and are valid for 75 mins from the time of being stamped on all forms of transport. Confusingly, however, they can only be used once on trains and metros. For €4

you can buy a *giornaliero* ticket which lasts all day. The bus system is relatively efficient, though routes from the station to the Vatican have a reputation for pick-pockets. The metro is also efficient, but less useful to visitors since it mostly links the suburbs to the city centre. Licensed taxis are white and have meters. Don't use anything else purporting to be a taxi.

Tourist information Azienda per il Turismo Roma, via Parigi 5, T06-3600 4399, www.romaturismo.com, near the train station. There are equally useful *Punti Informativi Turistici* around the city centre at locations such as at piazza delle Cinque Lune, T06-6880 9240, near piazza Navona.

In Roman mythology, Romulus and Remus were twins who founded the city of Rome. Their mother, Rhea Silvia, despite being a Vestal Virgin, was raped by Mars, the god of war and conceived the twins. Their uncle, Amulius, ordered a servant to kill the twins but instead they were cast adrift in a boat on the river Tiber. They were found by Tiberinus, the river god, and suckled by a she-wolf on the Palatine Hill, before being discovered by a shepherd who raised the children as his own. Once they became adults, Romulus and Remus returned home, killed their uncle and then built a settlement on the Palatine Hill, according to tradition in 753 BC. Remus killed Romulus but then, feeling remorse, named the city after his brother.

The extent to which Romulus and Remus were historical figures is unclear, and it seems that there was a settlement on the Palatine Hill which predates the traditional date of the founding of the city. However, such apparent facts haven't stopped the she-wolf becoming a symbol of the city – a bronze of her suckling the twins can be seen in the Capitoline Museums. A similar image was used on Second World War propaganda posters.

information, however, and a map of the ruins is useful in order to make out what is what. Highlights include the **Temple of Castor and Pollux**, the **Arch of Septimus Severus** and the **Arch of Titus**. The **Arch of Constantine**, next to the Colosseum, is the best preserved of all of Rome's ancient triumphal arches.

The Palatine hill has remains of grand palaces, as well as the 16th-century **Hortus Farnese**, Europe's oldest botanical gardens.

Colosseo

ⓘ *piazza del Colosseo, T06-3996 7700,* 🚇 *C4*. *Summer daily 0900-1930; winter daily 0900-1630. €9 includes Palatine. To avoid the queues, it's quicker to buy the joint ticket at the Palatine.*

Rome's most iconic building, sold in plaster miniature by souvenir sellers all over the city, the Colosseum is an impressive structure. Built from AD 72 to 90, the city's ancient amphitheatre once seated 50,000 people. Used for gladiatorial combat, 9000 animals are reported to have been killed during its 100-day opening celebrations.

Built by Emperor Vespasian and his son Titus, it sits on the site of one of Nero's palaces, the Domus Aurea. A floor has been constructed at the level where the original would have been but you can still see into the underground section where animals and combatants were kept.

Foro Romano

Colosseo

The remaining marble with which it was once clad was removed during the Renaissance and baroque periods and used to build houses, and to construct St Peter's.

Musei Vaticani

ⓘ *viale Vaticano 100, T06-6988 4947, www.vatican.va,* 🚇**A1**. *Mar-Oct Mon-Fri 0845- 1645 (last entry 1520), Sat and last Sun of month 0845-1345 (last entry 1220); Nov-Feb 0845-1545 (last entry 1220). €12.*

The Vatican Museums have an extraordinary wealth of art, including the masterpieces of Michelangelo in the **Capella Sistina** (Sistine Chapel), and those of Raphael in the **Stanze di Raffaello**. Michelangelo famously lay on his back for four years, between 1508 and 1512, to create his astonishing *Creation* on the ceiling. (Goethe said of it: "Without having seen the Sistine Chapel one can form no appreciable idea of what one man is capable of achieving.") He returned 23 years later to spend another six years painting the darker *Last Judgement* on the end wall above the altar. There is a self-portrait in it – Michelangelo paints himself as a flayed skin in the hand of St Bartholomew.

Both paintings were subject to a controversial restoration in the 1980s and 1990s which some claim now makes the frescoes too colourful.

The **Raphael Rooms** are only slightly less astounding: four rooms are frescoed with themes of Truth and Beauty as well as the achievements of popes. The most famous image includes depictions of Leonardo as Plato, Michelangelo as Heraclitus and Raphael as himself.

Start early and, especially in high season, be prepared for a long wait to get in. Once inside, colour-coded routes help find a way through the Papal treasure troves. Most head straight for the Sistine Chapel but there is plenty more to see.

Basilica di San Pietro

ⓘ *piazza San Pietro, T06-6988 1662,* 🚇**B1**. *Apr-Oct daily 0700-1900; Nov-Mar daily 0700-1800. Free. Cupola, Apr-Oct 0800-1800; Nov-Mar 0800-1700. €5. Those with bare shoulders or knees will not be allowed into the basilica.*

The biggest church in Christendom, **St Peter's** can hold 60,000 people. The basilica's current incarnation was started in 1506. The original plans were drawn up by Bramante but then changed by Raphael, who took over after the original architect's death. Michelangelo then took charge and changed the plans again and it was largely his Greek cross design and his enormous dome that was finally consecrated in 1626.

Inside, the enormity of the Vatican's church is emphasized by a line in the floor displaying the lengths of other big churches around the world. Of the many highlights Michelangelo's *Pieta* (a depiction of Mary holding the dead body of Jesus on her lap), sculpted from marble when he was only 24 years old, is the most affecting. Regrettably now behind glass, the sculpture loses some, but not all, of its disarmingly human qualities. Another highlight not to be missed is the climb up into the dome and out onto the terrace. From here there are great views down into the Vatican gardens in one direction and, in the other, over the 140 statues of saints on the colonnade to the piazza below. Note that there are 320 steps to climb even if you opt to take the lift up the first stage.

If you're here on a Wednesday morning, you can get a glimpse of a distant Pope addressing enthusiastic crowds in piazza San Pietro.

Capella Sistina

Basilica di San Pietro

Il Vittoriano

Il Vittoriano

ⓘ *piazza Venezia,* **B3**. *Monument and museum daily 0930-1730 in summer; 0930-1630 in winter. Free.*

The Monumento a Vittorio Emanuele II, more often called simply il Vittoriano, or, with less deference, the wedding cake or the typewriter, is one of Rome's most memorable monuments, if not its most beautiful. Always controversial, its construction involved the demolition of an old part of the city and many Romans consider it out of proportion and out of style with its surroundings.

Built at the turn of the 20th century in honour of King Victor Emmanuel, it now serves various purposes – the tomb of the unknown soldier is here, with an eternal flame, as are various exhibition spaces and the **Museo del Risorgimento**, with information about the unification of Italy.

Fontana di Trevi

ⓘ *piazza di Trevi,* **B3**.

Made especially famous by Anita Ekberg, who took the plunge in *La Dolce Vita*, the Trevi Fountain sits at the end of the Aqua Virgo, one of the aqueducts that

Fontana di Trevi

supplied ancient Rome with crucial pure water from outside the city. Rome's grandest, the baroque Trevi Fountain follows a Roman tradition of building fountains at the ends of aqueducts. Designed by Nicola Salvi in 1730 using elements of an earlier design by Bernini, the fountain is these days purified with chlorine and semi-permanently surrounded by a sea of coin-throwing tourists.

Scalinata di Spagna

In some ways an unlikely candidate for tourist must-see status, the 18th-century **Spanish Steps** consist of 138 stairs originally built into the hill to connect the Spanish embassy with the Holy See. At the top of the monumental stairs is the church of **Trinità dei Monti** from where the views across the city's rooftops are spectacular. Shoppers gather for a rest in the piazza di Spagna at the bottom. **John Keats** lived in a house at the bottom of the steps

Spanish Steps

and died there in 1821. There is now a museum dedicated to the poet.

Pantheon

ⓘ *piazza della Rotunda, T06-6830 0230,* **B2**. *Mon-Sat 0830-1930, Sun 0900-1800. Free.*

Built in AD 125 by Emperor Hadrian to replace an earlier building that had been destroyed by fire, the Pantheon is ancient Rome's most complete monument. A perfectly circular rotunda, the building is 43 m wide and 43 m high. A central oculus in the dome is open to the sky and lets through striking shafts of sunlight into the shadows. The dome was the largest in Western Europe until Brunelleschi's dome in Florence's Duomo was built in 1436.

The building was consecrated in AD 609 as a Christian church. Partly for this reason the pantheon was spared the damage inflicted on other Roman structures. The reason for the dome's survival may also have something to do with the composition of Roman concrete.

Since the Renaissance the building has been used as a tomb for the famous. Those buried here include Raphael and two Italian kings.

Pantheon

Piazza Navona

The central piazza of Rome, piazza Navona was built on top of the first-century Stadium of Domitian, which explains its rectangular shape. Surrounded by baroque architecture, the main points of interest in the piazza are its fountains, notably Bernini's central **Fontana dei Quattro Fiume** (Fountain of the Four Rivers), representing the Danube, the Ganges, the Nile and the Río de la Plata. The **Fontana Nettuno** (Fountain of Neptune), to the northern end of the piazza, is by Giacomo della Porta.

Campo de' Fiori

A more proletarian counterpoint to piazza Navona's aristocracy, the campo de' Fiori (commonly referred to simply as Il Campo) has a lively and high-quality market and plenty of equally lively bars and restaurants. In recent years Il Campo has been increasingly gentrified but it retains some of its down-to-earth feel. It really comes into its own in the evenings, once

Piazza Navona

Campo de' Fiori

the stalls are cleared away and locals descend to drink *aperitivi* at the outdoor tables and watch the world go by. The central statue is of Giordano Bruno, a philosopher burned at the stake here in 1600 for suggesting that philosophy was superior to religion. Julius Caesar also died nearby.

The Ghetto

ⓘ *Museo Ebraico di Roma, Lungotevere de' Cenci, T06-6840 0661, www.museoebraico.roma.it,* ⬛C2. *Jun-Sep Sun-Thu 1000-1900; Oct-May Sun-Thu 1000-1700.* €6.

Jews have lived in Rome for over 2000 years, meaning that the Roman Jewish community is the oldest in Europe. The relative security of Roman Jews through the ages came at the cost of a tax imposed by the Catholic church from the 14th century onwards.

Shops offer kosher pizza and there is an attractive synagogue in which the **Jewish Museum** details centuries of maltreatment by the Vatican as well as the rounding up of 2000 Jews in 1943.

Trastevere

The name Trastevere (the stress is on the first 'e') comes from the Latin *trans Tiberim*, meaning over the Tiber, and being on the other side defines much of the area's left-bank, bohemian identity.

The area of Trastevere is at its best in the evenings, when many Romans come and visit its lively bars and relatively cheap restaurants. It is also worth a wander during the day, however.

The church of **Santa Maria in Trastevere** ⓘ *piazza Santa Maria in Trastevere, T06-5814802,* ⬛C2, *daily 0730-2100,* is the area's most obvious sight and has some glitteringly spectacular 13th- century mosaics. It is one of the oldest churches in Rome and is set in a cobbled piazza.

To the north is a green area of parks around the Gianicolo hill, including the **Orto Botanico** (Botanical Gardens) ⓘ *largo Cristina de Svezia 24,* ⬛C1. Originally established in 1833, it hosts over 3500 species and includes a section of a 'scent and touch' garden.

Santa Maria in Trastevere

Sleeping

Many of Rome's cheaper sleeping options are grouped around the station, though few can be wholeheartedly recommended. The southern part of the *centro storico* offers many of the best mid-range options, while further north, around the Spanish Steps, prices and standards of service rise still further. In general the city's hotels are expensive compared to the rest of Mediterranean Europe.

€€€ **Hotel Art by the Spanish Steps**, via Margutta 56, T06-328711, www.hotelart.it. Sleekly modern and self-consciously hip, Hotel Art sometimes tries too hard, but generally its efforts pay off. It has micro-lighting, wooden floors and colour schemes in place of floor numbers.

€€€ **Hotel Eden**, via Ludovisi 49, T06-478121, www.hotel-eden.it. This hotel has refined old-fashioned elegance, a stylish bar and restaurant and great views from the terrace garden. If money is no object you may want to consider booking the penthouse – a snip at €3600 a night.

€€€ **Ripa**, via degli Orti di Trastevere 1, T06-58611, www.ripahotel.com. A relatively early exponent of the design hotel, Ripa has the feel of an old-fashioned view of the future – a take on the sort of futuristic designs to be found in 1970s science fiction movies. Curvy minimalism and muted colours are used through the 170 rooms. The downside is that it's a little out of the way on the western side of Trastevere.

€€€-€€ **Astoria Garden**, via Bachelet 8, T06-446 9908, www.hotelastoria garden.it. One of the best options near the station, the Astoria Garden has smart if rather generic rooms and, as the name suggests, a garden. Good value out of season.

€€€-€€ **Campo de Fiori**, via del Biscione 6, T06-6880 6865, www.hotelcampodefiori.com. A decent mid-range option with great views from the roof terrace; the hotel also has apartments for rent nearby.

€€€-€€ **Casa Howard**, via di Capo Le Case 18 and via Sistina 149, T06-6992 4555, www.casahoward.com. The name is the Italian title of EM Forster's novel, *Howard's End*, from which you might imagine a staid attempt at Englishness – you'd be wrong. This excellent-value designer B&B is now in 2 houses where the design is bright and colourful and the attention to detail commendable, from the slippers and the fresh breakfasts to the carefully sourced soap.

€€€-€€ **Hotel Santa Maria**, vicolo del Piede 2, T06-589 4626, www.htlsanta maria.com. Near the Villa della Fonte hotel in Trastevere, Santa Maria has an attractive central courtyard with orange trees, where a good breakfast is served.

€€ **Hotel Navona**, via dei Sediari 8, T06-686 4203, www.hotelnavona.com. Very central and good value, Navona is plain, but you'd be hard pushed to find anything else as reasonable within a stone's throw of piazza Navona itself. The same owners also run the more upmarket *Residenza Zanardelli*.

€€ **Villa della Fonte**, via della Fonte dell'Olio 8, T06-580 3797, www.villa fonte.com. With only 5 en suite rooms and a garden terrace, Villa della Fonte often fills up quickly. Not far from the piazza Santa Maria in Trastevere, simple rooms look out onto greenery-draped walls.

Best of the rest

Fontana delle Tartarughe ⓘ *piazza Mattei*, ⊿C2. Giacomo della Porta's attractive fountain dates from the 1580s. The eponymous turtles were added a century later.

Teatro di Marcello ⓘ *via del Teatro Marcello*, ⊿C3. Once a 15,000-seat theatre built by Julius Caesar, the ruins of the Teatro di Marcello were turned into Renaissance palazzi which fuse two architectural styles, with ancient Roman arches making up the lower half of the construction.

Castel Sant'Angelo ⓘ *Lungotevere Castello 50, T06-681 9111*, ⊿B2. *Tue-Sun 0900-1930. €5.* Hadrian's final resting place was built in AD 135 and has great views as well as a chapel designed by Michelangelo. Over the centuries it has served as both a refuge and a prison for popes and it was the setting for Puccini's opera *Tosca*.

San Luigi dei Francesi ⓘ *piazza San Luigi dei Francesi, T06-68 8271*, ⊿B2. *Fri-Wed 0830-1230, 1530-1900; Thu 0830-1230.* Rome's French church has three Caravaggio paintings in its Contarelli Chapel.

Eating

Many of the best restaurants in the centre are in the area around campo de' Fiori or across the river in Trastevere, where eating out is traditionally a little cheaper. Rigatoni all'amatriciana (pasta with sausage and a spicy tomato sauce) is a traditional dish you'll find nearly everywhere.

Lunch

Il Forno di Campo de' Fiori, campo de' Fiori 22, T06-6880 6662. Simple but notoriously delicious white or red pizza by the slice attracts lots of local workers at lunchtimes. Closes for the afternoon at 1430, so don't leave it too late.

La Grotta, via delle Grotte 27, T06-686 4293. Just south of the campo de' Fiori, and much quieter, this is a great lunch spot. Traditional Roman food and generous portions.

Margutta Vegetariano, via Margutta 118, T06-3265 0577. A rare Italian vegetarian restaurant, the Margutta, near piazza del Popolo, has art, a busy, friendly atmosphere and good, though not ground-breaking, vegetarian food.

Òbikà, via dei Prefetti 26a, T06-683 2630. A restaurant based entirely around one ingredient – mozzarella. The real buffalo milk stuff arrives fresh daily from Naples, Salerno and Caserta. The design mixes steely minimalism with ancient Roman touches.

Dinner

Magnolia, campo de' Fiori 4/5, T06-6830 9367. A more modern take on the traditional campo trattoria, Magnolia does great big bowls of salad and is also a good place to sit on the tables outside for a drink.

Supperclub, via de' Nari 14, T06-6880 7207. All the lighting and style of a chilled but colourfully lit club but serving modern international cuisine as well as trendy cocktails.

Al Bric, via del Pellegrino 51-52, T06-687 9533. A well-informed wine list is the centrepiece of this *enoteca* (wine bar), which also serves imaginative food, combining the traditional and the modern. Dishes include swordfish stroganoff and duck pappardelle.

Filetti di Baccalà, largo Librai 88, T06-686 4018. Closed Sun. A Roman institution, this battered cod joint has changed very little in a very long time. The menu consists of not much other than its trademark Roman dish but what it does it does very well.

Trattoria da Augusto, piazza de' Renzi 15, T06-580 3798. On communal tables outside in a less smart piazza than the nearby Santa Maria, Trattoria da Augusto can be chaotic but is never less than good-natured. The food is excellent and traditional fare. You'll do better with some Italian – menus are mostly of the spoken variety. Be prepared to hang around in the piazza for a table. Very Trasteveran.

Cafés and gelaterias

Il Gelato di San Crispino, via della Panetteria 42, T06-679 3924. Some have suggested that the exceedingly good ice cream served here from under stainless steel lids might be the best in the world. Try the trademark *gelato di San Crispino*, flavoured with honey, and you may never be able to eat a Cornetto again.

🌙 Nightlife

Bars and clubs

Trastevere and the area around campo de' Fiori are usually considered the liveliest for nocturnal Roman activities but **Testaccio**, a previously working class area to the south, is catching up fast. Wine bars are becoming trendier but in general are places to eat as much as to drink. **Campo de' Fiori** is an especially good location for an early evening *aperitivo*.

Many of the city's nightclubs are smart and pricey and the live music scene is limited, though the number of alternative venues is increasing. Interesting events often happen at the city's *centri sociali*. During the summer months some clubs move out to the coast. Nights start (and finish) late – don't expect much action before midnight. Listings magazines like *Roma C'è* give up-to-date details of what's on.

Live music

Classical music and opera tends to fare better than other music, especially in summer, when festivals mean that events sometimes take place in great outdoor settings, from Testaccio's ex- slaughterhouse to the Baths of Caracalla and the Botanical Gardens. The Renzo Piano-designed **Auditorium Parco della Musica**, via P de Coubertin 15, www.auditorium.com, which opened in 2002, has injected new life into Rome's music scene.

🛍 Shopping

Rome still has plenty of small shops run by local families rather than big chains – **Trastevere** and in the streets around **campo de' Fiori** are great areas for discovering bookshops, delicatessens, and shops selling antiques and garden tools. Rome's most famous products are shoes and other fashion accessories, such as bags and gloves. For fashion, **via del Corso** and the roads that run off it make up Rome's main shopping area and you'll find the headquarters of brands such as Gucci and Bulgari here.

Via Frattina, via Condotti and via del Babuino are especially good for burning holes in wallets.

"Here shall be a town", declared Peter the Great at the dawn of the 18th century and what a town it has turned out to be. St Petersburg is where East meets West. In its canals, squares, monuments, cathedrals and bridges you'll see an elaborate mix of European and Russian styles. The old capital of the Tsarist empire oozes history from its pores: it witnessed the opening shots of the Russian Revolution; the storming of the Winter Palace; Lenin's return from exile; and the enlightened days of Catherine the Great, who began the process of gathering the many treasures that can now be seen in its myriad museums. It is with good reason that St Petersburg is referred to by its residents as the *gorod muzei* – the city of museums.

St Petersburg

Arts & culture
★★★★
Eating
★★
Nightlife
★★
Outdoors
★★
Romance
★★★★★
Shopping
★★
Sightseeing
★★★★★
Value for money
★★★★
Overall score
★★★

At a glance

St Petersburg forms a sort of bushy tree, looped by the River Neva, with the main thoroughfare **Nevsky Prospekt** forming the trunk and canals and streets branching off. The river separates the north part of the city from the main centre and is lined with grand buildings from its golden days. The **Peter and Paul Fortress** is along the river on the **Petrograd Side**, one of the Neva delta's many islands. Cross back over the river to the south and the famous **Bronze Horseman statue**, a city icon, can be seen. **St Isaac's Cathedral**, with its huge brassy dome, dominates the skyline nearby. Head east from here and you'll find the **Winter Palace** and the **Hermitage Museum** beside the large, imposing **Dvortsovaya Ploshchad** (Tsar Alexander square). Further down Nevsky Prospekt on the right is the impressive bulk of **Kazan Cathedral**

The Russians said that Peter made his city in the sky, then lowered it, like a giant model, to the ground.

Orlando Figes, 'Natasha's dance: A cultural history of Russia'

and further down and off to the left is the stunning **Church of Our Saviour on Spilled Blood**, with its onion domes.

★ *Don't leave town without tasting* blini *and* ikra krasnaya *(pancakes and red caviar) – with vodka.*

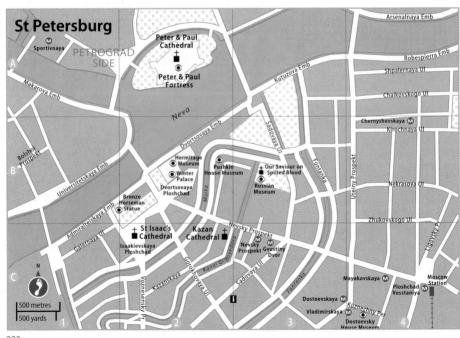

St Petersburg

Arsenalnaya Emb
Peter & Paul Cathedral
Sportivnaya
PETROGRAD SIDE
Robespierra Emb
Shpalernaya Ul
Peter & Paul Fortress
Makarova Emb
Kutuzova Emb
Chaikovskogo Ul
Neva
Bolshoi Prospekt
Chernyshevskaya
Kirochnaya Ul
Dvortsovaya Emb
Universitetskaya Emb
Hermitage Museum
Pushkin House Museum
Our Saviour on Spilled Blood
Sadovaya Ul
Fontanka
Nekrasova Ul
Winter Palace
Russian Museum
Uteiny Prospekt
Dvortsovaya Ploshchad
Bronze Horseman Statue
Moika
Zhukovskogo Ul
Admiralteiskaya Emb
Galernaya Ul
St Isaac's Cathedral
Kazan Cathedral
Nevsky Prospekt
Isaakievskaya Ploshchad
Nevsky Prospekt
Gvostiny Dvor
Ligovsky Pr
N
Voznesensky Pr
Kazanstaya
Gorokhovaya Ul
Kanal Griboed
Sadovaya Ul
Fontanka
Mayakovskaya
Ploshchad Vosstaniya
Moscow Station
500 metres
500 yards
Dostoevskaya
Kuznechny Per
Vladimirskaya
Dostoevsky House Museum

● Sights

Hermitage Museum

ⓘ *2 Dvortsovaya Ploshchad (Tsar Alexander square), T812-710 9625, www.hermitagemuseum.org,* ⬛JB2. *Tue-Sat 1030-1800, Sun and holidays 1030-1700. RUB 350 plus RUB 200 for each additional building in the complex. Metro Kanal Griboyedova, Nevsky Prospekt and Gostiny Dvor.*

St Petersburg's most famous attraction, the Hermitage Museum, consists of five connecting buildings: the Little Hermitage, the Old and New Hermitages, the Hermitage Theatre and the **Winter Palace**, the Russian tsars' largest and main residence. The Palace rooms, decked out in marble and some gold leaf, are well worth exploring for themselves, let alone for the stunning wealth of art that they contain.

The museum houses seven massive collections: art and culture of Western

Winter Palace

European, Russia and the Middle and Far East; antiquities of the former Soviet Union and near and Middle East; classical antiquities; and a coin collection.

The collection of Western Art includes an impressive array of well-known artists such as Poussin, Renoir, Degas, Monet, Matisse, Gauguin, Van Gogh and Picasso. Renaissance artists include da Vinci, Michelangelo and Titian. Spanish painters are represented by El Greco, Velázquez, Murillo and Goya, and Flemish and Dutch art by Van Dyck, Rubens, Rembrandt and Hals. An excellent display of statuary from ancient Greece and Rome is also here.

Though undeniably dazzling, make sure you at least sample the six other collections. Highlights include the Golden Treasures Gallery, with Greek Byzantine and Scythian jewellery, and ancient artefacts from Central Asia and Siberia, including Altai and Scythian relics.

Russian Museum

ⓘ *Inzhenernaya str, 4, T812-595 4248, www.rusmuseum.ru,* ⬛JB3. *Wed-Sun 1000-1700, Mon 1000-1600. RUB 300 (combined ticket for 4 palaces RUB 600). Metro Gvostiny Dvor and Nevsky Prospekt.*

● Travel essentials

Getting there Pulkovo Airport is 17 km south of St Petersburg's centre. There are 2 terminals 5 miles apart: Pulkovo 1, T812-104 3827, for domestic flights, and Pulkovo 2, T812-104 3444, for international flights. A free shuttle bus runs between them, (journey time 15 minutes).

There are various options for getting to the centre from the airport. A taxi will cost about RUB 1000. The shuttle bus T-39 runs from both terminals to Moskovoskaya metro station and then into the centre. Bus No 13 runs to Moskovoskaya metro station (journey time 30-40 mins), from where you can take the metro into the centre in 25-30 mins (RUB 10). There are also *mashrutnoye* (minibuses) to Moskovoskaya, costing little more than

the bus fare (around RUB 5). If you are driving, head for Pulkovskoe Shosse (E95, M20), which becomes Moskovsky Prospekt and then Sadoyova St and Nevsky Prospekt.

International trains from Berlin (with connections to London), via Belarus, arrive at Vitebski station. See also page 12.

Getting around The centre of St Petersburg is walkable but public transport around the city is cheap and efficient. Choose from metro, trolleybus, trams or buses. The metro is open 0545-0000/0030 and is a fast and convenient way to get about. Tokens can be bought at ticket offices and inserted into automatic barriers. 1 trip costs RUB 12; a pass for 7 days/10 trips costs RUB 98; 15 days/20 trips costs RUB 188. Trolleybuses, trams and buses operate from 0530-2400. There is a flat fare of RUB 4 per trip and you can buy tickets from the

conductor or driver. Hopping on the No 10 trolleybus will take you the length of Nevsky Prospekt, from Ploschad Aleksandra Nevskovo all the way over to Vasilievsky Island, allowing some good sightseeing opportunities. Taxis are plentiful and are typically yellow but private car drivers will also offer taxi rides (negotiate the fare before the journey). From June to September, boat trips along the St Petersburg canal leave from Fontanka at Nevsky Prospekt every 30 mins (RUB 200).

Tourist information A City Tourist Information centre can be found at Sadovaya ulitsa 14/52, T812-310 2231, Mon-Sat 1000-1900. See also www.petersburgcity.com.

Exchange rate Russian Ruble (RUB). £1 = RUB 51.15. €1 = RUB 34.83.

Though overshadowed by the Hermitage, the Russian Museum (Russki Musei), off Nevsky Prospekt, is worth visiting and is the world's largest museum of Russian art. Housed in the former Mikhailovsky Palace, it features the work of artists who would otherwise never, or rarely, be seen in the West, including the likes of Shishkin, Repin, Levitan, Fedotov, Kripensky, Bruni and Goncharova. Occasionally the museum stages a visiting exhibition, such as on Russian *skazka*, or fairy tales, and illustrations.

Peter and Paul Fortress

ⓘ *Petrograd Side*, ⬛**A2**. *Thu-Mon 1100-1800, Tue 1100-1700, grounds open every night till 2200. Tickets (RUB 80) can be bought from the Ioannovsky Gate or Boat House.*

Standing on one of the islands in the Neva delta, Peter and Paul Fortress (Petropavlovskaya Krepost) is the oldest building in St Petersburg. Built by Peter the Great to defend his new town, it served more as a prison for Russians than as a bulwark against invaders. Inside is **Peter and Paul Cathedral** (Petropavlovsky Sobor), constructed

Peter and Paul Fortress

1712-1732, with its golden needle spire and baroque interior. The cathedral is also the burial site for many Russian Tsars including Peter I and, in 1998, the last Tzar Nicholas II and the Romanov family were laid to rest here. The grounds outside the fortress are a major venue for several city festivals held throughout the year.

St Isaac's Cathedral

ⓘ *Isaakievskaya Ploschad 1, T812-315 9732, www.eng.cathedral.ru/isaac,* ⬛**C2**. *Thu-Tue 1100-1900, colonnade observation point Thu-Tue 1100-1800. RUB 600. Metro Nevsky Prospekt and Gvostiny Dvor.*

With its massive golden dome, St Isaac's Cathedral is one of the most familiar landmarks of the St Petersburg cityscape. Built in the first half of the 19th century, the church became a museum in 1931. The huge red granite columns, grey marble, bronze statutes and domes clad in gold make it an imposing building to visit and the colonnade offers superb city views.

Church of Our Saviour on Spilled Blood

ⓘ *Nabetrezhnaya Kanala Griboyedova 2, T812-314 4053,* ⬛**B3**. *Thu-Tue 1100-1800. RUB 200; buy ticket from inside church, not outside. Metro Nevsky Prospekt and Gvostiny Dvor.*

Near the Ekaterinsky Canal is the magnificent Church on the Spilled Blood (Khram Spasa-na-Krovi), also known as Cathedral of the Resurrection of Christ or Khram Voskreseniya Khristova. The cathedral was built on the placewhere the Tsar Alexander II was killed by terrorists in 1881. There's an exhibition about him inside. Make sure you take time to study the wonderful mosaics.

Pushkin House Museum

ⓘ *Naberezhnaya Reki Moika 12, T812- 570 6511, www.museum pushkin.ru,* ⬛**B2**. *Wed-Mon 1030-1730. Apartment Museum RUB 20, Lyceum RUB 20; other areas free. Metro Nevsky Prospekt and Gvostiny Dvor.*

On the southern bank of the Moika is the Pushkin House Museum (Pushkinsky Dom), in the original apartment (built in

Russian Museum

St Isaac's Cathedral

Going underground

St Petersburg's metro has been hostage to the fortunes of Russia's turbulent history. It was planned in 1899 but, due to the outbreak of the First World War and the Russian Revolution, building was postponed. Spurred on by the construction of the Moscow metro, in 1933, building began again just as Hitler's stormtroopers burst through the Russian frontier. After the Great Patriotic War the first metro line opened in 1955. While not as grand as Moscow's, St Petersburg's metro remains impressive as a feat of construction. It is the deepest subway in the world, has 61 stations and is 122 km long. Engineers also had to overcome stiff geological challenges such as the existence of several underground rivers and the proximity of the Finnish Gulf. The nature of these difficulties are reflected in the collapse of the tunnel between Lesnaya and Ploschad Muzhestva. Despite this, the metro is a fast and efficient way of getting about St Petersburg: trains pass every 95 seconds during the rush hour and every four minutes for the rest of the day.

Pushkin metro station

There are four lines set out in a London Underground-style format on the metro map: Line 1 – Kirovsko-Vyborgskaya – the red line; Line 2 – Moskovsko-Petrogradskaya – the blue line; Line 3 – Nevsko-Vasileostrovskaya – the green line; Line 4 – Pravobereznaya – the yellow line.

---

the 18th century for a court dignitary) where the great poet wrote such pieces as *The Bronze Horseman* and *The Captain's Story*. It was here that he died in 1837, after having been wounded in a duel over his beautiful wife, Natalia Goncharova. Founded in 1879, the museum displays portraits of the poet, an extensive book collection and Pushkin's personal items.

and the writings of contemporaries, especially those of his wife and secretary, Anna Grigorievna. Here you'll find Dostoevsky's personal belongings and his books.

Church of Our Saviour on Spilled Blood

Dostoevsky House Museum
ⓘ *Kuznechny per 5/2, T812-117 4031,* 🕓 *. Tue-Sun 1100-1800. Metro Vladimirskaya and Dostoevskaya.*

Not far from Vladimirskaya metro station is the house where, in 1878, the writer Fyodor Mikhailovich Dostoevsky moved with his family and stayed till his death, in 1881. It was here that he wrote *The Brothers Karamazov*. The house was later turned into communal apartments during Soviet times and had to be reconstructed from original plans

Pushkin House Museum

● Sleeping

There are some good deals in the top-end luxury hotels but there are very few cheap or mid-range places in the city centre, and those few are generally modern and bland.

€€€ Grand Hotel Europe, Mikhailovskaya ul 1/7, T812-329 6000, www.grandhoteleurope.com. The city's oldest hotel with sumptuous art nouveau interiors, shopping arcades and several bars and restaurants.

€€ Dostoevsky Hotel, Vladimirsky Pr 19, T812-331 3200, www .dostoevsky-hotel.ru. Modern 3-star hotel in the historic centre offering comfortable accommodation. The hotel occupies part of the building of one of the better shopping centres in the city (Vladimirsky Passage).

€€ Matisov Domik Hotel, Pryajka River Emb 3/1, T812-219 5441. Opened in 1993 and one of the first private hotels in the city, Matisov Domik is in a quiet district of town, close to the Mariinsky Theatre and 25 mins from Nevsky Prospekt; ideal for those who prefer peace and quiet to convenience. It has an intimate and bucolic feel and the staff strive to maintain a homely atmosphere.

€€ Neva Hotel, Tchaikovskovo St 17, T812-278 0504. In the fashionable Letney Sad (Gardens) district, it's nothing fancy but a good, comfortable 3-star hotel and reasonable value.

€€ Oktyabrskaya Hotel, Ligovsky Prospekt 10, T812-578 1515, www.oktober-hotel.spb.ru. Metro Ploshchad Vosstaniya. Opposite Moscow Station is this huge 563-room 3-star hotel in a mid-19th century building. Ask for one of the upgraded rooms.

● Eating

St Petersburg now offers plenty of choice in terms of cafés and restaurants serving a wide range of cuisines, from Russian to French and Chinese, often all on the same menu. Cafés often serve the best food and most are open from morning well into the evening. Most restaurants are open from 1200-1430 and 1800-2330/2400.

††† Shinok, Zagorodny Prospekt 13, T812-311 8262. This restaurant is decked out like a Ukrainian village and offers typical dishes such as *borsht* (beetroot soup), *kyshka* (sausage) and *kutya* (special wheat). In the evenings musicians provide entertainment.

†† Ketino, 8th Line 23, Vailevsky Island, T812-326 0196. This place offers excellent Caucasian dishes such as Georgian cheese bread served with an egg in the middle and also has a display of Georgian art.

†† Staroe Café, Fontanka Embankment 108, T812-316 5111. Good Russian food (tasty soups and *blini*) in a cosy, intimate setting with 19th-century decor and a pianist in the evening. There's only a small number of tables available for dining, so make sure you book or come early.

† Café Idiot, Moika 82, T812-315 1675. Named after Dostoevsky's novel, this delightful café offers bags of atmosphere in the basement of a house on a canal, minutes from St Isaac's cathedral and Nevsky Prospekt. A cosy, 1950s-style interior with sofas and jazz music in 5 vaulted rooms, including an art gallery and a library with English language books and magazines. The restaurant serves vegetarian and Russian food, coffee and speciality teas. Free vodka with every meal, RUB 300.

† Troitsky Most, Malaya Posadksaya Ul 4, Kronvergsky Prospekt 29, T812-232 6693. High quality vegetarian cuisine available at great value prices.

● Nightlife

There's plenty of varied nightlife on offer in St Petersburg. The famous **Mariinksy Opera and Ballet Theatre**, Teatralnaya Ploshchad 1, Bolshoi Concert Hall, Mikhailovskaya Ulitsa 2, box office T812-326 4141, www.mariinsky.ru, is home to the St Petersburg Philharmonic Orchestra. The **Maly Concert Hall**, Nevsky Prospekt 30, box office T812-312 4285, has performances by smaller ensembles, while the **Bolshoi Oktyabrsky Concert Hall**, Ligovsky Propsekt 6, box office T812-275 1175, concentrates on Russian classical music.

St Petersburg also offers a large range of clubs, divided into Dance, Music, Art and Erotic. Strict dress codes apply so dress up like young Russians do. Most clubs open between 2200 and 0600. Typical admission prices are RUB 250 before 2300 and RUB 300 after 2400; at weekends, expect to pay RUB 350-400. Most clubs are on or around Nevsky Prospekt and the embankment areas and include **Metro**, Ligovsky Pr, T812-166 0210; the stylish **Purga**, Neberezhnya Reki Fontanki 13, T812- 313 4123; and **Plaza**, Neberezhnya Makarov 2, T812-323 9090, which is popular with Russians and tourists.

Check the *St Petersburg Times*, www.sptimes.ru, for up-to-date entertainment listings.

Unusually for an inland city, Seville was once the most important port in the world. It directed the whole of Spain's trade with its New World colonies and the merchants and Crown salivated over the arrival of the gold- and silver-laden treasure convoys fresh from its mines. Today, the bristling ramparts of the Torre del Oro still dare invaders to do their worst, while many of the streets of Triana, the one-time sailors' barrio, still bear the names of the brave mariners who set forth into the unknown. You can find spots where Columbus prayed before his voyages or the ill-fated Magellan set forth to put a girth on the world. While the city's fortunes have waxed and waned, its allure has not diminished; within Spain it remains a word laden with sensuality and promise.

Seville

Arts & culture
★★

Eating
★★★★

Nightlife
★★★

Outdoors
★★

Romance
★★★★

Shopping
★★

Sightseeing
★★★

Value for money
★★★★

Overall score
★★★★★

At a glance

The historic hub of Seville is dominated by two awesome symbols of power and wealth, the **Real Alcázar**, and the **cathedral** with its emblematic **Giralda** – a sublime tower in beautiful brick. Nearby, Seville's Moorish and Jewish heritage is still elusively alive among the narrow streets of **Barrio Santa Cruz**, just east of the cathedral, and home to some fine tapas bars. South of the cathedral, the optimistic buildings erected for the 1929 Exhibition have been put to fine use; students bustle about and cityfolk stroll in the blessed shade of the **Parque María Luisa**, with its improbably-grand **Plaza de España** and two museums. **El Arenal**, west of the cathedral and once the sandy, seedy, flood plain of the Guadalquivir river, was built up around Seville's bullring and is now a riverside area with a theatre, good tapas and the fine art of the Hospital de la Caridad. To the south, **Triana**'s trendified riverbank is a mass of bars and restaurants; its backstreets full of tradition and beautiful tiles. A cluster

A city that waylays rhythm, and coils it into labyrinths, like tendrils of the vine aflame.

Federico García Lorca

of plazas and shopping streets fill Seville's old town (**Centro**), with baroque churches tucked away in its side streets. Nearby, quiet **San Vicente** offers the fine Museo de Bellas Artes. **La Macarena**, to the north, has friendly local bars, lively markets and quiet lanes brimming with Gothic- Mudéjar convents and churches. The river island of **Isla de la Cartuja** was the site of World Expo 1992.

★ *Don't leave town without a long meandering evening route through the city's tapas bars.*

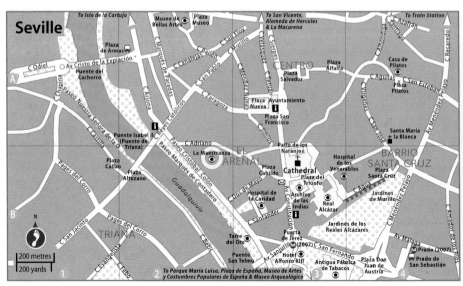

Seville

⦿ Sights

Cathedral and La Giralda

ⓘ *Pl del Triunfo s/n, T954-214971,* 🚌B3.
*Mon-Sat 1100-1800 (last entry 1700),
Sun 1430-1900 (last entry 1800).
Mon-Sat €7.50, free Sun.*

At the beginning of the 15th century,
150 years after the fall of Seville to the
Christians, a cathedral was erected over
the site of a mosque. **Santa María de
la Sede** is the result: a Gothic edifice of
staggering proportions and crammed
full of artistic treasures in nearly 50
chapels and its massive five-naved
central structure. The mosque's minaret,
the superb **Giralda** tower (and the city's
symbol), was retained as the bell tower,
and can be climbed via a series of ramps,
while pretty **Patio de los Naranjos**,
the Moorish ablutions area, has also
survived. The interior, combining
grandeur, space and solemnity, is
magnificent, while the exterior arguably
has more merit than all the cathedrals
of Andalucía put together.

La Giralda

Real Alcázar

ⓘ *Pl del Triunfo s/n, T954-502323, www.
Patronato-alcazarsevilla.es,* 🚌B3. *Oct-Mar
Tue- Sat 0930-1800, Sun 0930-1430;
Apr-Sep Tue-Sat 0930-2000, Sun
0930-1800, last entry 1 hr earlier.
€7, students free.*

The present Alcázar owes its Moorish
look (horseshoe arches, stucco, Arabic
calligraphy and coffered ceilings) not
to the Moorish rulers (little remains from
that period) but to the Castillian kings
Alfonso X and his son Pedro I. As well
as being a sumptuous palace and
a popular residence for visiting
Spanish royalty, the Alcázar was once
a considerable fortress, as you can see
when you pass through the chunky
walls of the red **Puerta del León**.
From here you emerge into a large
courtyard where the king's hunt once
assembled. It's dominated by the
impressive façade of the main palace
of the Castillian kings (inscriptions
about the glory of Allah – Pedro I was
a pretty enlightened man – adjoin more
conventional Latin ones proclaiming
royal greatness). To the left is the
Patio del Yeso, one of the few
remaining Moorish structures. Across
the courtyard are chambers built by
Fernando and Isabel to control New
World affairs. Magellan planned his trip
here and there's an important *retablo*
from this period of the Virgen de los
Navegantes. There's also the vast and
fantastic garden to stroll in; enjoy the
leafy shade and take a peaceful break
from the sometimes frenetic centre.

⊖ Travel essentials

Getting there Seville Airport,
T954-449000, is 10 km northeast of the
centre. A bus runs to and from the airport
to central Seville (Puerta de Jerez) via the
train and bus stations every 30 mins
weekdays (less frequently at weekends)
and coincides with international flights.
It takes 30 mins to Puerta de Jerez (€2.40).
The last bus leaves the airport at 2330.
A taxi to the city is around €19, slightly
more at night or on public holidays.

Sevilla's modern train station, Santa
Justa, is a 15-min walk from the centre on
Av Kansas City. For train information
contact RENFE, T902-240202, or see their
excellent website, www.renfe.es. A handy
central RENFE office is on C Zaragoza 29.

Getting around Although Seville's
old town with the main sights is a large
area, walking is by far the best way to get
around. A stroll from the cathedral to the
Museo de Bellas Artes takes 15-20 mins,
from the Plaza de España to the Alameda
de Hércules about 30 mins. The most
useful **TUSSAM bus** services are the
circular routes: C1 and C2 run via the train
station and Expo site (C1 clockwise, C2
anti-clockwise), while C3 (clockwise) and
C4 (anti-clockwise) follow the perimeter
of the old walls, except for C3's brief
detour into Triana. A single fare
is €1 (drivers will give change up to a
point), but a *BonoBus* from newspaper
kiosks costs €5 and is valid for 10

journeys. A **taxi** across town costs
around €6. The city's new **metro** is
currently under construction and line 1
is scheduled to open in late 2007.

Tourist information Junta de
Andalucía, Av de la Constitución,
T954-221404, Mon-Fri 0900-1930, Sat
1000-1400, 1500-1900, Sun 1000-1400.
Near the cathedral, this is the handiest
tourist office, but it is usually busy. Other
tourist offices are by the Puente de Triana
at C Arjona 28, T902-194897, Mon-Fri
0800-2045, Sat-Sun 0900-1400; Plaza de
San Francisco 19, T954-595288, Mon-Fri
1000-2000, Sat 0900-1400; the airport
and Santa Justa train station, Mon-Fri
0900-2000, Sat-Sun 1000-1400.

Museo de Bellas Artes

ⓘ *Plaza del Museo 9, T954-221829,* **A2**.
Tue 1430-2000, Wed-Sat 0900-2000,
Sun 0900-1430. Free for EU citizens.
€1.50 for others.

Seville's major art gallery is a must-see,
housed in a picturesque 17th-18th
century convent. Thoughtfully laid out
and thankfully uncluttered, it's a
treasure trove of Spanish art from the
15th-20th centuries including El Greco,
Velásquez, Murillo, Zurbarán – and a late
portrait by Goya.

Barrio Santa Cruz

Once home to much of Seville's Jewish
population, atmospheric Santa Cruz is the
most charming of the city's barrios: a
web of narrow, pedestrian lanes linking
attractive small plazas with orange trees
and shady terraces aplenty. There is a
fairly standard tourist beat but you can
easily get away from it. It's also a good
place for hotels, restaurants and shopping.
While there are a few sights of interest,
such as the excellent baroque church of
Santa María la Blanca and the
Hospital de los Venerables ⓘ *T954-*

Real Alcázar

● Best of the rest

Archivo de las Indias ⓘ *Pl del*
Triunfo s/n, T954-50052, **B3**.
Mon-Sat 1000-1600, Sun
1000-1400. Free. In the 18th
century this square and sober
Renaissance building was
converted into the state archive.
It's a fascinating record of the
discovery and administration of
empire; from the excited jottings
of Columbus to mundane book-
keeping of remote jungle outposts.
Casa de Pilatos ⓘ *Plaza de Pilatos*
s/n, T954-225298, **A4**. *Daily 0900-1*
900. €5 lower floor, €8 both, free
Tue from 1300. A stunning 15th-
century blend of Renaissance
classicism and Mudéjar styles.

562696, **B3**, *daily 1000-1330, 1600-1900,*
€4.75, the main enjoyment
to be had is wandering around and
trying to guess where you'll end up.

South of the cathedral

Much of the area south of the cathedral
is taken up with the large green space of
Parque María Luisa. It was used as the
site for the grandiose 1929 Ibero-
American Exhibition that the Primo de
Rivera dictatorship hoped would return
Seville and Spain to the world spotlight.
The legacy is a public park and a beautiful
series of buildings. The **Plaza de España**
is an impressive colonnaded space and
the **Hotel Alfonso XIII** to the northwest
is one of the most sumptuous in Spain.
Next door, the **Antigua Fábrica de
Tabacos** ⓘ *C San Fernando 4,*
T954-551000, **B3**, *Mon-Fri 0800-2030,*
free, is the cigarette factory made
famous in the late 19th century by

Carmen; it's now used by the university.
In the park beyond, two of the pavilions
have been converted into outstanding
museums: the colourful **Museo de
Artes y Costumbres Populares de
Sevilla** ⓘ *Pl de América 3, T954-232576,*
Tue 1430-2030, Wed-Sat 0900-2030, Sun
0900-1430, free to EU residents, €1.50 for
others; and the rich **Museo Arqueológico**
ⓘ *Pabellón de Bellas Artes, Pl de América*
s/n, T954-232401, same opening details.
A walk through this part of town
provides a fascinating view of an
architectural ensemble built just years
before the Civil War that plunged the
city and country into decades of
poverty and monoculturalism.

El Arenal

Built up in the 19th century, El Arenal
has some of Seville's major landmarks.
The **Torre del Oro** ⓘ *Paseo de Colón*
s/n, T954-222419, **B3**, *Tue-Fri*
1000-1400, Sat-Sun 1100-1400, €2, is
a beautiful Moorish tower. The exhibition
is mediocre but worth seeing for the
prints of Seville in the late 16th century.
La Maestranza ⓘ *Paseo de Colón 12,*
T954-224577, www.realmaestranza.com,

Barrio Santa Cruz

Semana Santa and Feria de Abril

Seville's Holy Week processions are an unforgettable sight. Mesmeric candlelit lines of hooded figures and cross-carrying penitents make their way through the streets accompanied by the mournful notes of a brass band and two large *pasos* (floats), one with a scene from the Passion, one with a statue of Mary. This isn't unique to Seville but what makes it so special is the Sevillians' extraordinary respect for, and interest in, the event. Members of nearly 60 *cofradías* (brotherhoods) practise intensively for the big moment, when they leave their home church and walk many hours through the streets to the cathedral and then home again. Some of the brotherhoods have well over a thousand in the parade; these consist of *nazarenos*, who wear pointed hoods (adopted by the KKK, but designed to hide the face of a man repentant before God), *penitentes*, who carry crosses, and *costaleros*, who carry the *pasos*. The first brotherhoods walk on Palm Sunday and the processions continue up until Easter Sunday, when a single *cofradía* celebrates the Resurrection.

Feria de Abril (usually in April, depending on Easter), originally a livestock market but now a major event in the Seville calendar, provides a lively antidote to the solemnity of Semana Santa. Line upon line of colourful marquees (*casetas*) reverberate to the slurping of manzanilla and the gyrations of pairs of dancing *sevillanas*.

B2, *daily 0930-2000 except fight days (spring and summer Sun and all week during Feria), when it's open 0930-1500*, €4, is one of Spain's most important temples to bullfighting.

The **Hospital de la Caridad** ⓘ *C Temprado 3, T954-223232,* **B3**, *Mon-Sat 0900-1330, 1530-1930, Sun 0900-1300, €5*, is a nursing home with a remarkable collection of 17th-century Sevillan art including haunting masterpieces by Juan de Valdés Leal. The **Río Guadalquivir** itself is also a major attraction here; although there are no longer galleons bound for the Spanish Main, there are several outdoor bars, river cruises, and a place to hire canoes.

Torre del Oro

Triana

Triana is many people's favourite part of Seville. It has a picturesque riverfront lined with bars and restaurants, and was for a long time the gypsy barrio and home of flamenco in Seville (its backstreet bars are still the best place to catch impromptu performances). Triana is also famous for ceramics; most of the *azulejo* tiles that so beautifully decorate Seville's houses come from here, and there are still many workshops in the area. It's got a different feel to the rest of the city, and *trianeros* are still a tight-knit social group. Many residents once lived in *corrales de vecinos*, houses centred around a common courtyard and there are still a few around to see. While the riverfront and surrounds are fairly trendy these days, venture into some of the smaller backstreets and you'll find that Triana preserves more of its history and associations than any other part of Seville.

⊙ Sleeping

With dozens of hotels in renovated old Seville mansions, there's a wealth of attractive, intimate lodging to choose from.

€€ **Las Casas de la Judería**, Cjón Dos Hermanas 7, T954-415150, www.casasypalacios.com. Spread across several old *palacios*, this hotel has sparkling patios, pretty nooks and hanging foliage.

€€ **Las Casas de los Mercaderes**, C Alvarez Quintero 9, T954-225858, www.casasypalacios.com. A beautifully renovated hotel and sibling to Las Casas de la Judería. Built around a beautiful arcaded patio.

€€ **Las Casas del Rey de Baeza**, Pl Jesús de la Redención 2, off C Santiago, T954-561496, www.hospes.es. An enchanting old *corral de vecinos* near Casa Pilatos, superbly restored. Rooftop pool and terrace as well as a beautifully decorated library and lounges.

€€-€ **Hotel Amadeus**, C Farnesio 6, T954-501443, www.hotelamadeus sevilla.com. A lovely small hotel with a classical music theme. Some rooms are fabulous, some merely excellent. Roof terrace with views of the centre and the Giralda. Highly recommended.

€ **Hotel Simón**, C García de Vinuesa 19, T954-226660, www.hotelsimon sevilla.com. Very attractive hotel built around a beautiful, airy courtyard with a fountain. There are plenty of *azulejos* and neo-Moorish features. Rooms are smallish but welcoming. Very well priced for the decor and ambience.

€ **YH Giralda**, C Abades 30, T954-228 324, www.yh-hoteles.com. Not to be confused with a youth hostel, this is a minimalist marble-decorated hotel in a great but quiet location. Good service and elegant and comfortable rooms.

⊙ Eating

Your best moments in Seville are likely to be spent eating. Tapas was invented here and it's the place in Spain where it is done best. There's little distinction between tapas bars and restaurants, so we've listed them all together. A standard tapa will cost €1-2. The *menú del día*, a filling, set price 3-course lunch (1330-1530 roughly) normally costs €6-12.

₮₮₮ **Egaña Oriza**, C San Fernando 41, south of Alcázar, T954-227254. Mon-Fri 1330-1530, 2030-2330, Sat 2030-2330. A smart restaurant mixing Andalucían and Basque cuisine. Try the *salmorejo*, stewed wood pigeon, sole with saffron sauce and a great ceviche of monkfish and grouper.

₮₮ **Kiosco de las Flores**, C Betis s/n, T954-274576. Dining on the riverfront in Triana is a classic Sevilla experience. This is one of the best places to do it, with an enormous range of seafood and a lovely outlook.

₮₮ **Taberna del Alabardero**, C Zaragoza 20, T954-502721. Hospitality school and one of the city's best restaurants, with a delicious seasonal menu. House specials include *corvina* (sea bass). Downstairs is an atrium bar serving snacks and *raciones*.

₮ **Bar Pepe Hillo**, C Adriano 24, T954-215390. 1200-0100. A legend in its own tapas time, especially for stews such as the *caldereta de venao* (venison). High-ceilinged and buzzing.

₮ **Bodega Santa Cruz**, C Rodrigo Caro 2, T954-213 246. 1200-2400. A busy and cheerful bar serving some of Seville's choicest tapas and *montaditos* (delicious little toasted sandwiches).

₮ **Casa Morales**, C García Vinuesa 11, T954-221242. Great old traditional place with big sherry jars, *montaditos* served on wooden trays, and the tab chalked up on the bar in front of you.

₮ **La Goleta**, C Mateos Gago, Barrio Santa Cruz, T954-218 966. Tue-Sun 0900-1500, 2000-2300. Tiny bar with loads of character. Limited but excellent tapas, particularly the 'candid' tortilla.

⊙ Nightlife

Seville's nightlife can't compete with Barcelona or Madrid but around Plaza Alfalfa and Calle Betis in Triana it's usually lively into the wee small hours. While much of the flamenco is geared to tourists, the quality of these performances is usually high, even if the atmosphere's a bit sterile. It's also possible to track down a more authentic experience; many bars have dedicated flamenco nights. The quality varies but the cost is minimal and occasionally you'll see something very special.

⊙ Shopping

Seville's main shopping area is the Centro around **Calles Sierpes**, **Tetuán**, **Velásquez**, **Cuna** and **Plaza del Duque**. This busy area is the place to come for clothes, be it modern Spanish or essential Seville Feria fashion: shawls, flamenco dresses, *mantillas*, ornamental combs, fans and castanets. Head to the **Alameda de Hércules** area for more offbeat stuff, either in the area's lively markets (Sun and Thu) or the smaller shops along Calles Amor de Díos, **Jesús del Gran Poder** or **Trajano**. If it's ceramics you're after, **Triana** is the place to go; there are dozens of attractively decorated shops. Most can arrange reasonably priced secure international delivery.

Elegantly built over several small islands, Stockholm can lay a fair claim to having one of the world's most beautiful city locations. In recent years it has shed its reputation as a provincial backwater and transformed itself into a far more cosmopolitan and dynamic place. No longer blond or bland, the city now pulsates with a creative energy that has helped form an urban culture with its sights firmly set on the world stage. Synonymous with both high design and hi-tech, it remains an eminently manageable and civilized place whose laid-back charm is reflected in its friendly, confident inhabitants, around a quarter of whom were born outside Sweden. Predominately young, these "new Swedes" are changing the way Stockholm thinks about itself.

Stockholm

Arts & culture
★★★

Eating
★★★

Nightlife
★★★

Outdoors
★★★★★

Romance
★★★

Shopping
★★★

Sightseeing
★★

Value for money
★★

Overall score
★★★

At a glance

The most important of Stockholm's 14 islands are those on which the city centre is built, only a few metres from the mainland. Stadsholmen, better known as **Gamla Stan**, is a mixture of narrow lanes and grand buildings, while adjacent **Riddarholmen** is also rich in historical associations. **Skeppsholmen**, to the east, has the ultra-cool modern art museum, while **Kungsholmen** to the west, houses the iconic City Hall. To the south, **Södermalm** is the biggest island and one of the city's main entertainment districts. Here, around the central **Medborgarplatsen**, you'll find bars and restaurants that reflect the cosmopolitan, design-led influences of 'new' Sweden. This is also the centre of Stockholm's relaxed gay scene.

The modernist-inspired **city centre** is on the mainland to the north, 10 minutes from Södermalm. The streets around **Stureplan** offer exclusive clubbing and shopping and **Vasastaden** is a busy commercial hub centred around T-Centralen train station.

I have never ceased to admire the genius who arranged that Stockholm be enclosed in a frame of wild nature.

Carl Jonas Love Almqvist (1793-1866)

Heading east from the city centre along the waterfront to the island of **Djurgården** is one of the most beautiful walks in any European city. Boasting three of Sweden's biggest attractions (Gröna Lund amusement park, Skansen and the Vasa museums), Djurgården is also a great place to relax in rural tranquillity.

★ *Don't leave town without buying gravad sauce, elk ham and surströmming at Östermalms Saluhall.*

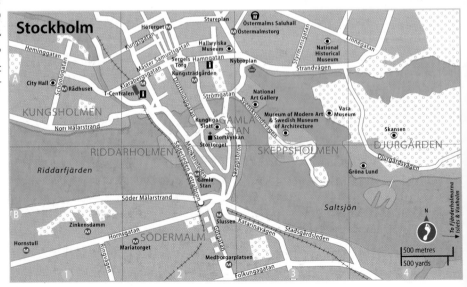

⊙ Sights

Gamla Stan
ⓘ *Metro Gamla Stan,* **☐B2**.

This island is the site of the majority of Stockholm's historic buildings and has been the stage on which much of Swedish history has been played out. Gamla Stan combines a residential area with a selection of government and royal buildings, not to mention plenty of cafés in its narrow streets with gabled roofs.

Just behind the main square, **Stortorget**, is Stockholm's impressive Cathedral and Royal Church, **Storkyrkan** ⓘ *Trångsund 1,* **☐A2**, *daily 0900-1800, guided tours Thu 1100, free.* It is ornately decorated and has a number of important Baroque artworks including the outstanding *St George and the Dragon* (Berndt Notke) from 1489.

Gamla Stan

Royal Palace (Kungliga Slott)
ⓘ *www.royalcourt.se,* **☐A2**. *Times vary; some sections closed during state visits. SEK 130 for all parts of the palace or SEK 90 for individual sections. Metro Gamla Stan.*

The massive bulk of Nicodemus Tessin's building dominates central Stockholm and is a powerful statement of the ambitions of the Swedish monarchy in the 18th century. Replacing an earlier palace which burnt down, it was completed in several stages and finally occupied in 1754. The austere façade is guarded by several stone lions. Its sumptuous interior is undeniably impressive and about as far as you can get from modern Swedish minimalism.

During state visits the Royal Apartments are closed but the three museums within the palace stay open and contain some interesting collections associated with the monarchy. The changing of the guard, which takes place at 1215 every day (1315 on Sunday), is a well-drilled reminder that the Swedish monarchy is still solidly in place.

⊙ Travel essentials

Getting there Stockholm is served by four international airports. The main one, **Arlanda**, T08-797600, www.lfv.se, is 45 km from the city. **Arlanda Express** trains, www.arlanda express.com, depart from from underneath the terminal to T-Centralen (20 mins; SEK 380 return). Buses run by **Flyggbussarna**, www.flygbussarna.se, leave every 15 mins for the 40-min journey to the centre and cost SEK 95 single, SEK 175 return. A taxi will cost SEK 480 and takes around 45 mins. **Stockholm Taxi**, T08-150000, www.taxistockholm.se.

Skavsta airport, T01-552804, www.skavsta-air.se, is 100 km from the city and is the base for budget airlines. Buses to and from Stockholm take 80 mins and cost SEK 199 return, SEK 130 single. A taxi will cost around SEK 1300. Contact **Nyköping Taxi**, T01-5521 7500.

Västerås airport, T021-805600, www.vasterasflygplats.se, is 85 km from the city. **Flyggbussarna** take 75 mins and charge SEK 199 return. A taxi will cost about SEK 1500 and take an hour. **Västerås Taxi**, T021-185000.

From **Bromma Airport**, T08-797 6874, www.lfv.se, the 20-min journey with **Flyggbussarna** costs SEK 130 return. A taxi (**Stockholm Taxi**, T08-150000) will take 15 mins and cost about SEK 250.

Mainline train services all run from **T-Centralen** and are operated by either **Swedish Rail** (www.sj.se) or **Connex** (www.connex.se). The high-speed **X2000** tilting train links Stockholm with Copenhagen in around 5½ hrs.

Getting around Central Stockholm is compact and easily walkable. **Stockholm Transport**, www.sl.se, operates the efficient metro system as well as local buses and commuter trains. Tickets valid for 24 or 72 hrs (SEK 60 or SEK 180) allow unlimited access to the whole network. Ferries to the archipelago (see box on page 237) are run by **Waxholmsbolaget**, T08-679 5830, www.waxholmsbolaget.se, and **Strömma Kanalbolaget**, T08-587140, www.strommakanalbolaget.com, and depart from Nybroplan on the mainland. **Rentabike**, T08-660 7959, www.renta bike.se, is well established and reliable. Canoe hire from **Djurgårdsbrons Sjöcafé**, T08-660 5757.

Tourist information The main tourist office, **Sverigehuset**, Hamngatan 27, T08-5082 8508, www.stockholm town.com, Mon-Fri 0900-1900, Sat 1000-1700, Sun 1000-1600, will deal with all enquiries. They also have a hotel booking service in T-Centralen T08-5082 8508.

Exchange rate Swedish Krona (SEK). £1 = SEK 13.44. €1 = SEK 9.20.

Best of the rest

Stadshuset (City Hall)
ⓘ *Hantverkargartan 1, T08-5082 9058, www.stockholm.se/cityhall,* ⓈⒶ¹. *SEK 60 with tours everyday at 1000 and 1200. Metro T-Centralen.*

The Blue Room, modelled on an Italian Piazza, and the Byzantine-inspired mosaics are the highlights of this iconic building which hosts the Nobel Prize dinner; you can try the menu in the Stadshuskälleren cellar restaurant (see page 238).

National Historical Museum
ⓘ *Narvavägen 13-17, T08-5195 5600, www.historiska.se,* ⓈⒶ³. *Daily 1100-1700. Free.* Ancient gold, art from the Romanesque and Gothic periods plus the world's oldest carpet and a unique Viking collection out in Östermalm.

Hallwylska Museum
ⓘ *Hamngatan 4, T08-519555, www.hallwylskamuseet.se,* ⓈⒶ². *Tue-Sun 1200-1600. Free.*
A remarkably opulent house standing as a monument to the various collections built up over a lifetime by its magpie-like owners.

Vasa Museum
ⓘ *Galärvarvsvägen 14, Djurgården, T08-5195 4800, www.vasamuseet.se,* ⓈⒶ³. *Daily 1000-1700, longer hours in summer. SEK 80. Bus 47 or 69 from Central Station.*

In 1628, at the height of Sweden's military power, the warship *Vasa*, which was to be the flagship of the Swedish navy, made its maiden voyage. It sank barely one mile out to sea. The story of the building of the *Vasa*, its demise and ultimate rescue from the seabed is well told in this purpose-built museum on

Vasa Museum

Djurgården. There is plenty of historical background and multimedia displays but the main draw is the ship itself. It is surprisingly large and bulky and its stern has an impressive number of warlike figures and martial symbols.

Skansen
ⓘ *Djurgården, T08-442 8000, www.skansen.se,* ⓈⒶ⁴. *May daily 1000-2000; Jun-Aug daily 1000-2200; Sep daily 1000-1700; Oct-Apr daily 1000-1600. SEK 70. Bus 47 from Central Station or 44.*

The prototype of all open-air museums, Skansen holds a sentimental place in every Swede's heart. A kind of Noah's Ark for Swedish rural buildings and industry, it first opened its doors in 1892. All the buildings were moved here from other parts of Sweden in an attempt to preserve a rural heritage that was rapidly disappearing with industrialization. There are displays of traditional crafts and a collection of Scandinavian animals including bears and elks. The summer-only open-air theatre hosts sing-a-long concerts which are an unmissable celebration of all things Swedish.

National Museum of Fine Arts
ⓘ *Södra Blasieholmshamnen, T08-5195 4300, www.nationalmuseum.se,* ⓈⒶ³. *Tue and Thu 1100-2000, Wed, Fri-Sun 1100-1700. Free. Metro Kungsträdgården.*

The paintings housed in this elegant building reflect all periods of art history. Highlights include Lucas Cranach's portrait of Martin Luther from 1526 and some fine Rembrandts. Swedish painters such as Larsson and Zorn are also well represented. The other permanent collection focuses on Swedish design and is a must-see for anyone who has ever bought IKEA furniture or marvelled at a cleverly-designed household appliance.

Museum of Modern Art and Swedish Museum of Architecture
ⓘ *Exercisplan, Skeppsholmen, T08-5195 5200, www.arkitekturmuseet.se, www.modernamuseet.se,* ⓈⒶ³. *Tue-Wed 1000-2000, Thu-Sun 1000-1800. Free. Metro Kungsträdgården.*

Skansen

Stockholm's archipelago

With picturesque red houses, perfect beaches and beautiful scenery, the thousands of islands which make up Stockholm's archipelago make an excellent place for an excursion from the city. No matter how short your time in Stockholm a day trip should be a priority. Stockholmers are very proud of having the islands on their doorstep and the lucky ones try to commute by boat during the summer.

The islands vary in size and character. Some, like **Vaxholm**, are lived on all the time, while others have no permanent population. Geographically they are divided into the Northern, Middle or Southern archipelago depending on their position in the Baltic. The closest are the **Fjärderholmarna islets**, about 25 minutes by boat. Vaxholm is a year-round option and a good introduction to the archipelago.

Some of the islands can be reached by ferry throughout the year from Nybroplan on the mainland. The main companies operating ferries to the archipelago have detailed information on their websites. Waxholmsbolaget and Strömma Kanalbolaget are the biggest operators (see Travel essentials box, page 235). The tourist office website, www.stockholm town.com, has details of individual islands and accommodation options. For longer stays in wooden cottages, Dess, T08-5424 8100, www.dess.se, has an online booking service.

Located on the city centre island of Skeppsholmen and housed in the same converted military building, these museums are rapidly becoming Swedish design icons. The Modern Art museum's permanent collection include Magritte's *The Red Model* and paintings by Picasso, Dali and Matisse.

The outstanding Museum of Architecture has a permanent display illustrating the history of Swedish urbanism as well as temporary exhibitions. There is an excellent restaurant and café.

Östermalms Saluhall

Östermalmstorg, www.saluhallen.com. Mon-Thu 0930-1800, Fri 0930-1830, Sat 0930-1600. Metro Östermalmstorg (take the Östermalmstorg/Nybrogatan exit).

This superb indoor market, in a late 19th-century characterful building, is the place to visit for good food, either in the form of ingredients or handmade meals, including takeaways that are perfect for a picnic. Choose anything from sushi to Swedish specialities at over 20 stalls, delis, cafés and restaurants.

National Museum of Fine Arts

Museum of Modern Art

● Sleeping

Finding reasonably-priced accommodation in Stockholm can be a challenge and you are advised at all times to book well in advance. Most places to stay in the centre have discounted weekend rates or other special offers. Try the tourist office website, www.stockholmtown.com, for bed and breakfast accommodation.

€€€ **Grand Hotel**, Södra Blasieholmshamnen, T08-679 3500, www.grandhotel.se. Metro Kungsträdgården. Stockholm's most famous hotel has an unrivalled position on the waterfront and is unsurpassed for class and service. Its exquisite bar is a good place to spot a famous face.

€€€ **Rival Hotel**, Mariatorget 3, T08-5457 8900, www.rival.se. Metro Mariatorget. Stylish and classy hotel in central Södermalm with individually designed rooms. The hotel is owned by Benny (from Abba) and if one of his musicals is in town there are good-value packages on offer.

€€ **Nordic Sea Hotel**, Vasaplan 7, T08-5056 3000, www.nordicsea hotel.se. Metro T-Centralen. One of a brace of hotels owned by Nordic Hotels, the Nordic Sea has a modern, efficient ambiance. The famous **Ice Bar** is on the ground floor (see below).

€ **Log Inn Hotel**, Kajplats 16, Södermälarstrand, T08-442 4420, www.loginn.se. Metro Slussen. A 10-min walk from Slussen, this is the best value of Stockholm's nautically themed hotels. Cabins are a little small but manage to squeeze in a bathroom. The location, with a view across to City Hall, make this an excellent option.

€ **STF Hostel af Chapman**, Flagmansvägen 8, Skeppsholmen,

T08-463 2266, www.stfturist.se. Metro Kungsträdgården. Deservedly famous central hostel. Most of the rooms are land-based but some are aboard an old clipper moored to Skeppsholmen. Book well in advance if you want one of these. There is also a bar.

● Eating

Swedish food has undergone something of a revolution in the past few years with the opening of a wave of international restaurants. Södermalm is the best place to find these, while Gamla Stan has traditional Swedish food of a high quality and price.

▼▼▼ **Den Gyldene Freden**, Österlånggatan 51, T08-249760, www.gyldenefreden.se. Mon-Fri 1700-2400, Sat 1300-2400. Metro Gamla Stan. Sweden's oldest restaurant has been around for over 200 years. The fish-heavy menu always has some Nordic influences. Romantic and classy.

▼▼▼ **Gondolen på Södermalm**, Katarinahissen, Stadsgården 6, T08-641 7090. Mon-Fri 1130-0100, Sat 1600-0100. Metro Slussen. Sitting on top of the KF Huset at Slussen (take the lift from the waterfront), this is one of Stockholm's best restaurants. The modern menu competes with the decor for sophistication and the view from the restaurant is spectacular.

▼▼ **Koh Phangan**, Skånegatan 57, Södermalm, T08-642 5040. Mon-Fri 1100-0100, Sat and Sun 1400-0100. Metro Medborgarplatsen. Wildly popular Thai-inspired place in Södermalm, complete with beach hut decor. Booking essential at weekends.

▼ **Jerusalem Kebab**, Gåsgränd off Västerlånggatan, Gamla Stan, T08-659 3900. Tue-Thu 0900-0100, Fri-Sun

0900-0300. Metro Gamla Stan. Hidden away off Västerlånggatan, this Palestinian-owned place serves up tasty and cheap Middle Eastern food with vegetarian options. A small courtyard terrace is a few metres away.

▼ **Stadshuskälleren**, Stadshuset, T08-5063 2200. Metro Stadshuset. A good lunchtime option, this restaurant in a corner of City Hall has a competitively priced menu at SEK 125. However, its star offering is the menu from the Nobel Prize dinner which weighs in at a hefty SEK 1350.

● Nightlife

Going out in central Stockholm is an expensive, flashy affair with a lot of queuing involved. The pubs around Medborgarplatsen and Frihemsplan are more relaxed. The best option is to pick a place with live music and spend the evening there. Note that all Swedish bars are non-smoking. For clubs, **Berns**, Berzelii Park, T08-5663 2222, Metro Östermalmstorget, is an impressive complex tucked away at the back of Berzelii Park with a relaxed atmosphere and a young crowd. Book in advance to get to the **Ice Bar**, Nordic Sea Hotel, T08-5056 3124, www.nordic seahotel.se. SEK 150 entrance including drink. You're only likely to go here once but it's an unforgettable experience. After donning your silver parka you will be served a drink in a bar where everything is made of ice.

Spy Bar, Birger Jarlsgatan 20, T08-5450 3701, Metro Östermalstorget, is the Armani-clad ruler of Stockholm designer nightclubs. For live music, **Stampen**, Stora Nygatan 5, T08-205794, www.stampen.se, has a jazz-club feel.

Tallinn, the medieval, upwardly mobile capital of Estonia, owes its fortunes and seemingly endless misfortunes to its strategic location on the eastern shore of the Baltic Sea. The city has been moulded by a combination of Teutonic efficiency and Russian extravagance, and has shaken off decades of Soviet occupation with astounding success. Although its architecture is often described as 'fairy-tale', there's nothing twee about it: the soaring spires and narrow Hanseatic merchants' houses, leaning perilously into the streets and washed with watery limes, lemons and pinks, are unfussy, even austere. The Old Town, encircled by forest and rugged city walls, spirals down to the silvery Bay of Tallinn, and is especially alluring in the snow, when hotels slash rates and the cobbles seem coated with crushed diamonds.

Tallinn

Arts & culture
★★★

Eating
★★

Nightlife
★★★★

Outdoors
★★★★

Romance
★★★★

Shopping
★★

Sightseeing
★★★

Value for money
★★★★

Overall score
★★★

At a glance

The heart of the city is the **Vanalinn** (Old Town), which is ringed by a rough limestone city wall. Traditionally the haunt of nobles, politicians and administrators, **Toompea** (Upper Town) sits in splendid isolation on the hill dominating the city, with spectacular views of the sea and the maze of medieval streets below. East of Toompea and down the hill, the kidney bean-shaped **All-Linn** (Lower Town) extends north from Harju Street along Pikk (Long) Street to the sea. Wedged between the wider streets is a higgledy-piggledy scrawl of cobbled lanes and medieval houses. Its focal point at all hours of the day and night is **Raekoja Plats** (Town Hall Square). Beyond the walls of the Old Town, bastions and a former moat have been transformed into lush parkland.

The leafy seaside suburb of **Kadriorg**, with its baroque palace, is a 10-minute tram ride away. Further east, near the 1980 Olympics Centre,

Tallinn is probably the only foreign city in the world outside Finland where a poetry reading in Finnish can attract a crowd.

The Economist

you can hit **Pirita** beach, take to the river and admire the skeletal ruins of St Birgitta's Convent. On the other side of town, a short bus ride away, is the cliffside Rocca Al Mare Open Air Museum, where you can get a unique insight into Estonian peasant life.

★ *Don't leave town without enjoying the views from Toompea in the early morning.*

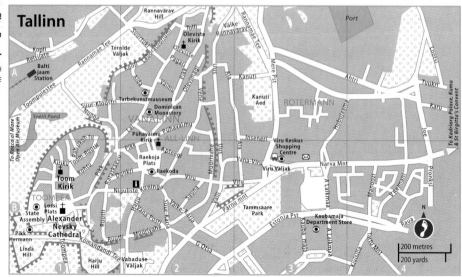

👁 Sights

Raekoja Plats (Town Hall Square)

Raekoja Plats is one of Europe's most appealing squares, especially on a summer evening, when the shade of the sky seems tailor-made for the gentle pinks, whites and blues of the façades. The Gothic **Raekoda** (Town Hall) ⓘ *T645 7900,* **J.B2**, *Jul-Aug Mon-Sat 1000-1600, Sep-Jun guided visits by appointment, EEK 35,* has been scrubbed clean to reveal the original creamy colour of the limestone, much to the surprise of the locals, who'd grown up with it being grey. The superb view from the **tower** ⓘ *Jun-Aug 1100-1800, EEK 25,* is well worth the slightly perilous ascent.

Pühavaimu Kirik (Church of the Holy Ghost)

ⓘ *Pühavaimu, T644 1487. EEK 10,* **J.B2**.

Raekoja Plats

Just north of Raekoja Plats, this modest yet prodigiously pretty church was completed in 1360. The only hints of flamboyance on its façade are an alluring copper spire (added in 2002) and the city's oldest public clock, carved by Christian Ackermann in the 17th century. The interior has an intimate feel and contains one of the city's most prized medieval works of art, the 15th-century altar by Berndt Notke.

Katariina Käik (St Catherine's passageway)

East of Pühavaimu Kirik and next to the **Dominican Monastery ruins** ⓘ *Vene 16, T644 4606,* **J.A2**, *May-Sep daily 1000-1800, EEK 90,* is the city's most romantic alley. It's a narrow passageway with overhead vaulting, wrought-iron lamps and artisan workshops (where you can watch people at work). Look out for the medieval tombstones, too.

Tarbekunstimuuseum (Applied Arts Museum)

ⓘ *Lai 17, T627 4600,* **J.A2**. *Wed-Sun 1100-1800. EEK 30.*

Towards the north of the Lower Town, housed in a former granary, storehouse and powder magazine, is one of the city's best museums. Three floors are devoted to ceramics, glassware, leather, metalwork, textiles and jewellery.

⊖ Travel essentials

Getting there Ulemiste Airport, www.tallinn-airport.ee, is 4 km southeast of the city centre. Taxis charge about EEK 100 to central Tallinn. Bus 2 leaves every 20 mins, 0700-2400, and stops near the Kaubamaja department store; EEK 15, one-way. The journey takes 15 mins.

Getting around The Old Town is easily negotiable on foot; a gentle stroll around the historic centre takes about 4 hrs. Outside the city walls, there's a reliable network of buses, trolleybuses and trams (1-day card EEK 45, 3-day card EEK 85). The city bus terminal is under the Viru Keskus shopping centre. Pick up

a transport map from the tourist office, bookshops or kiosks. Taxis are cheaper than in most western cities; there are ranks at road intersections and outside the bigger hotels. The Old Town is hilly and cobbled, but elsewhere there is a good system of cycle lanes. Further information is available at www.tallinn.ee.

Tourist information Tallinn's main tourist office is at Kullassepa 4/Niguliste 2, around the corner from Raekoja Plats, T645 7777, www.tourism.tallinn.ee. Open May and Jun Mon-Fri 0900-1900, Sat 1000-1700, Sun 1000-1700; Jul and Aug Mon-Fri 0900-2000, Sat and Sun

1000-1700; Sep Mon-Fri 0900-1800, Sat and Sun 1000-1700; Oct-Apr Mon-Fri 0900-1700, Sat 1000-1500. It can put you in touch with specialist guides and provides a free map and information about sights and excursions around Estonia. White posters displayed around the city list cultural events. The **Tallinn Card**, available from the tourist office, offers free entry to museums, unlimited public transport and other activities; from EEK 130 for 6 hrs to EEK 450 for 72 hrs. Many museums are closed Mon and Tue.

Exchange rate Estonian Kroon (EEK). £1 = EEK 23. €1 = EEK 15.65.

Oleviste Kirik (St Olaf's Church)

ⓘ *Lai 50, T641 2241,* **JA2**. *Spire Apr-Oct daily 1000-1800. EEK 25.*

Two blocks northeast of Raekoja Plats is the dazzlingly white Oleviste church, once the tallest building in Europe. The dizzyingly high, needle-thin copper tower was used as a radio transmitter by the KGB. The viewing platform has breathtaking views.

Toompea (Upper Town)

Toompea's main square, **Lossi Plats** (Castle Square), has been the seat of power since ancient times. The only remains of its once imposing medieval castle, however, are the west and south walls and three grey towers, including the iconic **Pikk Hermann**. The square is dominated by the fudge-coloured, onion-domed **Alexander Nevsky Cathedral**, erected in 1900 as a symbol of Russian authority. Much older and altogether more dignified is the austere but alluring **Toom Kirik** (St Mary's Cathedral) ⓘ *www.eelk.ee/tallinna.toom,* **JB1**. The pink confection next to Nevsky Cathedral

St Olaf's Church

is the **State Assembly Building** ⓘ *T631 6357, www.riigikogu.ee,* **JB1**, *book in advance for tours Mon-Fri 1000-1600, free,* home of Estonia's parliament, with an expressionist interior that belies the demure façade.

Kadriorg Palace

ⓘ *Wezenbergi 37, T606 6400, www.ekm .ee/kadriorg. May-Sep Tue-Sun 1000-1700, Oct-Apr Wed-Sun 1000-1700. EEK 45.*

Kadriorg Palace Park

Located east of the Old Town, in a delightful park, the palace was designed in 1718 for Peter the Great by Italian architect Nicolo Michetti. Mulberry-coloured, with cream pillars and graceful oval windows, it is modest, sober baroque at its best, and a fine setting for the Estonian Art Museum's foreign section. Just north stands **Kumu** ⓘ *Weizenbergi 34/Valge 1, T602 6000, www.ekm.ee, summer Tue-Sun 1100-1800, winter Wed- Sun 1100-1800, EEK 75 for all shows,* the new Art Museum of Estonia. It's a superb glass and concrete structure, with Estonian art from the 18th century to the present, and temporary shows.

St Birgitta's Convent, Pirita

ⓘ *Kloostri 9, T605 5044. Apr, May, Sep-Oct daily 1000-1800; Jun-Aug daily 0900-1900; Nov-Mar daily 1200-1600. EEK 20.*

The skeletal silhouette of this ruined convent, founded in 1407 by a trio of widowed merchants, is a spectacular sight. The gable was a useful orientation point for seamen. Damaged by Ivan the Terrible's troops, it was reduced to ruins during the Northern War. The remains have been sensitively restored and the nuns now live in an award-winning modern building with a guest house.

Rocca al Mare

ⓘ *Vabaõhumuuseumi tee 12, T654 9100. May-Sep daily 1000-2000, buildings until 1800; Oct-Apr daily 1000-1700, buildings closed. EEK 50 summer, EEK 25 winter.*

The 'Rock by the Sea' is a collection of 18th-century Estonian farm buildings, including thatched barn dwellings and windmills, assembled on a serene cliff-top site overlooking Kopli Bay. From May to August at weekends, folk dancers give comic shows at 1100. The sometimes inelegant moves involve male dancers bumping against each other's bottoms.

Rocca al Mare

European City Breaks Tallinn

Given the number of sieges, attacks and aerial bombardments Tallinn has endured, it's little short of miraculous that 80% of the city fortifications, including 29 towers, have survived. The bumpy limestone walls, splashed with orange-topped turrets, are the city's most distinctive feature – a reminder that this was once one of the most impregnable stongholds in northern Europe. Tallinn was further fortified in the 16th century, with earthen embankments and ramparts. In the 17th century, the Swedes planned to surround the city with 12 bastions; in the end, only a handful were built. For Peter the Great, Tallinn's strategic importance lay at sea and, following Russia's decision to strike Tallinn off the list of fortified towns in the mid-19th century, the bastions were handed over to the municipality, which had the good sense to transform them into parks and public gardens. The only surviving scraps of the Swedish bastions are Rannavärav, Harju and Linda hills. One of the best views of the city towers is from Rannamäe, to the west, while the loveliest stretch of reclaimed parkland runs from the manicured Tornide Väljak (Square of Towers),

between Rannamäe tee and the Old Town (reach it via Suurtuki Street, where cannons were once repaired), to the more romantic, rambling area around Šnelli Pond. Named after a local gardener, the pond is all that remains of the medieval moat. Watch out for pickpockets, who are sometimes a problem here.

🌓 Sleeping

Prices are low by European standards and, in winter, they plummet even further with the temperature. Early reservation is, however, essential in summer, especially during the National Song Festival and around midsummer.

€€€ Three Sisters, Pikk 71, T630 6300, www.threesistershotel.com. A boutique hotel in a cream and yellow trio of medieval merchants' houses. Sleekly designed, with large glass windows that sit well with the old beams and vaulted ceilings. The soft cream furnishings are of superb quality, and the bathrobes and bed linen are to die for.

€€ Merchant's House Hotel, Dunkri 4/6, T697 7500, www.merchantshousehotel.com. The city's most central boutique hotel has fresh, modern interiors and wooden floors in a medieval setting of painted and beamed ceilings, arranged around a pretty inner courtyard. Some rooms are on the small side. Cheaper summer rates in Aug and Sep.

€€ Old Town Maestro's, Suur-Karja 10, T626 2000, www.maestrohotel.ee. This former merchant's dwelling, rebuilt in historicist style in 1928, has spacious, high-ceilinged rooms with large mirrors and dark wooden furniture. Unusually in Tallinn, most rooms have baths. The owners also have a villa in Kadriorg.

€-€€ UniqueStay, Paldiski maantee 3, T660 0700, www.uniquestay.com. A fun, fresh hotel at the northwest foot of Toompea Hill, with bright colour schemes and crisp design throughout. Arty photos lend a touch of gravitas. The Zen rooms have NASA-designed chairs and whirlpool baths. Free parking, free 24-hr internet access.

€ Eurohostel, Nunne 2, T644 7788, www.eurohostel.ee. One of Tallinn's newest and freshest-looking hostels. The rooms are sparse but reasonably stylish, and there's a guest kitchen.

€ Old House Guesthouse, Uus 22, T641 1464, www.oldhouse.ee. Simple rooms on a quirky street at the northeastern edge of the Vanalinn. Very quiet at night.

❼ Eating

Tallinn is packed with eateries serving everything from hearty German-influenced Estonian dishes to fine French cuisine with a local twist. The restaurant scene has developed pretty much from scratch in the past 15 years and establishments come and go at breakneck speed.

Gloria, Müürivahe 2, T644 6950, www.gloria.ee. Genuine pre-war nostalgia, with a resolutely retro interior and plush crimson furnishings. Serves French and Russian classics, with nods to local tradition and Italian cuisine: beluga caviar, borscht, fillets of sole, duck with mango and local lamb dishes. The best wine cellar in the Baltics to boot.

Vertigo, Rävala puistee 4, T666 3456, www.vertigo.ee. Top Tallinn chef and TV personality Imre Kose's chic but cosy restaurant, in a modern building south of the Old Town, has a seafood bar, lounge and fine dining section, as well as a rooftop terrace and stunning views. Expect inspired cuisine that makes the most of local produce as well as top-quality imports.

Olde Hansa, Vana turg 1, T627 9020, www.oldehansa.com. Themed medieval restaurant with a summer terrace popular with Tallinners and foreigners alike. Try authentic Hansa-era dishes, such as slow-baked Wittenberg pork in beer or dried elk meat with juniper-ripened beef, all without a chip in sight. The huge portions are best washed down with a pot of honeyed beer.

Pegasus, Harju 1, T631 4040, www.restoranpegasus.ee. For most locals, this is the place to see and be seen but, though its sleek, white,

1970s-referencing decor is perfect for posing, Pegasus is utterly without pretension. The British chef makes splendid curries and is forever creating new dishes, among them scallops with asparagus and lime, sea bass with truffle sausage, or beef tenderloin with morel sauce. Great views from the terrace and the upstairs dining area.

Café Spirit, Mere puiestee 6e, T661 6151, www.kohvikspirit.ee. Good sushi is one of the main attractions at this trendy but relaxed café, which combines minimalism with comfy sofas. The salads are some of the best in town. Popular with fashionable

> 66 99 **They say pre-war Tallinn never slept, not even in winter. After the blip of the Soviet era, that is pretty much the case again …**

locals and no doubt deliberately difficult for tourists to find (the entrance is round the back).

Eesti Maja, Lauteri 1, T645 5252, www.eestimaja.ee. An unpretentious institution south of the Old Town, serving traditional Estonian food: cabbage soup, chanterelles in cream, spiced sprats and pearl barley.

❶ Nightlife

They say pre-war Tallinn never slept, not even in winter. After the blip of the Soviet era, that is pretty much the case again, making the city a paradise for 24-hour party people. Admission and

drinks are a bargain, with most venues attracting an up-for-it, unpretentious crowd. You'll find sophisticated sounds in the hippest places and more idiosyncratic music policies in the Old Town's cellar bars, notably the grunge-tastic **Levist Väljas**, Olevimögi 12. Visit www.mutantdisco.com or www.stereo88.com for the best parties in town. For unfussy dancefloor fun, head to **Hollywood**, www.club-hollywood.ee, in an old Stalinist cinema. At the other extreme, **Võit**, www.lovesexmoney.ee, is a low-key underground venue with techno, drum 'n' bass and rock nights.

Classical, contemporary and choral music concerts are inexpensive and of exceptional quality: don't miss performances by **Hortus Musicus** (early music), **NYYD Ensemble** (contemporary), the **Estonian Philharmonic Chamber Choir** or **Ellerhein Girls' Choir**.

❷ Shopping

Visiting Tallinn today, it doesn't seem possible that only 14 years ago you had to queue for overpriced, over-ripe tomatoes or make do without toothpaste and toilet paper. Now the Old Town is awash with shops selling amber, Russian dolls, juniper-wood butter knives and impossibly thick winter socks. Viru Tänav, in All-Linn, is the main shopping street. There are regular handicraft markets on Raekoja Plats. For genuine Estonian handicrafts try the **Estonian Folk Art and Craft Union**, www.crafts.ee, which has several outlets. For cutting-edge Estonian design and clubwear, try **Nu Nordik**, Vabaduse Väljak 8, T644 9392, www.nunordik.ee.

Turin

With its baroque castles and royal palaces, regal arcaded squares and stately tree-lined boulevards, all crowned by a breathtaking alpine backdrop, Turin displays all the grace of the Savoy family. It was in the aristocratic and artistic cafés of this sophisticated salon society that the idea of an Italian Republic was converted from a twinkle into a reality. Beneath Turin's classic exterior lurks the rebellious and possessed soul of an awkward child prodigy. It is the product of an incongruous collection of assets and eccentric character traits that combine to cast a peculiar sense of alchemy, like a shroud, over the city. These attractions, so long veiled in alpine mist and black magic mythology, were newly showcased as the city underwent a complete revamp for the 2006 Winter Olympics.

Arts & culture
★★★

Eating
★★★★

Nightlife
★★★

Outdoors
★★★★

Romance
★★★

Shopping
★★

Sightseeing
★★★

Value for money
★★★

Overall score
★★★

◉ Sights

Turin is a long oblong of a city with north-south boulevards traversed by a grid of side streets. With a few exceptions, most of the city's sights, shops and nightlife lie within the boundary of corso Regina Margherita to the north and corso Vittorio Emanuele II to the south, piazza Statuto to the West and the River Po to the east.

Piazza Castello

In a city symmetrically balanced by many fine squares, **piazza Castello** is Turin's most majestic, a visual recorder of the city's history. Cloistered by a quadrangle of porticoes, three sides of it are flanked by the baroque and neoclassical façades of the former residences of the House of Savoy and Turin's main theatre. On the northern side is the **Palazzo and Giardini Reale** ① *T011-436 1455*, ⅍A3,

Piazza Castello

Tue-Sun 0900-1930, €6.50, the Savoy royal palace and gardens. Annexed to the Palazzo Reale is **Duomo di San Giovanni Battista** ① *T011-436 1540*, ⅍A2, *Mon-Sat 0700-1230, 1500-1900, Sun 0800-1230, 1500-1900*, the only remnant of Renaissance architecture in the city. The **Cappella della Santa Sindone** was once home to the city's most famed

asset: the **Shroud**. Since a fire in 1997 the chapel has been closed and the Shroud firmly guarded, only making the most occasional of appearances. At the centre of the piazza stands the **Palazzo Madama** ① *T011-443 3501, www.palazzo madamatorino.it*, ⅍A3, *Tue-Fri and Sun 0900-1900, Sat 0900-2000*. The former Savoy castle, built on the original eastern Roman city gate, is a synthesis of the story of Turin and contains the **Museo Civico d'Arte Antica**.

East of piazza Castello

Between the atmospheric arches of via Po and corso Regina Margherita is the heart of Turin's university life, a tight network of lively and youthfully shabby streets. At the end of via Po the street opens out into **piazza Vittorio Veneto** which slopes down to the river and the **Murazzi**, scene of riverside cafés and subversive nocturnal activities. Rising

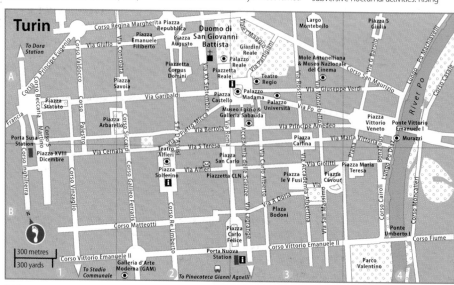

Turin

Mole Antonelliana

above this quarter, a lone spire towering above the city, is the **Mole Antonelliana** ① *via Montebello 20, T011-812 5658,* 🚇A3, *Tue-Sun 0900-2000, Sat until 2300,* Turin's equivalent of the Eiffel Tower. Inside, the acclaimed **Museo Nazionale del Cinema** ① *T011-813 8560, www.museo cinema.it,* 🚇A3, *Tue-Sun 0900-2000, Sat until 2300, €7.60,* is considered by many to be the most spectacular cinema museum in Europe.

Around the narrow streets south of via Po are some unexpected but world-class museums. The **Museo Egizio** ① *via*

Murazzi riverside cafés

Accademia delle Scienze 6, T011- 561 7776, www.museoegizio.org, 🚇A3, *Tue-Sun 0830-1930, €6.50,* has the largest collection of Egyptian artefacts outside Cairo; while **Galleria Sabauda** ① *via Accademia delle Scienze 6, T011-547440,* 🚇A3, *Tue-Thu 0830-1930, Fri-Sun 0830-1200 (until 2330 on public holidays that fall on Sat), €4,* contains many classics by the old masters. Further south, across corso Vittorio Emanuele II and east of porta Nuova, is **Parco Valentino**, complete with botanical garden, a majestic baroque palace and a faux-medieval castle. Fiat, the city's most famous company, was based around here. South along via Nizza is the former **Lingotto** factory, its rooftop testing track made famous by *The Italian Job*. It now houses a super-modern Renzo Piano museum, the **Pinacoteca Gianni Agnelli**, www.pinacoteca-agnelli.it, home to masterpieces from Canaletto to Picasso.

West of piazza Castello

South of piazza Castello, **via Roma** is a catwalk home for the flashiest boutiques, while west of here Turin is at its most Parisian, with an area of art nouveau architecture appropriately on **corso Francia**. At the heart of a more modern corner of Turin, south of corso Vittorio Emmanuele II, **Galleria d'Arte Moderna** (GAM) ① *via Magenta 31, T011- 562 9911, www.gamtorino.it,* 🚇B2, *Tue-Sun 1000-1900, €7.50,* is at the very cutting edge of modern art. South of the centre on corso IV Novembre is **Stadio Comunale**, training ground of once-glorious but fallen football club, Juventus FC, and now an Olympic theatre.

The alleyways north of **via Garibaldi**, the area of the original Roman

⚙ Design city

The dukes of Savoy may have given Turin its baroque splendour, but it was the city's industrial importance that shaped much of what it was to become. In promoting the car, Turin celebrated values of the artists and architects of the early 20th- century avant-garde movements that were being theorized in Paris: the new, the fast and the marriage of design with function. The grand city of arcades and palazzi had to expand and adapt to its new vocation and many of the early industrial buildings, such as the Lingotto factory, were praised by Marinetti – founder of Futurism – for they were not merely simple industrial spaces but important pieces of a modernist architectural legacy. Due to its proximity to France and historic openness to French influence, Turin was the gateway through which many modernist inventions and movements such as art nouveau, pret-à-porter fashion and cinema first came to Italy.

settlement, see a weekly weekend **market**, while north of piazza Repubblica is Turin's monthly flea market, **Il Gran Balon**. Further north around the freight station are post- industrial warehouses, which have been turned into clubs and late lounges.

⊖ Travel essentials

◓ Sleeping

€€€ Grand Hotel Sitea, via Carlo Alberto 35, T011-517 0171, www.thi.it. A refined and elegant luxury hotel in an 18th-century palazzo with an understated decor that oozes charm. It also has a fine restaurant.

€€€ Le Meridien Art & Tech, via Nizza 262, T011-664 2000, www.lemeri dien-lingotto.it. A little detached from the Turin of arcades, museums and shops, but nevertheless the number one choice for contemporary design.

€€ Dogana Vecchia, via Corte d'Appello 4, T011-436 7272. A former 17th-century customs house, this is one of the most atmospheric of Turin's hotels. The wood-panelled rooms are full of baroque furniture.

€€ Liberty, via Pietro Micca 15, T011-562 8801, www.hotelliberty-torino.it. On a road of fine art nouveau buildings, this beautifully restored palazzo attracts an arty, film-world clientele.

€ Des Artistes, via Principe Amedeo 21/d, T011-812 4416. A good value hotel in one of Turin's most evocative addresses. It's quiet and comfortable and the atmosphere both in and around the hotel does not disappoint.

---

❷ Eating

⫼⫼⫼ Neuv Caval 'd Brons, piazza San Carlo, T011-545354. One of the city's gastronomic classics offering a menu that has kept up with the times.

⫼⫼⫼ Ristorante del Cambio, piazza Carignano 2, T011-546690. Open since 1757 and one of Turin's most illustrious eateries. The decor is operatic, the food and service very much the same.

⫼ Le Vitel Etonne, via San Francesco de Paola 4, T011-812 4621. More of a winery than a restaurant but the food is delicious and the servings substantial – it's just a question of priorities and the rustic atmosphere emphasizes this.

⫼ Caffe San Carlo, piazza San Carlo 156. With the air of a museum, this grand café's columns, sculptures and paintings could grace a royal court. Unmissable for its regal atmosphere.

◑ Nightlife

When clubbing in Turin, don't expect the slightly dodgy techno of Milan or other Italian cities. Turin's edge is its grungy youth culture based on reggae, drum'n'bass and jazz. The late-hour meccas are the Po-side **Murazzi**, where former boathouses are now riverside clubs (many summer only), and the jazz venues of **Docks Dora** in the northwest. The revitalized *quadrilatero romano*, north of via Garibaldi, is virtually wall-to-wall with funky new bars, many sponsored by Martini (the original aperitif, born in Turin) who have created the concept of the 'drinner' (a Martini with food and music). These are Turin's late lounges with St Germain and their imitators turned up high on the speakers.

European City Breaks Turin

Valencia once languished in the shadow of flashy Madrid and trendy Barcelona but its days as a wallflower are long over. The word is out: Valencia, with its vibrant medieval core, its fantastic nightlife, shopping and restaurants, its sandy beaches and some of the most spectacular new architecture in Europe, is the hottest destination on the Mediterranean. The 2007 America's Cup has brought a new marina and several slick new amenities to the city, all cementing Valencia's position as one of the most forward-looking destinations in Spain. But its traditional charms – the palm-lined boulevards, baroque belltowers, Modernista markets and golden beaches – still assert their pull. It's a city in which old and new, shabby and sleek, co-exist peacefully.

Valencia

Arts & culture
★★★★

Eating
★★★★

Nightlife
★★★★★

Outdoors
★★★

Romance
★★★

Shopping
★★★

Sightseeing
★★★

Value for money
★★★

Overall score
★★★★

At a glance

Valencia divides neatly into three general areas, each with a distinctive atmosphere. The **Old City**, 4 km inland, is still the heart of Valencia, home to most of the sights and the best selection of nightlife and shopping. It's the perfect neighbourhood for a wander – you won't need public transport. Spreading out from the Old City eastwards to the sea is the **New City**, a largely anonymous area of bland offices and apartments, but also the site of the glittering **Ciutat de les Arts i les Ciències** (City of Arts and Sciences). It's quite a walk (around 3 km) from the Old City, but a pleasant stroll along the gardens which line the former riverbed of the Riu Túria. The New City links the Old City with Valencia's vast working **port** (El Grau), its glossy new marina and the main city beach of **Malvarrosa**. This long, golden stretch is lined with a modern promenade, behind which are the scruffy, cheerful neighbourhoods of Malvarrosa and Cabanyal which once belonged to the dock workers and fishermen.

I have tried to get close to the frontier between architecture and sculpture and to understand architecture as an art.

*Santiago Calatrava,
architect of the City of
Arts and Sciences*

★ *Don't leave town without checking out the obscene sculpture on the doorway to La Llotja.*

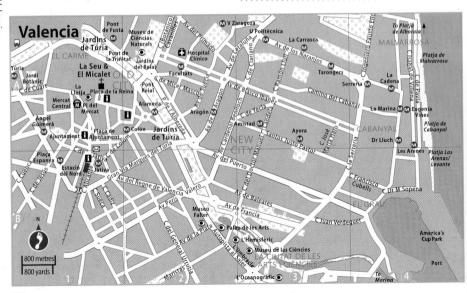

◉ Sights

La Seu and El Micalet (Catedral and El Miguelete)

ⓘ Pl de la Reina 1, T963-918127, www.archivalencia.org, **NA1**. Cathedral: Mon- Sat 1000-1730, Sun 1400-1730; free. Museu de La Seu: Mon-Sat 1000-1300, 1630-1900; €1.20/ 0.80. Micalet 1000-1300, 1600-1900, Sun 1000-1300, 1700-1930; €2/ €1. Bus 6, 16, 28.

Plaça de la Reina, a long, elegant space surrounded by cafés and palm trees, is one of the city's most important squares. (It's also the most touristy: you can't miss the horse-drawn carriages clattering around the narrow streets for a fat fee.) It's dominated by Valencia's vast and imposing **cathedral**, topped with the city's much-loved symbol, the octagonal bell tower known as the Micalet. It was largely completed by the end of the 15th century but, in the late 1700s, baroque craftsmen added the florid façade, with its thickly encrusted sculptural decoration and swooping lines.

Plaça de la Reina

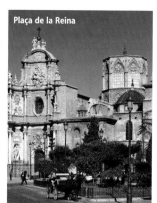

The cathedral's greatest treasure is kept in the **Capilla del Santo Cáliz**, where a jewel-encrusted chalice carved from agate is set into a pale alabaster altarpiece that fills an entire wall. (Drop a euro in the machine to light up the altarpiece for full operatic effect.) The chapel sits next to the Sala Capitular, which houses the cathedral **museum** with a fascinating collection of religious art, statuary and sculpture.

A separate entrance leads to the

Micalet, the slim bell tower with lacy Gothic tracery. Huff and puff up the 207 steps for staggering views across the blue-tiled cupolas, baroque towers and higgledy-piggledy maze of the Old City.

Mercat Central (Mercado Central)

ⓘ Pl del Mercat, T963-829101, www.mercadocentralvalencia.es, **NA1**. Mon-Sat 0730-1430. No fish market on Mon. Bus 26, 27.

Southwest of the cathedral in the other main square of the old city, Valencia's central market is one of the most beautiful in the country; a vast, Modernista concoction of wrought iron and stained glass surmounted with cupolas and whimsical weathervanes. The Comunitat Valenciana isn't known as 'Spain's orchard' for nothing and inside you'll find a breathtaking array of colourful, fresh produce with almost 1000 stalls to choose from. Ceramic mosaics twist around the walls, spilling over with fruit and flowers, in a hymn to Valencia's abundance, and light pours

⊖ Travel essentials

Getting there Valencia's International Airport, T961-598500, www.aena.es, is in Manises, 8 km west of the centre of town. The Aerobus runs into the centre every 20 mins daily 0600-2200 (€2.50) and is more direct than the local bus. Taxis from outside the departures hall cost €15-18 to the city centre. Trains, including the high-speed Euromed service from Barcelona, arrive into the Modernista Estació del Nord, near the Old City, T902-240202, wwww.renfe.es.

Getting around The Old City is best explored on foot; most of the main sights are within walking distance of each other. An excellent **bus** network will take you to places further afield like La Ciutat de les

Arts i les Ciències, the port and beaches, and the Llac Albufera. The N1 night bus connects the seaside neighbourhoods with the centre. A single ticket (available on the bus) costs €1.10. **Bus Turístic** runs a hop-on/hop-off city tour; tickets are €12 and valid for 24 hrs. The **metro** system is largely aimed at commuters, but Line 4 (a tram-line above ground) is handy for the beach at Malvarrosa. Single metro or tram tickets (€1.10) are available from machines in stations. Useful **travel passes** include: **BonoBus** (10 single rides for €5.20) and **T1/2/3** (1-, 2- or 3-day tickets valid for unlimited transport on bus, tram and metro for €3.10, €5.50 and €8 each). The **Valencia**

Card is valid for 1, 2 or 3 days (€6/€10 /€15) and offers unlimited public transport, plus discounts in museums, shops and restaurants. It is available from tourist offices, metro stations, some tobacconists and hotels.

Tourist information Offices at: Pl de la Reina, T963-153931, Mon-Sat 0900- 1900, Sun and hols 0900-1400; Pl de l'Ajuntament, T963-510417, Mon-Fri 0830-1415 and 1630-1815, Sat 0915-1245; C de la Paz 48, T963-986422, Mon-Sat 1000-1830, Sat 1000-1400; and Estació del Nord, C Jàtiva 24, T963- 528573, Mon-Fri 0900-1830, www.turisvalencia.es, www.valencia.es.

in through huge stained-glass windows. A massive cupola, encrusted with more elaborate mosaics, drenches the stalls in the main hall with sunlight. But perhaps the prettiest section of all is the fish market, a semi-enclosed hall, with a spectacular array of fresh seafood glistening on slabs beneath another cupola, this one adorned with playful, ceramic fish. The market is always busy, but get there early to catch it in full swing – breakfast at one of the dozens of stalls inside the market or tucked around the edges is an institution.

La Llotja (La Lonja)

ⓘ Pl del Mercat, T963-525478, ⧉A1. Tue-Fri 1000-1400, 1630-2030, Sun 1000-1500. €2/€1. Bus 26, 27.

The silk exchange is quite simply the most beautiful building in Valencia. Sitting squarely opposite the main entrance to the central market, it is one of the finest examples of civic Gothic architecture in Europe and was declared a World Heritage Monument by UNESCO in 1996. Construction began in 1483 under the direction of the brilliant Pere Compte, a master stonemason, engineer and

La Llotja

architect. The project was completed in just 15 years. The splendid main hall, the Sala de Contratación, is vast, with a lofty, vaulted ceiling which reaches almost 18 m at its highest point. To feel an echo of the buzz that would have animated the Llotja 500 years ago, visit it on a Sunday morning when a popular stamp and coin market is held in the Sala de Contratación.

La Ciutat de les Arts i les Ciències (La Ciudad de las Artes y las Ciencias)

ⓘ Av Autopista al Saler 1-7, T902-100031, www.cac.es. Museu de les Ciències: mid Sep-mid Jun Sun-Fri 1000-1800, Sat and hols 1000-2000; mid Jun-Jul and early Sep daily 1000-2000; Aug daily 1000-2200; €7.50/€5.80. L'Hemisfèric: daily 1000-2100; €7.50/€5.80. L'Oceanogràfic: Jan-mid Jun and mid Sep-Dec Sun-Fri 1000-1800, Sat and hols 1000-2000; mid Jun-Jul and early Sep daily 1000-2000; Aug 1000-2400; €22/€16.80. Combined tickets also available. Bus 35, 95.

Having seen how new architecture revitalized the fortunes of Barcelona up the coast, Valencia commissioned the glossy La Ciutat de les Arts i les Ciències in

order to raise its international profile. The futuristic complex designed by local celebrity architect Santiago Calatrava has been an overwhelming success and you may need to book in advance to get into some of its attractions in the high season. There are five main sections: **Museu de les Ciències** (a science museum that looks more like a 23rd-century airport), **l'Hemisfèric** (laser shows, IMAX and planetarium), **L'Umbracle** (a palm-lined walkway), **L'Oceanogràfic** (an aquarium in a series of beautifully sculpted pale pavilions, the biggest in Europe), and the **Palau de les Arts** (a venue for the performing arts). The buildings – although that seems too tame a term for these bold, graphic shapes – seem to emerge from the cool, blue pools which surround them.

Platjas (Playas/Beaches)

ⓘ North: bus 1, 2, 19, 31 and summer-only services 20, 21, 22. South: to El Palmar with Autocares Herca Mon-Fri 0700, 1200, 1400, 1500, 1800, 2000, 2100. Sat-Sun 0700, 0900, 1300, 1600, 2000. Bus is marked Valencia-El Saler-El Perellò; €1.70, 30 mins.

L'Umbracle

Mercat Central

Las Fallas is one of the most important fiestas in Spain. It dates back to the Middle Ages, when carpenters used to light a bonfire in honour of Sant Josep, their patron saint. Gradually, effigies were thrown into the fire, often depicting rival organizations. Now, the vast creations take all year to build and are paraded through the streets from 13-19 March. They can be of anything – cartoon characters, politicians, buxom ladies, animals – and each neighbourhood vies to create the best. They are accompanied by mini-versions (*Ninots*), the winning *Ninot* being the only one to escape the flames. Each day, firecrackers blast out over Plaça de l'Ajuntament, bullfights are held and the evenings culminate with a massive firework display. The fiesta finishes with a

bang on 19 March when the Fallas are thrown into an enormous pyre, the *Cremá*. You can find out more about the event at **Museu Faller (Museo Fallero)** ⓘ *Pl Monteolivete 4, T963-525478, Tue-Sat 1030-1500, Sun and holidays 1000-1500. €2/ €1, free on Sat, Sun and holidays. Bus 13 from Pl de l'Ajuntament.*

Heading north of the port is a long sandy beach which runs for several miles. Valencianos usually just call the whole stretch **Platja de Malvarrosa**, but in fact it is divided into sections: nearest the port is **Platja de Levante** or **Platja Las Arenas**, with a string of restaurants, hotels and bars squeezed next to each other on the Passeig

Neptuno. It quickly becomes the **Platja de Cabanyal**, before turning into the **Platja de Malvarrosa**, and finally the **Platja de Alboraia**. The water is a tad murky, owing to the proximity of the port (the beaches south of the city are cleaner), but it is still fine for swimming. There are rows of stripy beach huts, loungers for rent, snack bars and showers, and the whole length of the beach is backed by a modern promenade lined with palms and an outdoor market in summer. The further north you trek, the fewer people you'll find, but this is still a city beach and you won't find a quiet corner in the height of summer.

The beaches south of the port are quieter, cleaner and wilder than the main city beach of Malvarrosa. They are also harder to get to, unless you have your own transport, and have fewer amenities, so bring a packed lunch and lots of bottled water. The beach of **El Saler** becomes the beach

of **La Devesa**, with a small nudist section at its most southerly end. These beaches are backed by beautiful sand dunes and a dense, gnarled pine forest. There are walks through the forest and opportunities to see the birds which make their home around Llac Albufera.

L'Oceanogràfic

Platja Las Arenas

😑 Sleeping

€€€ **Palau de la Mar**, C Navarro Reverter 14-16, T963-162884, www.hospes.es. A handsomely converted 19th-century mansion and one of the city's most stylish hotels. Chic cream and black decor, a pool, gym, sauna and excellent restaurant. It's near the City of Arts and Sciences.

€€ **Ad Hoc**, C Boix 4, T963-919140, www.adhochoteles.com. A chic little hotel in a converted 19th-century mansion. Service can be frosty. The restaurant (expensive) has become a very fashionable haunt.

€€€ **Cónsul del Mar**, Av del Puerto 39, T963-625432, www.hotelconsuldel mar.com. The whitewashed Modernista former consulate's residence has beautifully decorated rooms some with the original plasterwork and fittings. It overlooks a busy street, but is not too far from the beaches or the City of Arts and Sciences.

€€ **Parador El Saler**, Platja del Saler, T961-611186, www.parador.es. Yellow metrobus services 190a, 190b, 191, 290 to El Perelló. Ask to be dropped off at the parador. A modern hotel overlooking sand dunes and surrounded by pine forest. There's an 18-hole golf course, swimming pool and good restaurant and the beaches are empty (well, sometimes) and golden. It often has special deals, so check the website before you go.

€ **Antigua Morellana**, C/En Bou 2, T963-915773, www.hostalam.com. Excellent *hostal* in an 18th-century mansion just a step from the Llotja and the Mercat Central, with charming owners and clean, well-equipped rooms, all with bathrooms.

😑 Eating

Restaurants

¶¶¶ **Ca Sento**, C Méndez Núñez 17, T963-301775. Tue-Sat 1330-1530, 2100-2330, Sun and Mon 2100-2330. Closed Aug. One of the most talked-about restaurants in the city. Tuck into classic, regional recipes given a creative new twist

¶¶¶ **Joaquín Schmidt**, C Visitació 7, T963-401710. Tue-Sat 1330-1530, 2100-2330, Sun and Mon 2100-2330. Quirky and highly original, both in its decor and cuisine. Offers distinctive variations on Mediterranean and international food.

¶¶ **Casa Mario**, C Roters 3, T963-924452. Mon-Sat 1200-1600, 2000-0100. An elegant, relaxed restaurant and tapas bar tucked behind the cathedral, specializing in fresh and tasty seafood. The *revueltos* (scrambled egg dishes) are also good.

¶¶ **Casa Roberto**, C Maestro Gozalbo, T963-951361. Tue-Sat 1300-1600 and 2100-2300, Sun 2100-2330. Closed Aug. Pictures of famous bullfighters set the scene in this traditional stalwart on the Valenciano restaurant scene. All kinds of rice dishes (*arroces*) are on offer; a great place to try an authentic paella.

¶ **Corretgeria 33**, C Corretgeria 33, T963-924161. Tue-Fri and Sun 1330-1700 and 2100-2400; Sat 2100-2400. A stylish and cosy choice in the Barri del Carme serving innovative Mediterranean specialities.

Tapas bars and cafés

Bar Pilar, C Moro Zeit 13, T963-910497. Daily 1200-2400. A timeless, old bar just off the Plaça del Tossal, where the thing to do is order up a portion of mussels and toss the shells in the orange buckets ranked underneath the bar. Give your name to the waiter if you want to get a seat.

Bodega Casa Montaña, Closep Benlliure 69, T963-672314. Tue-Sun 1000-1530, 1900-2300. Traditional, buzzy tavern still going strong thanks to its excellent wines and tapas.

Café Lisboa, Pl Dr Collado 9, T963-919484. Daily 0900-0230. A favourite, this arty café looks out over a pretty square with an ancient olive tree and serves great sandwiches and salads as well as cocktails in the evenings.

Café Sant Jaume, C Cavallers 51, T963-912401. Daily 1200-0200. Beautiful little café set in a former pharmacy, with swirling Modernista woodwork. In the centre of the city's main nightlife street so it's perfect for people watching.

La Edad de Oro, C Don Generoso Hernández 1, T963-924724. Mon 1900-0100, Tue-Sat 0900-0100. Laid-back café in the Barri del Carme, with changing art exhibitions and special events, serving snacks.

😑 Nightlife

Valencia's nightlife is concentrated in different areas, but the best place to start is the hip **Barri del Carme** in the Old City, where stylish restaurants, clubs, and bars are nudged up against each other. The heart of the gay scene is here on C Quart. There are also bars and clubs near the **university** in the new part of town: check out the streets around the Pl Honduras, near Avinguda Blasco Ibáñez and look out for the following favourites: **Radio City** (Old City), **La Indiana**, **Jam Disclub**, **Akuarela**, **Jimmy Glass**, **Roxy Club** (New City). In summer, everyone heads to big outdoor clubs (*terrazas*) in the suburbs. The beachside scene should also pick up, following regeneration.

Venice

Peerlessly photogenic, Venice can seem like a beautiful relic – a vulnerable novelty without much of a contemporary purpose. A one-time global sea power, Venice may or may not actually be sinking but its precarious hold on dry land is increasingly at risk from rising sea levels – high tides in winter regularly flood its piazzas and streets. At the very least, however, it is an extraordinary and gorgeously unlikely city, built on shifting sands, filled with great art, churches and palaces, and with a wonderfully peaceful absence of road traffic. And if you can get away from the massed tourists in piazza San Marco to one of the city's less popular corners, you'll find that, despite the *acque alte*, there is life in Venice, and no small amount of pride.

Arts & culture
★★★★★

Eating
★★★

Nightlife
★

Outdoors
★★★

Romance
★★★★★

Shopping
★★★

Sightseeing
★★★★★

Value for money
★★

Overall score
★★★★

At a glance

Most visitors to Venice arrive in the city's far west, from where, once you leave the train or car, all transport is by water or on foot. From here, the **Canal Grande** snakes in a reverse 'S' through the city, crossed only by the **Ponte degli Scalzi** (by the station), the arcaded **Ponte Rialto** and the **Ponte Accademia**. The new **Ponte di Calatrava**, designed by Santiago Calatrava, is scheduled to open in 2007 between the station and the road terminus at piazza Roma. To the north of the canal are the generally quieter districts of **Cannaregio** in the west and **Castello** to the east. In the second bend of the canal is the busy central area of **San Marco** and many of the city's main sights. On the southern side, **Santa Croce** and **San Polo** are nestled into the first bend of the Grand Canal, with another, more residential area, the **Dorsoduro**, on Venice's southern edge. Orientation in the narrow winding streets is famously hard, though you can get an excellent overview of the city from the

Venice is like eating an entire box of chocolate liqueurs in one go.

Truman Capote

top of the Campanile in **piazza San Marco**. Many visitors start here to follow a series of signposts that mark out a circuitous route to and from the station, via the Rialto. Around the Venetian lagoon a ferry ride away are the islands of **Giudecca**, **Murano**, with its glass-blowing industry, colourful **Burano** and the packed but fashionable beaches of **Lido**.

★ *Don't leave town without getting hopelessly lost along the winding backstreets and canals.*

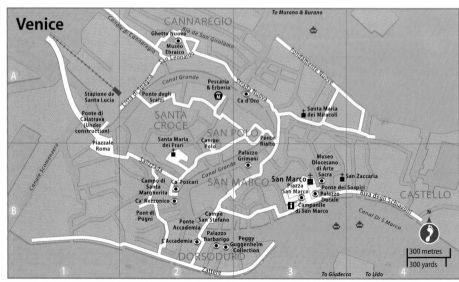

24 hours in the city

Venice is at its best early in the morning, so get up with the sun, when only locals and workers will be around. Have a *caffé* and *cornetti* in a café (the touristy ones won't open until the trains start arriving a bit later) and check out the fruit and vegetable markets and, especially, the *pescaria* (fish market) in the **Rialto**. Starting early will also enable you to get to **San Marco** before the tour groups and hordes of pigeon feeders. Have a look in the basilica and, perhaps, the **Palazzo Ducale** and then climb to the top of the **Campanile** before the crowds get too big. For lunch, pick one of the cafés and restaurants on or around the busy **campo Santa Margherita** in the Dorsoduro, such as Il Caffe. From here you are well placed for a wander along the waterside **Zattere** and to take in some art at either the **L'Accademia** or the **Peggy Guggenheim Collection**. Next, head slowly across the city to reach atmospheric **Cannaregio** by supper time, perhaps

Vaporetto **on the Grand Canal**

looking in on a church, such as **Santa Maria dei Frari** in San Polo, and having an ice cream or an *aperitivo* along the way. A boat ride is probably best left until the evening; avoid the twee temptation of a gondola and opt instead for a *vaporetto* up the **Grand Canal**.

European City Breaks Venice

⊖ Travel essentials

Getting there Venice Marco Polo, T041-260 9240, www.veniceairport.it, is the city's main airport, 19 km by road and 8 km by sea from the city, to the north of the lagoon. It is connected by boat to San Marco and the Zattere every hour (www.ali laguna.it, 1 hr, €12). Water taxis are much more expensive (up to €100) but will take you right to your hotel. Or travel by bus to piazzale Roma, every 30 mins (40 mins, €1).

About 32 km from the city, **Venice Treviso**, T042-231 5131, is a small airport used by Ryanair. Buses run to and from piazzale Roma to coincide with flights (45 mins; €5 single, €9 return). Alternatively, bus 6 (10-15 mins; €1) runs from to Treviso train station every 30 mins for frequent train connections to Venice.

Special day and night rail services connect **Venice Santa Lucia** train station with Paris, Nice, Vienna and Salzburg (www.trenitalia.it). The **Venice Simplon-Orient Express** (www.orient-express.com) luxury train service runs from London or Paris.

Getting around Despite the canals, the best way to get around is on foot. *Vaporetti* are fairly large passenger boats which ply several routes around and through the city, primarily up and down the Canal Grande and the Canale di Cannaregio and to other islands. *Traghetti* are gondolas without the silly hats, which cross the Canal Grande at places where there are no bridges. *Vaporetti* tickets cost €3.50 single, €12 for 24 hrs or €25 for 72 hrs and are available from booths at the stops. *Traghetti* cost €0.50 per

crossing – pay the boatman and stay standing, if you can. Gondolas cost €80 for 40 mins, maximum 6 people per gondola. The price rises to €100 after 1900.

Tourist information Azienda di Promozione Turistica, www.turismo venezia.it, has 2 central offices: in piazza San Marco, S Marco 71/f, T041-529 8711, daily 0900-1530, and in the Ex Giardini Reali, T041-529 8711, daily 1000-1800.

Venice Discovery Tours, http://venice.city-discovery.com, combine a walking tour in the morning with a boat tour (limited to 8 people) in the afternoon, €60 per person. You can also hire a private boat and a driver to take you around the canals or out into the lagoon, although this is significantly more expensive.

Sights

San Marco

ⓘ www.basilicasanmarco.it, ◥B3.
Apr-Sep 0945-1700; Oct-Mar 0945-1645.
Museum €3, Treasury €2,
Pala d'Oro €1.50.

Originally built in the ninth century to house the body of St Mark (stolen from Alexandria), the ornate and spectacular basilica of San Marco is the city's cathedral and its piazza is a magnetic gathering point for Venice's pigeons and tourists. John Ruskin called San Marco a 'treasure-heap' and it is indeed a bewildering collection of styles and ornamentation, from the Gothic spires of its façade and 19th-century mosaics, to a group of porphyry figures (the Tetrarchs), probably from fourth-century Egypt.

The centrepiece of the city, it has a large dome surrounded by four marginally smaller ones. Despite having been rebuilt and redecorated over the years, its form has changed little, though much of it dates from the 11th century.

The **Pala d'Oro** – the extravagantly rich golden altarpiece – is the highlight of the interior. The **Loggia**, complete with

Basilica of San Marco

Palazzo Ducale

life-size horses (the original bronzes, probably second-century Roman, are now in the Museo), is well worth the climb for the view over the piazza below.

Palazzo Ducale

ⓘ T041-271 5911, ◥B3. Apr-Oct 0900-1900, Nov-Mar 0900-1700. Musei di Piazza San Marco ticket (€12) also allows entrance to other museums around the city: Museo Correr, Museo Archeologico and the Sale Monumentali della Biblioteca Marciana.

Adjacent to the basilica, the Doge's Palace – largely a result of 14th- and 15th-century construction – combines Verona pink marble with ornate Gothic porticos to great effect. Doges were crowned at the top of the so-called Giants' Staircase. Inside, Domenico and Jacopo Tintoretto's Paradiso covers the end wall of the Great Council Hall.

The **Ponte dei Sospiri** (Bridge of Sighs) is an enclosed passageway through which prisoners once walked between their cells and the interrogation rooms in the palace. The best view of it is from Ponte della Paglia, at the palace's southeastern corner.

Campanile di San Marco

ⓘ T041-522 4064,
www.basilicasan marco.it, ◥B3.
Apr-Jun 0930-1700, Jul-Sep 0945-2000,
Oct-Mar 0945-1600. €6.

Until the smaller but more ornate **Torre dell'Orologio** ⓘ T041-522 4951, reopens, the 99 m-high Campanile is easily Venice's top tower. Originally ninth- century, the present incarnation of San Marco's bell tower dates from 1514. Views from its summit are fantastic – big vistas are rare in the city and here is nearly the whole island laid out in one broad sweep. The Campanile collapsed in 1902 and was subsequently rebuilt.

L'Accademia

ⓘ Dorsoduro 1050, T041-522 2247, ◥B2.
Mon 0815-1400, Tue-Sun 0815-1915.
€6.50.

Across the wooden Ponte dell' Accademia, Venice's art school occupies an ex-convent on the south side of Canal Grande and houses one of Italy's great art collections, including works by Titian, Canaletto, Giovanni Bellini, Tintoretto, Andrea Mantegna and Paolo Veronese.

Campanile di San Marco

That sinking feeling?

That Venice is sinking is a fact that has been repeated so often as to be accepted by almost all visitors to the city. However, most recent studies have suggested that the subsidence of the city from 1920 to 1970 has all but stopped. Venice is probably sinking by only 0.5 mm a year – roughly in line with the rest of the Adriatic coast.

That may not be much consolation to local residents as they wade through their city or move their valuables upstairs. The *acque alte* (high waters) are an increasingly frequent problem in winter – high tides combined with wind from the wrong direction brings the sea sweeping across Venice's *campos* and streets and into its buildings. Sirens and a network of raised walkways mean that life goes on but it's far from a happy situation in which to live.

In part the flooding can be blamed on rising sea levels. The loss of 10 cm of height during the 20th century also contributed. (Most now accept that this was due to the industrial extraction of water from rocks below the surface – a practice that was outlawed in the 1960s.) There is much less agreement about the solution, however. In 2003 the Italian government under Silvio Berlusconi gave their approval to MOSE (nominally the Modulo Sperimentale Elettromeccanico, but with a biblical nod to the holding back of the Red Sea), a grand plan to block the high water with a series of pontoons at the entrances to the lagoon. Costing around €3 billion and due to be completed around 2011, environmentalists think the pontoons would destroy the important ecosystem of the Venetian lagoon. Others point out that a project originally designed in the 1980s may be ineffective to cope with sea levels that are now predicted to rise with global warming. The Romano Prodi government is reviewing the project.

European City Breaks Venice

Canal Grande

Venice's most famous canal is its biggest: a watery highway cutting the city in two. Currently crossed only by three bridges, a trip on the canal is a must. Apart from

Canal Grande

being the quickest way to travel, it's also the best way to see some of Venice's greatest buildings: baroque **Ca' Rezzonico**, decorative **Ca d'Oro**, Michele Sanmicheli's frescoed **Palazzo Grimani**, Gothic **Ca' Foscari**, and **Palazzo Barbarigo** with its Murano glass mosaics. Also on the canal is the **Peggy Guggenheim Collection** ⓘ *Palazzo Venier dei Leoni, 701 Dorsoduro, www.guggenheim-venice.it,* **JB2**, *Mon and Wed-Sun, 1000-1800, €10.* Once the collector's home, there's now Picasso, Kandinsky, Pollock and a notoriously erect horse rider on view.

Pescaria

For a glimpse of Venice as it might be without tourists, head to the fish market near the Ponte Rialto early in

the morning. Next door in the **Erberia** market the abundant fruit and vegetables of the Veneto are sold with equal panache. Venice's market moved here to the Rialto area in 1097.

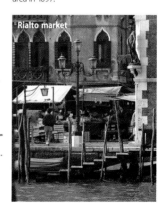

Rialto market

Ponte Rialto

The city's oldest bridge, originally made of wood, collapsed in 1444 and again in 1524. Antonio da Ponte's stone design was completed in 1591 and has stood ever since, becoming one of Venice's icons. The jewellery shops which line the arcades of the bridge are expensive and best avoided.

Museo Diocesano di Arte Sacra

ⓘ *Castello 4312, T041-522 9166,* ⬛B3. *Daily 1000-1800. Free (donations accepted).*

The beautiful Romanesque Chiostro di Sant' Apollonia, inside the Museum of Sacred Art, is one of Venice's less well-known architectural beauties and dates from the early 14th century. The museum itself is less impressive, but it does contain some remnants of an earlier version of the Basilica of San Marco which are nearly 1000 years old.

Cannaregio

With fewer sights than most other Venetian *sestieri*, Cannaregio is perhaps

Ponte Rialto

Dorsoduro

the least touristy of the city's quarters, except along its southern edge. Long parallel canals retain some of their working class feel and it can be one of the most rewarding parts of the city in which to wander. It also has some of the best restaurants. The **Canale di Cannaregio** was once the main way into the city and has some suitably grand buildings. East of here, three parallel canals have less ostentatious charms. Just south off the Rio di San Girolamo, the **Ghetto Nuovo** was the original Jewish ghetto and the origin of the name. The **Museo Ebraico** ⓘ *www.museoebraico.it,* ⬛A2, *Jun-Sep Sun-Fri 1000-1900, Oct-May Sun-Fri 1000-1730 €3,* tells the story of Venetian Jews. In the far east of the district, **Santa Maria dei Miracoli** is an exquisite early Renaissance church built in the 1480s.

Le Zattere and the Dorsoduro

The Zattere, the 2 km of quayside at Venice's southern extremity, is one of the city's best spots for the evening *passegiata*, with great views across to Giudecca island. North of here, the

ⓔ Best of the rest

Lido ⓘ *vaporetti from San Zaccaria.* Venice's famously fashionable beach sits on the far side of an island dedicated almost entirely to it. Just about every grain of sand is occupied in summer and you have to pay (or be staying at smart hotels) for access to many parts.
Frari ⓘ *campo dei Frari, T041-275 0462,* ⬛B2, *€2.50.* An enormous church filled with art by Titian, Giovani Bellini and others, Santa Maria Gloriosa dei Frari is almost always referred to by its shorter name.
Ca' Rezzonico ⓘ *Fondamenta Rezzonico 3136, T041-241 0100,* ⬛B2, *€6.50.* Perhaps the best chance to experience the interior of one of Venice's baroque palaces. Giorgio Massari's enormously grand ballroom and paintings by Canaletto and Tiepolo are some of the highlights.
Murano ⓘ *vaporetti from Fondamente Nuove.* On this island, a near neighbour of Venice, there is a museum dedicated to Venetian glass and you can visit glass-blowing factories. There are also some interesting churches.

Dorsoduro is Venice's youngest, hippest quarter, centring on buzzing **Campo di Santa Margherita**, which has some great bars and is especially lively in the evenings. The **Ponte di Pugni** (Bridge of the Boxers) still has engraved footprints where those taking part in east (*castellani*) versus west (*nicolotti*) punch-ups were supposed to stand.

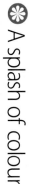

A splash of colour

Exactly why the houses in **Burano** are painted such bright colours may be lost in myth – the story most often told is that it was so that fishermen could recognize their houses from the sea. What is clear is that the island's colour scheme is now its biggest selling point and permission to paint one's house is closely controlled. But there are attractions other than the colourful houses: the ferry journey across the northern lagoon gives a good perspective to Venice's seafaring roots and its lagoon position. The island's lace industry, which began in the 16th century, means there is a school, a museum and lace shops, though genuine hand-woven Burano lace is hard to find. The Church of San Martino has a tall campanile and a Tiepolo painting of the crucifixion. The whole place has a slow, quiet charm. Neighbouring Mazzorbo is connected by a wooden bridge and has orchards and a 14th-century church with its original 1318 bell. ⓘ *Vaporetto No 12 from Fondamente Nuove, 40-50 mins, sometimes via Torcello,* **》A3** *.*

Sleeping

Venice's accommodation is, by reputation, expensive and over-booked. It's certainly worth reserving ahead at busy times, and during the Biennale or the Film Festival rooms may be hard to find but at other times a little ringing around should suffice. Most of Venice's visitors are day trippers and the advantages of being able to wander around the relatively unfrequented city in the evenings or early mornings far outweigh the price of a room.

€€€ Bellini, Cannaregio 116/a, T041-524 2488, www.boscolo hotels.com. Right on the Grand Canal and near the station, the Bellini has plenty of sophisticated antique Venetian elegance, but it all comes at a price.
€€€ Ca' Pisani, Dorsoduro 979/a, T041-240 1411, www.capisanihotel.it. A Venetian rarity, Ca' Pisani is a chic modern hotel in a 16th-century building. Sharp lines and hip colour schemes contrast effectively with the Dorsoduro surroundings.

€€€-€€ Hotel Flora, San Marco 2283/a, T041-520 5844, www.hotel flora.it. Venetian opulence abounds – lots of antiques and a vine-covered courtyard in a building where Titian may have painted.
€€€-€€ Locanda ai Santi Apostoli, Cannaregio 4391/a, campo Santi Apostoli, T041-521 2612, www.locandasantiapostoli.com. Some of the city's most reasonably priced views over the Grand Canal, from wooden-beamed rooms.
€€ Ca' delle Acque, San Marco 4991, T041-241 1277, www.locanda delleacque.it. About as central as you can get, halfway between piazza San Marco and the Rialto, Ca' delle Acque is a pretty place with apartments sleeping up to 8 as well as rooms.
€€-€ Pensione Seguso, Zattere 779, T041-528 6858. On the corner of a canal and the Zattere waterfront in the Dorsoduro, the smart Seguso has an English colonial air, very proper service and some excellent views.
€€-€ Villa Rosa, C della Misericordia 389, T041-716569, www.villarosahotel.com. Very

convenient for the station yet far enough back from the tourist traps of Rio Terrá Lista di Spagna to be quiet, the flower-clad Villa Rosa is an attractive option on the edge of Cannaregio.

Eating

Venice's culinary reputation is not great but find a table outside in a piazza on a warm summer's evening or beside a canal watching the boats go by and the food will almost certainly taste good. It's worth bearing in mind that most places close much earlier in the evening (around 2100) than in the rest of Italy. Eating out is also expensive here. The Dorsoduro and the northwest parts of Cannaregio are the best places to get away from the trilingual menus and experience something cheaper and nearer Venetian tradition. Risotto is a Venice staple, as is seafood, but there are plenty of restaurants specializing in other Italian delights.

Harry's Bar, San Marco 1323, T041-528 5777. Closed Mon. Famous (and wealthy) enough to threaten legal action against places around the world who copy the name, Harry's is a Venetian institution on the Canal Grande. Frequented by film and opera stars, those who can afford the high prices for both food and drink, and those who come just to gawp.

All'Arco, San Polo 436, T041-520 5666. Closed evenings and Sun. One of Venice's *ombre* (dialect for a glass of wine) places which also serve *cicheti* (snacks and light dishes). Near the Rialto, you could accompany your Prosecco with crostini, ham and gorgonzola.

Aqua Pazza, campo Sant'Angelo, San Marco 3808/10, T041-277 0688. Open late, Aqua Pazza serves truly excellent southern Italian pizzas out in the campo for extortionate prices and with an authentic air of slightly surly chaos. There are also other good southern Italian options such as deep fried vegetables and a mixed fish grill which make putting up with the poor service worthwhile.

Osteria Alla Zucca, Santa Croce 1762, Ponte del Megio, T041-524 1570. Near San Giacomo dell'Orio, this friendly little trattoria is good for vegetarians. The 4 or 5 tables outside on the street fill up quickly.

Osteria Anice Stellato, Fondamenta de la Sensa, Cannaregio 3272, T041-720744. Closed Mon. A reminder of Venice's one-time status as an important port linking east and west, Anice Stellato uses more spices than are usual in Italian cooking, combining them with Venetian cuisine to good effect. Out of the way on one of Cannaregio's long, quiet canals, this colourful little place usually has more locals than visitors. If it's full, **Ai 40 Ladroni**, T041-715736, next door is also a good option.

Osteria Bea Vita, 3082 Fondamenta degli Ormesini. A rarity in that you can sit outside beside a canal and be as likely to share tables with locals as with tourists. The good value €10.50 lunch menu is pasta- and risotto-based.

Osteria Vecio Forner, Dorsoduro 671/B, campo San Vio, T041-528 0424. Closed Sun. A fashionably smart little bar on the corner of a campo near the Guggenheim museum with good food options, especially for a light lunch. Dishes of the day €8-15.

66 99 ...find a table outside in a piazza on a warm summer's evening or beside a canal ... and the food will almost certainly taste good.

Osteria da Toni, Fondamenta di San Basilio 1642, T041-528 6899. Closed Mon. A long hike from San Marco, da Toni is a traditional no-nonsense trattoria of a kind rarely found in Venice. Popular with students and locals it's an excellent place for Venetian seafood and simple pasta and wine lunches. Not far from the western end of the Zattere, there are a few tables outside beside the canal.

Taverna da Baffo, San Polo 2346, Campo Sant'Agostin, T041-520 8862. Closed Sun. A popular café which opens early and stays open until 0200 with good coffee early, live music late and decent food in between. Free buffet on Tue evenings.

☷ Nightlife

Bars
Venice's nightlife is infamously somnolent – wander around the city at an hour when most Mediterranean cities would be sparking into life and you will probably find dark empty streets. The **Dorsoduro** is the area which bucks this trend somewhat; campo Santa Margherita is the best for a *giro de ombre*. When performed by Venetians these bar crawls of local nightspots usually involve the over-consumption of glasses of *spritz*, a misleadingly cheap and quaffable combination of wine, soda water and a bitter, usually Campari, Aperol or Cynar.

Live music
Nightclubs are practically non-existent though some bars have live music (**Il Caffe**, campo Santa Margherita) and the jazz scene is perhaps the least moribund of the Venetian performing arts. **Paradiso Perduto**, Fondamenta della Misericordia in Cannaregio, has jazz and blues. **La Fenice**, www.teatro lafenice.it, is one of the country's top opera venues.

❀ Festivals

Venice comes into its own during festivals. There's the profusion of contemporary art in the **Biennale** (www.labiennale.org), the cinematic buffs of the **Film Festival** (late Aug, early Sep) or the masks and thicker-than-ever throngs of tourists during **Carnevale** (Feb). Look out too for lesser known festivals such as **Venezia Suona** (www.veneziasuona.it), a music festival in Jul, and **Festa di Liberazione**, the Communist Party's annual knees-up in late summer.

Red-roofed and pastel-shaded, on the edge of the mountains and the cusp of the plain, Verona likes to think of itself as both the beginning and the distillation of the real Italy. At the crossroads of the north-south route from the Brenner Pass to Rome, and the east-west Milan-Venice road, the city has long been of strategic importance. Apart from Rome itself, Verona is Italy's best-preserved Roman city (with a Roman amphitheatre, a bridge, gates and theatre) and also has richly decorated Romanesque, Gothic and Renaissance aspects, with spectacular frescoed churches and houses. All this antiquity is given an opulent sheen by a well-dressed 21st-century population who have, in the main, done very well out of wine, opera, European integration and a select brand of tourism.

Verona

Arts & culture
★★★

Eating
★★★★

Nightlife
★★

Outdoors
★★

Romance
★★★

Shopping
★★

Sightseeing
★★★

Value for money
★★★

Overall score
★★★

◉ Sights

Centro storico

Bordered on three sides by the River Adige, the streets of Verona's ancient centre follow the Roman layout. The city's main shopping streets, including the shiny **via Mazzini**, and most of the well-known sights are here, between **Ponte Pietra**, the bridge which predates the city, in the north, along narrow winding streets to the original Roman gates of **Porta Leoni** in the south and **Porta Borsari** in the west. The site of the old Roman forum is now the expansive **piazza Erbe**, the heart of the city and filled with Renaissance and Gothic buildings dating from the 14th to the 18th centuries. On the eastern side of the piazza, **Casa Mazzanti** has a cycle of allegorical frescoes by Cavalli from around 1530, which face onto the square.

Piazza Erbe

The portico, filled with cafés selling ice-cream concoctions, was built in 1480. In the cellars, 3.5 m below the present-day surface, the original paving of the Roman forum has been found. **Fontana Madonna Verona** in the piazza's centre and one of the beloved symbols of the city, is a mishmash of

local Roman remains: the basin was taken from the thermal baths of Sant'Anastasia, the statue from the Capitol. Originally erected in the fourth century in honour of the emperor's lifting of the city's debts, the fountain was added by Cansignorio della Scala in 1368.

   Piazza dei Signori, leading off piazza Erbe, is more refined; a celebration not of commerce and the market, but of power and of poets, and in particular of the Scaligeri family, rulers of the city in the 13th and 14th centuries. While the foundations are also Roman, much of what sits on top is Gothic, Romanesque and Renaissance, and narrow streets of ancient palazzi, many still frescoed, stretch up to the Adige. The piazza's most attractive building, and the best place to sit and watch the daily comings and goings, is the Renaissance **Loggia del Consiglio** (built between 1476 and 1492 by Fra' Giocondo).

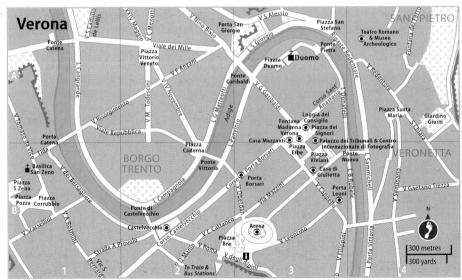

The **Duomo** ⓘ *piazza Duomo, T045-592813,* **⟍A3**, *Mon-Sat 0930-1800, Sun 1300-1800, €2.50, €5 for combined ticket for 5 main churches,* is just one of many spectacular churches in Verona. It has a beautiful façade, a stunning Titian (*Assumption* in the Cappella Cartolari-Nichesola, the first on the left), a Sanmicheli-designed bell tower, griffins, and plenty of historical interest. The stamp of the medieval rulers, the della Scala family, is visible most ostentatiously in their elaborate **Gothic tombs.**

The collection of ancient excavated remains under **piazza Viviani** and the cortile del Tribunale in the very centre of old Verona is the spectacular, if slightly damp, setting for excellent large-scale photography exhibitions at the **Centro Internazionale di Fotografia** ⓘ *T045-800 7490,, ⟍B3, Tue-Sun 1000-1900 during exhibitions. €4.10.* Recent exhibitions have included Giuliana Traverso and Willy Ronis.

Also within the walls of the old city is **Casa di Giulietta (Juliet's House)** ⓘ *23 via Cappello, T045-803 4303,* **⟍B3**, *Mon 1330-1930, Tue-Sun 0830-1930, entrance to the house €4, courtyard free,* an extraordinary indictment of modern

Duomo

tourism but also strangely magnetic. A heaving mass of day trippers throng in and out of the courtyard to take photos of the famous fictional balcony (added to the building in the 1930s).

Juliet's balcony

Arena

ⓘ *piazza Bra, T045-800 3204, www.arena.it,* **⟍B3**. *Mon 1345-1930, Tue-Sun 0830-1930, 0900-1530 during opera season. €4, €1 first Sun of month.*

At the other end of via Mazzini from the enormous spread of piazza Erbe, **piazza Bra** forms an alternative centrepiece to the city, with the giant elliptical Roman Arena dominating it. Verona's most famous sight is the third largest Roman amphitheatre still in existence after the Colosseum and the little-visited amphitheatre in Capua. Still dominating much of the city, it is used as a 20,000-seater stadium and a theatre for the summer opera season. To the west, **Castelvecchio** ⓘ *corso Castelvecchio 2, T045-592985, www.comune.verona.it/ castelvecchio/cvsito,* **⟍B2**, *Mon 1345-1930, Tue-Sun 0830- 1930, ticket office closes 1845, €4, free first Sun of the month,* has all the attributes you'd wish for in a

castle, plus a great bridge, and is now the Civic Museum of Art. Further west, the ornate 12th-century **Basilica San Zeno** ⓘ *piazza San Zeno, T045-800 6120,* **⟍B1**, *Apr-Oct Mon-Sat 0830-1800, Sun 1300-1800, Nov-Mar Tue-Sat 1000-1300 and 1330-1600, Sun 1300-1700, €2.50,* is justifiably the city's favourite church.

North and east of the Adige

The steep hill of San Pietro was the original site of settlement in the city. At its base, looking out across the river, sits the **Teatro Romano and the Museo Archeologico** ⓘ *Rigaste Redentore 2, T045-800 0360,* **⟍A4**, *Mon 1345-1930, Tue-Sun 0830-1930, ticket office closes 1845, €2.60, free first Sun of the month, information on summer events T045-807 7201.* From its top are fantastic panoramic views over the city. To either side of the hill are residential areas of the old city. There are atmospheric little districts of winding streets, especially in Veronetta to the south, with many of the city's best bars and restaurants. Beyond rise hills of olive trees and vineyards, with the first signs of the Alps to the north.

Arena

⊖ Travel essentials

Getting there Verona Villafranca Airport (Valerio Catullo), T045-809 5666, www.aeroportoverona.it, is served by APTV bus every 20 mins to and from the train station, 0635-2335. (Journey time is around 15 mins, €4.50 each way). Taxis cost around €20 to the centre. Tiny Brescia Montichiari Airport (Gabriele D'Annunzio) T030-965 6511, www.aeroportobrescia.it, used by Ryanair, is about an hour away from Verona by bus. Ryanair runs a service between the airport and Verona train station to coincide with their flights and costs €11 single, €16 return. Tickets are available from an office inside the arrivals/departures hall (or, on the return journey from Verona, on the bus).

International trains, including services from Paris and Munich, arrive at Porto Nuovo station, www.trenitalia.com.

Getting around The size of Verona's compact centre means that walking is by far the best way to get around and see the sights. Orange **AMT**, T045-887 1111, buses serve the city. All services centre on the sprawling bus station, opposite the train station, south of piazza Bra. Tickets must be bought (either from tobacconists, marked with a large 'T' outside or from AMT machines at the station) before boarding and stamped on board, after which they are valid on any bus for 1 hr. An ordinary ticket costs €1. A 10-journey ticket (*una tessera*) is also available for €9, and a day ticket (*giornaliero*) for €3.50. The most useful city services are likely to

be 11, 12, 13, and 14 between the station (from beside the AMT booth) and piazza Bra, continuing over the river to via XX Settembre. At weekends and on holidays these are replaced by services 91, 92 and 98.

Tourist information The main office is at via degli Alpini 9 (just behind the Arena), T045-806 8680, Mon-Sat 0900-1900, Sun 0900-1500, iatbra@tiscalinet.it. As long as you know what you want, they'll probably be more than willing to help. There's an 'office' at the railway station, Porta Nuova FS, T045-800 0861, iatfs@tiscalinet.it, Mon-Sat 0900-1800, Sun 0900-1500, which is no more than a man at a desk, but can nevertheless be useful for those arriving at the station.

⊙ Sleeping

€€€ Gabbia D'Oro, corso Porta Borsari 4a, T045-800 3060, www.hotel gabbiadoro.it. A stone's throw from piazza Erbe, luxurious Gabbia D'Oro has plush rooms as well as medieval features such as areas of bare wall and wooden beams.

€€ Aurora, piazza Erbe, T045-594717, www.hotelaurora.biz. Overlooking piazza Erbe, the friendly Hotel Aurora has a great sunny terrace and unfussy air-conditioned rooms.

€€ Torcolo, vicolo Listone 3, T045- 800 7512, www.hoteltorcolo.it. On a quiet road behind piazza Bra, Torcolo has charm and style. Attic rooms on the 3rd floor, with sloping ceilings, are particularly attractive.

€ Armando, via Dietro Pallone 1, T045-800 0206. In an attractive, quiet area between piazza Bra and Ponte Aleardi, Hotel Armando is plain but comfortable, and much better value than all the hotels further south.

⊘ Eating

The line between bars and restaurants is a fine one in Verona. Osterie serve food of varying complexity and trattorie often have good, and enormously long, wine lists. There is little tradition of drinking without eating but, having said that, Verona's student population adds a lively edge and some of the city's drinking spots stay open well into the early hours. (Via Sottoriva, around San Zeno and Veronetta are the best areas.) Wine predominates, though most places also have beer on tap.

♉ Al Bersagliere, via Dietro Pallone 1, T045-800 4824. Mon-Sat 1200-1430, 1930-2200, also open as a bar from 0800. Traditional Veronese and Lessinian food, plenty of polenta-based dishes as well as smoked goose breast, trout with Soave wine and lots of wine and home-made desserts.

♉ Hostaria la Vecchia Fontanina, piazzetta Chiavica 5, T045-591159. Mon-Sat 1200-1430, 1930-2230. An attractive little restaurant serving a mixed crowd of mainly Italians. A varied and interesting menu includes pasta with nettles and even the bread and house wine are a cut above the rest.

♉ Carro Armato, vicolo Gatto 2a, T045-803 0175. Mon, Tue, Thu-Sat 1100-0200, Sun 1100-0000. Generally considered a nightspot, Carro Armato buzzes in the evenings, has an excellent wine list and extremely good local dishes.

♉ Osteria Trattoria Al Duomo, via Duomo 7a, T045-800 4505. Mon-Sat 1100-1500, 1800-0000, kitchen 1200-1430, 1930-2230. One of the city's best trattorie. The service and the 1980s pop blasting out of the stereo might put you off but the excellent food makes up for this.

Caffè Tubino, 15d corso Porta Borsari, T045-803 2296. Daily 0700-2300. Excellent coffee and *cornetti* in a distinctive little café.

For centuries the most powerful city in continental Europe, Vienna oozes with the memories, traditions, riches and ambitions of Europe's most calculatingly expansionist dynasty: the Habsburgs. Imposing yet florid palatial architecture defines the city, whether lining grand boulevards or set among landscaped parks. The opera house, myriad concert halls and art collections bear testimony to a taste for high culture in a city that harboured Beethoven, Mozart, Brahms, Klimt and Schiele. Traditionally straight-laced and uptight, this one-time outpost of the Cold War now finds itself again at the heart of an expanded Europe that it once would have ruled. Blowing off its cobwebs and newly alive with the influences of its position at a cultural crossroads, it is impossible not to have a good night in Vienna.

Vienna

Arts & culture
★★★★

Eating
★★★★

Nightlife
★★★

Outdoors
★★

Romance
★★★★

Shopping
★★★

Sightseeing
★★★

Value for money
★★

Overall score
★★★

At a glance

The cultural core of Vienna lies within the city's old town (Altstadt), defined by the **Ringstrasse**, formerly the medieval walls. A tram ride will cast you back to fin de siècle Habsburg times and past the famous **Opera** that echoes with Mozart, Brahms and Beethoven. The **Museums Quarter** (MQ) lies in the southwest of the Ring and consists of the Imperial Palace (now the Kunsthistoriches Museum – one of the most important fine arts museums in the world), the former Imperial Stables with their unique balletic Lippizaner white stallions, and also the MUMOK and Leopold museums of contemporary and modern art. Between your Brueghels and Klimts, you'll be able to enjoy a host of atmospheric, relaxed and even hip bars, restaurants and shops in the ultimate meeting of high art and high life. For film aficionados (and kids) the **Prater funfair** and Ferris wheel of *Third Man* fame lie to the northeast across the Danube. If you'd rather just recline and be Austrian for the weekend,

> The best coffee in Europe is Vienna coffee, compared to which all other coffee is fluid poverty.
>
> *Mark Twain*

the elegant, tightly packed streets of the Altstadt are the home of Vienna's unsurpassable cafés. By day you can follow in the footsteps of Trotsky and Freud with some cake and a whipped-cream coffee, and by night enjoy the studied melange of new-imperial and ultra-modern. Vienna is a long way from the waltzes of Johann Strauss and that famous 1980s pop video by Ultravox.

★ *Don't leave town without a slice of your own delicious* Sachertorte.

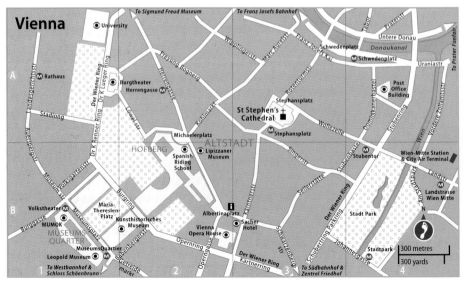

◉ Sights

Der Wiener Ring

In 1857 the Habsburgs razed the city's medieval wall to create a monument to their vanity. This took the form of a grand boulevard circling the centre, lined with extravagant and imposing royal buildings, private residences, vast squares and parks, puffed up monuments and elegant cafés. One hundred and 50 years on it acts as a walk-by window on the Habsburg dynasty and is best viewed by hopping on either the number 1 or number 2 tram. In doing so you will be able to take in, at least from the outside, Otto Wagner's Post Office building, the Vienna Opera House, the Imperial Palace, Museum of Fine Arts, the Burgtheater and the University.

St Stephen's Cathedral

St Stephen's Cathedral

ⓘ T01-515 523526, www.stephans kirche.at, **A3**. Mon-Sat 0600-2200. €1. U-bahn Stephansplatz, bus 1A, 2A, 3A.

Austria's most important Gothic building, Vienna's cathedral was begun in the 12th century although the oldest remaining parts are the Romanesque Great Gate and the Towers of the Heathens, dating from the 13th century. If you have a head for heights, climb the 343 steps to the top of the 137 m-high South Tower (*Steffl* to locals). Gothic was out of vogue by 1579 when the North Tower was capped by a cobbled-together Renaissance spire. Inside are a number of treasures, notably the red marble sepulchre of Emperor Frederick III, sculpted from 1467 to 1513 by Niclas Gerhaert van Leyden.

Imperial Palace and Museums Quarter (MQ)

ⓘ MQ, T01-523 5881 1730, www.mqw.at, **B1**. Daily 1000-1900, individual museum times vary. U-bahn MuseumsQuartier, Volkstheater. Bus 2A, 48A, tram 49.

⊖ Travel essentials

Getting there Schwechat Airport, T01-70070, www.viennaairport.com, is 19 km southeast of the city centre. The **City Airport Train** (CAT), www.cityair porttrain.com, takes you non-stop to the City Air Terminal at Wien-Mitte junction near Vienna Hilton and St Stephen's Cathedral. Journey time is around 15 mins, daily 0538-2335 (€9, €16 return). On the way back you can check in at the City Air Terminal. **Vienna Airport Lines** buses link the city to the airport from Schwedenplatz, Suedtiroler Platz, the City Air Terminal at Hotel Hilton and Westbahnhof (€6, €11 return). Journey time is around 20 mins, daily 0500-2400. The S-bahn is the cheapest option. Take line S7 (every 30 mins; journey time 35 mins). Get an *Aussenzonen* (outer zone) ticket for €4 (€2 if you have a Vienna Card, see

below) and have it punched before entering the train. A taxi costs around €15. Bratislava's **MR Štefánika Airport** in Slovakia is only 60 km east of Vienna and close enough to be an alternative to Schwechat. There are various options for shuttling to and from the airport as well as car rental desks.

As Central Europe's main rail hub, Vienna has good connections to most other major European destinations. **Eurostar**'s London-Vienna service via Paris takes around 14 hrs. Vienna has several train stations; check whether you're arriving at Westbahnhof, Südbahnhof or Franz Josefs Bahnhof.

Getting around Vienna is very pleasant for exploring on foot. The city's network of efficient and picturesque trams (especially Nos 1 and 2 which go clockwise and anti-clockwise around the

famous Ring), buses or the art nouveau underground system, is easy to use. A single trip costs €1.50, a 24-hr card costs €5 and a 72-hr card costs €12.

Tourist information Over 200 discounts are available in the city with the **Vienna Card** (€16.90), available at hotel and the Tourist Information Centre, 1 Albertinaplatz, T01-2111 4222, www.info .wien.at, daily 0900-1900. The card is also available at all sales offices or information booths of the Vienna transport system. It allows unlimited travel by underground, bus and tram, discounts on airport transfer services, reductions (see prices in brackets in Sights section) at museums, theatres, concerts, shops, restaurants, cafés and bars. There's another tourist office in the Arrivals hall at the airport, 0700-2200. **Wien-Hotels & Info**, T01-24555, 0900-1900, has a hotel booking service.

Until the end of the First World War, the Imperial Palace was the centre of the Austro-Hungarian empire. Since then it has been transformed into a veritable empire of the arts. The Museums Quarter ranks as one of the 10 largest cultural complexes in the world, complete with bars and restaurants in which to digest it all. The following are just some of the highlights the area encompasses.

Spanish Riding School (Spanische Hofreitschule)
ⓘ *1 Michaelerplatz, T01-533 9031, www.srs.at,* ◤B2◥ *. Daily 0900-1700. Free , 15-min guided tours Tue-Sat 1230-1700. Performances cost up to €22, see website. U-bahn Herrengasse, bus 2A.*

Even if you are not of an equine inclination it is impossible not to be moved by the beauty of the famous Yugoslavian Lippizaner white stallions on display. The art of classical riding taught by the school dates back to the Renaissance. (The stables are some of the few Renaissance buildings in Vienna.) Here you can live the history of these horses and admire gala balletic exhibitions of incredible precision.

Spanish Riding School

MUMOK

The impressive riding hall was furnished in baroque style by Joseph Emanuel Fischer von Erlach between 1729-1735 and was supposed to provide children of the aristocracy with the chance to take riding instruction. You can watch the morning training sessions and visit the stables. The nearby **Lipizzaner Museum**, www.lipizzanermuseum.at, provides further information.

Kunsthistorisches Museum
ⓘ *1 Maria-Theresien-Platz , T01-525240, www.khm.at,* ◤B2◥ *. Daily 1000-1800, Thu 1000-2100. Closed Mon. €10 (€9). U-bahn Volkstheater, Museumsquartier, bus 2A, 57A*

Vienna's Museum of Fine Arts was built in 1891 next to the Imperial Palace in order to house the extensive collections of the Habsburgs. During their reign they managed to amass the largest collection of Brueghel paintings in the world, including his *Farm Wedding*. Also among their collection are Raphael's *Madonna in the Meadow*, Vermeer's *Allegory of Painting*, Velazquez's Infanta paintings and masterpieces by Rubens, Rembrandt, Duerer, van Dyk, Holbein,

Titian and Tintoretto. As such, it must surely rank among the most important fine art museums in the world.

Leopold Museum
ⓘ *7 Museums platz, T01-52570,* ◤B1◥ *, www.leopoldmuseum.org. Wed, Fri-Mon 1000-1900, Thu 1000-2100. €9 (€8.10). U-bahn MuseumsQuartier, Volkstheater.*

The passionate art lover Dr Rudolf Leopold amassed hundreds of masterpieces and has his own museum to showcase, among other things, the world's largest collection of works by Egon Schiele. Other major artists featured here are Gustav Klimt and Oskar Kokoschka, and furniture and other pieces by Otto Wagner. Combined, they give an insight into early 19th-century Vienna.

MUMOK
ⓘ *T01-52500, www.mumok.at,* ◤B1◥ *. Tue-Sun 1000-1800, until 2100 on Thu. €8 (€6.50). U-bahn Volkstheater.*

The Museum of Modern Art traces the path of Vienna's avant garde through Pop Art, Nouveau Réalisme and Vienna Actionism. Warhol, Jasper Johns, Marcel

Schloss Schönbrunn

Location, location, location, location

In his 1949 story of drug racketeering in war-torn Vienna, film director Carol Reed masterfully turned the city into as towering and brooding a character as the film's central figure – Orson Welles' Harry Lime. With his sense of Impressionism coupled with stark chiaroscuro he produced some of the most iconic and memorable scenes in world cinema, the locations of which are easily visited to this day. Harry Lime first appears, or rather a white cat appears at his shiny feet, in the doorway of **number 8 Schreyvogelgasse** before the two set off in a nocturnal chase around the city. The famous Ferris wheel scene, which closes with Lime's immortal (but factually inaccurate) put-down about the Swiss and cuckoo clocks, takes places on the 19th-century **Riesenrad** ⓘ *Prater 90, T01-729 5430, www.wienerriesenrad.com, Oct-Apr 1000-2000, May-Sep 1000-2200, €8 (€7)*. The 65 m Ferris wheel with its wood cabins sits within the city's **Prater funfair park** where there are still many original and traditional carousel rides. The windblown cemetery where Lime is twice buried (alongside Beethoven and Brahms) is the **Zentral Friedhof** on Simmerigen Hauptstrasse. Joseph

Cotton stays at the **Sacher Hotel,** famous for its eponymous cake. If you can stomach it, parts of the sewers, where the film reaches its climax, can be visited by joining a guided **Third Man tour of the city**, www.viennawalks.tix.at.

European City Breaks Vienna

Duchamp, George Brecht and Otto Muehl are all here. MUMOK also presents art history from classic modern works up to the present, ranging from Kupka to Kandinsky.

Schloss Schönbrunn

ⓘ *Schönbrunner Schlossstrasse 13, T01-8111 3239, www.schoenbrunn.at. Apr-Jun and Sep-Oct daily 0830-1700; Jul-Aug until 1800; Nov-Mar 0830-1630. €11.50 (€10.20). U-bahn Schönbrunn, bus 10A, trams 10, 58.*

This mouthwatering baroque palace was built around 1700 and is now a UNESCO World Heritage Site. It includes 2000 rooms of wall-to-wall imperial splendour (only 40 can be visited), all set in a

symmetrical classically landscaped garden complete with maze and the world's oldest zoo. Emperor Franz Joseph

Sigmund Freud Museum

(1848-1916) was born here in 1830, later marrying the Empress Sisi and keeping her in unsustainable style, and spending the last two years of his reign here.

Sigmund Freud Museum

ⓘ *Berggasse 19, T01-319 1596, www .freud-museum.at. Daily 0900-1700. €8 (€6.50). U-bahn Schwarzspanierstrasse, or bus 40A, tram D or trams 37, 38, 40, 41, 42*

Psychology students or anyone who rails against the therapy culture should visit the apartments where it arguably all started. Freud lived and worked here from 1891 to 1938 and all his furniture, possessions, letters, documents, photographs and even an oedipal home movie by his daughter are here.

😑 Sleeping

Vienna is rich in stylish, sometimes overblown, hotels recalling its imperial past, as well as a new breed of design hotels more conscious of the city's contribution to modernism. However, there is not as much choice at the bottom end.

€€€ Hotel Imperial, Karntner Ring 16, T01-50 1100, www.luxurycollection.com/imperial. An extravagant converted palace famed for the visits of its politicians.

€€€ Hotel Sacher, Philharmonikerstrasse 4, T01-514560, www.sacher.com. Deliberately and eccentrically old fashioned, this family-run hotel likes to live in a 19th-century time warp. Romantic, at times camp, but never dull, this is the best address for a taste of Habsburg decadence.

€€€ Style Hotel, Herrengasse 12, T01-22780, www.stylehotel.at. Housed in an art nouveau building opposite the city's famous Café Central, the interiors are more art deco. The 78 well-appointed rooms offer every luxury while delicious Italian cuisine is served in the Sapor restaurant and the bar is increasingly attracting a stylish post-prandial clientele.

€€ Hotel Das Triest, Wiedner Hauptstrasse 12, T01-589180, www.das triest.at. Not for those wanting a slice of Old Vienna but bright, clean and comfortably modern; 17th-century on the outside but Conran on the inside.

€€ Hotel Riviera, Schönlaterngasse 13, T01-907 6149. A very laid-back, Mediterranean atmosphere with a lovely garden and an attractive and welcoming bar makes this a good mid-price option.

€ Alstadt Vienna Hotel, Kirchengasse 41, T01-522 6666, www.altstadt.at. Old-world pretentions at half the price. A historic patrician's house in the centre of the old city comfortably furnished with Italian furniture and a striking decor. Family-run, 25 rooms, some with lovely views and plenty of atmosphere.

66 99 A visit to at least one of Vienna's famous cafés should not be missed.

🅞 Eating and nightlife

The line between food and fun has been blurred in Vienna, as in many European cities. There are classic Viennese restaurants but as an alternative, or even after your Wienerschnitzel, the main focus is on a wide variety of hybrid bar-restaurants and restaurant-clubs. A visit to at least one of Vienna's famous cafés should not be missed.

₩₩ Steirereck im Stadtpark, Am Heumarkt 2A, Landstrasse,1030, T01-713 3168, www.steirereck.at. Mon-Fri 1130-1500 and 1900-2300. An old gourmet favourite of Vienna foodies. Choose your room for a formal or relaxed ambience. Always grand but refreshingly laid back.

₩ Café Central, Herrengasse 14. Daily 0900-2300. With its gaudy Gothic vaulted ceiling, this was a favourite of Trotsky and also allegedly where Hitler thought up *Mein Kampf*. A piece of the city's heritage as much as any museum.

₩ Café Landtmann, Karl Lueger Ring 4, T01-24100, www.landtmann.at. Daily 0730-2400. One of Vienna's many historic cafés set in an huge, high-ceilinged theatrical space with great views of the Burgtheater.

₩ Lutz/A1 lounge, 6-7, Mariahilfer Strasse, T01-585 3646/526 0026, www.lutz-bar.at, www.a1lo. 1000-0400 (Lutz), Mon-Wed 0930-2200, Thu-Fri 0930-2400 (A1). Two bar-restaurants in one. Lutz is elegant and classic, themed with wood panelling and a great cocktail and wine list. A1 is futuristic with glass, metal and dry ice, and packed with technical gimmicks.

₩ Palmenhaus, Burggarten, T01-533 1033, www.palmenhaus.at. Daily 1000-0200. A beautifully renovated palmhouse in the heart of the museum district. Summer seating outside and good quality nibbles year round. On Fri night, the sophisticated air is replaced by a groovy club scene.

₩ Santo Spirito, Kumpfgasse 7, T01-512 9998. Mon-Thu 1800-0200, Fri until 0300, Sat 1100-0300, Sun 1100- 0200. A modern take on Vienna's contribution to classical music, the volume rising through the evening, sets a great backdrop for a cultured if lively evening.

₩ Café Alt Wien, Bäckerstrasse 9, T01-512 5222. Daily 1000-0200. A studenty vibe ensures that the intellectual traditions of this café continue over illuminating drinks and a renowned goulash.

₩ Point of Sale, Corner Schleifmühl-gasse 12, Operngasse, T01-966 9891. Sun-Thu 1000-0100, Fri-Sat 1000-0200. Late breakfast is the principal attraction here, served into the afternoon as you watch life go by on the lively Schleifmuehlgasse.

With its clean, wide streets and reputation as home to Europe's pre-eminent banking 'gnomes', it's easy to stereotype Zurich in the familiar Swiss style. But the town has undergone quite the liberal transformation over the last decade, and it doesn't take long to start uncovering a surprisingly schizophrenic nature. Big enough to take its place on the world stage but small enough to comfortably walk around, this most commercial of all Swiss cities has a deceptively long tradition of artistic unorthodoxy, as befits the city that buried Joyce and saw the birth of the Dada movement. And Zurich is also an extremely active city. Split by the River Limmat, shored by Lake Zurich and surrounded by some of Europe's most impressive peaks, Zurichers live an attractive lifestyle that is beguilingly easy to slip into.

Zurich

Arts & culture
★★★

Eating
★★★

Nightlife
★★★

Outdoors
★★★★

Romance
★★★

Shopping
★★★

Sightseeing
★★★★

Value for money
★

Overall score
★★★

⊙ Sights

Niederdorf (Old Town) ◥B1

Zurich's beautiful old town straddles the Limmat and is roughly bookended by the Fraumünster and Grossmünster churches, the city's two most dominant landmarks. Its winding streets and hidden nooks are perfect for getting into the rhythm of the city. Cute, bijou cafés and restaurants sit next to shops and boutiques, and reflect the increasingly dichotomous nature of the city.

Cabaret Voltaire

ⓘ *Spiegelgasse 1, T043-268 5720,* ◥B1. *Tue, Wed, Fri-Sun 1300-1900, Thu 1300-2300. 10-min walk from Zurich station or trams 4 or 13 to Rathaus station.*

A short walk from its easterly banks of the Limmat you will find perhaps one of the most important venues for nascent modern art at the turn of the 20th century. As Switzerland remained neutral in First World War, it attracted scores of artists, writers, poets and actors who wanted no part in the

bloodshed. Two such were a German couple, Hugo Ball and Emmy Hennings, who were well aware of the rich artistic talent surrounding them. They contacted painters, players and poets and told the press they intended "beautiful things" to happen in the back hall of a Dutch restaurant on the Spiegelgasse. By February 1916 their cabaret was born, soon becoming the focal point for a new generation of artists known collectively as the Dadaists. The re-establishment of Cabaret Voltaire in 2002, when a group of artists successfully campaigned against its demolition, coincided neatly with the return of the liberal tradition to Zurich, and the newly refurbished Cabaret Voltaire is once again home to extraordinary art exhibitions and cabaret.

Fraumünster

ⓘ *Stadthausquai, T044-211 4100* ◥B1. *May-Sep Mon-Sat 0900-1600; Mar, Apr and Oct Mon-Sat 1000-1700; Nov and Feb Mon-Sat 1000-1600. Paradeplatz station, trams 2, 6, 7, 8, 9, 11, 13*

Of Zurich's three major places of worship, two dominate the skyline – Fraumünster

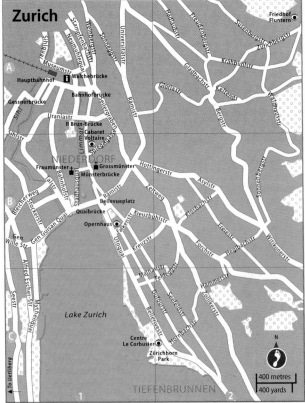

Zurich

Fraumünster

Designer building

Charles-Edouard Jeanneret, born in the Jura Mountains of northwestern Switzerland in 1887, became interested in design at an early age and spent his teenage years travelling around France, Germany, Turkey and Greece, where he studied the Parthenon. On his return, he took on the pseudonym Le Corbusier, meaning 'the crow-like one'. He became interested in concrete, a relatively new medium, and realised its potential. In this respect, he was one of the first Modernists and introduced his ideas of tower blocks and open-plan living in his book *Une verse de Architecture*. As well as buildings, he designed furniture, pioneering the use of chrome alongside leather. He also painted and was a founding member of the Purism movement alongside artist Ozenfant. Although he has been honoured by his country with his portrait on the back of the 10 CHF note, there seems to be little recognition of his final work, Le Corbusier Pavillion, now **Centre Le Corbusier/Heidi Weber Museum** ⓘ *Hoeschgasse 8, T044-383 6470, www.centerlecorbusier.com,* 🚋 *, Jul-Sep Sun 1430-1700,* next to the lake in Zurichhorn park. The building was finished after his death and, though it lay empty for years, it now houses a large collection of his writing, sketches and architectural drawings.

(Church of Our Lady) and Grossmünster. You'll probably gravitate towards both at some point, but make sure you visit this spectacular place. Whether it was was begun in the ninth century, with the original abbey, or the 13th century, is unclear, but its main draw is the incredible stained glass windows by Marc Chagall and Augusto Giacometti. Giacometti's work tends to be overshadowed by Chagall's array of magnificent windows, but both are must-sees – as the visiting hordes testify.

Freidhof Fluntern
ⓘ *Zurichberg,* 🚋 *. May-Aug daily 0700-2000, Mar, Apr, Sep and Oct daily 0700-1900, Nov-Feb daily 0800-1700.*

Although it might not be host to so many deceased luminaries, Zurich does have its own Père-Lachaise. The most famous incumbent by far is James Joyce, who lived with his family in Zurich during the two world wars. Joyce wrote most of *Ulysses* in Zurich. He returned at the outbreak of the Second World War and

died in January 1941. A statue marks his burial place. You can also find the grave of Nobel Prize winner Elias Canetti here.

Lake Zurich – Gold Coast
ⓘ *Bellevue station, trams 2, 4, 5, 8, 9, 11, 15; bus 912, 916.*

Ask any Zuricher to recommend somewhere in their city and chances are they'll mention the lake. Water is a

Lake Zurich

massive part of life in the city, and in the summer it seems as though the whole population decamps lakeside. The Gold Coast starts at Bellevue, where the lake meets the river, and follows a path along the lake towards Tiefenbrunnen. This is where Zurich locals come to relax, swim, sunbathe, socialise, wakeboard or simply just gawp at the huge sun-drenched houses that line this exclusive patch of Swiss real estate.

Uetliberg
ⓘ *S-Bahn from Zurich hauptbahnhof to Uetliberg.*

The classic excursion in Zurich is to head up to the summit of Uetliberg (871 m), which overlooks the entire city, Lake Zurich and the Alps. Take the S-Bahn train from Zurich Hauptbahnhof and Uetliberg is at the end of the line. There's enough to do here to make a worthwhile day trip, including the Planetenweg (a 1:1 billion scale version of the solar system) and a vertigo-inducing viewing tower, for the best views of the lake and the city.

Travel essentials

Getting there Zurich Airport, www.zurich-airport.com, is 13 km away. An efficient public transport system sees 6 trains an hour leave for the centre, a 10-min journey costing CHF 5.80. The bus station is also well served by 11 bus lines and departures every few minutes. Taxis (T0848-850852) cost about CHF 50.

Zurich has excellent rail links with many European cities, including Barcelona, Paris and Munich, www.sbb.ch. International trains arrive at Zurich Hauptbahnhof (HB) station. See also page 12.

Getting around Although the centre is small, trams and buses are so reliable that most people use them. Operating 0530-2400, they are extremely easy to follow; just remember to buy a ticket or a **Zurich Card** (offering discounts on travel and attractions) before boarding. See also www.vbz.ch for more public transport details.

Tourist information The main centre is in Zurich HB station, T044-215 4000, www.zuerich.com. May-Oct Mon-Sat 0800-2030, Sun 0830-1830; Nov-Apr Mon-Sat 0830-1900, Sun 0900-1830. All staff speak English and can help with accommodation, events, public transport and other information.

Sleeping

€€€ Alden Hotel Splügenshloss, Splügenstrasse, T044-289 9999, www.alden.ch. Built in 1895, this imposing edifice has been lovingly restored, re-opening in 2002, with 20 suites and 2 restaurants. Each individually designed suite has a drawing room large enough for meetings or private dinner parties.

€€€ Bar Hotel Seehof, Seehofstrasse 11, T044-254 5757 www.hotelseehof.ch. A prime example of new blood running through the veins of an old city, this hotel has simple and striking decor, a restaurant offering Japanese-influenced cuisine and staff who are young, cool and very much in the know.

€€€ Lady's First Design Hotel, Mainaustrasse 24, T044-380 8101, www.ladysfirst.ch. This is a 28-room boutique hotel with a twist; as the name suggests, it caters especially for women. Although men are equally welcome, the all-female team at the 19th-century former townhouse offer travelling ladies beautifully presented rooms, in-house masseuses, cosmetic and beauty specialists, a rooftop terrace and a rose garden.

€ City Backpacker/Hotel Biber, Niederdorfstrasse 5, T044-251 9015, www.city-backpacker.ch. As Europe's cleanest place to live, Zurich offers spotless accommodation regardless of the price bracket. This place in the Old Town has single, double and dorm rooms, communal kitchen, terrace, washing facilities and, interestingly, a discount on Swiss Army Knives.

Eating

Casa Aurelio, Langstrasse 209, T01-272 7744, www.casaaurelio.ch. A traditional Spanish family-run restaurant in the historical centre. International flavours and an appealing atmosphere create an exciting eating experience.

Kronenhalle, Rämistrasse 4, T044-262 9900, www.kronenhalle.com. One of the most famous restaurants offering traditional Swiss dining, Kronenhalle has fed the famous for years. Picassos and Matisses adorn the walls and reservations are essential.

Angkor, Kreis 5, Giessereistrasse 18, T043-205 2888. An awe-inspiring setting and sumptuous Thai food; for the ultimate dining experience choose one of the water tables and have fish swim past whilst you tuck in.

Lumière, Widdergasse 5, T01-211 5665. This French bistro serves arguably the best steak and French fries in Zurich. The service is extremely friendly and the wine list is excellent. The king prawns are also superb.

Nine Bar & Restaurant, Seefeldstrasse 40, T044-253 7070. Favoured by the city's beautiful people, Nine is testament to simple and elegant design. As much about the bar as the restaurant, Nine is a chic place to dine on fine Mediterranean dishes.

Nightlife

As well as apparently providing a 5th of Switzerland's income, Zurich reputedly has more clubs per head than any other European city and its thriving nightlife is an important part of the city's recent liberal resurgence. The obvious place to begin is the Niederdorf, although the Langstrasse area is probably the place to head for grittier clubbing. Recently, the Zurich West district has become something of an epicentre. In addition, Zurich is home to the **Zurcher Opernhaus**, Falkenstrasse1, www.opernhaus.ch, one of Europe's oldest operas, and a host of traditional and experimental theatre companies.

European City Breaks Zurich

Credits

Editors: Jo Williams and Sophie Blacksell
Picture editor: Robert Lunn
Publisher: Patrick Dawson
Editorial: Alan Murphy, Felicity Laughton, Nicola Gibbs
Cartography: Sarah Sorensen, Kevin Feeney
Cover design: Robert Lunn
Sales and marketing: Andy Riddle, Zoë Jackson, Hannah Bonnell
Advertising: Debbie Wylde
Finance and administration: Elizabeth Taylor

Contributors

Amsterdam	Francisca Kellett
Antwerp	Clare Thomson
Athens	Jane Foster
Barcelona	Mary-Ann Gallagher
Berlin	Nina Hamilton, Julie Campbell
Bilbao	Andy Symington
Bologna	Ben Donald
Bratislava	John Oates
Brussels	Clare Thomson
Budapest	Annie Dare
Copenhagen	Sean Sheehan and Pat Levy
Dublin	Sean Sheehan and Pat Levy
Edinburgh	Alan Murphy
Florence	Julius Honnor
Glasgow	Alan Murphy
Istanbul	Dominic Whiting, Julie Campbell
Krakow	Julius Honnor
Lisbon	Caroline Lascom, Julie Campbell
Ljubljana	Francisca Kellett, Rebecca Ford
London	Charlie Godfrey-Faussett, Julie Campbell
Lyon	Francisca Kellett, Ben Donald
Madrid	Mary-Ann Gallagher
Milan	Julius Honnor
Munich	Francisca Kellett, Esther Hölderle
Naples	Julius Honnor
Paris	Sophie Warne, Julie Campbell
Prague	Francisca Kellett Julie Campbell
Reykjavik	Laura Dixon, Julie Campbell
Riga	John Oates
Rome	Julius Honnor
St Petersburg	Patrick McConnell, Julie Campbell
Seville	Andy Symington
Stockholm	Sean Sheehan and Pat Levy
Tallinn	Clare Thomson
Turin	Ben Donald
Valencia	Mary-Ann Gallagher
Venice	Julius Honnor
Verona	Julius Honnor
Vienna	Ben Donald
Zurich	Matt Barr

Print

Manufactured in India by Nutech Photolithographers, Delhi.
Pulp from sustainable forests

This product includes mapping data licensed from Ordnance Survey® and the Ordnance Survey Complete Atlas of Ireland, with permission of the Controller of Her Majesty's Stationery Office © Crown Copyright 2005. All rights reserved. Licence number 100027877.

Footprint feedback

We try very hard to make each Footprint guide as up to date as possible but, of course, things always change. To let us know about your experiences – good, bad or ugly – go to www.footprintbooks.com and send in your comments.

Publishing information

Footprint European City Breaks
© Footprint Handbooks Ltd
September 2007
ISBN 978 1 906098 02 5
CIP DATA: A catalogue record for this book is available from the British Library

® Footprint Handbooks and the Footprint mark are a registered trademark of Footprint Handbooks Ltd

Published by Footprint
6 Riverside Court
Lower Bristol Road
Bath BA2 3DZ, UK
T +44 (0)1225 469141
F +44 (0)1225 469461
discover@footprintbooks.com
www.footprintbooks.com

The maps are not intended to have any political significance.

Every effort has been made to ensure that the facts in this guidebook are accurate. However, travellers should still obtain advice from consulates, airlines etc about travel and visa requirements before travelling. The authors and publishers cannot accept responsibility for any loss, injury or inconvenience however caused.

Photography

Cover: Alamy (Hideo Kurihara, Jon Arnold Images), Budapestinfo.Hu, Julius Honnor, Shutterstock (Alan James Ager, Aleksejs Kostins, Arnis Rukis, Astrid Van Der Eerden, Danilo Ascione, Felixfotografia.Es, Knud Nielsen, Robert Anthony).

Prelims, Ratings & Festivals: Alamy (Art Kowalsky, Hideo Kurihara, nagelestock.com), Shutterstock (Robert Anthony). **Essentials:** Shutterstock (Alex Stepanov, Christophe Testi, Manfred Steinbach, Pawel Klisiewicz, Thor Jorgen Udvang, Tito Wong). **Amsterdam:** Alamy Travel-Shots), Shutterstock (Olga Shelego), Netherlands Board Of Tourism & Conventions. **Antwerp:** Tourism Flanders-Brussels. **Athens:** Alamy (Robert Harding Picture Library Ltd), Hemisphere Bertrand Gardel/Monde), Shutterstock Asher, Wizdata, Inc), SuperStock (Alvaro Leivs, Chmura, Kevin O'hara), TIPS (Guido Alberto Rossi). **Barcelona:** Alamy (Aa World Travel Library, Kevin Foy, Vincent Lowe), Shutterstock (Astrid Van Der Eerden, Jorge Felix Costa, Jose Antonio), Spanish Tourist Office. **Berlin:** Shutterstock (Jarno Gonzalez Zarraonandia, Ulrich Buechsenschuetz, Yurok), Susannah Sayler. **Bilbao:** Alamy Mark Baynes), Hemisphere (Franck Guiziou/Monde), Shutterstock (Bruce Amos), TIPS (Andrea Pistolesi). **Bologna:** Julius Honnor, Fototeca ENIT (Vito Arcomano), SuperStock (Age Fotostock). **Bratislava:** Bratislava Tourist Office, John Dates. **Brussels:** Alamy (Art Kowalsky), Shutterstock (Hugo Maes, Ronald Sumners), Tourism Flanders-Brussels. **Budapest:** Alamy (Sergio Pitamitz), Budapestinfo.Hu, Shutterstock (János Gehring, Ls Kay), TIPS (Charles Mahaux). **Copenhagen:** Shutterstock (Alban Egger, Christian Noval, Knud Nielsen, Rudolf Lotulán, W.Ahrens, Warnock), SuperStock Nils-Johan Norenlind). **Dublin:** Alamy Andre Jenny, Danita Delimont, Fan Travelstock, Ian M Butterfield, Imagestate), visitdublin.com, Shutterstock (D.H.Snover, Joe Burns, Keith Levit, Michael J Thompson), Susannah Sayler. **Edinburgh:** Alamy (Arch White, David Robertson, Iain Masterton), Kevin Feeney, Nativa,

Photolibrary (Index Stock Imagery), Shutterstock (Bill Mckelvie), TIPS (Alberto Nardi). **Florence:** Alamy (Ken Welsh), Shutterstock (Peter Clark, Olga Skalkina, Wh Chow), Fototeca ENIT (Paola Ghirotti), SuperStock (Etienne, Javier Larrea), TIPS (Marvin Newman), Hemisphere (Franck Guiziou/Monde, Pawel Wysocki/Monde), Julius Honnor. **Glasgow:** Alamy (Stephen Saks Photography, Yadid Levy), Shutterstock (Bill Mckelvie, Rubiphoto), SuperStock (Brian Lawrence). **Istanbul:** Hemisphere (Patrick Frilet/Monde, Pawel Wysocki/Monde), Shutterstock (Andrew Skinner, Connors Bros, Roman Barelko, Svetlana Tikhonova), SuperStock (Bruno Morandi, Renaud Visag). **Krakow:** Shutterstock (Church_Puchan, Gate_Puchan, Piotr Przeszlo). **Lisbon:** Shutterstock (Aleksander Bochenek, Clara Natoli, Gary James Calder, Photooiasson), Hemisphere (Patrick Frilet/Monde), SuperStock. **Ljubljana:** Shutterstock (Simon Krzic). **London:** Alamy (Ace Stock Limited, Alan Copson City Pictures, David Pearson, Tim Gartside), Shutterstock (Bartlomiej K. Kwieciszewski, Cj Photography, Damaphoto.Ch, Deetone, Jacqueline Abromeit, James Ager, Jarno Gonzalez Zarraonandia, Jeff Gynane, Paul Cowan, Stephen Finn, Tyler Boyes, Vinicius Tupinamba). **Lyon:** Alamy (Images-Of-France, Nick Hanna), Shutterstock (Jakez), Hemisphere (Franck Guiziou/France, Laurent Giraudou/France). **Madrid:** Alamy (Ian Dagnall, Kevin George, John Stark), Shutterstock (Graca Victoria, J. Helgason, Photooiasson, Rubiphoto), Spanish Tourist Office, José Resino. **Milan:** Fototeca ENIT (Vito Arcomano), Shutterstock (Dino), Hemisphere (Philippe Renault/Monde). **Munich:** Alamy (Art Kowalsky), Shutterstock (Elena Kouptsova –Vasic, Radu Razvan, Yan Ke), SuperStock (Thomas Lauterback), Hemisphere (Maurizio Borgese/Monde, Patrick Frilet/Monde). **Naples:** Alamy (Culliganphoto), Julius Honnor, Shutterstock (Alfio Ferlito, Danilo Ascione), SuperStock (Doug Scott). **Paris:** Alamy (David L. Moore), Shutterstock (Aleksejs Kostins, Asher Welstead, Cornel Achirei – Achi, Elena Elisseeva, Enrique Sallent, Keith

Levit, Nikolay Misharev, Pete Hoffman, Taolmor), Susannah Sayler. **Prague:** Alamy (Humberto Olarte Cupas), Czechtourism, Shutterstock (Jaroslaw Grudzinski). **Reykjavik:** Alamy (Arctic Images, Bill Bachmann, Nordicphotos), Hemisphere (Romain Cintract/Monde), Shutterstock (Eirikur Kristjansson, Lukáš Hejtman). **Riga:** Shutterstock (Arnis Rukis, Dainis Derics, Edgars Dubrovskis). **Rome:** Alamy (Adam Eastland, Frank Chmura), Fototeca ENIT (Vito Arcomano), Shutterstock (Anthony Smith, David Davis, David Macfarlane, Eugene Mogilnikov, Faberfoto, Marc C. Johnson, Olga Shelego, Polartern), SuperStock (Javier Larre, Jon Ivern), TIPS (Sandra Baker). **Seville:** Shutterstock (Adriaan Thomas Snaaijer, Jarno Gonzalez Zarraonandia, Javier, Nick Stubbs, Soundsnaps), Susannah Sayler. **Stockholm:** Alamy (John Lens), Shutterstock (Mikael Damkier, Rubiphoto, Wizdata. Inc), SuperStock (Doug Scott), TIPS (Chad Ehlers, David W Hamilton). **St Petersburg:** Alamy (Imagebroker, Jon Bower, Robert Harding Picture Library Ltd), Shutterstock (Agb, Alexey Samarin, Sergei A. Tkachenko), SuperStock (Doug Scott, Wojtek Bliss). **Tallinn:** SuperStock (Age Fotostock), Shutterstock (Veronika Trofer), Tallinn City Tourist Office. **Turin:** Città Di Torino (Michele D'ottavio), SuperStock (Prisma), Fototeca ENIT (Vito Arcomano), Cape' Tabac (Adriano Bachella). **Valencia:** Shutterstock (Alberto Pérez Veiga, Felixfotografia.Es, Hannu Liivaar, Tom Cummins), Spanish Tourist Office. **Venice:** Alamy (Chuck Pefley, Worldwide Picture Library), Fototeca ENIT (Vito Arcomano), Kevin Feeney, Shutterstock (Marco Van Belleghem, Razvan Stroie, Wh Chow), SuperStock (Medioimages). **Verona:** Fototeca ENIT (Vito Arcomano), Shutterstock (Franziska Lang, Khirman Vladimir, Titus Manea, Willem Dijkstra). **Vienna:** Hemisphere (John Frumm/Monde, Maurizio Borgese/Monde), Shutterstock (Hermann Danzmayr, Monster, Puchan, Sean Nel), SuperStock (San Rostro). **Zurich:** Shutterstock (Andres Rodriguez, N.A., Switzerland, Reihe13).

There is a passion for travel and discovery at **Footprint** that has been reflected in our publishing since the *South American Handbook* was first published back in 1924. More than 80 years on, our aim is still simple: to give travellers a refreshingly different view that helps them to follow their own route and have a unique, memorable experience.

 Don't just take our word for it!

If 'the essence of real travel' is what you have been secretly yearning for all these years, then Footprint are the guides for you. **Under 26 magazine**

Who should pack Footprint–readers who want to escape the crowd. **The Observer**

Footprint can be depended on for accurate travel information and for imparting a deep sense of respect for the lands and people they cover. **World News**

I carried the South American Handbook from Cape Horn to Cartagena and consulted it every night for two and a half months. I wouldn't do that for anything else except my hip flask. **Michael Palin, BBC Full Circle**

The Publishers of the best travel guide in the world. **Graham Greene**

The guides for intelligent, independently-minded souls of any age or budget. **Indie Traveller**

Footprint
Travel guides

www.footprintbooks.com